Private Equity, Second Edition

History, Governance,
and Operations

Wiley Finance Series

Founded in 1807, John Wiley & Sons is the oldest independent publishing company in the United States. With offices in North America, Europe, Australia and Asia, Wiley is globally committed to developing and marketing print and electronic products and services for our customers' professional and personal knowledge and understanding.

The Wiley Finance series contains books written specifically for finance and investment professionals as well as sophisticated individual investors and their financial advisors. Book topics range from portfolio management to e-commerce, risk management, financial engineering, valuation and financial instrument analysis, as well as much more.

For a list of available titles, visit our Web site at www.WileyFinance.com.

Private Equity, Second Edition

History, Governance, and Operations

HARRY CENDROWSKI
LOUIS W. PETRO
JAMES P. MARTIN
ADAM A. WADECKI

John Wiley & Sons, Inc.

Library of Congress Cataloging-in-Publication Data:
Private equity : history, governance, and operations / Harry Cendrowski . . . [et al.]. — 2nd ed.
    p. cm. — (Wiley finance series)
  Includes index.
    ISBN 978-1-118-13850-2 (cloth); ISBN 978-1-118-22542-4 (ebk);
  ISBN 978-1-118-23885-1 (ebk); ISBN 978-1-118-26350-1 (ebk)
  1. Private equity. I. Cendrowski, Harry.
  HG4751.P744 2012
  332'.041—dc23

                                 2011052820

Printed in the United States of America

10 9 8 7 6 5 4 3 2 1

Contents

Preface   xvii

MODULE I
The Private Equity Model and Historical Information

CHAPTER 1
Introduction to Private Equity   3

Introduction   3
What Is Private Equity?   4
General Terms and Brief Overview   5
The Limited Partner Agreement and General Partner
    Incentives   12
Private Equity Firm Structure and Selected Regulations   15
Types of Private Equity Investment   20
The Private Equity Fundraising Process   22
Recent Fundraising Trends   25
General Partner Investment Restrictions   26
Conclusion   28
Notes   28

CHAPTER 2
Overview of Historical Trends   29

Introduction   29
A Brief History of Private Equity   29
Private Equity at the Turn of the Century   33
Venture Capital Investment and Returns by Fund Stage   39
Venture Capital and Buyout Returns by Fund Size   43
Secondary Funds   45
Conclusion   48
Notes   48

CHAPTER 3
Trends in Private Equity   **51**

Introduction   51
A Changing Tide   51
Overall Industry and Fundraising Trends   54
Selected Regulatory Changes and Proposals   60
Rise of Strategic Buyers   64
Conclusion   66
Notes   66

CHAPTER 4
Harvesting Private Equity Investments Through Initial
Public Offering   **69**

Initial Public Offerings   69
    Basics   69
    Initial Steps in the "Going Public" Process   72
    Role of the Securities and Exchange Commission and
        State Policing Bodies   75
    Post-IPO Underwriter Responsibilities   77
    Registration Documents   78
    Historical Trends   79
    Summary   83
Notes   83

CHAPTER 5
Legal Considerations in Initial Public Offerings   **85**

Introduction   85
Initial Public Offering   86
    Introduction   86
    Potential Advantages   87
    Potential Disadvantages   89
    Advance Planning Opportunities   91
        Selection of Advisors   91
        Securities Counsel   92
        Accountants   92
        Underwriters   93
        Corporate Housekeeping Matters   93
        Antitakeover Provisions 93
        Management   94
    The Initial Public Offering Process   94
        Principal Parties   94

Principal Documents 96
Selling Security Holder Documents 98
The Registration Process 100
Possible Liabilities Faced by a Company and Its
Directors and Officers 102
Liabilities under Federal Securities Laws 102
The Sarbanes-Oxley Act and Dodd-Frank Act 105
Public Company Filing Obligations 107
Initial Public Offering Alternative:
Reverse Mergers 107
Advantages 107
Disadvantages 108
Conclusion 109

CHAPTER 6
Harvesting Investments Through Mergers and Acquisitions

111

Introduction 111
M&A Basics 111
Types of Takeovers 112
Reverse Takeovers 113
The Takeover Process and Financial
Advisor Selection 114
Analyzing Potential Buyers 115
The Sale Process 116
The Bidding Process 118
Reaching an Agreement 119
Historical M&A Trends 120
Conclusion 122

CHAPTER 7
Legal Considerations in Sale Transactions

123

Introduction 123
Sale Transactions 124
Prior to the Sale Transaction 124
Use of an Investment Banker 124
Marketing Process 125
Due Diligence 125
Negotiations Phase 125
Key Deal Issues 126
Valuation and Pricing Issues 126

Special Issues in Sales of Private Equity
    Fund–Owned Businesses   132
Sale and Acquisition Structure   134
    Merger   134
    Asset Purchase   135
    Stock Purchase   135
Employee Incentive Issues   135
    Cash Retention Bonus   135
    Stock Bonuses   136
    Recapitalizations   137
The Sale Transaction Process   137
    Letter of Intent   137
    Disclosure of Acquisitions   138
    Time and Responsibility Schedule   138
    Definitive Agreements   139
    Necessary Consents   140
Conclusion   142

CHAPTER 8
Intellectual Property and Private Equity   143

Introduction   143
Intellectual Property Rights and Remedies   143
    Patents   144
    Trademarks   146
    Copyrights   147
    Trade Secrets   148
Pre-Acquisition Due Diligence   149
    Established Barriers to Entry—Evaluating
        Investment Value   149
    Freedom to Practice—Assessing Risk of
        Proposed Acquisition   151
Creating Intellectual Property Value During
    Management   152
    Leveraging and Monetizing Patent Rights   153
    Bolstering Technological Advantages   153
    Boosting Brand Development Efforts   154
    Preserving Knowledge-Based Resources
        of the Workforce   155
Positioning the Exit—Reverse Due Diligence   156
    Minimizing Exposure of Representations and
        Warranties   158
Notes   159

MODULE II
Governance Structures in Private Equity

CHAPTER 9
The Private Equity Governance Model   163

Introduction	163
A New Model for Corporate Governance	163
An Analogy to Physics	167
Corporate Governance and the Management of Crisis	168
Public Corporations and the Private Equity Model	171
The Magic of the Private Equity Governance Model	173
Conclusion	175
Notes	176

CHAPTER 10
Value of Internal Control   177

Introduction	177
Introduction to COSO and Internal Control	178
COSO Background	178
Internal Control Defined	178
Components of Internal Control	179
Control Environment	179
Risk Assessment	182
Enterprise Risk Management	183
Control Activities	184
Information and Communication	186
Monitoring	186
Limitations of Internal Control	188
Control Objectives and Control Components	189
Effectiveness of Internal Control	190
Internal Control and the Private Equity Firm	191
Value of Internal Control for Private Equity Fund Operations	191
Value and the Control Environment	193
Value and Risk	194
Value and Control Activities	194
Value and Information and Communication	195
Value and Monitoring	195
Value of Internal Control for Target Companies	195
Operational Value	196

Financial Reporting Value 197
Compliance Value 197
Conclusion 198
Notes 198

CHAPTER 11
Internal Control Evaluation **201**

Introduction 201
PCAOB Auditing Standard No. 5 203
Phase 1: Planning the Audit 204
Risk Assessment 206
Scaling the Audit 206
Fraud Risk 206
Using the Work of Others 207
Materiality 207
Phase 2: Using a Top-Down Approach 208
Identifying Entry-Level Controls 208
Control Environment 209
Period-End Financial Reporting Process 209
Identifying Significant Accounts and Disclosures and
Their Related Assertions 210
Understanding Likely Sources of Misstatement 211
Selecting Controls to Test 211
Phase 3: Testing Controls 211
Testing Design Effectiveness 212
Testing Operating Effectiveness 212
Relationship of Risk to the Evidence to Be Obtained 212
Special Considerations for Subsequent Yearly Audits 213
Phase 4: Evaluating Identified Deficiencies 213
Phase 5: Wrapping Up 215
Forming an Opinion 215
Obtaining Written Representations 215
Communicating Certain Matters 216
Phase 6: Reporting on Internal Controls 217
Conclusion 218
Notes 218

CHAPTER 12
Financial Statement Fraud and the Investment Decision **219**

Introduction 219
Money Laundering 219
Categories of Fraud 221

What Is Fraud?   222
The Required Elements of Fraud   223
Financial Statement Attestation   225
    Tax Return Preparation   225
    Compilation   226
    Review   226
    Audit   226
Recommendations   227
    Do Not Rely Solely on Financial Statements   227
    Pay Attention to Details   228
    Follow Up on Unexpected or Interesting Items   229
    Maintain Professional Skepticism   229
    Explanations Should Be Rational, Reasonable, and
      Verifiable   230
    What Do the Financial Statements Say about the Entity's
      Ability to Meet Its Objectives?   230
Fraud and Due Diligence Procedures   231
    Background Investigation of Key Employees   231
    Testing of Journal Transactions   232
    Check File Metadata   232
Conclusion   233
Notes   234

CHAPTER 13
Professional Standards   **235**

Introduction   235
Federal Trade Commission   235
    Federal Antitrust Legislation   235
      Sherman Antitrust Act (1890)   236
      Clayton Antitrust Act (1914)   236
      Federal Trade Commission Act (1914) 236
      Robinson-Patman Act (1936)   237
      Celler-Kefauver Antimerger Act (1950) 237
      Hart-Scott-Rodino Antitrust Improvement
        Act (1976)   237
    Federal Consumer Protection Legislation   238
Securities and Exchange Commission   239
    Securities Act (1933)   239
    Securities Exchange Act (1934)   240
    Public Utility Holding Company Act (1935)   241
    Trust Indenture Act (1939)   241
    Investment Company Act (1940)   242

Investment Advisers Act (1940) 242
Foreign Corrupt Practices Act (1977) 243
Sarbanes-Oxley Act (2002) 244
   Public Company Accounting Oversight
      Board 244
   Auditor Independence 245
   Corporate Governance 246
   CEO/CFO Certifications 247
   Enhanced Financial Disclosure 247
   Civil and Criminal Penalties 247
"Private" Equity Going Public 248
Introduction to Public Standards 248
Public Company Accounting Oversight Board Standards 249
   PCAOB Auditing Standard No. 1 249
   PCAOB Auditing Standard No. 2 249
   PCAOB Auditing Standard No. 3 250
   PCAOB Auditing Standard No. 4 250
   PCAOB Auditing Standard No. 5 250
      The Standard Is Less Prescriptive 251
      Scalable Audits 251
      Audit Focus 251
      Using the Work of Others 252
   PCAOB Auditing Standard No. 6 252
   PCAOB Auditing Standard No. 7 252
   PCAOB Auditing Standard No. 8 252
   PCAOB Auditing Standard No. 9 253
   PCAOB Auditing Standard No. 10 253
   PCAOB Auditing Standard No. 11 253
   PCAOB Auditing Standard No. 12 253
   PCAOB Auditing Standard No. 13 254
   PCAOB Auditing Standard No. 14 254
   PCAOB Auditing Standard No. 15 255
American Institute of Certified Public Accountants Auditing
  Standards 255
   SAS 99, "Consideration of Fraud in a Financial
      Statement Audit" 256
   SAS 1 Amendments 257
   SAS 85 Amendments 257
   SAS 82 Replacements 257
      Descriptions and Characteristics of Fraud 258
      Professional Skepticism 258
      Engagement Team Discussions 258

Fraud Risks   259
Identifying Risks   259
Assessing Risks   259
Responding to the Risk Assessment   260
Evaluating Audit Evidence   261
Auditor Communication   263
Audit Documentation   263
SAS 104, "Amendment to Statement on Auditing
    Standards No.1, 'Codification of Auditing Standards
    And Procedures ("Due Professional Care in the
    Performance of Work")'"   264
SAS 105, "Amendment to Statement on Auditing
    Standards No. 95, Generally Accepted Auditing
    Standards"   265
SAS 106, "Audit Evidence"   265
SAS 107, "Audit Risk and Materiality in Conducting
    the Audit"   265
SAS 108, "Planning and Supervision"   266
SAS 109, "Understanding the Entity and Its
    Environment and the Risks of Material
    Misstatement"   266
SAS 110, "Performing Audit Procedures in
    Response to Assessed Risks and Evaluation
    of the Audit Evidence Obtained"   267
SAS 111, "Amendment to Statement on Auditing
    Standards No. 39, 'Audit Sampling'"   267
SAS 112, "Communicating Internal Control Related
    Matters Identified in an Audit"   267
SAS 113, "Omnibus Statement on Auditing Standards"   268
SAS 114, "The Auditor's Communication With Those
    Charged With Governance"   269
SAS 116, "Interim Financial Information"   270
American Institute of Certified Public Accountants
    Accounting and Review Standards   270
    SSARS 10   271
    SSARS 12   271
Institute of Internal Auditors Standards   272
Information Systems Audit and Control
    Association   272
Conclusion   273
Notes   273

MODULE III

Understanding Operations

CHAPTER 14
Contemporary Business and Competitive Intelligence   **277**

Introduction   277
Contemporary Business Intelligence   278
   Sources of Information   278
      Public Records Searches   278
      News Archives   279
      Legal Proceedings   279
      Patent Awards and Applications   280
      Social Networking   280
      Employees   280
Competitive Intelligence and the External Environment   281
Normalizing Performance   282
Cost of Capital and the Option to Invest   285
Developing Unique Intelligence   287
An Economic View of Quality   289
Developing Relationships and Navigating Crises   290
Application to Private Equity   291
   Investment Decision   291
   Strategic Management of Portfolio Companies   291
   Exit Strategy   292
Conclusion   292
Notes   292

CHAPTER 15
Organizations as Humans   **293**

Introduction   293
Purpose of the Organization   294
Genesis   295
Development and Specialization   296
Parts of the Whole and Maturation   297
Environmental Adaptation   299
Environmental Influence and Interaction   302
Maturity Creates "The Machine"   303
Death of the Organization and Rebirth   304
Strengths and Weaknesses of the Organizations as
   Humans Metaphor   305
Conclusion   307
Notes   307

CHAPTER 16
Beginning the Lean Transformation 309

Introduction 309
    The Origins of Lean Operations:
        Lean Manufacturing 310
    Potential Pitfalls of Lean 311
    Organizational Development 312
    Discipline Building 315
    What Private Equity Means for Lean 317
Conclusion 318
Note 318

CHAPTER 17
Performing Manufacturing Due Diligence Assessments 319

Introduction 319
Performing the Assessment 319
    Employee Satisfaction 320
    Customer Satisfaction and Perceived Quality 322
    Corporate Vision and Mission 323
    Equipment and Facility Maintenance 324
    Visual Management 326
    Inventory Management and Product Flow 327
Operational Data and Cost of Sales 328
Conclusion 333
Notes 333

About the Authors 335

Glossary 339

Index 345

Preface

Shortly after the writing of this book's first edition, the U.S. economy was shaken by a catastrophic economic crisis, the likes of which had not been seen since the Hoover administration. A multitude of factors combined to cause falling stock markets, rising unemployment, and a general angst among the American public, who watched as once-iconic firms faded into history. Lehman Brothers and Bear Stearns were dissolved. Merrill Lynch sold itself to Bank of America for roughly one half of its prior year value. AIG sought billions from the federal government to preserve solvency. Industrial icons General Motors and Chrysler filed for bankruptcy. America's disease soon evolved into a worldwide pandemic, crippling economies that, three years later, are still attempting to regain their footing.

While the American economy was fighting the Great Recession, the Private Equity (PE) landscape was facing its own battle. Returns of PE portfolio companies, including buyout and venture-backed businesses, plummeted as harvest environments became challenging. Many PE investors faced liquidity issues and found themselves over-allocated in alternative investments as the value of their public securities degraded faster than illiquid assets. Investors subsequently moved to reduce PE investments, resulting in some of the leanest fundraising levels seen in recent times.

At the time of this writing, the U.S. economy appears to be on the mend, though European debt default worries continue to make investors skittish. The general environment for PE firms remains challenging and, in some instances, less lucrative than it was prior to the latest economic crisis. Except for a handful of occurrences, the multibillion dollar deals that grabbed headlines in 2006 and 2007 no longer exist. Debt is often less freely available, and acquisition prices are up as strategic buyers look to put some of their estimated $1 trillion in balance sheet cash to work. Investors hoping to quickly recover their 2008–2009 losses may be disappointed by near-term returns.

For comparative purposes and consistency, most chapters within this book contain graphs of annual data through December 31, 2010. While the first half of 2011 appeared promising for PE, European debt market jitters stemmed PE's rebound in the second half of 2011: Deal volume fell by roughly 23 percent in the third quarter of 2011 as compared with the second quarter of 2011, while exits fell by 54 percent over the same time period. Though deal volume and exits decreased, valuations remain aggressive, putting extreme pressure on PE firms to deliver returns.

PE firms have historically made money by leveraging a portfolio company and using its free cash flow to pay down and convert debt to equity over a five- or six-year holding period. In an environment with high acquisition prices and reduced debt availability, this model is not sustainable. We believe operational expertise, ingrained within a PE firm's culture, is necessary to generate high returns in today's environment. While many firms state they possess an operational focus, this focus must permeate the firm's culture and should be reflected in the backgrounds of its partners. An operational focus is likewise essential for venture capital firms. Venture-backed companies that are able to maximize capital efficiency through streamlined operational processes will be more likely to generate high abnormal returns for their parent funds and investors. Though the PE market is challenging, it remains a unique engine of the U.S. and world economies.

PE, including buyouts and venture capital, helps foster ingenuity, creativity, and an entrepreneurial spirit within the communities it reaches. It also provides a mechanism for older companies to reshape themselves into more modern entities. As the United States rebounds from the economic crisis, PE and its numerous forms, including fundless funds, can greatly assist in repairing the economy and the country's spirit: No other organizational form is endowed with a commensurate governance structure that aligns the incentives of all parties, helping achieve results that are optimal for society as well as for investors.

The exposition of PE is the focus of the treatise in your hands. More specifically, its purpose is threefold: to describe the history of PE; to illustrate how governance structures differ between PE portfolio companies and those of public corporations; and finally, to explain how the operations of PE portfolio companies can be improved. Along these lines, the text provides valuable information for numerous audiences: students unaccustomed to PE, PE professionals, and investors should all find valuable information in this book. Chapters have been designed on a standalone basis, although we highly recommend that readers unaccustomed to PE read the initial three chapters of the book before perusing other sections.

The book begins with Module I—The Private Equity Model and Historical Information, a comprehensive introduction to the PE process: The key players, terms of investment, and historical trends are described in detail. In reading these chapters, the PE novice will become accustomed to the terminology used by industry professionals along with the roles played by participants in this asset class.

Harvesting plays a pivotal role in PE investments. In this module we also introduce the reader to the harvesting mechanisms of the initial public offering (IPO) and the sale to a strategic or financial buyer—also known as a merger and acquisition (M&A) deal—as well as legal considerations in both harvest mechanisms and those pertaining to intellectual property.

From there, the book transitions into Module II—Governance Structures in Private Equity, a discussion of the unique governance structures that the PE model imparts on portfolio companies. Applicable professional standards, models of internal control, and contemporary business intelligence are also discussed. Though not all models directly apply to PE, they are expounded as best practices that may be employed by funds and their portfolio companies

The book concludes with Module III—Understanding Operations, which provides information devoted to assessing and improving the operations of portfolio companies. A metaphor for analyzing organizations is introduced in Chapter 15, that of organizations as humans. This philosophical framework provides the reader with a detailed methodology for understanding the complexities of today's organizations. Subsequent chapters discuss the topics of lean manufacturing and operations assessments; they are designed to assist PE professionals in understanding how to perform operations assessments, and also how to improve the manufacturing operations of portfolio companies.

After completing the book, it is our hope that the reader will have gained an understanding of the intricacies within the PE industry as well as an appreciation for the asset class.

Harry Cendrowski
Chicago, Illinois
January 10, 2012

The Private Equity Model and Historical Information

CHAPTER 1

Introduction to Private Equity

Harry Cendrowski
Adam A. Wadecki

INTRODUCTION

Private equity (PE), including buyout and venture capital (VC) transactions, is a critical component of modern finance. Since 1980, over $1.1 trillion has been raised by U.S. buyout funds and roughly $700 billion has been raised by VC funds. (See Exhibit 1.1 and Chapter 2 for additional information on fundraising trends.) Eight hundred thirty billion dollars was raised by U.S. buyout funds in the last 10 years alone, while $489 billion was raised by U.S. VC funds over the same time period.

While relatively small levels of PE capital were raised through the early 1980s, PE fundraising levels have experienced considerable growth—and

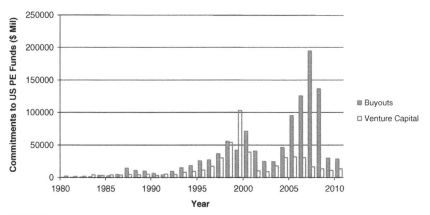

EXHIBIT 1.1 Historical Venture Capital and Buyout Annual Fundraising Levels, 1980–2010
Source: Thomson's VentureXpert database.

3

cyclicality—since that time. However, in spite of the large amounts of capital placed in PE, relatively few individuals have even modest knowledge of this central pillar of the contemporary financial system.

This chapter introduces PE, defines frequently used PE terms, provides an overview of the PE model, and describes the PE fundraising and investment processes. It is not comprehensive in nature but, instead, presents an introduction to numerous concepts that are discussed in greater detail in later sections of this book. Newly defined terms are italicized for the reader's convenience.

For comparative purposes, data within this text is generally examined on an annual basis; the latest period of data available prior to this book's publication was the year ending December 31, 2010.

Though many forms of PE exist, this book will largely focus on two types of such investments: buyouts and VC. Other types of PE investments, including mezzanine financing, private investments in public equity (PIPEs), and fund of funds (FoF) investments, will be discussed throughout the work; however, these will not be the primary focus of this text.

WHAT IS PRIVATE EQUITY?

Many definitions of PE exist, though, at the simplest level, PE is a medium or long-term equity investment that is not publicly traded on an exchange. PE includes VC and buyout transactions as well as investments in hedge funds, FoF, PIPEs, distressed debt funds, and other securities. It also includes angel financing or investments in very early stage companies. The focus of this text is VC and buyout transactions, and the funds originating such transactions as these funds manage a majority of PE capital.

The previous definition of PE generally holds, though exceptions exist. PE includes transactions structured with convertible debt; the purchase of publicly traded companies that are subsequently taken private and delisted from an exchange; and illiquid investments in publicly traded companies. However, while a business itself may be publicly traded, a PE fund's investment in such a business is generally not traded.

In the United States, PE investments are themselves not traded on the New York Stock Exchange (NYSE), NASDAQ, or other regional exchanges, though some PE firms, including The Blackstone Group (Blackstone) and Kravis, Roberts & Company (KKR), have gone public in recent years. Without an exchange on which to trade shares, and in the absence of market makers, PE investments are generally illiquid and held for between three and seven years before a liquidity event or harvest occurs. At this time, the PE fund is able to realize gains (or losses) from the sale of the company.

There exist two categories of PE investment: capital placed in funds (*fund investing*) and capital placed in *portfolio companies* (*direct investing*), or companies under direct ownership of an entity. For example, a pension fund rarely invests capital directly in portfolio companies, though some exceptions do exist. Pension fund managers and their staff instead generally focus their efforts on fund investing activities: they place capital with PE funds that act as appointed managers between the pension fund and portfolio company. PE funds, conversely, use their capital to make direct investments in portfolio companies.

GENERAL TERMS AND BRIEF OVERVIEW

To understand the PE arena is to understand the "man behind the curtain" in *The Wizard of Oz*—many details of the industry are shrouded in secrecy, and firms are often reluctant to divulge details of their funds to outsiders. Nonetheless, once understood, the complexities of the industry largely vanish, and the reader is left with a concrete understanding of the motivations that keep such a well-oiled machine running. The privacy in which the industry operates is essential to its function. Many of the PE transactions involve providing liquidity to family and privately held companies not at all interested in publicity. In the VC segment, many of the investees are technology based and careful guarding of private and proprietary business intelligence and intellectual property is essential until such investees reach critical mass and can lead or sustain novel market positions.

PE funds are usually organized as limited partnerships and are formed and managed by management companies, formed by the GPs of each limited partnership. These funds are—for the most part—private investment vehicles that permit investors to pool their capital for investment in portfolio companies, allowing investors to greatly increase their diversification, reach, and purchasing power in the marketplace. A PE firm may offer investors the opportunity to invest in multiple funds.

The limited partnership or limited liability company (LLC) structure affords PE funds a number of advantages, including the use of pass-through taxation. In other words, the income generated from such an organization is taxed only once, as it flows to the partners. This is in contrast to a C corporation, where a corporation must first pay corporate-level taxes on income, in addition to taxes paid by owners as ordinary or dividend income. PE funds, also frequently organized in such a manner as these types of organizations, have a finite lifetime.

As of the date of this writing, PE funds are frequently unregistered investment vehicles, meaning that, unlike publicly traded securities, their investment and financial reporting policies are not governed by the Securities and Exchange Commission (SEC) or another policing body. Regulation of the PE industry is an evolutionary process, and significant changes will soon affect larger PE funds. With the passage of the Dodd-Frank Wall Street Reform and Consumer Protection Act (Dodd-Frank) of 2010, many PE funds will be required to register with the SEC. Exemptions to registration requirements exist for VC funds, funds with under $150 million in assets under management, and foreign funds without a place of business in the United States.[1]

Managers of PE funds are often referred to as the *general partners* (GPs), while investors are known as the *limited partners* (LPs), the latter term signifying the limited liability of the investors: investors can lose, at most, the sum of their total committed capital contributions.

Capital for PE investments comes from a variety of LPs. Corporations, banks, and insurance companies were early investors in PE. More recently, pension funds, foundations, and university endowments have joined other LPs to place significant portions of capital with PE funds. These relative newcomers began flocking to PE in the late 1970s and early 1980s due to high historical returns and changes to investment regulations, and growing experience with the benefits of PE funds.

The California Public Employees' Retirement System (CalPERS) and Blackstone are prominent examples of limited and general partners, respectively. CalPERS manages nearly $240 billion of capital; $24 billion is committed to PE funds. CalPERS' portfolio includes investments in numerous buyout and VC funds, including those run by Apollo Management; Blackstone; The Carlyle Group; Kohlberg, KKR; Madison Dearborn Partners; TPG Capital; Khosla Ventures; and Alta Partners. Furthermore, as is often the case in PE, CalPERS has a close relationship with many of its PE fund managers. The organization has participated in at least three funds managed by each of the above-mentioned PE firms.[2]

PE fund investments in portfolio companies are made at the discretion of the GPs, to whom investors entrust their capital. LPs do not influence the day-to-day operations of the fund, as doing so may cause them to lose their limited liability status. Some LPs, having seen net returns diminish with the economic crisis, are demanding greater transparency in fund operations. LPs receive quarterly statements and reports from PE funds relating portfolio companies receiving investment, capital deployed to date, and investment returns, among other items. LPs may express their sentiments regarding these items, but they are not involved in day-to-day fund-level decisions. PE funds have annual meetings to account to LPs, and operate with advisory committees, which include LPs as members.

Unlike other investment vehicles, most PE funds are limited-life entities. They do not exist in perpetuity, and they have a legally bound, limited

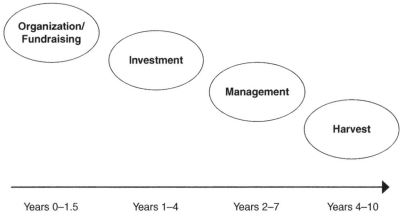

EXHIBIT 1.2 Typical Stages of a Private Equity Fund

lifetime; conversely, *evergreen funds*, as their name implies, are not limited-life entities. While a firm may exist for decades, the typical lifetime of a given PE fund is roughly 8 to 12 years, the average being 10 years. However, in some cases where prospective fund deals may already be scouted, a fund life of six years is not uncommon.

Throughout a fund's lifetime, it will typically go through four stages: organization/fundraising, investment, management, and harvest. See Exhibit 1.2 for further information.

During the organization/fundraising phase, a PE fund recruits investors and determines its strategy and investment focus. The latter point is especially important for VC funds, as they often target a specific area of the marketplace for investment. A fund's focus generally includes the industry, stage, and geography of companies in which it will invest. At least two of these three parameters are frequently held constant and may not be compromised in the investing process. For example, a VC fund may specifically focus on early-stage medical devices across the United States; generally this focus would not change without concurrence of a majority of LPs.

The fundraising phase is highly challenging, especially in times of economic turmoil. Unlike other types of entities, PE funds cannot place fundraising advertisements in newspapers, journals, or online sources, issue press releases, or grant interviews to the press in order to promote their funds, largely because they are not permitted to do so (fund regulations are discussed later in this section). Instead, fund promotion is generally accomplished through word of mouth among LPs, most of whom have a large network of peers. *Placement agents* may also be used by GPs to reach qualified investors.

In a typical, 10-year, limited-life fund, the organization/fundraising stage generally occurs over the first 18 months of the fund's life. The fundraising pace is dependent on numerous factors, including the overall macroeconomic environment and investors' appetite for PE. Some of PE's largest mega funds raised money at even faster levels throughout 2006, 2007, and the first quarter of 2008; fundraising since that time has taken considerably longer for most funds.

It is a primary goal of the PE firm to cultivate long-term relationships with its investors and *gatekeepers*, the latter denoting organizations that assist investors in allocating their PE capital. Gatekeepers are usually compensated with a 1 percent annual fee on committed capital. These agencies are used by LPs to locate PE partnerships that match their investment criteria. Investors with little previous experience in PE investment will often use gatekeepers, as will those with limited staff resources, as gatekeepers frequently provide ancillary services such as due diligence for their clients. Many gatekeepers today also act as FoF managers. An FoF is a partnership that invests capital in multiple PE funds. Because they cultivate long-term relationships with PE fund managers, an FoF manager may be able to access a PE fund not possible directly.

Once the organization/fundraising phase has been completed, the investment stage begins. During the investment stage, GPs scout deals and develop deal flow for their fund. This stage typically encompasses years one through four of the fund. While LPs make funding commitments to the GPs when they first join the fund, only a portion of their pledged capital is immediately taken at the fund's *closing*, or date at which fundraising concludes, nor invested. Once a closing has occurred (typically 12 to 18 months after the fundraising process begins), GPs require time to scout deals before they begin investing money. GPs usually time formal requests to LPs for pledged capital with the projected closing of actual investments. These requests are termed *capital calls*. Once a capital call has been executed, the funds from the capital call are invested in portfolio companies.

Though our previous example highlights *event-based capital calls*, other types of capital calls exist. For example, some funds draw down capital from investors on a prespecified time schedule. This permits the investor to budget for capital subscriptions with certainty.

Waiting to *draw down* capital from LPs, as opposed to demanding all capital up front, allows a GP to maximize the internal rate of return (IRR) of its investments. IRR is a function of the cash-on-cash return received as well as the amount of time required to generate such a return. By drawing down capital from LPs as it is needed, a GP is able to minimize the time element of the IRR calculation, boosting fund returns and the PE firm's reputation. The LP requires this so that it can retain its committed capital in its own investing cycle until called.

Beginning in approximately year two, a PE fund will focus on managing investments in portfolio companies. In some cases, GPs will replace the management team of such a company with professionals from inside the firm while, in other cases, the company's management team may remain in place. Throughout this time period, PE investors may also attract other funds to assist them in raising capital to take the firm to the next level. Such an investment, where multiple firms purchase equity stakes, is called a *club deal* or *syndicated investment*.

Syndicating investments allows GPs to:

- Form relationships with their counterparts.
- Ensure a portfolio company has enough *dry powder* or reserve capital to become successful.
- Diversify risk.
- Provide potential exit opportunities for an initial investor.

Though it may seem counterintuitive to form relationships with competitors, GPs benefit from such relationships by obtaining access to deals in which they might not otherwise participate and bring additional intelligence to benefit the investors. In exchange for this favor, it is expected that the GP who received access will reciprocate on his next deal. Syndication also broadens the base of investment, allowing the portfolio company to tap numerous sources of capital and permitting GPs to hedge investment risks through partnerships with syndicate investors. Lastly, syndication provides potential exit opportunities for GPs, as a GP may sell his interest in the portfolio company to another investor when the GP's fund enters its harvest phase.

In years 4 through 10, known as the *harvest* or *disinvestment period*, PE funds seek to realize the gains made on their investments as soon as feasibly possible. During this time, GPs focus on realizing returns on the fund's assets. Some investments in portfolio companies will pay off handsomely, while others will not. During the disinvestment period, it is the GPs' job to discern which investments are worthy of additional funding and which should be liquidated. This decision is influenced by the PE funds' finite lifetime and the natural life cycle for the investee's development.

Many PE firms, especially those within the VC industry, operate on the assumption that "lemons ripen faster than plums" or "lemons mature faster than pearls." In other words, portfolio companies that fail will be more rapidly discerned than those that succeed. Portfolio company failure is an inevitable fact of the PE business. GPs must mitigate this failure by quickly rooting out failing firms and deploying the majority of their capital to winners rather than losers. The disinvestment period for "lemons" hopefully begins before "plums" and "pearls." GPs distinguish themselves by how they add value to investees facilitating their success and how underperformance or failure is averted.

It is the GPs' goal to realize all investments prior to the fund's liquidation at the end of the fund's lifetime. *Liquidity events* take place as companies are *harvested* by GPs, usually beginning around the fourth year of the fund. (Note that the term "liquidity event" is generally viewed in a positive light by those in the PE arena.) Portfolio companies are harvested through many types of exit strategies: an outright sale (to a strategic or financial buyer), an initial public offering (IPO), and merger are three of the most common exit strategies. Once a company is liquidated, proceeds are typically handled as follows:

- First, LPs receive return of their committed capital.
- Second, LPs receive a hurdle rate (6 to 8 percent) of committed capital.
- Third, return on capital (profits) are allocated among LPs and GPs.

In the third step, the ratio is typically 80 percent to LPs and 20 percent to GP. The GP return on capital is referred to as the GP's *carried interest* or *carry.*

Proceeds from U.S. PE investments are generally split between GPs and investors on a deal-by-deal basis. This is known as the *American waterfall model*, where the term "waterfall" denotes the agreed sequence of distribution of exit proceeds. If distributions occur long before the fund is liquidated, some capital may be reinvested in other portfolio companies, rather than being returned to investors. This activity largely depends on the provisions set forth in the *limited partner agreement* (LPA). This document memorializes the relationship between the GP and its LPs and specifies legal terms, such as the lifetime of the firm, the split of profits, management fees, and expense reimbursements. In contrast to the American waterfall model is the *European waterfall model*, where proceeds are not distributed until the fund has been liquidated. The European waterfall model has gained notoriety in the United States as influential groups, including the Institutional Limited Partners Association (ILPA) have recommended an "all-contributions-plus-preferred-return-back-first" (i.e., European waterfall) compensation model.[3]

Both waterfall models have pros and cons, but GPs generally prefer the American waterfall model while LPs generally prefer the European waterfall model. The American waterfall model allows the GP to receive its carried interest sooner, and this interest can be distributed to the partners or used as an equity contribution for a *follow-on fund*, or a fund that is raised subsequent to one currently run by a GP. The American waterfall model is moderated by a *clawback provision* to address the possibility for a GP to receive a large amount of carried interest for a successful, early portfolio company harvest, and the carried interest received for a quickly harvested, successful deal may exceed the total carry the GP should receive at the end of the fund. For example, assume a GP runs a $100 million fund and the LPA specifies 20 percent carried interest. Let us further assume the GP paid $10 million for a portfolio company, the company grew rapidly, and the GP liquidated it for $110 million. This harvest generates $100 million of pretax capital gains, with the GP receiving $20 million pretax of carry. Let us now suppose the remainder of the GP's portfolio was composed of failed companies. In this instance, the $20 million of carry received by the GP would exceed 20 percent of the fund profits ($100 million of pretax capital gains from the initial harvest sale, less $90 million lost from the failure of the remaining companies). In this instance, a clawback provision in the LPA would be invoked, and the GP would have to return $18 million of previously received carry.

Despite the ubiquity of Internet stock trading among everyday investors, direct investment in PE funds is generally not possible for many investors. Indirect investments in public PE firms such as Blackstone or Fortress Investment Group are, however, possible for the individual investor. This is in large part due to the fact that nearly all PE funds have a substantial minimum contribution size that is required of investors in order to participate in the fund. Often this hurdle will be specified in the LPA separately for institutional (i.e., pension funds, banks, etc.) and individual investors. Generally, the GPs will require a smaller commitment from individual investors than from institutional investors. The LPA of most funds prohibits follow-on funds until the previous fund has completed its "new names" investment cycle. Often the LPA "flattens" the fee structure of the combined funds so the GPs remain focused on delivering results from prior funds before diverting attention to raising a new fund and getting mesmerized by the allure of additional fee income.

Though the previous process aptly describes the lifetime of many PE funds, a PE firm may have multiple funds under its stewardship at the same time. Raising multiple follow-on funds is a central goal for GPs and allows them to turn a collection of limited-life funds into a lifetime business—should they be successful. GPs may raise a follow-on fund two to four years after the start of a previous fund; the time period between fundraising decreases as the economic climate and previous fund returns improve.

Raising a follow-on fund is no easy task and requires that the GP deliver high returns to its LPs. When a follow-on fund is raised, it is often labeled with a scheme that lets investors—and the public—quickly recognize long-term success, in spite of rather lackluster naming conventions. For example, suppose that there exists a new PE firm, "Nouveau Equity." Often, the first fund raised by a firm will bear a name similar to "Nouveau Equity," with future follow-on funds being named "Nouveau Equity II," "Nouveau Equity III," and so on. While the naming scheme is banal, it offers investors an at-a-glance understanding of the age of the firm.

Such names are also a source of pride and credibility for management, as it is no easy task for a firm to raise a large number of follow-on funds—the ability to do so speaks highly of the management team in place at a PE firm.

Successful PE firms are no different than other professional firms; they consistently produce above-average returns and do so with a consistent strategy. Professional investors in PE firms measure the performance of the firm's funds. Successful PE firms meet or exceed benchmark measures, build their professionalism, reputations, name equity, and stature. This building process is painstaking in today's competitive environment. It does not happen by chance and requires strong discipline.

THE LIMITED PARTNER AGREEMENT AND GENERAL PARTNER INCENTIVES

The LPA contractually binds both the GPs and LPs in a single, limited partnership agreement. Most PE funds are organized as limited partnerships, as opposed to C corporations—or any other structure for that matter, though an increasing number of PE funds are being structured as LLCs, where an LLC operating agreement would contractually bind the parties. For expositional simplicity, we will assume GPs and LPs are bound through an LPA and not an LLC operating agreement; the limited partnership structure remains dominant in the U.S. PE industry due to a well-established body of laws and practices concerning this organizational form.

In addition to specifying the lifetime of the firm, how capital commitments will be drawn, allocations and distributions, covenants and restrictions, carried interest, management fees, and expense reimbursements, the LPA discusses investment restrictions placed on the GPs, provisions for extending the fund's lifetime, commitments made by LPs, and actions taken should LPs default on their commitment.

While the GPs unquestionably require funds for investment in portfolio companies, these funds are not required at the fund's closing, though a pledge from the LP stating its commitment is included in the LPA.

LPAs generally specify that investors contribute a given percentage of their pledged capital at the fund's closing, usually between 10 and 40 percent. Future contribution dates may be denoted in the LPA, or the GPs may select these dates at their discretion—the latter is likely the case. Most funds draw down more than 90 percent of their capital by the time the fund is three to four years old and has completed the original investment cycle.

The LPA may also contain special provisions designed as a check on the GPs' power. In most cases, the LPs can replace the GPs if a majority believe that the GPs are not handling the fund's investments properly. (In some instances, LPAs require a supermajority, say, two thirds, to agree on such an issue in order for it to take place.) In extreme cases, the LPs may vote to dissolve the fund.

Although unusual, for one reason or another, an LP may default on its commitments to the fund; the penalty associated with such an action is often determined by circumstances. For instance, if a public pension fund were forced to withdraw from a PE fund due to changes in government regulations, withdrawal penalties would likely be waived. However, should an LP fail to respond to a capital call, the investor may be liable for interest and penalties, and in extreme cases, the LP may have to surrender its stake in the fund. Penalties may also be less harsh if the GP has a long-standing relationship with a defaulting LP that it would like to maintain. In such a case, the GP may recruit investors or permit the LP to sell its stake in the fund to another investor for fair market value on *secondary markets*.

Secondary markets for LP interests have developed dramatically since their beginnings in the early 1980s. They provide liquidity for investors whose PE investing plans and allocations may change during the life of such investments. Secondary investing has become a subclass of PE and many long-term PE investors have allocations to this subclass either directly, through specialized advisors or FoFs with this capability. In recent years, the secondary market has included a secondary direct category to facilitate direct investments in VC or PE investees through purchases from VC or PE firms, directly with investees, or through private placements. A celebrated deal in this category is the recent series of Facebook secondary purchases.

In addition to commitment levels and recourse provisions for LPs, the LPA specifies the fund's carried interest and management fees. With respect to the latter, the GPs—especially those of buyout funds—typically receive such fees dependent on the size of the fund, although some of today's largest funds continue to charge management fees commensurate with those of lesser size. A standard management fee charged by a GP ranges between 1.25 and 3 percent per annum of the fund's committed capital, with a 2 percent fee being highly common in the industry. Larger funds generally will charge investors a smaller management fee representative of the administrative economies of scale associated with running such firms (e.g., less paperwork and staff per dollar of committed capital). However, venture funds may charge a standard 2 percent management fee irrespective of the fund size as the economies of scale are considerably less for these funds than for their buyout counterparts. *Breakpoints*, or fund sizes in excess of which the management fee rate drops, are common.

Buyout funds purchase mature companies with well-known pasts. In contrast, VC funds seek out small, newly formed companies with promising ideas and strong management teams. While the buyout model permits GPs to acquire larger companies as the fund size grows (e.g., Bell Canada, TXU Corporation, Chrysler), VC firms invest in smaller firms in spite of their fund size.

Management fees are frequently scaled down once the investment period is complete and may be adjusted according to the proportion of the portfolio that has been divested. There exist, however, numerous differences across funds pertaining to management fee structure and the ramp down schedule. For example, some funds will not receive management fees from LPs after the fund's five-year mark has passed. Management fees are used to reimburse some fund expenditures, though numerous expenses are borne by the fund itself.

In addition to management fees, GPs also receive carried interest. Carried interest represents the primary incentive mechanism for GPs. The standard carry used in many PE agreements is 20 percent of the fund's profits, although a carried interest of between 15 and 30 percent is not uncommon; the most successful funds will be more likely to obtain higher carry. This form of return on investment serves to align the interests of the GPs with those of the LPs, as it incentivizes the GPs to generate strong investment returns. LPs receive the remainder of the fund's profits after the carry has been deducted. Gompers and Lerner found that over 80 percent of PE funds charged a 2 percent management fee and 20 percent carried interest.[4]

Carried interest has caused quite a stir in recent years as members of Congress have questioned the current practice of taxing carried interest as capital gains (with a maximum federal rate of 15 percent in 2011), rather than as ordinary income (with a maximum federal rate of 35 percent in 2011). Even Warren Buffet has weighed in on the issue.[5]

It is, however, little understood that GPs generally purchase their carried interest and this becomes part of their risk or "skin in the game." As previously stated, carried interest is generally subordinated to LPs' returns and does not accrue until LPs receive a return of their capital plus a preferred return. In this manner, carried interest works in a similar fashion as the entrepreneur's own investment, aligning the interest of the GP with the LP's desire for above-average returns.

Exhibit 1.3 presents a diagram of the complete private equity process, along with the fees received by each party.

In recent years, many LPAs and LLC operating agreements have specified a *preferred return* for PE investors. This return represents an annual return LPs are entitled to receive on their invested capital before GPs can receive any carried interest. A typical preferred return is 8 percent per annum, though many preferred returns fall between 6 and 10 percent of invested capital.

There exists a tremendous push among PE funds to achieve returns in the top quartile of all investments made by similar funds. Similar funds include those participating of the same *vintage year* (or year the fund was activated), industry, stage, and geography. Some LPs will examine funds by vintage year and quarter as numerous macroeconomic shifts affecting PE

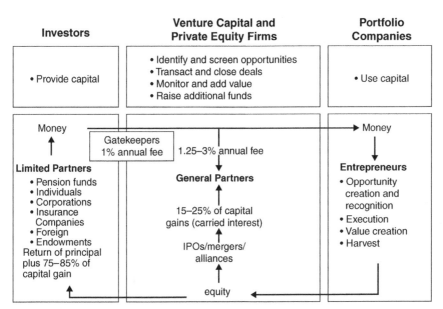

EXHIBIT 1.3 The Private Equity Process

fund performance might occur throughout a year (e.g., first quarter versus fourth quarter of 2000 or 2008).

As with a fine bottle of wine, PE firms with funds in the top quartile of their peers are revered by investors. When these firms seek to raise follow-on funds, they are generally oversubscribed, as investors attempt to gain access to these funds—past truly is prologue in PE. This is especially true in times where returns in other asset classes are subpar, as the "flight to quality" for many investors compels them to gain access to funds with strong track records. PE industry leaders distinguished themselves in the 2008–2011 period of extremely difficult economic times. The firms that intelligently supported investees during these times have demonstrated strong exits as the down cycle reversed.

PRIVATE EQUITY FIRM STRUCTURE AND SELECTED REGULATIONS

When compared with the total size of the companies that they invest in and oversee, PE firms are relatively small. Blackstone, KKR, and Texas Pacific Group (TPG) are three large firms at the center of the industry. Blackstone has a staff of 1,470 professionals in 22 offices around the world. This staff manages $150 billion in assets and portfolio companies with a total of

686,000 employees.[6] Smaller firms will often have significantly fewer personnel. A firm with $250 million in assets under management may have a staff of 20 to 40 employees; a firm with under $100 million in assets under management may have a staff of five to seven employees.

Many PE firms outsource functions to leverage their staff. Investment due diligence and operations assessments are sometimes performed by external advisors, effectively reducing the current staff size at PE firms.

In past decades, PE firms were composed almost wholly of GPs who were responsible for making all investment decisions, including portfolio company selection, management, and exit or harvest strategies. However, as the PE industry has grown, more staff-level employees and other executive staff members now comprise a significant portion of the employment in PE firms. Staff-level employees may include associates and principals, while a firm's executive staff now includes individuals with typical corporate-like titles, such as chief financial officer (CFO), chief executive officer (CEO), chief operating officer (COO), and chief legal officer (CLO), and chief recruitment officer (recruitment and HR are important value-add activities), among others.

While members of a firm's executive staff may play a role in the oversight of portfolio companies, these individuals are primarily focused on deal flow development of the PE firm; however, they are sometimes involved in *term sheet* (an initial document presented to a prospective portfolio company summarizing key terms of an *investment agreement*) negotiations and planning the harvest of portfolio companies.

In order to minimize administrative burdens placed on firms and to ensure that fund qualifies for exemption from numerous registration requirements, minimum capital commitment levels are kept relatively high. In this manner, many PE funds have few investors in order to qualify for an exemption available under Rule 506 of Regulation D of the amended Securities Act of 1933.[7] Exemption from this Act is favorable due to the considerable costs, public disclosure obligations, and compliance obligations associated with registration.

Many Regulation D exemptions require that securities or fund interests be offered only to *accredited investors* or a maximum of 35 unaccredited investors. Dodd-Frank changed the definition of "accredited investor." Prior to Dodd-Frank, a person was an accredited investor if (1) such person had an individual income in excess of $200,000 in each of the two most recent years or joint income with their spouse exceeding $300,000 in each of those years and has a reasonable expectation of reaching the same income level in the current year; or (2) such person's net worth, together with their spouse, exceeds $1 million at the time of purchase. For the purpose of determining net worth, individuals previously could include the value of their primary residence. Under Dodd-Frank, individuals may no longer include the value of their primary residence for the purpose of determining net worth under the accredited investor definition. Other provisions of the accredited investor definition remain unchanged. Large, 501(c)(3) organizations, corporations, business trusts, and partnerships not formed for the specific purpose of acquiring securities are accredited investors if they have in excess of $5 million in assets.

Regulation D imposes very specific restrictions on the solicitations funds may use to raise capital. Specifically, no mass mailings, advertisements, press releases, or informational seminars are permitted. However, funds may engage in solicitation with investors with whom they have preexisting business relationships and with investors who are believed to be accredited.

Furthermore, fund managers may not provide information to nearly any type of publication (those of both wide and limited circulation) for the purpose of fundraising; even general articles about a fund and its managers are frequently avoided given that they may be viewed as a promotion of a fund by the SEC. *Tombstone* ads and press interviews discussing the fund are generally permissible after the fund has ceased fundraising. Formal interviews with the press are rarely granted by GPs, as the GPs do not want to have their actions misconstrued as promoting their next fund.

Dodd-Frank significantly increases the regulation of PE firms, particularly those that manage one or more private funds. Per Dodd-Frank, a private fund is a fund that is exempt from the definition of investment company under the Investment Company Act of 1940 (IC Act). This exemption occurs due to Sections 3(c)(1) and 3(c)(7) of the IC Act, and generally includes VC and PE funds.

Prior to the passage of Dodd-Frank, PE funds commonly maintained exemption from registration as investment advisors by advising fewer than 15 clients. This exemption was permitted under Section 203(b)(3) of the IC Act. After July 21, 2011, this exemption was eliminated, meaning fund managers must register with the SEC unless they can rely on another exemption from registration.

Dodd-Frank also narrowed another exemption from the Investment Advisers Act of 1940 (IA Act). Under this exemption, a VC or PE fund was exempted from registration under the IA Act if the fund did not provide advice regarding securities listed on a national exchange and all of its clients were residents of the state in which the fund had its primary office and place of business. Dodd-Frank, however, does contain several new exemptions from registration with the SEC under the IA Act. These include exemptions for (1) an investment advisor to one or more venture capital funds and (2) an investment advisor that manages only one or more private funds and that has aggregate assets under management of less than $150 million.[8]

Other regulations, such as the Employee Retirement Income Security Act of 1974 (ERISA), weigh in heavily on investment in PE funds. ERISA was enacted primarily to protect the interests of participants in employee benefit plans and their beneficiaries, and it requires plans to supply participants with detailed information. Specific plan features and funding must be disclosed to participants. The act also "provides fiduciary responsibilities for those who manage and control plan assets; requires plans to establish a grievance and appeals process for participants to get benefits from their plans; and gives participants the right to sue for benefits and breaches of fiduciary duty." ERISA has been amended multiple times over its life. These changes, according to the U.S. Department of Labor, were aimed at "expanding the protections available to health benefit plan participants and beneficiaries."[9]

When originally passed in 1974, ERISA instructed pension plan managers that they should invest plan assets "with the care, skill, prudence, and diligence under the circumstances then prevailing that a prudent man acting in a like capacity and familiar with such matters would use in the conduct of an enterprise of a like character and with like aims." This is generally known as ERISA's Prudent Man Rule. As such terms were initially quite vague, some plan managers believed that the act forbade them to invest in risk capital such as PE. Institutional investments in the PE arena soon plummeted after the act's passage on September 2, 1974. It was not until 1979 that the Department of Labor clarified ERISA's Prudent Man Rule, explicitly permitting pension fund managers to invest in PE.

Despite the aforementioned clarifications to the Prudent Man Rule, ERISA still limits the participation of pension plans in PE. Aside from special exemptions, PE funds are not permitted to raise more than 25 percent of the capital for a given fund from pension "benefit plan investors." If the fund qualifies as either a VC, real estate investment, or distressed investment operating company, it may be exempt from the above requirements; however, these qualifications are not easy to achieve.

The U.S. Pension Protection Act of 2006 also bore significant influence on PE funds with respect to ERISA regulation, especially the act's revised definition of a benefit plan investor. Whereas previously the definition included employee benefit plans subject to ERISA, it also included government and foreign country benefit plans; these latter two types of benefit plans are now excluded from the definition. FoFs also benefited from this piece of legislation: Only 50 percent of an FoF's ERISA contribution to a PE fund is counted as part of the 25 percent rule.

As evidenced by the above-mentioned plethora of regulations (which still only represent a fraction of those to which PE funds must adhere), raising a PE fund is no simple task. Because of these regulations, the LPA often specifies a minimum and maximum number of investors, along with minimum commitment levels for investors. The targeted fund size is also specified in the agreement as a range, determined by both the general and limited partners.

If the GPs are not able to raise enough capital to meet the lower level of this range, the fund is not allowed to close, and commitments are released. In contrast, the LPs also have a vested interest in not allowing the fund size to grow too large. In such a case, the administrative duties of the GPs may become unbearable, and the GPs' management team may become stretched too thin managing many investors.

Investors will usually permit GPs to exceed the prespecified maximum fund size by a small amount (i.e., 5 to 15 percent), although all LPs must agree to such terms. In some instances, LPs have even permitted the GPs to reopen a formerly closed fund to raise additional capital (e.g., Blackstone Capital Partners V). Such a rare step might be taken because of the LPs' fears that they would be excluded from future funds should they vote against the fund's reopening.

This instance alludes to an important issue in the current PE arena: access to top-tier funds. While the number of PE funds has continued to grow in size, there continually exists a push for LPs to invest in follow-on funds managed by firms that have demonstrated superior past returns in previous funds. As discussed in a previous section, LPs usually look to invest their capital in firms that have demonstrated fund returns in the top quartile of all those in a similar investment area.

In addition to possessing strong historical track records, institutional-quality funds are run by GPs who have demonstrated an ability to "get deals done" in the past, and they generally accept contributions only from LPs with whom they've had ongoing relationships. The "star quality" of such funds and their managing firms frequently overshadows other, smaller funds in the PE market.

As such, start-up PE funds, or those with lesser track records, have a significantly harder time raising capital than do those funds with historical returns in the top quartile. However, one way in which new and smaller funds can attract first-time investors is by investing a considerable amount of their own capital in the new fund—this contribution will also be specified in the LPA.

Prior to the enactment of the Tax Reform Act of 1986, GPs were required to put up 1 percent of the total capital in a fund (the 1 percent rule). In these times, even in the top quality firms, LPs expect GPs to invest much more than one percent in their fund. Nonetheless, the GPs of well-established funds continue to finance approximately 1 percent of the new fund in order to provide investors tacit assurance that they have significant "skin in the game." Moreover, some LPs require that the GPs contribute more than 1 percent of the fund's capital in order for them to invest in the fund. This is generally true for small- to mid-market funds.

TYPES OF PRIVATE EQUITY INVESTMENT

There are many types of private equity investment; however, this book primarily focuses on VC and buyout transactions. Exhibit 1.4 presents a taxonomy of PE investments that will be described in this section.

At one end of the spectrum lies *angel investing*. The national angel market in recent years has grown dramatically and in 2008 was more than twice the size of the VC industry in financing early-stage investees. Although it has gained considerably more structure in recent years, the market for angel capital remains rather informal, as is often arranged by word-of-mouth. Frequently, lawyers or other business professionals will refer companies to investors through personal recommendations.

Angel investors are generally high-net-worth individuals who invest in companies with a feasible idea; prototypes of future products may or may not have yet been developed when the investor is first approached. In order to compensate these investors for the large risks they must bear, they generally require relatively large equity stakes or invest in convertible debt securities. Such convertible structures might allow an angel investor to forgo a valuation of the investee (a considerable task involving much guesswork at this stage of the company's life) and resist future cramdowns through recapitalization by subsequent investors. Convertible debt also allows an angel investor to "ride the upside" of his investment through conversion to equity.

Despite their interest in the company, the typical angel investor rarely exercises control over the business; the day-to-day operations of the business are left to the entrepreneur, or the management team, although the investor may provide the investee with advice.

Investors in firms with a little more maturity than those funded by angels are called seed investors. These individuals also make equity investments in fledgling firms, but the idea upon which the firm has been formed has a higher probability of success. Seed money may be used to recruit management or increase research and development expenditures so that a product may be refined for sale. Many PE professionals regard seed funding as the first level of early-stage VC.

More mature firms seeking early-stage VC will present complete sound business plans and prototypes of commercially feasible products. These

EXHIBIT 1.4   Private Equity Investment Categorized by Age of the Portfolio Company

firms will employ their funding to construct manufacturing facilities and establish a supply chain for their product so that it may be sold to retail customers. Such firms may also use their VC to build inventory.

The most mature of firms seeking early-stage VC may already be turning a profit, but they require further injections of cash in order to fund the fast-growing business; opportunities for investment may outstrip the current cash flow of the business. If they possess collateral and, at a minimum, a brief history of profits, these firms may also seek bank financing. Restrictions on banks have limited such loans in recent years except for those banks skilled in backing loans with SBA guarantees.

As is the case with angel investing, providing early-stage VC is a long-term commitment. Returns on investments may not be realized for many years, and the investments are highly illiquid. These risks are mitigated by the commensurate stakes these investors generally demand.

Firms that possess fully developed products with proven technology may seek later-stage VC. These firms have a track record of profitability, but may require further cash injection in order to grow the firm beyond what the current level of working capital permits. Also, if early investors wish to cash out of the firm prior to a liquidity event, later-stage VC can be used to facilitate this need.

Many VC investments are made in stages. A primary investment is made, and further capital is not committed until the portfolio company is able to meet a milestone specified by the terms of investment. This phenomenon of *staged capital* permits investors to limit their downside risk, while allowing entrepreneurs to retain larger equity stakes in their company.

If a portfolio company received all of its funding up front, investors would be squeamish about the entrepreneur squandering the cash, and, moreover, the entrepreneur would have to grant his/her investors a large equity stake to receive this funding. By injecting capital in stages, the business is allowed to appreciate in value before further cash infusions are required. As the business's value increases, the entrepreneur can give up a smaller piece of his/her equity in order to receive an infusion of cash. Successful VC investors use such staging to ensure their capital is used efficiently and focused on steps or milestones related to the investee's business plan.

At the opposite end of the spectrum from VC investments lie buyout deals. These transactions focus on the acquisition of mature public or private companies or subsidiaries of such companies that often have experienced a short-term "blip" in earnings. While historically the company may have produced strong returns for investors, because of market forces or poor management, they may have experienced a recent downturn that the buyout team believes they can remedy.

When searching for potential buyout targets, GPs look for firms with strong, stable cash flows, market leadership, a well-seasoned management team, and a low debt-to-equity ratio relative to industry peers (i.e., a conservative capital structure). Cash is king in leveraged buyout (LBO) transactions, as cash payments are used to service the debt raised in the deal—not earnings. Moreover, in possessing these qualities, banks will be more likely to lend large amounts of debt to the target firm, as each of these traits increases the probability that the company will make its interest payments in a timely manner. Because of the large amounts of debt used in buyout deals, they are often referred to as LBOs.

While VC investments are typically all-equity deals or use subordinated debt, buyout investments are often funded with large amounts of debt. Control of a company is assumed by buying out the current shareholders with capital derived from a combination of debt (from lenders such as banks) and equity (from PE funds). Due to the high level of debt in buyout transactions, buyout GPs strictly monitor their portfolio companies' cash flow.

In the late 1980s, leverage multiples were especially high as buyout funds pushed the limits on debt financing; average leverage multiple for all LBOs was 8.8 times earnings before interest, taxes, depreciation, and amortization (EBITDA). By 1992, however, this multiple had decreased to 6.0 times EBITDA with the savings and loan crisis and the subsequent recession that resulted from it.

As the economy continued to grow at record pace in the mid-to-late 1990s (real gross domestic product [GDP] growth averaged 4 percent per year from 1994 through 1999), banks became more lenient, increasing debt multiples, though today leverage multiples are well down from highs seen in 2006 and 2007.[10]

THE PRIVATE EQUITY FUNDRAISING PROCESS

One of the most important topics in the modern PE arena is fundraising. As many funds raised massive sums of money through the second quarter of 2007—some in the tens of billions of dollars—fundraising was often at the forefront of many news articles and discussions centered on the arena. Although the current credit markets and the macroeconomic climate have put a significant damper on current fundraising levels, it is nonetheless important to understand why some PE funds experienced such high rates of investment in recent times, and also how the fundraising process works.

There are four principal parties that are at the heart of all PE fundraising processes: GPs, LPs, gatekeepers, and placement agents. As discussed in a previous section, the LPs pledge capital commitments to the GPs, who are then responsible for investing these funds in portfolio companies. In some instances, third-party investment advisors (aka gatekeepers) may also be involved in the fundraising process. These advisors, such as Cambridge Associates, Abbott Capital Management, Credit Suisse First Boston, and Venture Economics, assist the LPs in making PE investments. They are extremely knowledgeable about the industry and generally track the performance of funds and firms, issuing recommendations to LPs about where they should invest their funds. The GP counterparts to these investment advisors are called *placement agents,* or firms that the GPs hire in order to attract capital. Some of the world's largest investment banks, such as Goldman Sachs, have placement agencies. The agents charge a fee for providing this service, with the cost largely being a function of the new fund's size and the GPs' current status as a PE investor. For instance, the fee charged to a smaller, new, non-follow-on fund with a fledgling management team may be as high as 3.5 percent of the fund's total committed capital; the fee for identical services for a large fund run by well-established GPs may be as low as 0.5 percent of committed capital.

While the majority of a PE fund's assets are put up by the LPs, the GPs almost always contribute some capital toward the fund, typically 1 percent of the fund's *corpus* or total fund size. As discussed above, GPs may contribute more than this customary amount.

Raising a new fund has never been an easy task. The recent popularity of well-established PE firms raising mega-follow-on funds has made such a task even harder, crowding out newer firms. Investors want to see top-quartile returns in previous funds and a seasoned management team as GPs with a track record of success, and they want to invest in a fund led by a PE firm with significant brand equity. Despite copious enticements (e.g., lower management fees and carried interest), LPs may still prefer to invest in a fund managed by a tried and true GP. Nonetheless, in order to encourage LPs to invest in new funds, GPs may put up a larger than normal portion of the fund's capital. Such an act serves to demonstrate to potential LPs that the GPs have significant skin in the game and, presumably, confidence in their investing abilities. Such an action may also help a fund surpass a threshold size, permitting it to garner more attention (e.g., the $100 million, $500 million, $1 billion, or $10 billion level). Additionally, the GPs of new funds may hire placement agents in order to raise additional capital. There currently exist agents who specialize only in new funds. Recognizing that some new funds have well-motivated GPs, several FoF Managers have charters to seek out newer and first-time funds. This has led to innovation in strategies and some regional funds to attract institutional investors.

In general, the GPs of new funds will likely find a pool of investors to help finance their funds if these GPs have previously worked for name brand firms, if they have executed and harvested many successful deals, and if the macroeconomic climate is favorable to their strategies. Without such a personal track record and a stable economic climate, GPs attempting to raise new funds will struggle.

LPs place capital with established GPs raising new funds for several reasons, one of which is the difficulty LPs experience in attempting to gain access to established, brand-name, top-tier funds. PE GPs and LPs seek to establish long-standing relationships with one another. Most firms overseeing top-quartile funds already have such relationships with large public body and corporate pension funds, insurance companies, foundations, endowments, family offices, and high-net-worth individuals. As such, when a new follow-on fund is raised by a top-quartile firm, the necessary commitments are generally oversubscribed. Not only do those firms with established relationships want an LP interest in the new fund, so, too, do a large group of investors attempting to gain access to these funds. Unfortunately, however, many of these investors are not granted access to such funds because of the enormous popularity that top-quartile funds generate—everyone is clamoring for a piece of those pies. For these reasons, some LPs may turn to less well-established funds to invest their money.

LPs might also place capital with well-established GPs raising new funds due to exemplary personal track records. New PE firms have been established when GPs break away from established firms to start new firms and funds to reap a greater portion of economic benefits from the investing process. While younger GPs might support a significant fraction of the workload at an established fund, they may not receive a proportionate share of carried interest; a large portion of carried interest frequently goes to partners with "their name on the door" and the co-founders of PE firms. By starting their own fund, an established PE professional will have a chance to reap greater rewards from managing LPs' capital.

When LPs invest in PE funds, they pay close attention to dealmakers at the fund level, and may, in some instances, entice an established professional to leave his current post by promising to commit capital to a new fund he manages. LPs want to place capital with those who are highly incentivized to deliver stellar returns; this might best be exemplified by a professional who has "earned his stripes" at an established fund, but now wants to break out on his own and establish a reputation.

GPs of new funds may also find investors by looking for LPs who have motivations beyond those of financial returns. For example, some university endowments may seek to invest a certain portion of their capital in funds that are located close to such universities; the same might be the case for state pension funds or even corporate pension funds. This is particularly true of LPs located in California, Colorado, Oklahoma, Indiana, and Ohio. These organizations believe that by setting aside a portion of their capital for such investments, they are contributing to the economic well-being of their home state. Individual investors—as opposed to institutional investors—may also be more receptive to investments in such funds, as many are considerably more risk-prone than institutional investors.

Some newer funds may also try to take a very specific industry focus with respect to new investments. This strategy caters to the fact that many LPs are now trying to achieve better portfolio diversification by amalgamating groups of specialized funds. Such a tactic has recently worked well for many mid-market funds.[9]

A final tactic GPs may use in trying to attract new investors is the use of a lead investor (aka special LP). In order to obtain such a title, a lead investor will contribute a large portion of the fund's capital, and may even help subsidize the GPs' marketing costs. In return for such services, the lead investor may receive a portion of the fund's carried interest, on top of an already substantial portion of the fund's distributions. However, it is important to note that the use of a special LP may scare away some potential investors who recognize that this investor will require a substantial portion of the firm's distributions in return for the risks it must bear.

RECENT FUNDRAISING TRENDS

The current trend toward investing capital with large PE funds is a direct result of the LPs' increasing desire to invest in funds with excellent historical track records, and also the aforementioned changes to the U.S. Pension Protection Act of 2006. Provisions of this act have made it possible for government pension funds to invest large sums of capital in funds, without having to maintain their contribution level below 25 percent of the fund's total assets. This has allowed some states with large pools of assets to contribute significant amounts of capital to top-tier funds.

PE *mega funds*, or funds generally managing more than $1 billion in capital, are also making it continually harder for funds of smaller size to find qualified investors, as these smaller funds may not possess the brand equity of their larger brethren. In the current PE arena, nearly all LPs want to invest in funds with firms that have historical top-quartile performance and high brand equity. As many GPs will maintain strong business ties with their LPs (recall the example at the beginning of the chapter of CalPERS and Blackstone), this makes it very difficult for new investors to contribute capital to top-quartile funds.

In some cases, GPs who had previously managed successful PE funds with a parent firm will leave the company and start their own fund—or GPs may elect to stay with the PE firm while starting a new fund using their own personal capital. An example is Vinod Khosla, a partner at the VC firm Kleiner Perkins Caufield & Byers, starting his own venture firm, Khosla Ventures. Khosla is known within the VC community as a prominent deal maker and had been highly recognized by both *Forbes* and *Fortune* magazines.[11] He was a co-founder of Daisy Systems and founding CEO of Sun Microsystems. Khosla focused his new firm on green technologies and launched the firm with the full support of Kleiner Perkins.

In some instances, GPs who leave large firms to start their own funds are highly successful, while others are not. When evaluating whether to invest in such a fund, LPs seek to discern if a GP's success was rooted in the firm's "secret sauce," or through the tenacity of the individual. Along these lines, the LPs will have intense discussions with the individual managing the new fund and attempt to discern just how much skin they had in the game on each of the deals listed on their resume.

LPs will grill the prospective fund manager about who specifically scouted the deal, who arranged the financing, and in what financing rounds the LP's firm participated. Was the deal actually originated and shaped by the individual or someone else in the firm? Did another investor participate in the first round and then bring in this individual's firm for the second round (a safer investment)? Questions such as these, supplemented by numerous phone calls from one LP to another, serve as a principal form of due diligence employed by investors.

Active due diligence pursued by LPs can also help weed out possibly naïve, new fund managers who are purely chasing trends. With so many alternative investment vehicles participating in today's financial arena—most of which were subject to little governmental regulation prior to Dodd-Frank—there are sometimes managers who will try to lure investors to a "flavor of the month" fund. These managers constantly vacillate in focus. They attempt to raise buyout-focused funds when the buyout market is hot (i.e., circa 2007), VC funds when venture is hot (i.e., circa 1997), real estate funds when they're hot, and so on. It is important that the investor be on the lookout for such managers and funds, and that due diligence is actively pursued before committing any capital to an investment.

GENERAL PARTNER INVESTMENT RESTRICTIONS

While the GPs are the administrators of PE funds, there are often restrictions placed on their activities, to which they are contractually bound. At first blush, one may think that the LPs can largely shape the investment decisions of the GPs, serving in somewhat of a board of directors role. LPs are not permitted to direct the day-to-day operations of the fund if they are to retain limited liability status. This detail highlights the extreme importance of the LPA provisions, as the LPs have little say in the fund investment strategy once they commit capital.

Within the LPA are frequently a series of covenants binding the GPs. Although such covenants have now become commonplace, they were virtually nonexistent until the 1980s when venture returns began to sag (see Exhibit 2.9 for further information). During this time period, some LPs felt that their investing counterparts had strayed from the original focus of the fund and, in the process, had invested money in areas where they lacked expertise; the result was lackluster returns and the genesis of covenants in LPAs. Today, in addition to restrictions on the types of investments GPs may make, covenants also specify other numerous restrictions, such as restricting the size of an equity investment a GP may make in a potential portfolio company.

LPs seek to maximize returns while minimizing risk. GPs are expected to deliver such returns.

If the GPs of a fund have invested only a minimal amount of money in the fund (i.e., 1 percent of the fund's assets at closing or less), then they are, in a sense, risk-prone investors. They have little to lose on their initial investment, and a large percentage of carried interest to gain should the investment pay off. In contrast, the LPs are considerably more risk averse than the GPs, since they stand to lose a substantial amount of capital should the fund not generate adequate returns.

In this way, covenants limiting GPs' contributions to portfolio companies are advantageous for LPs as they limit the GPs' ability to invest in a "walking dead" investment, one that requires a lot of cash but produces little in return. A GP may be motivated to invest significant portions of cash into such a company in the hopes that a capital infusion may set the business on track, while the LP would rather cut his/her losses and invest the capital elsewhere. Such covenants are usually expressed as a percentage of the fund's contributed capital or market value of the fund's assets (e.g., not more than 10 percent of the fund's contributed capital may be invested in a single portfolio company).

Furthermore, as many successful PE firms go on to raise follow-on funds, LPAs also contain covenants restricting the practice of having these funds invest in a previous fund's portfolio company. For instance, if "Nouveau Equity" invests in a portfolio company, "Nouveau Equity II" will likely be restricted by its LPA in investing in said company. These covenants are used to prevent GPs from infusing additional capital into a declining company.

As described in previous sections, GPs are under constant, unrelenting pressure to produce returns in the top quartile of all funds. Though many GPs possess high integrity, the quest for this lofty position can potentially entice GPs to make unethical decisions without the use of proper covenants.

Covenants may also restrict the GPs' use of debt in financing portfolio companies, requiring total debt levels to remain below a threshold value based on a percentage of the fund's assets. These covenants became popular after some PE funds in the 1980s used above-average levels of debt to finance portfolio companies with the hope that they would have a better chance of growing faster.

A final type of covenant that commonly appears in LPAs is one that relates to the reinvestment of fund profits. Without such covenants, GPs, motivated by yearly management fees, might attempt to increase their wealth by investing intermediate distributions in investments they well know will not pay off by the end of the fund's life. With the LPs' consent, the GPs may then try to extend the fund's life in order to obtain more yearly management fees. Furthermore, as some GP management fees are based on a percentage of the value of assets under management, returning distributions to investors may decrease these fees.

CONCLUSION

This chapter has presented an introduction to PE finance, including an overview of the PE fundraising process, recent fundraising trends, selected regulations, and investment restrictions placed on GPs. Key terms have also been introduced to the reader. While PE was a largely dormant asset class through the late 1970s, PE investments now represent a significant fraction of many institutional investors' portfolios.

NOTES

1. *Source:* http://www.sec.gov/news/press/2011/2011–133.htm.
2. *Source:* Thomson ONE Banker database.
3. Institutional Limited Partners Association, "Private Equity Principles: Version 2.0," January 2011.
4. P. Gompers and J. Lerner, "What Drives Venture Capital Fundraising?" NBER Working Paper No. 6906.
5. *Source:* http://www.nytimes.com/2011/08/15/opinion/stop-coddling-the-super-rich.html.
6. *Source:* http://www.blackstone.com/cps/rde/xchg/bxcom/hs/firm.htm.
7. *Source:* http://sec.gov/about/forms/regd.pdf.
8. For the Dodd-Frank definition of a VC fund, see http://blogs.wsj.com/venture-capital/2011/06/22/sec-adopts-vc-definition-gives-funds-20-latitude-to-do-other-deals/.
9. For further information, see www.dol.gov/dol/topic/health-plans/erisa.htm.
10. *Source:* Standard & Poor's LCD Comps reports.
11. For further information, see www.khoslaventures.com.

CHAPTER 2

Overview of Historical Trends

Harry Cendrowski
Adam A. Wadecki

INTRODUCTION

Through private equity (PE) has garnered significant attention in recent times, various forms of organized PE have been present for decades. This chapter provides the reader with a brief history of PE, along with historical data pertaining to VC and buyout funds. Fundraising, portfolio company investment, and net returns to limited partners (LPs) are explored on numerous dimensions, including fund size, fund stage, and portfolio company industry. Secondary funds are also examined, including the rise of this market circa 2008 and subsequent return to historical fundraising levels.

A BRIEF HISTORY OF PRIVATE EQUITY

Forms of PE finance are almost as old as history itself; however, in the United States, PE finance—specifically, venture capital (VC)—can largely trace its roots back to private financings employed by the railroad and textile mills in the nineteenth century. However, with the help of the federal government, VC largely jumped onto the investment scene after the turn of the twentieth century: The events of World War I were the setting for the beginnings of VC in the United States.

The War Finance Corporation (WFC), created by Congress on April 5, 1918, was charged with providing credit to essential war industries, largely through loans granted to banks. In its six months of wartime existence, the WFC advanced over $71 million. With its charter expanded during the subsequent peacetime, the WFC was instrumental in financing the railroad and agricultural industries. After the passage of the Agricultural Credits Act of 1923, which established the 12 regional banks of the Federal Reserve, the

WFC was ordered to close, eventually wrapping up its affairs in 1939. Even so, the WFC set the stage for other government-based entities that would fund private enterprises.

In 1932, the Reconstruction Finance Corporation (RFC) was created by President Herbert Hoover "to alleviate the financial crisis of the Great Depression."[1] The RFC was charged with lending money to "all businesses hurt by the Depression, large and small."[2] President Hoover's successor, President Franklin D. Roosevelt, strongly endorsed the RFC and continued to nurture the corporation in hopes of turning around the nation's economy. The Great Depression following the 1929 stock market crash had forced many small businesses to close their doors as individuals stemmed their discretionary spending.

The next decade saw the beginning of another milestone in U.S. history: World War II. While the RFC had not focused on businesses of any particular size, Congress gave a boost to small businesses when it created the Smaller War Plants Corporation (SWPC) in 1942. Although many large businesses deployed enormous amounts of capital to increase production and efficiency for the wartime effort, smaller businesses, lacking such resources, could not compete with their larger brethren. To ameliorate this issue, the SWPC became the first governmental body focused on loaning money expressly to private entrepreneurs. The SWPC also became an advocate for the nation's small businesses and "encouraged large financial institutions to make credit available to small enterprises."[3]

After the war ended in 1945, the SWPC was dissolved, and its duties became part of the RFC, while the Office of Small Business began producing educational programs to assist entrepreneurs in getting their businesses off the ground.

With the beginning of the Korean War in 1950, Congress created the Small Defense Plants Administration (SDPA), a body similar to the SWPC, but with direct oversight from the RFC. The SDPA was charged with certifying small businesses and referring them to the RFC for government contracts, when the administration deemed such entities were ready to perform the work. However, by 1952, "a move was on to abolish the RFC," and in its place, President Dwight D. Eisenhower proposed the creation of the Small Business Administration.[4] The administration was officially created by the Small Business Act of 1953 to "aid, counsel, assist, and protect, insofar as is possible, the interests of small business concerns."[5] The administration was up and running by the next year, providing educational programs and financial assistance to entrepreneurs and advocating for small businesses to receive government contracts.

In 1958, the Investment Company Act created the Small Business Investment Company (SBIC) Program, which "regulated and helped provide funds for privately owned and operated VC investment firms."[6] The SBIC was the offspring of a study performed by the Federal Reserve that "discovered, in the simplest terms, that small businesses could not get the credit they needed to keep pace with technological advancement."[7] The SBIC was now a prime force in the genesis of the modern VC industry.

Several years prior to the SBIC's creation—in 1946—General Georges Doriot founded what many regard as the first organized VC firm in the United States, American Research and Development Corporation (ARD). Doriot, a former French Army man who emigrated to the United States in the 1920s, formed ARD while teaching at Harvard University. In its early years, ARD invested roughly $70,000 of equity into a company named Digital Equipment Corporation, founded by two MIT engineers, Ken Olsen and Harlan Anderson, working on a mini-computer. In September 1970, the company went public and raised over $38 million by an initial public offering (IPO).[8]

Doriot, along with two other notable figures in the venture industry, J. H. "Jock" Whitney, an investor in Minute Maid, and Lawrence Rockefeller, an investor in Eastern Airlines, are largely credited with propelling VC onto the scene in its early years. What was once a cottage industry financed primarily by high-net-worth individuals soon became an organized, alternative asset class.

In the 1960s, a bull IPO market further assisted VC in growing its popularity. Top venture firms, like ARD, were now able to realize significant returns on their investments through lucrative exit events. The leveraged buyout (LBO) industry also came to prominence in the 1960s with the growing popularity of what were then called "bootstrap" transactions. Lewis Cullman is generally credited with orchestrating the first U.S. LBO: the 1964 takeover of Orkin Exterminating Company.[9]

Nonetheless, in the subsequent decade, the PE industry suffered a large blow as the stock market went into a slump in the 1970s and investors were unable to realize the returns they had come to expect through IPOs. Things already looked bleak for PE when the industry was dealt an unintentional knock-out punch in 1974 with Congress's passage of the Employee Retirement Income Security Act (ERISA).

ERISA was aimed at tightening regulations for pension funding and vesting (specifically, with respect to defined-benefit plans), but had the unintended effect of causing pension managers to halt the placement of capital in "high-risk" investments. Because of ERISA, PE fundraising hit a nadir in 1975. In this year, the entire VC industry raised just $10 million.

Clarifications to ERISA's Prudent Man Rule in 1978, however, curbed the downward spiral and explicitly permitted pension managers to invest in PE; investment in VC and buyout-backed companies began a resurgence.

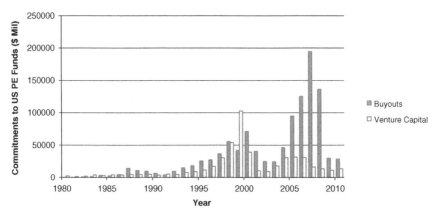

EXHIBIT 2.1   Historical Venture Capital and Buyout Annual Fundraising Levels, 1980–2010
Source: Thomson ONE Banker.

Shortly thereafter, Congress slashed the maximum capital gains tax rate from 49.5 to 28 percent with the passage of the Stieger Amendment, greatly enabling PE investors to realize better net returns. The Tax Act of 1981 further lowered the maximum capital gains tax rate to 20 percent.

The IPO market also experienced a resurgence with star companies like Apple Computer, Genentech, and Federal Express all going public in the late 1970s and early 1980s. As shown in Exhibit 2.1, VC and buyout fundraising, or commitments from LPs to general partners (GPs), surged through the 1980s and varied cyclically though the 1990s and 2000s as an ever-growing number of institutional investors and high-net-worth individuals began to allocate portions of their portfolios to PE investments.

In the late 1980s, buyout fundraising eclipsed VC fundraising, as mammoth takeovers, such as Kohlberg, Kravis, Roberts & Company's (KKR) 1988 acquisition of RJR Nabisco, came to popularity and investors viewed them favorably. Low capital gains tax rates coupled with high availability of bank debt helped the buyout industry experience strong growth. The establishment of the junk bond market in the 1970s and 1980s by individuals like Michael "Junk Bond King" Milken only helped fuel this boom. However, excessive use of debt, such as that employed in Robert Campeau's takeover of Federated Department Stores, where debt comprised over 95 percent of the transaction, generated skepticism among investors—some wondered if the buyout industry had gone too far in its borrowing practices. Numerous companies began adding "poison pill" provisions to their charters in an attempt to scare off would-be raiders like Carl Icahn, who acquired TWA in a hostile takeover in 1985.

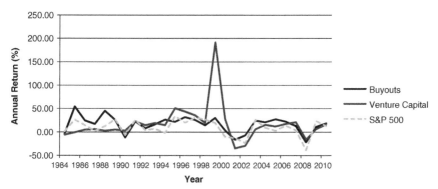

EXHIBIT 2.2 Historical Venture Capital, Buyout, and S&P 500 Annual Returns, 1984–2010
Source: Thomson ONE Banker.

The 1970s/1980s surge in PE capital forced net returns to investors back to near-market levels in both the VC and buyout industries. As shown in Exhibit 2.2, VC returns plummeted, from an average of 33 percent per year from 1979 to 1983, to an average of less than 12 percent per year over 1983 to 1987. Even worse, returns averaged just 2 percent per year from 1984 to 1990, well below the average Standard & Poors (S&P) 500 return during that time period.

Although somewhat delayed with respect to the ebb in VC returns, buyout funds experienced a similar retreat in returns as they fell from a five-year average of nearly 35 percent in 1985 to 1989, to an average of less than 13 percent over the 1989 to 1993 period.

Throughout the late 1980s, and into the early to mid-1990s, commitments to VC and buyout funds continued to plummet. Institutional investors failed to renew commitments in follow-on funds, and new funds were unable to find investors willing to lend capital. Moreover, an economic recession in the early 1990s did not help either arena generate stable returns. Real GDP, shown in Exhibit 2.3, remained relatively flat from 1989 through 1993. In the mid-1990s, however, the U.S. economy, PE, and PE-backed portfolio companies experienced a previously unseen boom in investor and consumer popularity.

PRIVATE EQUITY AT THE TURN OF THE CENTURY

PE market fluctuations from the mid-1990s through current day can largely be broken into four time periods: (1) dot-com boom (1995 through first quarter of 2000); (2) dot-com bust (second quarter of 2000 through 2004);

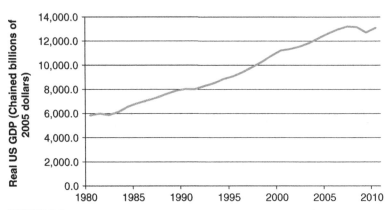

EXHIBIT 2.3 Historical Real U.S. GDP in Chained Billions of 2005 Dollars, 1980–2010
Source: U.S. Bureau of Labor Statistics.

(3) buyout boom (2004 through first quarter of 2008); and (4) buyout bust (second quarter of 2008 through today). Commitments to U.S. VC and buyout funds from 1995 through 2010 are presented in Exhibit 2.4.

In the mid-1990s, an economic recovery was in the making. After remaining flat in the early 1990s, real U.S. GDP grew at a compound annual growth rate (CAGR) of 3 percent from 1992 through 1995 (see Exhibit 2.3), and many thought the U.S. economy was fast approaching a new era of growth. The IPO market gained steam, and investors appeared particularly enamored with IPOs centered on the "new economy" of

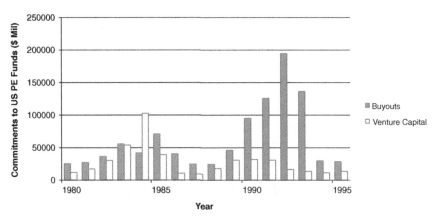

EXHIBIT 2.4 Historical Venture Capital and Buyout Annual Fundraising Levels, 1995–2010
Source: Thomson ONE Banker.

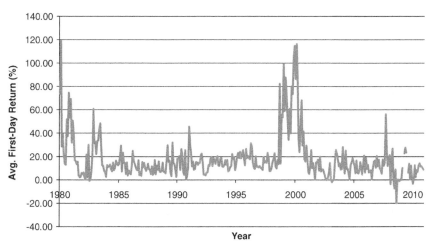

EXHIBIT 2.5 Historical Average First-Day Return to U.S. Initial Public Offerings, 1980–2010
Source: Professor Jay Ritter's IPO Database.[10]

high technology and the Internet: dot-com companies. New issues were delivering first-day returns near 100 percent to investors in the midst of this euphoria. This level of first-day returns had not been seen in nearly 20 years. (See Exhibit 2.5.)

In addition to becoming the darlings of PE, dot-coms, with a label denoting their intense focus on Internet-based services, began invading popular culture. Sixteen of the 33 ads featured during the 2000 Super Bowl promoted dot-com web sites. That 16 Internet-based firms, many with relatively weak operating cash flows, paid a then-record $2.2 million each for 30-second television ads, demonstrates the public hysteria surrounding these companies.[11]

In response to the public's seemingly insatiable appetite for dot-com services, investors poured large amounts of money into VC. VC fundraising levels grew from about $12 billion in 1995 to over $111 billion in 2000, a CAGR of over 55 percent. Buyout funds also experienced high growth levels, though not as extreme as those seen in the VC industry: Buyout fundraising increased from around $26 billion in 1995 to $72 billion in 2000, a CAGR of 22 percent. (See Exhibit 2.4.)

With the growth in fundraising came extremely high levels of capital deployment by VC and buyout funds. In the year 2000 alone, 8,300 VC-backed portfolio companies received $102 billion of VC, up from 2,000 companies receiving $7 billion of VC in 1995. Buyout investment also increased during this time period. In 1995, 500 companies received

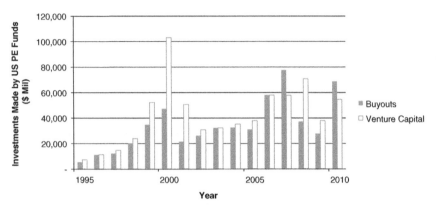

EXHIBIT 2.6 Historical Venture Capital and Buyout Annual Investment Levels, 1995–2010
Source: Thomson ONE Banker.

$5.5 billion of buyout capital; by 2000, nearly 2,600 companies received $47 billion of capital. (See Exhibits 2.6 and 2.7.)

The infamous dot-com era, a time in which stock valuations seemed to decouple from fundamentals, had arrived. By 2000, commitments to U.S. VC funds exceeded 6 percent of the total market value of the combined New York Stock Exchange, NASDAQ, and American Stock Exchange,[12] over four times the historical average of 1.5 percent from 1980 through 1999. VC outshone many asset classes as dot-com fever set in. Investors believed that the new Internet-driven economy was going to push the status quo ahead by leaps and bounds. Unfortunately, many investors strayed

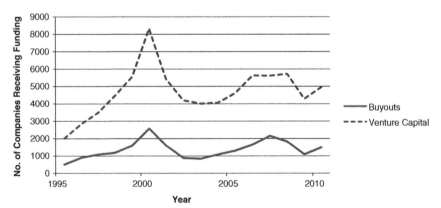

EXHIBIT 2.7 Historical Number of Companies Receiving Funding, 1995–2010
Source: Thomson ONE Banker.

from fundamental models of valuation when analyzing VC portfolio companies, believing that even companies projected to run in the red for many years were worth millions of dollars. Typical market-based valuation methods, including price/earnings and price/revenue multiples, were cast aside in favor of price/clicks and price/web site hits multiples.

Many such dot-com companies based their business models on the power of "network effects," believing that if they could build market share, they could eventually charge a fee for the service they were providing. However, growing the business to such a state usually required numerous years of considerable losses. Venture investors stepped in to help offset these losses and assist companies in generating operating funds through IPOs.

From 1995 through the first quarter of 2000, venture funds deployed enormous amounts of capital to numerous start-ups that did not possess particularly savvy entrepreneurs at the helm, and the dot-com bubble eventually crashed on Monday, March 13, 2000. On this day, the NASDAQ exchange dropped from 5,038 to 4,879 points, a one-day return of −3.2 percent. Though seemingly insignificant in light of the exchange's fivefold increase in value from 1995 to 2000, the drop signaled that the effervescent dot-com era had gone flat. As of this writing in fall 2011, the NASDAQ continues to hover at about half its peak value set in 2000.

Venture returns soon began to sag. In 2000, the average venture fund generated net annual returns of nearly 200 percent for investors; by 2001, the tide had turned, and venture investors lost an average of 40 percent of their capital in just one year. Buyout fund returns also declined, from a multiyear high of 30 percent per year in 1999 to −16 percent per year in 2002. (See Exhibit 2.2.)

For several years subsequent to the dot-com bust, PE—especially the VC industry—possessed a weak pulse. VC fundraising levels plummeted from $111 billion in 2000 to just $29 billion in 2003. As fundraising levels decreased, so too did the number of portfolio companies receiving VC. By 2003, 4,000 companies received VC, less than 50 percent of the level that had received funding just three years earlier. The buyout industry was also hit hard. Fundraising collapsed, dropping to $21 billion in 2002 from $72 billion in 2000. Investments decreased similarly. PE largely went into hibernation until 2004, when fundraising and investment levels once again began to rise. (See Exhibits 2.4 and 2.6, respectively.)

The late 2000s would play out in remarkably similar fashion to the decade prior, with a pronounced asset boom followed by a subsequent bust. This time, however, it was the buyout industry's chance to shine—and, later, to be spurned by investors. In 2005, buyout funds raised nearly $130 billion of capital, up from $53 billion one year prior. In the span of just one year, the buyout market arose from its 2001 through 2004 slumber. Credit markets were flowing as liquid as ever, and buyout shops employed this leverage to purchase ever-larger companies.

By the early part of 2007, the buyout industry was enjoying a renaissance never before seen by investors. Investments spiked to $80 billion and fund sizes, returns, and distributions were at or near record highs. Investors' quest for access to top buyout funds had never been fiercer. "Buying big companies" appeared relatively easy for "any large buyout shop," though it seems some buyout professionals underestimated the limited options for harvesting these large portfolio companies. Harvest options included "a smaller community of prospective buyers and a fickle market for public offerings."[13] What many investors did not yet know was that the IPO market would soon become an even more difficult harvest mechanism once the credit markets crashed in 2008.

From March 2008, when Bear Stearns was rapidly sold to JP Morgan Chase, through March 2009, the S&P 500 lost over 50 percent of its value. (See Exhibit 2.8.) Within this time period, numerous additional shake-ups in the financial sector occurred, including the events of September 15, 2008, when Lehman Brothers filed for bankruptcy. Uncertainty permeated the public markets and the offices of PE investors. Shocked by the marked decrease in their portfolios over a short period of time, many investors began to curb investments in alternative assets, including PE. This decision was made due to liquidity as well as the *denominator effect.*

When allocating capital to alternative assets, many LPs had a strict rule that no more than a certain percentage of their assets (generally between 5 and 10 percent) could be allocated to PE. When the stock market collapsed, investors saw the values of their total portfolios erode; however, because PE

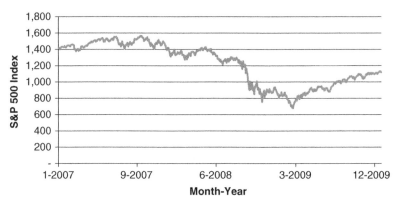

EXHIBIT 2.8 Historical S&P 500 Index Level, 2007–2009
Source: Center for Research in Security Prices.

investments are not liquid and, at that time, LPs were not required to adhere to current mark-to-market standards for asset valuations (i.e., Accounting Standards Codification 820), many investors saw the proportion of PE investments to their total portfolios increase beyond prespecified thresholds. To mitigate this issue, investors put the brakes on PE fund commitments in the years following the credit crisis. (See Exhibit 2.4.)

Today, PE fundraising remains below recent historical levels, and investors are generally tepid about the asset class. Net returns from 2008 to 2010 were less than stellar, though both VC and buyout funds slightly outperformed the S&P 500 in 2010. (See Exhibit 2.2.) Buyout and VC fundraising levels are just above those from 15 years ago and did not top $20 billion in 2010. Already left with a bad taste in their mouths from the dot-com bust, many investors are pushing GPs to lower management fees and carried interest as well as provide more favorable terms in exchange for commitments. A recent survey indicated 50 percent of LPs believe this shift in terms would "persist in the longer term."[14] Though the near-term outlook for PE seems somewhat bleak, 72 percent of PE investors are signaling they will place capital with PE funds between the summer of 2011 and the end of 2012.[15] Whether or not investors will follow through with their intentions remains to be seen.

VENTURE CAPITAL INVESTMENT AND RETURNS BY FUND STAGE

The PE industry has evolved significantly during the past few decades. This section explores selected historical trends in the VC arena, affording the reader a unique perspective on previous data and trends in the industry, beginning with a historical analysis of VC investment and returns by fund stage.

Decades ago, many VC funds had a balanced focus and selected investments in companies at varying stages of development. LPs, in general, viewed the asset class as one entity, rather than an amalgamation of numerous entities as they do today.

When placing capital with GPs in the current market, LPs generally select a fund to fill a very specific piece of their investment pie, and funds are highly specialized to meet this task. Exhibit 2.9 illustrates the historical percentage of capital placed with various types of VC funds. In this era of increased fund specialization, the amount of capital placed with balanced VC funds has decreased significantly over the past few decades. Recently, however, balanced funds have experienced a resurgence, garnering over 60 percent of VC in 2010 versus less than 40 percent just one year prior.

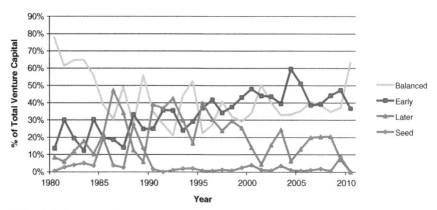

EXHIBIT 2.9   Historical Commitments to Venture Capital by Stage, 1980–2010
Source: Thomson ONE Banker.

Though early-stage funds raised roughly 22 percent of all VC from 1980 to 1989, 45 percent of VC raised between 2000 and 2009 went to early-stage funds. In contrast, later-stage and balanced VC funds have experienced marked declines in fundraising over the past three decades. Thirteen and forty percent of all VC raised went to later-stage and balanced VC funds, respectively, from 2000 to 2009; each figure is roughly 10 percent below its average from 1980 to 1989.

Exhibit 2.10 presents VC investment by sector as a percentage of total VC investment over the past three decades. Perhaps most notable is the rise of computer-related and communications-focused VC investment during the dot-com era and the subsequent decline of funding for these sectors thereafter. Though VC investment in communications-focused companies has decreased since 2000, computer-related VC is again on the rise, in part

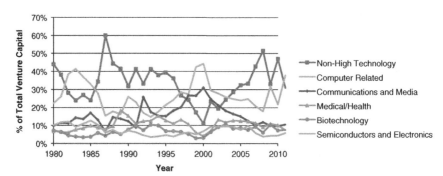

EXHIBIT 2.10   Historical Venture Capital Investment by Sector, 1980–2010
Source: Thomson ONE Banker.

due to the surging popularity of social networking and related applications. Exhibit 2.10 also demonstrates that, despite their popularity in the press, investments in medical and biotech companies comprise a relatively small fraction of total VC investment. The heyday for these VC-backed industries predates the dot-com era, though funding levels in the medical and biotech sectors have stabilized recently. Lastly, non-high-technology investment has surged in recent times. This sector includes VC placed in consumer products companies as well as "low-tech" cleantech and industrial ventures. Though investment in non-high-technology portfolio companies has recently burgeoned, a number of indicators suggest some elements of the sector are becoming less attractive for VCs.

Long an ardent supporter of cleantech investments, Kleiner Perkins Caufield & Byers has stemmed investments in cleantech firms, as have other VCs, including Draper Fisher Jurvetson. Overall, investments in cleantech are down 10 percent in the second quarter of 2011 versus one year ago, and numerous reports indicate this trend will continue.[16]

Venture returns, including those for early-stage funds, spiked in the late 1990s with the dot-com boom. However, since the dot-com bust, many funds have struggled to regain their footing, especially seed-stage funds. In fact, $1 invested in the average early-stage fund in 2005 would be worth little more than $1 today. A similar story prevails for seed-stage funds.

While these venture funds have struggled to deliver superior returns to investors over the past decade, returns to later-stage funds have increased since the early 2000s. Over the past decade, returns to later-stage funds outpaced those of all other VC funds. As evidenced by Exhibit 2.11, later-stage funds did not experience especially high returns during the dot-com era.

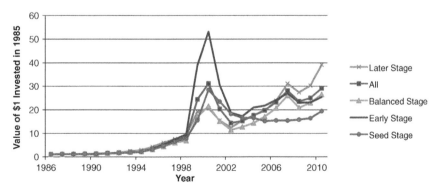

EXHIBIT 2.11 Value of $1 Invested in 1995 in an Average Venture Capital Fund by Fund Stage, 1996–2010
Source: Thomson ONE Banker.

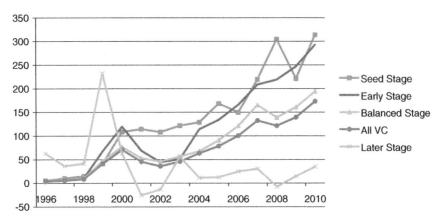

EXHIBIT 2.12 Value of $1 Invested in 1995 in the Average First Quartile Venture Capital Fund by Fund Stage, 1996–2010
Source: Thomson ONE Banker.

Since that time period, however, they have provided investors significantly positive returns well above market levels.

Of course, not every investor receives the average return on capital he/she has invested in a VC fund. Returns have a distribution, and though this distribution is not explicitly tabulated for VC funds, it is possible to infer conclusions about the distribution with existing data.

Exhibits 2.12 and 2.13 illustrate first and fourth quartile returns, re-spectively, to the VC funds listed in Exhibit 2.10. (Note that fourth quartile return data for seed-stage funds was not available.)

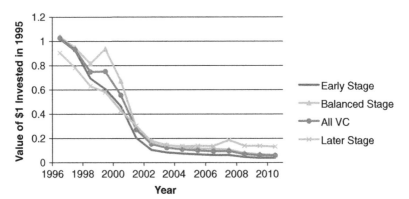

EXHIBIT 2.13 Value of $1 Invested in 1995 in the Average Bottom Quartile Venture Capital Fund by Fund Stage, 1996–2010
Source: Thomson ONE Banker.

Comparing Exhibits 2.11, 2.12, and 2.13 simultaneously, several conclusions become evident: (1) returns to later-stage funds have a relatively tight return distribution; (2) early-stage funds exhibit relatively large return distribution; and (3) balanced funds possess a return distribution between later- and early-stage funds. While later-stage funds delivered high average returns, first quartile later-stage funds did not exhibit returns that favorably compared with other first quartile VC funds from 1995 through 2010. Winners and losers in later-stage funds exhibit more stable returns than early-stage counterparts. For investors looking for relatively predictable VC returns, later-stage funds may offer the return profile they desire. The steadiness of later-stage returns is likely due, in part, to the relatively high level of certainty VC firms have regarding a portfolio company's future cash flows. This certainty mitigates downside risk, but it may also curtail the upside of returns as the strongest portfolio companies could forego VC financing and instead fund operations through internal cash flows or, perhaps, nondilutive financing such as venture debt.

At the opposite end of the spectrum, early-stage funds provide relatively volatile returns that offer investors the chance at large gains (this was especially true in the dot-com boom), but also sizeable losses. Early-stage funds invest in companies with highly uncertain cash flows. This uncertainty can play to the advantage of an investor. At most, a VC fund can lose the sum of its investment; the upside potential for returns, on the contrary, is unbounded. If an early stage-fund includes enough winners to outpace the negative returns generated by losers, investors could realize handsome returns.

VENTURE CAPITAL AND BUYOUT RETURNS BY FUND SIZE

While the previous analysis examined historical VC returns by stage, we now examine both VC and buyout returns by fund size. Exhibit 2.14 presents return information for small (under $250 million), medium ($250 million to $500 million), large ($500 million to $1 billion), and mega (over $1 billion) VC funds from 1996 (the latest data available) to 2010. Perhaps most striking about the results presented in Exhibit 2.14 is the relatively poor performance of mega VC funds over this period of time. Returns to mega VC funds generally trailed those of all other fund sizes until 2007, and have remained in second-to-last place of all fund sizes since that time. Though numerous investors often attempt to gain access to mega buyout funds due to their sterling reputation, our analysis demonstrates that other VC funds may offer more attractive net returns for investors.

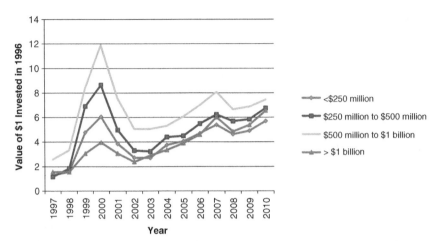

EXHIBIT 2.14   Value of $1 Invested in 1996 in Various Venture Capital Funds by Fund Size, 1996–2010
Source: Thomson ONE Banker.

Over the past few decades, numerous mega funds have also arisen in the buyout arena as investors have sought to place capital with brand-name funds, including The Blackstone Group and KKR. In spite of their astronomical size, many mega buyout funds are oversubscribed by investors hoping to gain access to such a fund.

Exhibit 2.15 presents evidence that may cool the optimism of some mega buyout fund investors. More specifically, the exhibit demonstrates that over the past 15 years, medium-size buyout funds, those $250 to

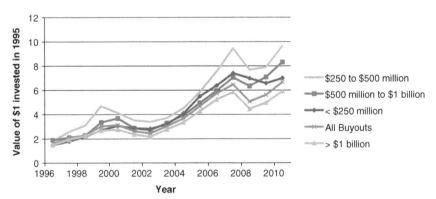

EXHIBIT 2.15   Value of $1 Invested in 1995 in Various Buyout Funds by Fund Size, 1996–2010
Source: Thomson ONE Banker.

$500 million in size, have delivered returns superior to those of other buy-out funds, including mega funds. The strong performance of medium-size funds has sustained itself over much of the past 15 years.

At the bottom of the performance rankings are mega buyout funds. Though numerous investors place capital with these brand-name funds, Exhibit 2.15 demonstrates they have failed to deliver returns superior to their counterparts in recent times. Perhaps most surprising, though, is the strong performance of small buyout funds, those under $250 million in size. These funds and their portfolio companies have generally outperformed all buyout funds over the past 15 years, though in 2009 and 2010 they delivered returns inferior to those of other buyout funds. The reason behind this recent erosion in small buyout returns is unclear, though one reason may be the economic crisis and its documented effect on small businesses.

Years after the crisis began, many small business owners remain jittery about their economic future. A recent survey by U.S. Bancorp indicated 70 percent of small businesses have no plans to expand their staffs in the near-term future. Another recent survey indicated credit deployed to small business continues to decline; this could prove disastrous for any business, especially in light of current raw material and commodity prices.[17]

SECONDARY FUNDS

PE investments are generally illiquid and, in some ways, represent a blind leap of faith by investors. LPs place capital with PE funds, and this commit-ment is often locked up for a number of years before LPs receive distribu-tions or have the option to recall the monies they placed. While waiting for either of these events to occur, LPs cannot turn to a public market to liqui-date their assets in the event they require liquidity. With many PE investors facing a liquidity crunch in today's economy, a mechanism that affords these investors liquidity is sometimes beneficial.

The secondary market has evolved in response to LPs' demand for im-mediate liquidity and greater transparency. From 2000 to 2010, nearly $60 billion in capital was raised by secondary funds, or funds that specialize in acquiring PE portfolios several years after the fund's direct investments have been made. Nearly $20 billion of capital was raised by secondary funds in 2008 as a number of noted LPs publicly struggled to achieve liquidity with PE investments. (See Exhibit 2.16.) The struggles of these LPs, in part, helped increase market supply and, indirectly, demand for secondary funds.

Most recently, commitments to secondary funds have dropped from historic highs to below-average levels. A significant amount of interest in the secondary markets existed in 2008, when numerous university

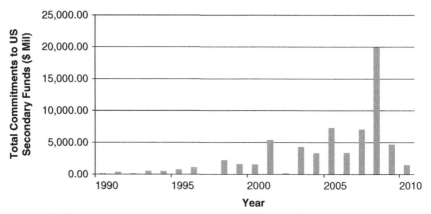

EXHIBIT 2.16   Historical Commitments to Private Equity Secondary Funds, 1990–2010
Source: Thomson ONE Banker.

endowments, including Harvard and Yale, were looking to divest PE assets. It appeared the "floodgates on the secondary private equity market would swing open." However, "as the value of buyout fund investments" declined throughout 2008 and 2009, "the gap between buyer and seller expectations" increased and "left the market in limbo."[18]

When Jane Mendillo became President and CEO of Harvard Management Company, a subsidiary charged with managing the university's endowment and pension assets, she redesigned the school's investment strategy. In 2008, Harvard had "about 13% of its endowment assets in private equity," a significant fraction by any measure.[19] The school, along with Yale University, had "pioneered an investment approach that de-emphasized U.S. stocks and bonds and placed large sums in more exotic and illiquid investments, including timberland, real estate, and private-equity funds. That strategy, which was widely copied, helped the schools avoid significant losses after the technology boom ended in 2000."[20] Unfortunately, it also put them in a bind as the value of the university's liquid assets dwindled with the most recent economic recession.

As the public markets began their fall in the second quarter of 2008, Harvard's endowment saw its liquidity dry up. The university borrowed $1.5 billion in taxable debt to shore up liquidity, "froze faculty salaries, slowed campus expansion plans, and enacted other cutbacks."[21] Harvard also sold some PE investments on the secondary market, including a $150 million interest in Denham Capital Management LP. While initial demand for its PE interests was poor,[22] Harvard was, in part, able to sell stakes in PE funds as the markets recovered and investors realized Harvard's secondary interests afforded them access to funds to which they might not otherwise have access. Furthermore, some of the funds in which Harvard participated had already begun to realize tangible returns, a significant benefit to secondary investors.

Purchasers of secondary interests are afforded a unique benefit uncommon to other PE investors. As secondary investors purchase PE fund interests years after the fund's initial close, they are afforded better knowledge of the fund's potential returns. For example, if an investor purchased a secondary interest in year six of a PE fund, it is highly likely that a portion of the fund's investments would have been liquidated, potentially allowing the investor a glimpse at the remaining returns. Secondary investors also benefit from an increased level of liquidity when compared with other PE investments, as a smaller amount of time exists until the fund's mandatory liquidation. For example, if a secondary investor purchases a fund interest in year six of a ten-year fund, the GP must liquidate investments within a four-year timeframe (barring a fund extension approved by its LPs); the secondary investor need not tie his capital up for the fund's entire lifetime.

Lastly, secondary investors generally do not see negative returns in the early years of their stakes. The typical PE investor with an interest in a ten-year fund will experience what is frequently known as the *J-Curve* or *hockey stick* nature of returns. These labels denote the distinct decline in value of PE fund interests, followed by a subsequent rise. (See Exhibit 2.17.) For some investors, the initial portion of the J-curve makes them uneasy, as charges can eat into the fund's principal even before investments are made. Secondary investors are able to circumvent this portion of the J-curve by entering PE funds in later years, reaping the benefits of increased return certainty.

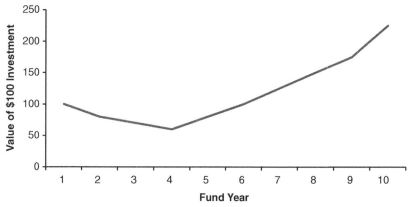

EXHIBIT 2.17 Sample Private Equity J-Curve

Furthermore, though secondary investments have carved out a significant place in PE, investors must remain vigilant in purchasing such assets. Investment due diligence coupled with a solid understanding of the fund-in-question's assets are fundamental to achieving strong secondary returns—perhaps even more so than in standard PE investments themselves.

A 1970 paper written by Nobel Laureate George Akerlof titled "The Market for Lemons" presents a near-perfect analogy to PE secondary markets. The paper highlights the effects of uncertainty and information asymmetry in the used car market, where a poor-quality car is often referred to as a "lemon." In brief, Akerlof concludes that owners of good cars, knowing their cars are of high quality, will not sell their vehicles while owners of poor-quality cars will place them up for sale to dispose of them.[23]

When purchasing secondary investments, investors must make certain they are not purchasing an unwanted "lemon" that a previous LP has cast aside. Given that most notable LPs have a large basket of PE assets which they might sell in the secondary market, a potential purchaser, in addition to rigorous due diligence, should seek to understand why an LP chose a specific PE interest to liquidate, and take moves to ensure a newly purchased fund interest possesses the asset quality initially represented to the buyer.

CONCLUSION

PE fundraising has experienced considerable cyclicality in the past 30 years. During that time, investors and GPs have lived through two buyout booms, occurring in the late 1980s and late 2000s, as well as the dot-com era of the late 1990s. Each of these periods of ebullience was followed by a significant retreat in PE fundraising and investment.

VC and buyout returns have also ebbed and flowed, though it appears many mega funds do not deliver the high abnormal returns investors are seeking.

While secondary funds garnered much attention in 2008 as many notable LPs attempted to liquidate PE assets, secondary fundraising levels in 2009 and 2010 were relatively weak when compared with historical levels.

NOTES

1. *Source:* Small Business Administration, http://www.sba.gov/about-sba-services/our-history.
2. *Id.*
3. *Id.*

4. *Id.*
5. *Id.*
6. *Id.*
7. *Id.*
8. *Source:* Thomson ONE Banker.
9. C. Sullivan, "Lewis Cullman Works Hard to Give It Away," *Newsweek,* January 11, 2005.
10. *Source:* http://bear.warrington.ufl.edu/ritter/ipoisr.htm.
11. A. Edgecliffe-Johnson and J. Martin, "Dot com advertising invades the Super Bowl," *The Financial Times,* January 28, 2000.
12. *Source:* Authors' analysis of data from Thomson ONE Banker and the Center for Research in Security Prices.
13. L. Kreutzer, "Growing Fat on Mega Deals, Firms May Starve for Exits," *Dow Jones' Private Equity Analyst* (November 2006).
14. *Source: The Prequin Private Equity Quarterly,* Q2 2011.
15. *Id.*
16. M. Lynley, "Kleiner Perkins leads slower Q2 cleantech investing," July 6, 2011, http://venturebeat.com/2011/07/06/q2-cleantech-investing-2011/.
17. D. Mattioli and S. Neddleman, "For Small Businesses, Recession Isn't Over," *Wall Street Journal,* July 6, 2011.
18. K. Holman, "Secondary Slowdown? This Corner of the PE Market Was Expected to Be Brisk in 2009, but for Now it Remains in Limbo," *The Investment Dealers' Digest,* March 6, 2009.
19. C. Karmin, "Harvard Endowment Regroups—Facing 30% Loss, Investment Chief Seeks to Manage More Money Internally," *Wall Street Journal,* August 9, 2009.
20. J. Hechinger and C. Karmin, "Harvard Hit by Loss as Crisis Spreads to Colleges," *Wall Street Journal,* December 4, 2008.
21. C. Karmin, "Harvard Endowment Regroups—Facing 30% Loss, Investment Chief Seeks to Manage More Money Internally," *Wall Street Journal,* August 9, 2009.
22. *Id.*
23. G. Akerlof, "The Market for Lemons: Quality and Uncertainty in the Market Mechanism," *Quarterly Journal of Economics* 84, no. 3 (1970).

CHAPTER 3

Trends in Private Equity

Harry Cendrowski
James P. Martin

INTRODUCTION

Private equity (PE) investments have garnered significant attention in recent times as the industry raised vast sums of capital from 2005 to 2007 and now faces increased regulatory scrutiny. This chapter presents a summary of selected topics facing the industry and provides the reader with a comparison of how the current PE environment compares and contrasts with the 2005 to 2007 "golden age" of PE.

A CHANGING TIDE

Many important PE milestones have been set in the past several years as the industry has experienced exuberance, pessimism, and recovery. In 2007, buyout firms were raising record amounts of capital, and VC funds saw fundraising levels increase from post-dot-com era lows. (See Exhibit 3.1.)

Although first used by the Fortress Investment Group, the 2007 initial public offering (IPO) of The Blackstone Group drew wide publicity, as the event seemed to coincide with what may be seen as the zenith of PE. Even though many home investors were effectively boxed out of the Blackstone IPO, the event was nonetheless an important milestone in the history of PE: It further opened the doors to everyday investors wishing to invest in PE funds. Blackstone sold 133.3 million shares—10 percent of the company's stock—of their limited partnership in the IPO offering at about $30 per share, raising nearly $4 billion for a publicly held fund. The firm also sold an additional 10 percent stake to the Chinese government for $8 billion. For his part, Blackstone co-founder and CEO Stephen Schwarzman received 23 percent of the company's stock, worth $7.5 billion, in addition to $677 million in cash proceeds. Shortly after Blackstone's IPO event, another PE

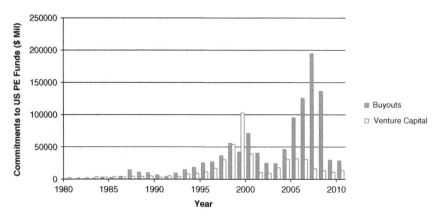

EXHIBIT 3.1   Historical Venture Capital and Buyout Annual Fundraising Levels, 1980–2010
Source: Thomson ONE Banker.

heavyweight, Kohlberg Kravis Roberts (KKR) filed an S-1 document with the Securities and Exchange Commission (SEC) expressing to raise a publicly subscribed fund. While KKR postponed their IPO after the public markets began their descent in 2008, the firm eventually went public in July 2010.

With the benefit of hindsight, one might argue that the Blackstone IPO marks a significant turning point in the PE arena and perhaps signaled the over-exuberance of investors to the asset class. Despite the fact that Blackstone had amassed 17 underwriters for its IPO, it is hard to imagine that these firms had to put on much of a road show to sell shares of the PE giant; investors were already clamoring for shares after Mr. Schwarzman had hit the road for only a few days.[1] Moreover, the event also illustrated the avarice displayed by some individuals who run PE's top firms.

PE is hardly a partnership of equals. Instead, the arena's most notable individuals reap the majority of the spoils, while less notable partners are left to wrangle for their share. As reported in the *Wall Street Journal,* "No founder of any of the major private-equity firm[s] had ever kept as much of the equity in the firm as Mr. Schwarzman."[2]

Though the offering was oversubscribed by investors, today Blackstone stock trades at a fraction of its initial issuance price. As of the time of this writing in October 2011, shares of Blackstone have fallen over 50 percent from the firm's June 2007 IPO price of $31, and have fallen nearly 60 percent from the stock's all-time high, set shortly after the IPO. Blackstone's depressed share price compares similarly with those of other publicly traded

PE firms, including KKR and Apollo Global Management, whose stocks have sagged in the latter part of 2011.

One might additionally argue that Blackstone's IPO touched off the current wave of Washington-based regulatory reforms and proposals centered on PE. At the time of its IPO, some in Congress believed the company's current structure allowed it to largely skirt the current tax code. Many members of Congress share this belief about PE firms today. Even some buyout leaders have spoken out about the current tax code, which allows "buyout barons to pay lower taxes than a 'cleaning lady,'"[3] and magnate Warren Buffet, himself a buyout artist with a permanent source of capital, has opined that the "super rich" need to pay more taxes.[4]

In any event, it is clear that market sentiment has greatly changed in the years following Blackstone's IPO. In April 2007, Henry Kravis of KKR said that we were living in PE's "golden age."[5] Mr. Kravis, whose firm was looking to undergo an IPO in the latter part of 2007, likely has since changed his tune. Shortly after his remarks were made, Mr. Kravis's cousin George Roberts, also a cofounder of KKR, stated that the immediate future will bring difficulties to the PE arena.[6] Roberts's prediction could not have been more accurate.

Amassing large quantities of cheap debt, PE's secret weapon, has become extremely tough to obtain, as credit markets remain tight. It appears that even PE's "800-pound gorillas" are struggling to secure large quantities of debt for their transactions. Exhibit 3.2 shows the average equity contributions to leveraged buyouts from 1987 through the third quarter of 2011. Equity contributions remain near all-time highs, and significantly above levels seen decades ago.[7]

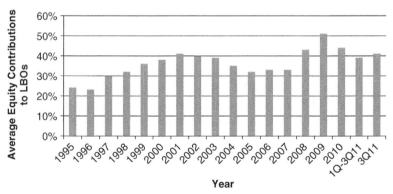

EXHIBIT 3.2   Historical Average Equity Contributions to Leveraged Buyouts, 1995–2011
Source: Standard & Poor's.

However, lending market difficulties are not the only issues facing PE professionals; instead, these difficulties can be seen as a harbinger of a range of difficulties facing the PE industry in this challenging economic environment.

OVERALL INDUSTRY AND FUNDRAISING TRENDS

As detailed in Chapter 2, fundraising in today's PE environment is especially challenging, with 2010 fundraising levels roughly equivalent to those of 15 years ago. (See Exhibit 3.1.) According to London-based Preqin, of the 1,676 funds worldwide attempting to raise $680 billion in the second quarter of 2011, only 120 funds closed with a combined $66 billion.[8] Deal volume is also down, as it appears the third quarter of 2011 will see volume at roughly half of second quarter of 2011 levels. As many PE firms struggle to raise capital, the balance of power has shifted from GPs to LPs, resulting in lower management fees, carried interest, and more favorable terms for investors. "Even marquee firms have resorted to lowering fees, easing terms and reducing fund sizes."[9]

To combat the difficult fundraising environment, some PE firms are "turning to the public markets, forming business development companies [BDCs] and other publicly traded vehicles to invest alongside shrinking private funds." BDCs afford PE partners a "more liquid way of investing in debt strategies, but could also dilute the focus of" fund managers.[10]

In short, a BDC is a form of publicly traded private equity that was created by the U.S. Congress in 1980 through amendments to the Investment Company Act of 1940. Unlike a typical PE fund, BDCs "face no restrictions on the type of investor they may attract. 'It is essentially a vehicle through which the investment manager can make Private Equity investments and get access to the public markets to find investors and capital.'"[11]

While PE funds must generally raise capital from accredited investors (see Chapter 1 for additional information), there exists no such restriction on BDCs. In fact, a BDC is required to "invest at least 70% of the portfolio in small, privately traded companies, which generally leads to greater investment diversity."[12]

BDCs may possess tax advantages over typical PE funds—especially if Congress is able to raise the tax rate on carried interest as originally proposed in the American Jobs and Closing Tax Loopholes Act of 2010. In this act, Congress proposed taxing 50 percent of carried interest at ordinary income and 50 percent as capital gains until 2013; thereafter, 75 percent of carried interest would be taxed at ordinary income levels.[13] This tax change, however, was not implemented when Senator Max Baucus (D-MT) eliminated it from the final version of the act.

While BDCs may one day possess tax advantages over traditional PE funds, they currently are advantageous for several reasons. Money raised by BDCs represents a permanent source of capital that cannot be redeemed by investors. Though PE funds generally have a finite lifetime, BDCs do not. BDCs can also allow managers to access public capital markets, affording both investors and general partners greater liquidity than that which exists in a typical PE fund. From the perspective of investors, BDCs may be less prone to volatility than PE investments. "This is in part because of strict leverage rules which require total debt to be no more than half of total assets, effectively setting a 2:1 asset coverage ratio. Over leveraging was identified as one of the problems that contributed to the global financial crisis."[14]

On the downside, access to public markets means BDCs are subject to numerous securities laws, including the Sarbanes-Oxley Act of 2002. They must file regulatory documents, such as 10-K, 10-Q, and proxy statements with the SEC. Adhering to these regulations may prove costly, but it appears some PE funds are willing to pay necessary compliance costs in order to obtain permanent sources of capital.

Overall, the number of BDCs grew to 29 in August 2011 from just six in 2000. Funds that have, or will shortly launch BDCs include buyout heavyweights Apollo Global Management LLC, BlackRock Inc., Thomas H. Lee Partners LP, and Kohlberg Capital Corporation.[15]

PE funds may structure BDCs as a "sidecar fund," or a fund that co-invests with a typically organized PE fund. "Since BDCs are required to maintain investment diversity or the amount of capital they can invest per deal, a traditional private mezzanine fund can cost-effectively provide the remainder of the money that is needed." Some argue BDCs are "becoming the dominant model for issuing junior capital and mezzanine (debt) in the marketplace." BDCs typically charge 1.5 to 2 percent in management fees plus a performance fee. Sidecar funds charge 1 to 2 percent but without the overhead of a public company and perhaps a lower performance fee.[16]

While PE fundraising has remained relatively bleak in recent years, a recent Dow Jones survey indicates some investors are again warming to the idea of PE investment. Fourteen out of 29 institutional investors surveyed by Dow Jones' Private Equity Analyst publication said they expected to increase their PE commitments slightly from 2010 levels. Another 8 out of 29 stated they expected to increase commitments significantly. None saw their commitment levels dropping year over year.[17]

Many LPs appear to be favoring small buyout funds, VC funds, and funds with a focus on the BRIC countries (Brazil, Russia, India, and

China).[18] Investors are becoming increasingly wary of large buyout funds as some of the world's largest funds struggle to renegotiate terms on 2006 and 2007 era debt issuances. Even though some funds were able to renegotiate this debt, the "overhang" issue continues to loom large in LPs' minds. Seventy-two percent of investors in a recent industry survey planned to commit more capital to small buyout funds, while only 17 percent planned to increase their commitments to large buyout funds; over 50 percent of investors planned to slow down commitment levels to large buyout funds.[19] In another recent survey, only 6 percent of LPs found "large to mega buyouts" as an area of the market viewed as presenting attractive investment opportunities; 49 percent believed small to medium-sized buyouts presented attractive investment opportunities.[20]

The damped spirits for mega fund investment stand in stark contrast to fundraising trends of 2005 through the second quarter of 2008, when an increasing fraction of investors' capital was being committed to funds over $1 billion in size. As a percent of total capital raised, commitments to funds over $1 billion in size grew from 40 percent in 2000 to 76 percent in 2007. Through the first half of 2011, 57 percent of all capital raised by PE funds went to funds over $1 billion in size. (See Exhibit 3.3 for additional information.)

LPs appear to be relatively pessimistic about mega fund returns, perhaps for good reason. In Chapter 2, our analysis demonstrated mega funds did not deliver higher-than-average returns in either the venture capital or buyout arena. Other research corroborates this evidence. Within the VC community, fund-of-funds manager Industry Little Hawk released a

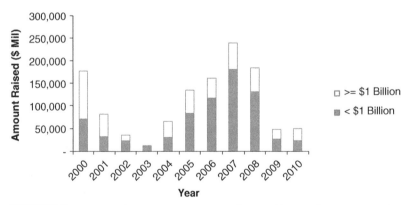

EXHIBIT 3.3 Historical Private Equity Capital Raised by Fund Size, 2000–2011 (2011 data through October 2011)
Source: Thomson ONE Banker.

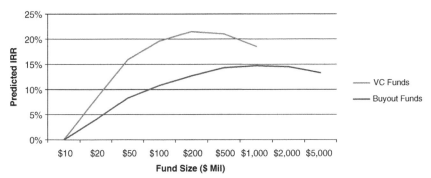

EXHIBIT 3.4 Predicted Internal Rate of Return by Fund Size
Source: Josh Lerner and Antoinette Schoar, referenced in November 2009 issue of
Private Equity Analyst magazine.

white paper in 2009 demonstrating small VC funds outperformed large VC
funds by 11.3 percentage points over a 20-year period ending in March
of that year.[21]

Harvard University's Josh Lerner and MIT professor Antoinette Schoar
arrived at a similar conclusion. They found a VC fund of $300 million in
size appears to generate peak performance. Lerner and Schoar also found
that buyout funds of roughly $1 billion in size (well below the size of some
near-$20 billion buyout funds raised in the years preceding the economic
crisis) provided optimal returns. The authors noted that firms tend to stum-
ble as they get bigger: "While large funds do not necessarily perform dramatically worse than small funds, the process of getting larger seems to be
associated with a deterioration of returns."[22] Lerner and Schoar's values for
predicted IRRs by fund size are shown in Exhibit 3.4.[23] These predicted returns were based on calculations associated with the market power of firms,
fees, and the risks fund general partners bear in making investments, and
were based on data through 1999, a time in which VC firms were performing quite well relative to nearly any benchmark.

While Lerner and Schoar's research showed strong returns to VC funds
of many different sizes, returns, most recently, to investors of many VC
funds have not met expectations in recent years. As shown in Exhibit 3.5,
venture returns have hovered near an annual IRR of 0 percent for the past
10 years, considerably below the expectation held by 69 percent of LPs that
their PE fund holdings generate net returns somewhere near those of the
public market plus at least four percentage points.[24]

LPs, however, appear slightly unfazed by these historical data, with
many indicating they will increase allocations to VC funds in the near future. Over 72 percent of survey respondents in a recent Dow Jones survey

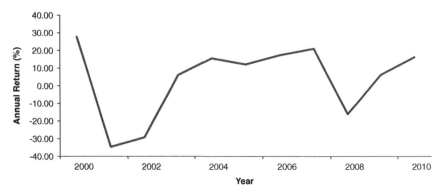

EXHIBIT 3.5 Historical Net Returns to Venture Capital Limited Partners, 2000–2010
Source: Thomson ONE Banker.

stated they planned to increase commitments to VC in 2011 or keep them consistent with 2010 levels.[25] Increasingly favorable market conditions have allowed the IPO to once again become a potential exit vehicle for LPs, though IPO volume remains a fraction of what it was roughly 10 years ago (see Chapter 5 for additional information).

VC funds might also reap benefits due to provisions in the Dodd-Frank Wall Street Reform and Consumer Protection Act of 2010 (Dodd-Frank) forbidding banks and other financial institutions from (1) investing more than 3 percent of tier 1 capital into private equity funds and (2) investing more than 3 percent of the total capital of a given PE fund. These limitations are part of what is popularly called the Volcker Rule, named for former Federal Reserve Chairman Paul Volcker, and pose significant implications for numerous PE funds that have come to rely on steady bank capital in the fundraising process. "Many private equity funds currently have banks as anchor investors representing 20% or more of the fund's capital. Restricting each bank's investment to 3% may leave a number of private equity funds with significantly less capital to invest."[26]

However, the Volcker Rule may have an unintended side effect that could give small businesses and venture-backed firms an added boost. "There are no limitations under the Volcker Rule on a bank's investment in SBIC Funds. For middle market PE funds seeking capital commitments, a license to operate as an SBIC could produce the tremendous advantage that banks could continue to serve as anchor investors not subject to the Volcker Rule's 3 percent cap. In addition, Dodd-Frank eliminates the exemption from SEC registration for investment advisors to funds with fewer than 15 clients. However, among the exceptions to this newly required registration

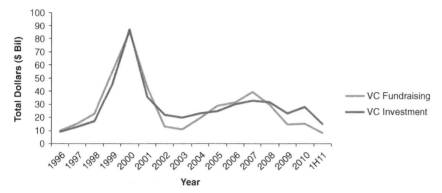

EXHIBIT 3.6 Venture Capital Fundraising and Venture Capital Investment Based on All Venture Capital Fund Closings
Source: Dow Jones VentureSource.

is that an adviser to SBIC Funds need not register with the SEC."[27] Given the implications of the Volcker Rule, one would expect the number of PE funds licensed by the Small Business Administration (SBA) to increase in the coming years, potentially providing an unintentional boon to small businesses and venture-backed firms that receive financing from SBA-licensed funds.

Increased investment in venture-backed companies could not come soon enough for start-ups, many of whom are bracing for a rough end to 2011. Until commitment levels ramp up, the VC industry remains in contraction mode, with VC investment exceeding fundraising levels from 2009 through the first half of 2011 (see Exhibit 3.6). During this time period, investment totaled roughly $65 billion while fundraising totaled approximately $37 billion. Unless fundraising picks up, investment activity must decline, meaning tough times lie immediately ahead for entrepreneurs.

While "Hot start-ups and growth-stage companies can raise capital all day . . . the classic Series B round is hard."[28] Moreover, as mentioned previously, PE investors are becoming enticed by overseas investment opportunities, with one recent survey indicating 78 percent of LPs were open to investing in emerging economies. The same survey indicated 61 percent of LPs expected to increase emerging-market investments in the long term. "Asia remains attractive to a high proportion of investors,"[29] with many LPs believing that "Asia is currently offering the best opportunities for investment." More specifically, 40 percent of LPs believe attractive investment opportunities are available in China, and 35 percent believe attractive investment opportunities exist in India.

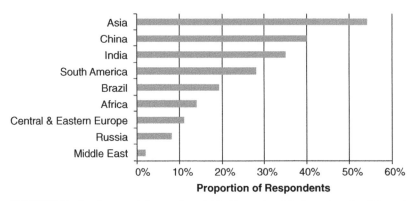

EXHIBIT 3.7   Regions and Countries within Emerging Markets that Are Viewed by Limited Partners as Presenting Attractive Opportunities in the Current Financial Climate
Source: The Preqin Private Equity Quarterly, Q3 2011.

Exhibit 3.7 presents additional information on regions and countries within emerging markets that LPs believe present attractive investment opportunities.

SELECTED REGULATORY CHANGES
AND PROPOSALS

Many PE funds are primarily concerned with delivering strong returns to limited partners. In recent years, however, funds have found themselves under increased scrutiny from governmental bodies, and numerous regulations appear on the horizon. Compliance with these new or revised regulations increases fund costs at what is perhaps the most inopportune time for those in PE. Funds and their investors are reeling from the Great Recession; many feel these new regulations will increase costs and further decrease net returns to limited partners. Few, if any, in the business expect regulatory change to positively impact PE, and some believe regulatory changes will drive many small funds out of the business completely.

One element that has become relatively clear in recent months is that nearly all PE firms will need to register as investment advisers with the SEC. According to the SEC, an "investment adviser" means "any person who, for compensation, engages in the business of advising others, either directly through publications or writings, as to the value of securities or as to the advisability of investing in, purchasing, or selling securities, or who, for compensation and as part of a regular business, issues or promulgates analyses or reports concerning securities; but does not include one of several exemptions."[30] PE firms meeting certain stipulations were previously exempt from registration (see Chapter 2 for additional information).

While initial proposals, including one introduced by Senator Jack Reed (D-RI) in 2009, effectively required "private investment firms, including hedge funds, private equity firms and venture firms, with more than $30 million in assets under management to register,"[31] the final requirement for registration, included in Dodd-Frank, was more lenient.

Included in Dodd-Frank was a requirement that all PE firms, or "investment advisers" in SEC parlance, register with the SEC, save those that (in layman's terms):

- Are classified as venture capital advisers
- Have less than $150 million in assets under management
- Do not have a place of business in the United States[32]

Though some surveys indicated 60 percent of PE professionals once believed VC funds would be required to register as investment advisers,[33] VC funds were, in fact, provided with an exemption in the final version of the legislation.

In registering with the SEC, PE firms must provide information that "is not only used for registration purposes, but that is used by the Commission in its regulatory program to support its mission to protect investors."[34] This information includes:

- Basic organizational and operational information about each fund they manage, such as the type of private fund that it is (e.g., hedge fund, PE fund, or liquidity fund), general information about the size and ownership of the fund, general fund data, and the advisor's services to the fund.
- Identification of five categories of "gatekeepers" that perform critical roles for advisers and the private funds they manage (i.e., auditors, prime brokers, custodians, administrators and marketers).[35]
- Additionally, the SEC is adopting amendments to the adviser registration form. All registered advisers will have to provide more information about their advisory business, including information about:
- The types of clients, their employees, and their advisory activities.
- Their business practices that may present significant conflicts of interest (such as the use of affiliated brokers, soft dollar arrangements, and compensation for client referrals).[36]

While some larger PE firms, including The Blackstone Group and KKR, are already registered with the SEC, Dodd-Frank will have significant implications for many PE funds, save those that fall into a prespecified exemption.

In addition to the information above, registered PE funds will be subjected to a higher degree of disclosure, both to limited partners and the SEC, than other PE funds. "For example, firms would have to disclose agreements made with investors in side letters . . . [and] could also find their fund and portfolio company valuations subject to SEC scrutiny and verification."[37] Firm-level record keeping will need to be bolstered, and firms will be subject to regular examination by the SEC. For small and medium-sized PE firms, some have estimated compliance costs in the hundreds of thousands of dollars.[38]

Firms will also be required to designate a chief compliance officer and all reforms must be in place by July 21, 2011, the one-year anniversary of the passage of Dodd-Frank.[39] A recent study by Dow Jones' Private Equity Analyst publication found 17 percent of PE funds had a dedicated compliance officer, while nearly 59 percent relied on a chief financial officer, chief operating officer, or chief administrative officer to fulfill the role, and nearly 25 percent gave the task to a senior professional.[40] For these professionals who already have a full slate, Dodd-Frank could present yet another unwanted thorn in their side. While not a knock-out punch, new regulations will also provide a hurdle that may disincentivize new firms from entering the market.

Dodd-Frank has unquestionably garnered a significant amount of attention in PE circles and has perhaps distracted national attention from an issue that today remains in the background: carried interest taxation. Carried interest taxation generated such a national buzz in 2009 that the Obama Administration specifically addressed the issue in its budget proposal that year. Though momentum regarding the issue has slowed, industry professionals, including Douglas Lowenstein, head of the Private Equity Council, believe the issue will creep up as the economy recovers and public pressure to reduce government debt increases.[41]

To review, carried interest represents the portion of capital gains retained by PE firms as compensation for managing limited partners' capital. PE funds typically received carried interest of 20 percent[42] in addition to an annual management fee of 2 percent of committed capital as well as other fees. The management fee is subject to ordinary income tax, while carried interest is taxed at the capital gains level. The top tax rate on capital gains held longer than a year (as of this writing) is 15 percent, less than half the top 35 percent tax rate on ordinary income. Moreover, carried interest is not subject to Federal Insurance Contributions Act (FICA) or Medicare taxes.

The current tax framework for carried interest has largely remained unchanged for over 50 years.[43] Industry professionals generally voice their support for the current system of taxation—and disdain for changes to it. Some feel that changes to carried interest taxation could push some U.S.-based funds abroad or encourage funds to change compensation schemes in ways that are more tax favorable.

Irrespective of opinions, "At least twice Congress has come close to raising taxes on carried interest but backed off, and President Barack Obama also has pushed for a change."[44] Some skeptics believe carried interest is not an investment, but rather "compensation to partners in exchange for their services."[45] As such, they contend, it should be taxed at ordinary income levels—and the national Tax Court may agree.[46] It is "compensation for services and, like any other form of remuneration, should be taxed as ordinary income."[47]

A recent ruling in the case of *Dagres v. Commissioner* was not directed at opining specifically on the issue, but nonetheless addressed it. VC fund manager Todd Dagres "wound up in court over a $3.6 million deduction he took for a loan to a business associate that went sour . . . The case hinged in part on whether Mr. Dagres's share of profits meant he was engaged in a trade or business, or was acting as an investor." The Tax Court sided with Dagres and allowed him his deduction because his carried interest "was compensation from a trade or business." The body even likened Dagres's compensation to that of "stockbrokers, financial planners, investment bankers, business promoters, and dealers,"[48] all of whom pay taxes at ordinary income rates when proceeds from investments are realized.

While taxing carried interest as ordinary income has arguably garnered the lion's share of attention surrounding the issue, other methods of carried interest taxation have also been proposed, for example, taxing carried interest as property when granted. This proposal "would force carried interest to be valued when issued, and that value would be taxed [at that time] as ordinary income to the recipient."[49] As carried interest is sometimes distributed in the form of stock or options, its value may fluctuate between the time it is granted and the close of the fund. This proposed method of taxation would tax carried interest as ordinary income when granted and would tax the gain between the time carried interest was granted and the close of the fund at the capital gains tax rate. "For example, if carried interest was valued at $75 million when granted and ended up being worth $100 million at the close of the fund, the general partner would be taxed on $75 million of ordinary income when receiving the carried interest and $25 million of capital gain when receiving the $100 million."[50] Of course, issues arise in this method of taxation as well, most notably the determination of the fair market value of any distributed carried interest.

However, irrespective of the form of change to carried interest taxation, increased carried interest taxes will affect PE investors as well as general partners and possibly have a significant impact on PE compensation structures. Nonetheless, industry insiders feel any taxation changes will be worked out through creative schemes designed to minimize their impact, including burdening carried interest with some offsetting expenses, such as staff salaries. A definitive stance on changes to carried interest taxation continues to evolve.

RISE OF STRATEGIC BUYERS

During the buyout boom of 2005 to 2007, financial sponsors acquired numerous portfolio companies much to the chagrin of strategic buyers (aka strategics). Replete with cash from record-setting fundraisings, PE firms moved to deploy capital at record paces—and at record valuations. These valuations were, in part, buoyed by free-flowing capital markets and investors' appetite for not only PE, but for the debt employed in PE portfolio companies as well.

Today, the tides have turned significantly in favor of strategic buyers. Corporations today have learned from years past and are moving with renewed urgency to close deals. Through October 2011, $515 billion of acquisition volume has been completed by strategic buyers compared with $66 billion for PE firms.[51] With interest rates at historic lows, record-high cash balances are being scrutinized by executives and investors alike and are providing a motivational tool for strategic acquirers. Moreover, the slow pace of the economic recovery has decreased many sellers' once-lofty expectations for their business's valuations. "Investment bankers say strategic buyers are coming at auctions more aggressively with a higher success rate than in previous cycles." It certainly helps that U.S. strategics have nearly $1 trillion of cash on hand to deploy.[52]

Through September 2011, strategics purchased 4,269 companies in 2011 compared with 5,046 in all of 2010; PE firms purchased 532 companies through September 2011 versus 706 companies last year.[53] The pendulum does not appear to be swinging back in favor of PE firms anytime soon. Corporations are now equipped with corporate development staffs that include, among other individuals, former PE professionals. Furthermore, "in addition to deal savvy, corporations benefit from lower borrowing costs as a result of their existing business . . . " They are able to combine "earnings before interest, taxes, depreciation, and amortization with those of the acquisition target, therefore forming 'a better lending base' that has easier access for financing. Financial sponsors, by contrast can only borrow against the business of the potential target, without any benefit from the combination."[54]

Many aggressive strategic acquirers have acquired firms at a far greater pace than even some of the industry's largest financial sponsors. For example, Pfizer Inc. has made $75 billion of acquisitions in the past three years, more than three times the amount of deals performed by the top financial sponsor, Blackstone Group. Even the 10th most active strategic buyer, Sanofi-Aventis US, has been more active than the Blackstone group.

Aggressive strategic buyers provide a ripe harvest environment for PE firms. An exit to a strategic is a valuable option given the uncertainty surrounding the PE IPO market, though the IPO is once again becoming a viable exit option for PE investments. However, while strategic mergers and acquisitions activity can assist PE firms in achieving higher harvest valuations, it also serves to depress returns by inflating purchase prices, forcing financial buyers to cough up more cash and leverage to acquire businesses. Through October 2011, financial sponsors only accounted for roughly 11 percent of total acquisition volume, down from a high of roughly 35 percent during the peak of the buyout boom in 2007 and 2008 (see Exhibit 3.8).[55] Choppy public markets have contributed in part to the rough ride experienced by financial sponsors in the past few years. Among other things, public market fluctuations make banks especially cognizant of their liquidity positions and capital ratios; in environments of uncertainty, banks are generally risk averse and cut back on lending. With the credit markets remaining

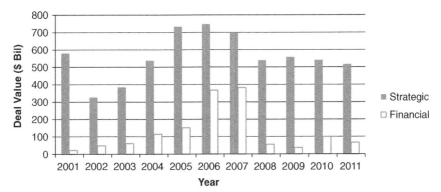

EXHIBIT 3.8 Strategic and Acquisitions Deal Volume, 2001–2011
Source: Deallogic.

considerably less liquid than they were in 2007, financial sponsors are simply not able to find adequate levels of debt at terms that are attractive enough to get many deals done.

CONCLUSION

This chapter has presented a summary of current issues, including those pertaining to fundraising, regulations, and the harvest environment, facing PE investors and general partners. While PE experienced rapid growth in fundraising from 2005 to 2007, today's environment is a challenging one for PE firms.

NOTES

1. "Blackstone's Lengthy List." *Wall Street Journal,* June 14, 2007.
2. H. Sender, "How Blackstone Will Divvy Up Its Riches." *Wall Street Journal,* June 12, 2007.
3. "Loeb's European Challenge." *Wall Street Journal,* June 15, 2007.
4. W. Buffett, "Stop Coddling the Super Rich." *New York Times,* August 14, 2011.
5. "A Short-Lived Golden Age." *Wall Street Journal,* July 23, 2007.
6. H. Sender, D. Berman, and G. Zuckerman, "Debt Crunch Hits Deals, Deal Makers and Key IPO." *Wall Street Journal,* July 27, 2007.
7. *Source:* Leveraged Lending Review–3Q11. Standard & Poor's.
8. *Source: The Preqin Quarterly,* Q2 2011.
9. A. Jacobius, "Private Funds Turning to Public Vehicles," *Pensions & Investments,* September 19, 2011.
10. *Id.*
11. *Source:* http://www.eisneramper.com/uploadedFiles/Resource_Center/Articles/Articles/PE_Direct_SUMMER_2011.pdf.
12. *Id.*
13. *Source:* http://www.natlawreview.com/article/carried-interest-tax-provisions-american-jobs-and-closing-tax-loopholes-act-2010.
14. *Source:* http://www.eisneramper.com/uploadedFiles/Resource_Center/Articles/Articles/PE_Direct_SUMMER_2011.pdf.
15. A. Jacobius, "Private Funds Turning to Public Vehicles," *Pensions & Investments,* September 19, 2011.
16. *Id.*
17. L. Kreutzer, "LPs Have Brass in Pocket, but Few GPs Will Benefit," *Private Equity Analyst,* January 2011.
18. *Id.*
19. *Id.*

20. *Source: The Preqin Private Equity Quarterly,* Q3 2011.
21. R. Garland, "VC 2.0 Group Argues for Smaller Funds," *Private Equity Analyst,* November 2009.
22. *Id.*
23. *Id.*
24. "Meeting LP Demand," *The Preqin Private Equity Quarterly,* Q2 2011.
25. L. Kreutzer, "LPs Have Brass in Pocket, but Few GPs Will Benefit," *Private Equity Analyst* (January 2011).
26. *Source:* http://www.mcguirewoods.com/news-resources/item.asp?item=5582.
27. *Id.*
28. R. Garland, "Start-Ups Brace for Dark VC Winter," *Private Equity Analyst* (October 2011).
29. *Source: The Preqin Private Equity Quarterly,* Q3 2011
30. *Source:* http://www.sec.gov/rules/extra/ia1940.htm.
31. L. Kreutzer, "As Curtain Opens on Regulatory Change, PE Firms Not Quite Applauding," *Private Equity Analyst* (October 2009).
32. *Source:* http://www.sec.gov/news/press/2011/2011–133.htm.
33. L. Kreutzer, "As Curtain Opens on Regulatory Change, PE Firms Not Quite Applauding," *Private Equity Analyst* (October 2009).
34. *Id.*
35. *Source:* http://www.sec.gov/news/press/2011/2011–133.htm.
36. *Id.*
37. L. Kreutzer, "As Curtain Opens on Regulatory Change, PE Firms Not Quite Applauding," *Private Equity Analyst* (October 2009).
38. *Id.*
39. H. Canada and C. Chung, "New Compliance Rules are Headache for Small Firms," *Private Equity Analyst* (January 2011).
40. *Id.*
41. *Id.*
42. A. Metrick and A. Yasuda, "The Economics of Private Equity Funds," September 8, 2008, http://ssrn.com/abstract=996334.
43. *Source:* http://thehill.com/the-executive/q-a-with-eric-solomon-assistantsecre-tary-for-tax-policy-with-department-of-the-treasury-2007–11–02.html.
44. L. Saunders, "Tax Report: 'Carried Interest' in the Cross Hairs," *Wall Street Journal,* August 6, 2011.
45. *Id.*
46. *Id.*
47. C. Livingston, "Finding the Right Balance: A Critical Analysis of the Major Proposals to Reform the Taxation of Carried Interests in Private Equity," *The Tax Lawyer* (Fall 2008), 241–258.
48. *Id.*
49. *Id.*
50. *Id.*
51. S. Dai. "Revenge of the Strategics: Corporations Gain Upper Hand in Quest for Deals," *Private Equity Analyst* (October 2011).

52. *Source:* Represents aggregate of S&P 500 non financials Cahs holdings of 416 companies as of the end of the second quarter 2010. Data included in S. Dai, "Revenge of the Strategics: Corporates Gain Upper Hand in Quest for Deals," *Private Equity Analyst* (October 2011).

53. S. Dai, "Revenge of the Strategics: Corporations Gain Upper Hand in Quest for Deals," *Private Equity Analyst* (October 2011).

54. *Id.*

55. *Id.*

CHAPTER 4

Harvesting Private Equity Investments Through Initial Public Offering

Harry Cendrowski
James P. Martin

A "harvest" or "exit" is an event whereby the investors and management of a company sell at least a portion of their shares to public or corporate buyers. The harvest provides an opportunity for private equity (PE) funds to realize returns for their investors, while enabling managers with equity stakes to have a "liquidity event" for their shares—in other words, an opportunity to sell their shares by making them "liquid."

Along these lines, there are three primary methods by which PE funds harvest companies: initial public offerings (IPOs), mergers, and acquisitions. The latter two exit methods (discussed in subsequent chapters) are frequently discussed in parallel and are collectively known as M&A transactions. This chapter will exclusively present an introduction to the IPO process.

INITIAL PUBLIC OFFERINGS

Basics

The IPO is seen by many private firm managers and entrepreneurs as a potential milestone for their company and also for their career. There is undoubtedly a sense of prestige and pride that comes from taking a company public, as it signifies that a firm has achieved a high level of historical or expected growth. Customers and suppliers will also look at a firm differently if it has achieved public company status. Some may believe the firm to be more stable than its competitors, and, hence, they may elect to pursue more future business opportunities with the company.

In general, a public company is often perceived as a more enduring competitor than its private company counterpart. Therefore, customers who wish to purchase products from firms that either require periodic service or are sold with warranties often seek new business with public firms. However, despite the cachet associate with taking a firm public, there exist more substantial motivations for a company to undergo an IPO.

First and foremost, the IPO process permits firms to (rather) quickly and cheaply raise large amounts of capital. This is especially important for growing firms whose management team wishes to take their company to "the next level." Such firms may not internally possess the necessary capital to fund new, profitable projects that require intensive outlays of funds. For instance, some start-up pharmaceutical companies require extensive capital in order to maintain liquidity while new drugs are reviewed by the Food and Drug Administration.

In some cases, a growing firm may resort to an IPO out of necessity when projects cannot be funded internally. Lending institutions may refuse to grant loans to a private firm due to the idiosyncratic risks associated with the company and/or its lack of hard assets or cash flow. Even if the firm were offered a loan by a bank, large interest payments—buoyed by relatively high interest rates (when the riskiness of the loan is considered)—could serve to diminish the profitability of the sought project and constrain the firm's free cash flow.

By going public, a firm will generally be able to obtain financing with better terms than if it were private. Since public firms open themselves to much more scrutiny than their private peers, debt rating agencies, such as Moody's, Standard and Poor's, or Fitch, will generally accord higher ratings to firms with publicly traded stock.

The decision to go public also brings liquidity, as an IPO creates a public market where stakeholders can trade shares with other investors. This liquidity is especially beneficial to both entrepreneurs and PE investors, as they can easily sell their shares to other investors—with a few caveats. In some cases, PE firms will distribute shares directly to their limited partners, rather than sell them on the open market, in order to maximize the internal rate of return (IRR) on their investment.

However, it is important to note that liquidity for some shareholders, including venture capitalists and entrepreneurs, may not be attained at IPO. Many underwriters—investment banks who market the IPO to investors—will require "lock-up" periods ranging from 60 to 360 days, with 180 days being the norm. During this time period, insiders are not permitted to sell shares on the open market.

Underwriters require this lock-up on the sale of shares in order to maintain stability in a newly public company's stock price during its initial trading period. If investors were to cash out large amounts of shares, a glut would ensue, with the share price dropping steeply. Furthermore, the lock-up period serves to reassure investors that management will retain "skin in the game" for a finite time period after the company goes public.

With respect to growth strategies, an IPO also permits a firm to more easily finance M&A deals, as a company can elect to sell shares to the public in order to finance such transactions. Without this source of capital, a firm may be unable to profitably fund such a deal if it possesses weaker debt ratings.

For growing firms, the decision to go public also creates a new method of luring top-notch talent to the company: employee stock and stock options. While more fledgling firms may not be able to offer distinguished executives lucrative cash remuneration packages, stock-based compensation can serve to "sweeten the deal" for these individuals. Moreover, such compensation serves to align the interests of executives with the company, as they may benefit greatly from the appreciation of equity stake.

But for all the advantages an IPO brings, there also exist numerous, less publicized pitfalls, two of which are the one-time cost of going public and the ongoing cost of securities law compliance. In today's market, the cost of going public can be in excess of 10 percent of the overall IPO offering amount. This expense reflects the fees associated with compensating under-writers (historically 7 percent of the offering amount), legal and filing fees for registering the IPO, and the value associated with the time a management team must reserve for going on the "road show" and drawing up the IPO prospectus.

Furthermore, the sale of publicly traded stock also forces a firm to register with the Securities and Exchange Commission (SEC) and subjects the company to an immense amount of securities laws and regulations, including the well-publicized Sarbanes-Oxley Act of 2002.[1] Some firms, especially those in the financial sector, might be subject to the Dodd-Frank Wall Street Reform and Consumer Protection Act of 2010. Adherence to securities laws, and the attestation of such adherence, requires a considerable amount of time and capital. The filing of publicly available quarterly statements and the creation of a board of directors are two SEC requirements for public companies that may be novelties for a formerly private firm.

Private companies enjoy a considerable amount of privacy, especially when compared to their publicly traded peers. Such companies are not scrutinized by Wall Street analysts, who often request to talk with top-level executives about a company's performance. As Bill Gates, chairman of Microsoft Corporation, once told *Fortune* magazine, "To have a stock trader call up the chief executive and ask him questions is uneconomic—the ball bearings shouldn't be asking the driver about the grease."[2] Gates was particularly irked by the notion that he would be required to entertain calls from outsiders who knew little about the inner workings of his soon-to-be-public software company.

Analysts like to see steady, predictable earnings growth from the companies that they monitor, and, accordingly, they exert pressure on corporate executives to deliver results commensurate with their expectations. In some cases, executives may be impelled to set aside long-term goals in order to meet those required by analysts in the short term. Some private company executives, like Bill Gates circa 1986, would rather manage their company as they see fit than have it face the perusal of Wall Street analysts.

Moreover, executives of public firms face considerably more scrutiny with respect to their personal lives and perquisites. The appropriateness of salary packages and business expenses will be debated at length by shareholders, along with other fundamental business practices. It is important to remember that the management team of the once-private company is now obliged to make decisions in the interests of *all* shareholders. In this role, a management team is substantially more vulnerable when overseeing a public firm, as public shareholders wield significant power. In extreme cases, a bloc of shareholders may attempt to take over the firm if they are dissatisfied with management's performance.

Initial Steps in the "Going Public" Process

The decision to go public is made with considerable deliberateness. While many firms will look to outsiders for advice regarding their decision, it is important to remember that these individuals—and the firms they represent—all have their own interests at stake in an IPO. For instance, if a private company currently employs a non–"Big Four" accounting firm as its primary auditor (PricewaterhouseCoopers, Deloitte & Touche, Ernst & Young, and KPMG are often referred to as the "Big Four" auditors), a partner from this smaller firm may advise against going public, since Wall Street typically likes to see audits performed by a "Big Four" firm. If the company were to go public, the smaller auditing firm would risk losing its account. On the other hand, investment bankers may advise a private firm to go public solely because they stand to collect sizeable fees from underwriting the deal. As an anonymous person once said, "Never ask a barber if you need a haircut," and firms should always keep in mind the motives of those they counsel for going public.

Selecting an appropriate underwriter is the first step a private company must take in order to go public. Investment banks frequently court successful, private firms in the hopes of subsequently underwriting their IPO or providing financial advisory services. With the rise in notoriety of league tables (published rankings of investment banks based on the dollar volume of deals on which they work), the investment banking industry has become particularly competitive in the past few decades.[3] Given this environment, private firms are now more readily able to negotiate underwriting services with several banks.

When selecting an underwriter, a management team should first analyze the investment banking firm's reputation: How have its past IPOs performed in the market? Has the firm underwritten IPOs in industries similar to the company seeking to go public? Do its research analysts possess good reputations on Wall Street? Will it make commitments to provide analyst coverage after the offering? Are the underwriting fees and fee structure commensurate with those of other firms (some underwriters will require compensation in the form of warrants in addition to cash)?

As the underwriter's name will appear on publicized documents highlighting the offering to potential investors, it is essential that the firm possess a sound reputation. Without a strong reputation, an underwriter may struggle to woo investors, including other investment banks, for the offering. Moreover, it is important for management to understand the network in which a potential underwriter participates.

Another important issue managers should consider when selecting an underwriter is the share price of the offering proposed by the investment bank. Underwriters generally employ a rather uncomplicated model when determining the price at which a security should sell when it goes public. As a first step, the underwriter will estimate future earnings for the IPO candidate and calculate an approximate earnings per share (EPS) value based on this figure and the size of the offering. This EPS estimate will then be multiplied by a price-to-earnings (P/E) ratio in order to compute a price per share.

The P/E ratio imputed by an underwriter is derived from an exhaustive analysis of competitive public company P/E ratios based on firm revenues, earnings, and industry, among other factors. However, as P/E ratios fluctuate heavily over time—and hence, over the course of offering negotiations—underwriters may change their share price estimate as the offering nears. By this stage, however, the soon-to-be-public company has little choice but to go along with the underwriter's new price estimate; the only other alternative is to cancel the offering completely.

Underwriters also use a process known as "book building" in order to determine the price of an offering. In this approach, the underwriter will solicit bids from investors who apprise the investment bank of the number of shares they wish to buy for a prespecified range of prices. Using this information, the underwriter sets an appropriate offering price.

Many firms select multiple underwriters for their offering, although only one firm will be deemed the *lead underwriter* or *book-running manager*. This firm's primary responsibility is to maintain a logbook of all the aforementioned investors who have expressed interest in the offering. Often, a firm will hire a smaller, *boutique* investment bank and pair it with a *bulge bracket* firm to underwrite the offering: The boutique bank is one that specializes in offerings of companies in a particular industry, while the bulge bracket bank is a large firm like Goldman Sachs or JPMorgan that possesses a marked ability to lure investors to the offering. However, all firms involved in the offering will attempt to recruit brokerage houses and other investment banks that can sell shares in the offering to their clients; this group of firms is often called the *syndicate*.

Once a firm has selected its underwriter(s), and prior to the filing of disclosure statements with the SEC, a nonbinding *letter of intent* is signed between the parties. This document specifies a target price range for the firm's shares (usually in conjunction with a range of P/E ratios used in deriving such prices), the fees charged by the underwriters, and the type of underwriting activity the investment bank will follow: either *firm commitment* or *best effort*. Firm commitment underwritings denote those in which the underwriter promises to sell the entire offering at a predetermined price, whereas best effort underwritings are those where the underwriter uses its best effort to sell offering shares at the specified price. (In today's market, best effort underwritings are virtually nonexistent; nearly all underwritings are of the firm commitment type.)

Aside from marketing the IPO, underwriters provide many crucial services to nascent firms: they are responsible for conducting due diligence on the private firm, assisting lawyers with regulatory filings, and determining the size of the IPO offering. As such, selection of the proper underwriter is paramount to the success of the IPO and the future success of the company.

Some investment banks sell many of their shares to institutional investors (e.g., insurance companies, pension funds, etc.) as opposed to private retail investors (e.g., high-net-worth individuals). While institutional investors can purchase large amounts of shares in an offering, they often have little tolerance for underperforming companies; in some cases, they may dump their shares in a company if the investment managers believe a portfolio company will struggle in the near-term future. Furthermore, these investors are constantly evaluating and rebalancing their portfolios attempting to maximize their returns while minimizing risk. Retail investors, conversely, are generally more loyal to a company and trade securities less aggressively.

Aside from underwriter selection, management should also discuss the size of the IPO offering and those of desired subsequent rounds. The size of the IPO, also called the primary offering, should be based on management's estimate of the capital required to take the firm to the next level. Offering too much stock at one time could dilute ownership and decrease the firm's ability to procure future capital through seasoned equity offerings, that is, sales of stock that occur after an IPO; in a primary offering, many companies elect to sell around 10 percent of their total stock to the public. However, aside from the primary offering, where capital is raised expressly for use by the firm, newly public companies often have a secondary offering where firm principals may sell their shares to the public, personally pocketing the proceeds of the sale. This offering occurs after the previously mentioned lock-up period set by the underwriting investment bank(s).

Role of the Securities and Exchange Commission and State Policing Bodies

Registration with the SEC and state regulatory bodies is a necessary process for any private company looking to go public, the first step of which is the preparation of a *registration statement.* This statement is divided into two parts: the *prospectus* or "selling document," which is available only to investors in the offering, and a second portion that may be viewed by anyone on the SEC's web site. This second portion may take one of many forms, but most companies looking to go public file what is called an *S-1 registration document.*

Once the S-1 has been filed, SEC staff members will comb through these disclosure documents and frequently make requests for revisions and/or clarifications. (These requests are centered on disclosures of material information and do not represent the SEC's personal approval or disapproval of the offering.) After these issues have been addressed to the SEC's satisfaction, the Commission will declare the registration *effective*, at which point the shares in the offering may be sold to investors.

Over the course of the offering and after it has been deemed effective by the SEC, the underwriter(s) market the security to potential investors—both institutional and retail. This activity is primarily accomplished through the distribution of the above-mentioned prospectus, which is generally called a *red herring* by investors; the document has historically featured disclaimers printed in red on its cover. In addition to this document, the management team frequently travels on a *road show* to promote the offering and discuss the prospectus.

In between filing the offering and the date the SEC declares it effective is a time frequently called the *quiet period* by investors. Although federal laws do not explicitly define the term "quiet period," for securities, federal laws limit the information a company and its underwriters can convey to investors during this juncture. However, in 2005, the SEC liberalized the laws governing the quiet period, permitting "offering activity and communications to allow more information to reach investors by revising the 'gun-jumping' provisions under the Securities Act."[4] The following bullet points express the effect of these revisions, as defined by the SEC[5]:

- Well-known seasoned issuers are permitted to engage at any time in oral and written communications, including use at any time of a new type of written communication called a *free writing prospectus*, subject to enumerated conditions (including, in some cases, filing with the Commission).
- All reporting issuers are, at any time, permitted to continue to publish regularly released factual business information and forward-looking information.
- Nonreporting issuers are, at any time, permitted to continue to publish factual business information that is regularly released and intended for use by persons other than in their capacity as investors or potential investors.
- Communications by issuers more than 30 days before filing a registration statement will be permitted so long as they do not reference a securities offering that is the subject of a registration statement.
- All issuers and other offering participants will be permitted to use a free writing prospectus after the filing of the registration statement, subject to enumerated conditions (including, in some cases, filing with the Commission).
- The exclusions from the definition of prospectus are expanded to allow a broader category of routine communications regarding issuers, offerings, and procedural matters, such as communications about the schedule for an offering or about account-opening procedures.
- The exemptions for research reports are expanded.

Nonetheless, despite these revisions, firms looking to go public must monitor the statements of management during the quiet period and ensure that no optimistic assertions are made about the status of the corporation or its future; if such statements are made, the SEC may rule that the firm was trying to precondition the market (frequently called *gun jumping*).

In previous years, namely, prior to 1996, state regulatory bodies were also required to approve the offering for sale to investors based within the state. However, while the SEC has perennially focused on disclosures, state regulatory bodies formerly assessed offering prices. Along these lines, some states previously barred firms from purchasing IPOs when they felt the offering prices were too high (this occurred multiple times in the early 1980s with IPOs of high-technology firms like Genentech and Apple Computer). Since 1996, all securities registered on the New York Stock Exchange (NYSE) or NASDAQ have been absolved from state-level requirements.

Once an offering has been deemed effective, the underwriters of the IPO will frequently place a *tombstone ad* in major financial periodicals to advertise the offering. The ad is so named because it is typically printed in unadorned black-on-white text, complete with a centered headline, resembling a tombstone.

Post-IPO Underwriter Responsibilities

In addition to marketing the IPO, the underwriter generally attempts to ensure stock price stability in the days following the offering, with special emphasis on protection against stock price attrition. In order to accomplish this objective, underwriters frequently employ a complicated tactic informally called the *Green Shoe* or, in legal parlance, the *overallotment option*. This option permits the underwriter to oversell generally up to 15 percent of the prespecified amount of shares in an offering with little consequence. (The Green Shoe option derives its name from the IPO of the now-defunct Green Shoe Company in the 1930s, the first IPO to employ this option.) This activity is known as *shorting*, since the investment bank essentially short sells shares to investors, with the option to call back the shares in the days following the offering. If, in the coming days, the newly public stock's price declines (referred to as *breaking issue* or *breaking syndicate bid*), the underwriting investment bank can call in its shorts and repurchase the oversold 15 percent of shares at the offering price.

If, however, the price of the stock appreciates, the underwriter can exercise its Green Shoe option and purchase up to 15 percent of the total amount of shares available in the offering from the parent company *at the original offering price*; without this option, the underwriter would be forced to eventually purchase these short-sold shares in the open market at a price higher than that in the offering.

In addition to maintaining stock price stability, the underwriter also generally commits to providing analyst coverage and financial advice for the firm in the coming months and years following the IPO. Aside from being a good business practice, the underwriter seeks future business from the newly public company, namely, that should the firm elect to raise money through a seasoned equity offering in the future, the underwriter will again be contracted to handle this event.

Registration Documents

The basic IPO registration statement is the S-1, which must be filed with the SEC. This document must contain essential information on the future public company, generally organized in the following manner:

- *Business summary.* Discusses the company's current line of business, its products and/or services, intellectual property, and supply chain distribution processes.
- *Management.* Identifies all corporate officers and directors, along with their ages, positions, and a brief biography.
- *Financial data.* Includes audited balance sheets from the previous two fiscal years, and three years of audited income statements. These statements must be prepared in accordance with U.S. generally accepted accounting principles.
- *Risk factors.* Describes the idiosyncratic and systematic risks associated with investing in the company. For instance, perhaps the company participates in a particularly competitive industry or is heavily influenced by government regulations and policies. These risks should all be included in the S-1.
- *Description of capital stock.* Describes the size of the offering and the number of shares to be sold at IPO.
- *Use of proceeds.* Explains how the company plans to deploy the capital it raises from the offering.
- *Management's discussion and analysis of financial condition and results of operations.* Historically analyzes audited balance sheets and income statements, highlighting one-time disclosures and other nonrecurring items so as to dispel confusion surrounding their circumstances.

In lieu of filing an S-1, a company may elect to file a Form SB-2 if the offering meets certain conditions: more specifically, the total value of all shares sold at the offering may not exceed $25 million, and the company's annual revenues must also be below this threshold.

Filing a Form SB-2 has several advantages for smaller companies. Companies may file this registration document at an SEC regional office, as opposed to the SEC headquarters in Washington, DC. Moreover, only one audited balance sheet, for the most recent fiscal year, is required (as opposed to two years of audited balance sheets for an S-1), and only two years of audited income statements are required (versus three years of audited statements for an S-1). The Form SB-2 also has simplified disclosure requirements when compared to its larger S-1 brother.

Furthermore, offerings for firms seeking financing of less than $5 million from an IPO may elect to be classified as a Regulation A offering with the SEC, often called a *mini-public offering*. This offering procedure is rather similar to the process followed when filing a Form SB-2, although it is considerably less complex in one particular aspect: there is no requirement for audited financial statement disclosure in Regulation A offerings. Additionally, issuers of Regulation A offerings can distribute solicitation prospectuses so long as they are preapproved by the SEC and a 20-day "cooling-off" period is observed. During this time, issuers may not solicit potential investors of the offering. Regulation A offerings are not permitted for entities that:

- have one or more classes of securities registered under Section 12 of the 1934 Act or file reports pursuant to Section 15(d) of the 1934 Act;
- are not U.S. or Canadian domiciled issuers;
- are investment companies;
- are blind pools or shell companies or involve fractional oil/gas interests;
- are any company where an officer, director, or 10 percent or more stockholder is a "bad boy" under Rule 262 of the 1933 Act or where any such person at a broker-dealer that sells the offering is such a person.

Historical Trends

The market for both venture capital (VC) and buyout-backed IPOs has long been cyclical, as evidenced by the numerous peaks and valleys in Exhibit 4.1. Throughout the 1980s, the number of VC and buyout-backed IPOs steadily increased. VC and buyout-backed IPOs peaked at 352 and 116, respectively, in 1986, after which the IPO market for both forms of equities began tapering off. Both numbers were significantly above the number of PE-backed IPOs just five years earlier: in 1975, just two PE-backed IPOs took place. As stated in Chapters 1 and 2, the Employee Retirement Income Security Act of 1974 (ERISA) had a profound effect on the PE industry, bringing investment in PE-backed firms to a virtual standstill until 1979 (when the U.S. Department of Labor clarified ERISA's language and explicitly permitted pension managers to invest in PE); the effects of this Act are manifested by the dearth of PE-backed IPOs during the mid-to-late 1970s as well as the high number of PE-backed IPOs subsequent to the Department of Labor's clarification.

The U.S. economy began to slow down in the late 1980s, officially entering a recession in July 1990.[6] Once the economy emerged from this

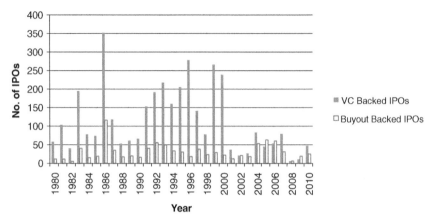

EXHIBIT 4.1   Number of Venture Capital and Buyout-Backed Initial Public Offerings per Year, 1980–2010
Source: Thomson ONE Banker.

recession in March 1991[7] and the IPO market stabilized, the number of PE-backed IPOs recovered and again began to surge. VC-backed IPOs increased from 61 in 1989 to 278 in 1996 and remained strong through the end of the 1990s. Many investors, believing that a new, Internet-based economy was going to revolutionize the future, jumped heavily into VC-backed IPOs and high-technology companies during the dot-com era. In fact, one study from this time period showed that when corporations changed their name to a more "Internet-related dot-com name," this slight alteration produced "cumulative abnormal returns on the order of 74 percent for the 10 days surrounding the announcement day."[8] It is hard to believe such fanfare was associated with only a simple change in nomenclature and was not necessarily indicative of a change in business strategy.

Buyout-backed IPOs increased steadily from 16 in 1990 to 55 in 1992, though the market's appetite for buyout-backed IPOs did not increase as rapidly as it did for VC-backed IPOs. Many of the buyout-backed IPOs during this time were so-called reverse leveraged buyouts, the name referring to the act of offering new, publicly traded shares in a firm that was previously taken private through a buyout transaction.

Since 2000, the number of VC-backed IPOs has remained significantly below previous historical levels. From 1991 through 2000, there were an average of 193 VC-backed IPOs per year; from 2001 through 2010, this figure decreased to 41 per year. Many investors continue to have a lingering bad taste in their mouth from money lost in IPOs during the dot-com bust. During this time period, many IPOs, especially those backed by VC firms, experienced extreme first-day run-ups in price, followed by significant losses

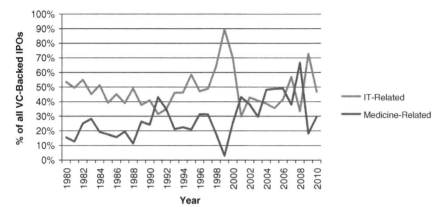

EXHIBIT 4.2 Historical Percentage of Information Technology and Medicine-Related Venture Capital–Backed Initial Public Offering, 1980–2010
Source: Thomson ONE Banker.

once the dot-com bubble burst. In contrast to the marked decrease in VC-backed IPOs, the number of buyout-backed IPOs has remained relatively steady over the past 20 years.

Exhibit 4.2 presents the number of information technology (IT) and medicine-related (biotech, life science, medical device, and pharmaceutical-related) VC-backed IPOs. While a very high percentage of VC-backed IPOs were IT focused during the 1998 to 2000 period, the dot-com bust temporarily caused a significant decrease in the number of IT-related IPOs. However, subsequent to the dot-com bust, VC-backed IPOs in the medical arena increased significantly, peaking at over 65 percent of all VC-backed IPOs in 2008. Most recently, medicine-related IPOs have decreased, though they did regain their footing in 2010.

Exhibit 4.3 presents the median age at IPO for VC and buyout-backed portfolio companies. Today, the median age at IPO for buyout-backed firms is higher than ever and is nearly 30 years of age. As buyout funds grew larger throughout the 2000s, they acquired increasingly large, and often, older companies. The harvest of these established firms began several years ago and is driving up the median age at IPO of buyout-backed companies.

The median VC-backed IPO age has also increased in recent years, and is now nearly 10 years of age. From the early 1980s through the dot-com era, the median age at IPO for VC-backed firms was roughly six years of age. Most recently, however, investment banks will only take companies public that have a history of stable cash flows; developing this history of cash flows requires a considerable amount of time and is increasing the median age at IPO.

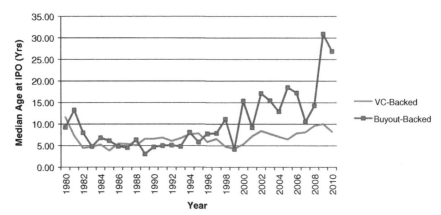

EXHIBIT 4.3 Median Age at Initial Public Offering for Venture Capital and Buyout-Backed Offerings, 1980–2010
Source: Thomson ONE Banker.

The investment banking landscape has changed significantly in recent years as the "four horsemen" investment houses that historically supported smaller public offerings (Robertson Stephens, Alex Brown & Sons, Hambrecht & Quist, and Montgomery Securities) have gone out of business. The remaining investment banks are rather large and are generally only interested in promoting stocks that will raise at least $100 million or are known brand-name companies like Facebook or LinkedIn. This is reflected in Exhibit 4.4, which plots the median offering amount for VC and buyout-backed IPOs since 1980; the average offering amount for VC-backed firms

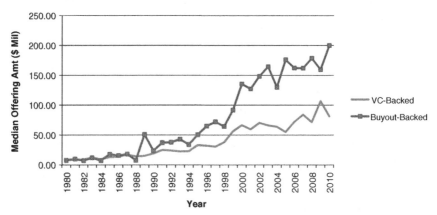

EXHIBIT 4.4 Initial Public Offering Median Offering Amount, 1980–2010
Source: Thomson ONE Banker.

is roughly double the offering level 10 years ago when the "four horsemen" were in business.

So far, a new crop of "four horsemen" has not arisen, even though many VC firms are "split on whether they get the marketing support for their stocks from the big banks or whether it is better to go with a small boutique."[9]

Summary

The IPO is a key milestone in the history of both a company and its management team. By going public, a firm may expand its business with both customers and suppliers, as these companies will generally view a public firm as an enduring part of their supply chain. Moreover, underwriter selection is an essential part of an IPO offering and will bear heavily on the success of the offering.

In recent years, the PE IPO market has continued to rebound from its rock bottom in 2008; however, many VC-backed firms are still looking to harvest their investment via other means. PE-backed firms that go public today are generally older than they were in the recent past; this attribute seems to bolster the confidence of investment banks and investors in the offering.

NOTES

1. For further discussion of the effects of the Sarbanes-Oxley Act of 2002 on private equity finance, see D. Brophy and A. Wadecki, "Fraud Deterrence in Private Equity," in *The Handbook of Fraud Deterrence*, ed. H. Cendrowski, J. P. Martin, and L. W. Petro. (Hoboken, NJ: John Wiley & Sons, 2007).
2. B. Uttal, "Inside the Deal that Made Bill Gates $350,000,000," *Fortune* 14 (1986): 23–30.
3. For further information, see http://markets.ft.com/investmentBanking/tablesAndTrends.asp.
4. *Source:* www.sec.gov/answers/quiet.htm.
5. *Id.*
6. Data from the National Bureau of Economic Research, http://www.nber.org/cycles.html.
7. *Id.*
8. M. Cooper, O. Dimitrov, and P. Rau. "A Rose.com by Any Other Name." *Journal of Finance* 56. Issue 6. December 2001.
9. A. Jacobius, "Rough Road for Venture-Backed IPOs," *Pensions & Investments,* March 8, 2010.

CHAPTER 5

Legal Considerations in Initial Public Offerings

Phillip D. Torrence

INTRODUCTION

Initial Public Offerings (IPOs) are one mechanism by which PE funds may realize liquidity for their investments. This chapter will focus on the straightforward IPO model, rather than the details of some of their variants, such as post-IPO registered offerings, Rule 144 exchanges, recapitalizations, reverse mergers with public shell companies, and so on.

In general, a PE fund will look to an IPO as its exit strategy because it believes, based on market conditions in existence at the time, that it can obtain a significantly higher return on its investment as compared to a sale transaction. Nonetheless, the following factors may make a sale transaction more favorable than an IPO:

- *Infrastructure.* To go public and maintain its stock price, the target generally must have established a consistent, stable pattern of growth and profitability. To do that, the target will need to establish professional manufacturing, distribution, finance, and administration and management. Building the infrastructure necessary to operate as a successful, publicly traded company is time consuming, expensive, and dilutive to the present equity holders. While in a particular case the target may command a higher valuation in an IPO than it can in a sale transaction, the potential for a higher valuation may not be worth the expected dilution. Moreover, an independent growth strategy can be risky if the target is likely to be overtaken by better capitalized competitors.
- *IPO windows.* The IPO market is volatile and reacts to factors that are outside the target's control. IPO windows may open and close in a cycle different from the target's growth, capital, and liquidity needs. For example, the adoption of government regulation of, or bad press about, the target's industry can affect the target's ability to go public. It may

not affect the profitability of the target's business, however, or its potential attractiveness to an acquirer already in that industry.

■ *Public disclosure.* The process of going public requires that the target disclose important information about its strategy, competitive advantage, and finances that it might prefer to keep confidential. Once public, such disclosures continue as the target is required to file regular 10-Ks, 10-Qs, and proxy statements. Moreover, there is an increasing risk that the target will be sued by its shareholders if, with hindsight, the target's public disclosures prove to be materially inaccurate. The target may prefer to be acquired to avoid that public disclosure and potential liability.

■ *Cost.* A public offering is expensive. Underwriters typically take a commission ranging between 5 and 10 percent on the stock sold, and the legal, accounting, and printing fees can add up to significant amounts. Complying with the Securities and Exchange Commission's (SEC's) public reporting requirements imposes additional administrative burdens, requires substantial executive attention, and costs the target additional amounts annually.

■ *Liquidity for shareholders.* While the target may think that going public will provide its shareholders with liquidity, that liquidity may be initially illusory. Many targets sell relatively few shares in their IPO, and many more do not get serious analyst coverage. There may be little market interest in the target's stock, with few shares trading daily (target's *float*). Furthermore, underwriters will require the target's shareholders to sign market standoff agreements, agreeing not to sell any of their shares into the public market for at least 180 days after the target's IPO. The target's shareholders may find that, although the target is now "public," their stock is relatively illiquid. If the target's shareholders receive freely tradable acquirer stock that has a significant float, they may receive more real liquidity more quickly than is possible through a target IPO.

INITIAL PUBLIC OFFERING

Introduction

The Securities Act of 1933, as amended (the Securities Act), establishes the principal legal framework for the offer and sale of securities in the United States. The Securities Act relies on a combination of regulatory oversight and private litigation to ensure compliance with its requirements. The SEC carries out the regulatory oversight.

Pursuant to Section 5 of the Securities Act, it is unlawful to "offer" or "sell" securities absent compliance with the registration process (i.e., the filing of a registration statement with the SEC), unless an exemption is available. Issuers proposing to offer and sell securities to the public are required to file with the SEC, and disseminate to prospective investors, all material information concerning the issuer and the securities offered.

With respect to the registration requirements under Section 5 of the Securities Act, the IPO process is divided into three periods: (1) the "pre-filing period," during which the issuer begins preliminary negotiations with underwriters and issuer's counsel begins drafting the registration statement; (2) the "quiet period," during which the issuer files the registration statement, and the preliminary prospectus (a part of the registration statement) is used to market the securities offering (written offers may only be made through the use of a preliminary prospectus, which is often referred to as the "red herring," because it contains on its cover a legend, printed in red, stating that offers to buy may not be accepted, and sales may not be made, prior to the effectiveness of the registration statement); and (3) the "post-effective period," during which the issuer's registration statement is declared effective by the SEC, and sales of securities can be effectuated using the final prospectus .

A decision to take a PE fund portfolio public should not be taken lightly. In addition to the larger costs of an IPO when compared to a sale transaction, an IPO may not guaranty a PE fund its exit. It may very well be the start of a new life rather than an exit. Many underwriters will require major stockholders, including PE funds, to enter into lock-up agreements to refrain from reselling their shares for a specified period of time (typically for 180 days) after the effective date of a registration statement.

Potential Advantages

The main benefits of going public include

- *Cash.* A successful IPO by a company offering its securities to the public can generate substantial proceeds for a company. This large infusion of capital provides the company with the opportunity to expand its operations, build necessary infrastructure, deliver more products and services, and accelerate its growth.
- *Access to the public market for future financings.* A public company has the opportunity to raise additional cash more easily in the future in follow-on offerings. Follow-on offerings take less time and expense to complete than an IPO. Public companies are also in a better position to obtain debt financing in the public debt markets. Complying with the

periodic reporting requirements of a public company may enable the company to be a more attractive candidate for lending or debt investors. In addition, an IPO and the consequent decrease in equity relative to debt makes for a stronger balance sheet, which can make debt financing easier to obtain on more favorable terms.

- *Providing a liquid market for the company's shares.* Going public should make the company's shares more marketable because there is a regulated and liquid market on which the company's shares are traded. While a company is private, investors typically apply a significant liquidity discount in determining the price they are willing to pay for the company's stock. Going public should eliminate this penalty and permit pre-IPO investors to realize a greater value for their shares than they otherwise would. In addition, the elimination of the liquidity discount permits the company to obtain more cash per new share from the new investors.

- *Increasing the valuation of the investment.* Many stockholders in private companies invest expecting that they will earn a sizable return upon a liquidity event, such as an IPO. A public market for a company's securities gives the investors an opportunity to realize that appreciation in value of their investment. The timing of this liquidity depends on the terms under which the initial shares were acquired. If an investor has contractual registration rights to include its shares in the IPO, or is otherwise permitted to sell its shares in the IPO, that appreciation in value can be realized immediately. In other instances, realization of that appreciation may be delayed if all or some of an investor's shares are not included in the offering, and are subject to contractual lock-up provisions or holding period requirements under the federal securities laws.

- *Incentives for employees.* Many companies provide incentives to employees by granting them stock options. If stock options have been granted prior to the IPO, the completion of the IPO will enable the employees to participate in the appreciation in the value of the underlying stock. Liquidity for employees generally will not occur simultaneously with the completion of the IPO, as the company's underwriters are likely to "lock up" their shares following the company's IPO. A "lock-up" is an agreement between a company or the underwriters on the one hand, and a stockholder on the other hand, whereby the stockholder agrees to refrain from reselling his/her shares for a specified period of time (typically for 180 days) after the effective date of a registration statement. In addition, the public market in the shares of the company may encourage future employee ownership of the company through participation in post-IPO employee stock plans, giving the stock a visible value and employees a liquid market on which to trade their shares upon their options being converted into tradable shares. Historically, share and stock option plans have been important recruitment and retention tools for public companies. In addition, many public companies believe that widespread employee ownership of the company helps align employee objectives and interests with that of the company.

■ *Creation of a currency for acquisitions.* A public company should have greater access to capital and will also be able to offer publicly tradable shares rather than cash as consideration for an acquisition (shares in a private company may well be unacceptable to the seller). Under certain circumstances, a stock-for-stock acquisition may be eligible for favorable tax treatment that is unavailable in the case of a cash acquisition. However, stock issued in connection with an acquisition is not automatically freely tradable just because the company is public. If the shares issued in the acquisition are not registered with the SEC, the shares are restricted securities under the Securities Act and their resale needs to be registered or qualify for a specific exemption from registration.

■ *Enhanced public profile for the company.* Going public should improve the perception of a company's financial stability and transparency. In addition to the initial publicity associated with an IPO, an IPO should also increase public awareness of the company through greater ongoing press and analyst coverage. This may help sustain demand for and liquidity in the shares.

■ *Comfort for suppliers and customers.* The fact that a company has undergone the rigorous due diligence and other processes required to go public may help reassure some customers and suppliers as to the company's financial standing and overall stability. The company's position within its industry and among its competitors may be enhanced and the perceived risk of default is lower. Suppliers may believe a public company is a better credit risk, and, as a result, may be more likely to extend favorable terms to the company.

■ *Greater transparency and improved internal controls.* The continuous disclosure requirements applicable to a public company tend to promote transparency. Compliance with these requirements demands effective internal systems, procedures, and controls.

Potential Disadvantages

The benefits of an IPO must be weighed against the potential disadvantages:

■ *Potential loss of control.* The sale of a portion of the company's equity inevitably means a loss of control for the pre-IPO investors and management. Significant acquisitions and other strategic decisions may require the prior approval of stockholders.

- *Susceptibility to market conditions.* After going public, the stock price (and value) of a public company can be adversely affected by market conditions beyond its control. Management cannot control the fluctuations of the public market. In addition, the pressures of being a public company can cause management to stress achieving short-term performance for its stockholders at the expense of long-term, strategic goals.

- *Loss of privacy.* The greater accountability to stockholders puts many decisions of management and the board of directors under the spotlight. Important strategic decisions may be subject to market, if not also public, scrutiny. Underperformance of the company or management may attract adverse press or analyst comment and impact the stock price.

- *Time and cost of disclosure and reporting requirements.* Both during and after the IPO process, the company will be subject to extensive rules and regulations, including the SEC's periodic reporting requirements and Regulation Fair Disclosure. Preparation of required reports and other documents, and the design, implementation, and maintenance of the internal controls, procedures, and systems necessary to do so, will require significant expense and attention of company personnel. In addition, company insiders and large stockholders will become subject to the reporting requirements of Section 13 or Section 16 of the Securities Exchange Act of 1934, as amended (the Exchange Act), which will require preparation of filings and the assistance of counsel.

- *Increased exposure to litigation.* Public companies and their control persons, including directors and executive officers, also face increased exposure to lawsuits for securities fraud and other types of class actions. These lawsuits are usually brought after a company makes a public announcement that surprises the market and the stock price drops. They typically involve investors who traded in the company's stock during the period leading up to the announcement of the bad news, and are often initiated and coordinated by "plaintiffs bar" (law firms that specialize in these lawsuits). If the lawsuit survives a motion to dismiss, the resulting litigation can drag on for years before settlement or judgment for potentially millions of dollars and can further divert additional management time from running the company. In addition, public companies and their control persons are exposed to increasingly aggressive regulatory enforcement actions and investigations.

- *IPO and post-IPO expenses.* The IPO process is expensive. For some companies, the expenses involved in an IPO and in maintaining public company status may be prohibitive and outweigh the perceived benefits. In addition, the expenses associated with being a public company can be significant. These expenses include the costs of compliance with SEC reporting requirements, SEC and securities exchange corporate governance standards, and all internal controls, procedures, and systems required to ensure compliance.

■ *Distraction of management from the operations of the company.* A large amount of management time will be diverted from the main job of running the business, both during the IPO process itself and afterwards in order to fulfill the continuing obligations of being a public company, including managing investor relations. For example, the offering process can take three to five months and consists of many obligations for management that cannot be delegated (such as management presentations, drafting sessions, and road shows).

An IPO is a complex, time-consuming process, typically requiring 90 to 150 days or longer to complete from the time underwriters are selected. It requires a great deal of time, energy, and attention by management and staff and may be distracting (and possibly disruptive at times) to the normal operation of the business.

Early planning to prepare the company and management for an IPO can ameliorate some of these difficulties. For instance, preparation of SEC financial statements and analyses of financial reporting requirements and financial tests that will be important to investors and analysts are recommended. In addition, a company that starts acting like a "public company" in the sense of anticipating public disclosure of virtually all aspects of its operations and business; documenting transactions; gathering, assembling, and maintaining files; and updating corporate legal affairs will be better positioned to manage the IPO process. Likewise, understanding the financial and legal implications of a change in tax status and planning for any major recapitalization or reorganization that may be appropriate for a public company are also essential steps in planning for the process and may help to avoid surprises.

Advance Planning Opportunities

Selection of Advisors Paramount to an IPO's success are several issues: experienced securities counsel, accountants, and underwriters must be identified and selected as early as possible in the process. Federal securities regulations applicable to IPOs require detailed disclosures with respect to all material facets of the company's business (including its development over the five years prior to the offering or longer periods if material to an investor's understanding of the business), a summary of the company's financial information over the same period, a thorough analysis of the company's financial condition and results of operations on a comparative period-to-period basis for the three years before the offering, and detailed disclosures with respect to executive compensation and related party transactions.

Securities Counsel   Compliance with federal and state securities regulations and managing the offering process (including the sometimes differing interests of the underwriters) requires counsel with substantial securities law expertise. Securities counsel will assist the issuer in preparing the registration statement and prospectus and in negotiating the underwriting arrangements with the underwriters. Involving securities counsel in the process at an early stage is important: the earlier counsel becomes involved, the more familiar he/she can become with the issuer, its management, and business, which will facilitate earlier identification and resolution of legal and disclosure issues.

In addition, securities counsel can assist in "housekeeping" matters that require updating, consult on corporate recapitalization and structural changes that may be necessary or appropriate for a public company, and help to prepare the issuer to respond to due diligence requests from the underwriters. A well-prepared, organized, "clean" company will be better received by the underwriters and will enable the company to avoid groundless concerns and needless follow-up due diligence that can be extremely time consuming and distracting to management.

Accountants   If the company's regular accountants do not have public company clients, it may be prudent to change to a firm with significant SEC experience. Federal securities regulations require that the financial statements and schedules that will be filed with the registration statement and those required to be filed with the SEC on an ongoing basis comply with special rules. In addition, experienced auditors are important in anticipating and responding to SEC accounting comments in the registration process. Since changes in accountants during the two years before the offering must be disclosed and explained in the prospectus, the involvement of qualified auditors early in the company's development may be appropriate. They can provide important business and financial planning advice to better position a company for a future public offering. Even if the company has no specific plans or timetable for an IPO, it may be wise to have the accountants perform certain procedures (like observing inventory) that cannot be done after the fact since the financial statements required for the registration statement include two years of audited balance sheets and three years of audited income statements (less for an issuer that qualifies as a "small business issuer").

Underwriters The underwriters often provide financial advisory services to companies with no specific plans for an offering. They can give useful advice on market expectations and reactions to business planning issues, management, and other matters that may eventually be important to an offering.

Corporate Housekeeping Matters Securities counsel should be involved at an early stage (and certainly well before the underwriters' due diligence begins) in reviewing and assisting in corporate housekeeping matters. These include, for example, a thorough review of governing documents, stock records, past offerings, corporate minutes, documentation of material transactions, and licenses.

Antitakeover Provisions Securities counsel can also assist in assessing whether antitakeover provisions are appropriate for the protection of the existing shareholders. While such provisions should not be considered as absolute protection against a loss of control, these provisions are intended to encourage a bidder to negotiate with the board of directors. Whether these devices are necessary or appropriate will depend on whether existing shareholders will be in control following completion of the offering. The market's perception (particularly institutional investors) and state securities or "blue sky" regulations may have an impact on whether these types of provisions can be employed. Examples of these types of provisions include

- Classified board of directors.
- Removal of directors only for cause.
- Cumulative voting for directors.
- Supermajority vote requirements for certain matters, including mergers, sales of substantially all assets, and certain other types of business combinations.
- Blank check preferred stock.
- Large amounts of authorized, but unissued common stock.
- Shareholder rights plan (so-called *poison pill*).
- Elimination of, or restrictions on, taking action by shareholder written consent in lieu of a meeting.
- Fair pricing provisions (intended to ensure that all shareholders receive comparable consideration in a business combination transaction).
- Special procedures for nominations of directors.
- Special procedures for setting record dates.
- Elections by the issuer to be subject (or to not be subject) to the business combination and control share acquisition laws of its state of incorporation.

Management   Underwriters often recommend the addition of outside directors to the board of directors who have significant business experience. If the securities are to be listed on a national securities exchange or the NASDAQ National Market, at least two independent directors will be required. Even though the additional directors will usually join the board after the offering is completed, underwriters generally want them disclosed in the prospectus, so it is thus important to start considering candidates early in the process. The five-year business background of each director must be disclosed in the prospectus. Additional disclosure is required in the event any director (or any affiliated business) has been involved in any bankruptcy proceedings, convicted in a criminal proceeding (other than traffic violations and other minor offenses), enjoined from engaging in any type of business practice, or found to have violated any securities laws. Although involvement in these types of proceedings does not necessarily preclude a person from serving as a director or executive officer of a public company, it is important to know that appropriate disclosures will be required and that they could affect the stock market's reception to the offering. In any event, the underwriters should be made aware of these issues as early as possible.

Disclosures with respect to the five-year business background of executive officers are required. Employment and noncompetition agreements with executives who are important to the success of the business should be considered. Any golden parachute arrangements will need to be fully disclosed. The potential impact of the IPO on any existing arrangement should also be considered.

The cost, availability, and coverage of directors' and officers' liability insurance should be investigated as well. In some cases, such insurance may be required by outside directors as a condition to serve on the board of directors.

The Initial Public Offering Process

An IPO is a complex and time-sensitive process that involves the combined efforts of company personnel, experienced securities counsel, accountants, and underwriters. The process typically requires 90 to 120 days to complete from the time underwriters are selected. Exhibit 5.1 presents a diagram of the key components of the IPO process.

Principal Parties   The principal parties in an IPO are:

- *Registrant.* The company—the entity that will issue the securities to be sold to the public.

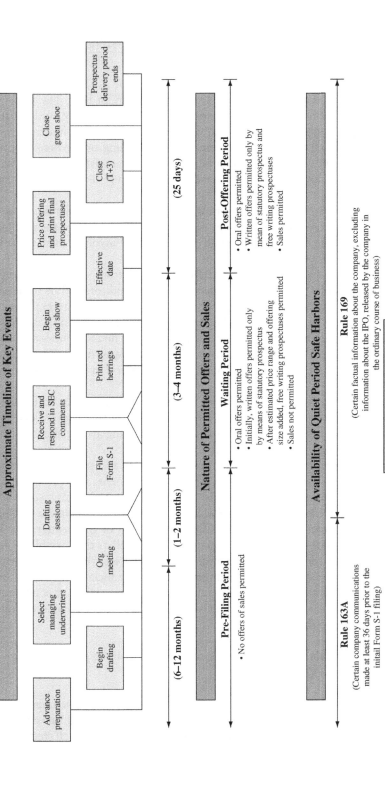

Approximate Timeline of Key Events

| Advance preparation | Select managing underwriters | Drafting sessions | Receive and respond in SEC comments | Begin road show | Price offering and print final prospectuses | Close green shoe | Prospectus delivery period ends |

| Begin drafting | Org meeting | File Form S-1 | Print red herrings | Effective date | Close (T+3) |

(6–12 months)   (1–2 months)   (3–4 months)   (25 days)

Nature of Permitted Offers and Sales

Pre-Filing Period
• No offers of sales permitted

Waiting Period
• Oral offers permitted
• Initially, written offers permitted only by means of statutory prospectus
• After estimated price range and offering size added, free writing prospectuses permitted
• Sales not permitted

Post-Offering Period
• Oral offers permitted
• Written offers permitted only by mean of statutory prospectus and free writing prospectuses
• Sales permitted

Availability of Quiet Period Safe Harbors

Rule 163A
(Certain company communications made at least 36 days prior to the initail Form S-1 filing)

Rule 169
(Certain factual information about the company, excluding information about the IPO, released by the company in the ordinary course of business)

Diagram not to scale

EXHIBIT 5.1   Key Components of the Initial Public Offering Process

■ *Selling security holders.* It is not unusual for some of the existing security holders to sell a portion of their holdings in an IPO. The underwriters will, of course, want to know the reason the security holders are selling (presumably liquidity) and will want to be involved in determining how much will be sold. Sometimes, depending on market conditions, the amount of capital to be raised by the registrant, and other factors, it is not advisable or possible to include any security holders in the IPO.

■ *Underwriters.* The underwriters will agree to purchase the securities (normally on a firm commitment basis) and to resell them to the public. The managing underwriter and its counsel will be involved in all phases of the IPO process.

■ *Auditors.* The auditors will normally be the registrant's long-time independent public accountants. Occasionally, new auditors will be selected if the existing firm does not have sufficient public company expertise. The auditors certify the annual financial statements included in the prospectus, assist in preparing and reviewing other financial information included in the prospectus, and provide the underwriters with certain assurances (in the form of so-called comfort letters) in connection with the closing.

■ *Registrant's counsel.* Counsel with securities law experience will be required to assist the registrant in the preparation of the required disclosure documents and in negotiating the underwriting arrangements with the managing underwriter and its counsel.

■ *Financial printer.* The financial printer typesets and prints the selling documents—principally the registration statement and prospectus. There are numerous national and regional financial printers, some of which have offices located in Michigan. The cost of printing the selling documents can be substantial. Careful selection of the printer and a clear understanding of the anticipated cost, as well as the variables that may impact the cost, is important. Experienced securities counsel can assist registrants in making arrangements with financial printers and in reducing printing charges by maintaining the selling documents through the early drafting and revision process. Exhibit 5.2 presents the key parties to the IPO process.

Principal Documents   The principal documents that will be prepared in connection with an IPO are as follows:

■ *Registration statement.* The registration statement is the document that is filed with the SEC and state securities (or "blue sky") administrators to register the securities for sale to the public. It is often referred to as

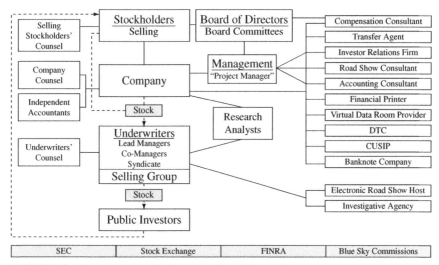

EXHIBIT 5.2 Key Parties in the Initial Public Offering Process

the S-1, which relates to its title as the Registration Statement on Form S-1, the form used by an issuer registering an IPO. The registration statement consists of a cover page, a prospectus, and certain additional information relating generally to the estimated expenses of the offering; recent unregistered offerings by the registrant; indemnification of officers, directors, and others; undertakings by the registrant; and exhibits.

- *Preliminary prospectus.* The prospectus is the principal selling document. Prior to the registration statement's being declared effective by the SEC, the prospectus is commonly called the *red herring*, which refers to the language appearing on the spine of the prospectus cover page, in red, indicating that the document is subject to completion. Officially, the red herring is called the *preliminary prospectus* and is used by the underwriters to solicit interest in purchasing the securities. It will contain a range of the public offering price (for example $10 to $12 per share). The final price and other information relating to the price and the underwriting syndicate and compensation will be blank in the red herring.

- *Final prospectus.* Shortly before or after the registration statement is declared effective by the SEC, the registrant and the underwriters will agree on the public offering price and specifics of the underwriting compensation, sign the underwriting agreement, and prepare and file the final prospectus (sometimes called a *black*, to indicate that the red printing on the cover of the preliminary prospectus has been removed).

The final prospectus is the definitive offering document for the securities.

■ *Underwriting agreement.* The underwriting agreement is the definitive agreement pursuant to which the underwriters agree to purchase the securities from the registrant and any selling security holders. It will contain detailed representations and warranties by the registrant and the selling security holders with respect to all facets of the business; capitalization, litigation, and other matters concerning the registrant and the security holders; covenants with respect to actions to be taken before and after the offering; and indemnification and contribution provisions whereby the registrant and the selling security holders will agree to indemnify the underwriters in respect of federal or state securities law liabilities in connection with the IPO and other specified matters. Each managing underwriter has its own preferred form of underwriting agreement. Careful negotiation of the terms of the underwriting agreement with experienced securities counsel is important.

The underwriting agreement will be signed immediately after the initial offering price and underwriting compensation are agreed upon by the managing underwriter and the registrant (and, if applicable, the selling security holders). Until the underwriting agreement is executed, the underwriters do not have any commitment to purchase the securities. (Sometimes an underwriter will insist on a letter of intent as a condition to going forward with the IPO process to ensure that it will be reimbursed for expenses if the IPO does not eventually get completed).

Other underwriting documents typically include an agreement among underwriters and a selected dealer agreement. The agreement among underwriters is an agreement between members of the underwriting syndicate and specifies the rights and obligations among the members. The selected dealer agreement is an agreement between the underwriters and certain securities dealers and specifies, among other things, the commission (referred to as a *concession*) dealers in the syndicate are to receive. The registrant normally does not have any input into, and may not even receive copies of, these documents.

Selling Security Holder Documents   The principal documents that will be prepared in connection with an IPO are as follows:

■ *Lock-up agreement.* This is an agreement typically required by all underwriters in which the selling security holders (and other substantial security holders) agree to not sell or dispose of any of the company's securities held by them for a period of time (typically 90 to 180 days) after the offering is completed without the consent of the managing underwriter. The purpose of the agreement is to prevent significant amounts of securities from being sold into the market shortly after the IPO, which could adversely impact trading prices.

■ *Power of attorney and custody agreement.* This is a document pursuant to which each selling security holder irrevocably appoints one or more persons to hold in custody the securities to be sold to the underwriters under the underwriting agreement and authorizes the attorney(s)-in-fact to execute the underwriting agreement and to deliver the securities at the closing. The agreement will normally provide for the person also to receive payment from the underwriters and to deduct the selling security holder's aliquot share of the offering expenses before paying the balance to the security holder. The purpose of the agreement is to ensure that the transaction can be completed in the event the security holder becomes incapacitated or otherwise unavailable.

■ *Directors and officers questionnaire.* This is a document that will be executed by each director, officer, controlling person, and selling security holder. Its purpose is to solicit and confirm information contained in the registration statement. It is an integral part of the due diligence process.

■ *Other documents.* Various other documents must be prepared, including, for example, the form of the stock certificate; application(s) for admission or listing on NASDAQ National Market or New York Stock Exchange (NYSE); and various closing documents, opinions, and certificates.

■ *Offering expenses.* The IPO process is expensive. The actual expenses incurred will be dependent on many factors, including the size and complexity of the offering, and are very difficult to predict. Final amendments to registration statements are required to include a good faith estimate of various offering expenses. A review of recently completed, comparable transactions can often provide a reasonable estimate of overall expenses for a planned IPO. Expenses that will be incurred by the registrant include
  ■ SEC filing fee.
  ■ NASDAQ/NYSE listing fees.
  ■ National Association of Securities Dealers fee.
  ■ Accounting fees.
  ■ Legal fees.
  ■ Underwriting discounts and commissions.
  ■ Printing fees (prospectus).
  ■ Engraving fees (stock certificates).
  ■ Directors' and officers' liability insurance premiums.
  ■ Transfer agent fees.
  ■ Blue sky fees.

The Registration Process

- *Timeline.* The amount of time from start to finish is inherently difficult to predict due to the many uncertainties in the process, including the SEC's current review schedule, any unique characteristics of the offering or special issues (particularly accounting) that may arise, and the current condition of the IPO market. A timeline of 120 days from the time the principal parties are selected to closing may be useful as a guide.
- *Due diligence.* Due diligence is the process by which underwriters, auditors, and counsel conduct investigations of the registrant and its business for the purpose of verifying information required for and statements made in the registration statement. The registrant has absolute liability under the federal and state securities laws for false or misleading statements made in the registration statement. Others involved in the offering process, including directors and principal officers of the registrant, underwriters, and accountants, may also have liability, but may have a defense if they did not have knowledge that the statements were false or misleading and they exercised due diligence in ascertaining the relevant facts.

  The due diligence process will be very time consuming, and will begin at about the time the working party is formed and continue through closing. The underwriters' counsel will prepare a detailed due diligence checklist of legal documents and information it wants to review. The underwriters will also want to engage in significant financial and business due diligence investigations.

  The registrant's securities counsel will be involved in the due diligence process at each step and will help to assemble due diligence documents and serve as a "clearing house" for due diligence requests.
- *Confidentiality.* It is important that the registrant, its directors, officers, and others involved in the IPO process and selling security holders understand the need for confidentiality of all aspects of the IPO process, including that the registrant is even considering an offering. The SEC has published guidelines with respect to the disclosure of information about the registrant and the offering beginning with the time a preliminary understanding is reached with the underwriters until 90 days after the effective date of the registration statement. Different guidelines apply during different phases of the registration process. The SEC has the authority to delay or stop an IPO under certain circumstances, and, accordingly, it is important that all forms of publicity be cleared with experienced securities counsel during this period (even new advertising can be a concern under some circumstances).

- *Registration statement.* The drafting of the registration statement will be managed and coordinated by the registrant's securities counsel. Once an initial draft is prepared, it will be circulated among the working group and revised. Normally, a series of drafting sessions will take place in which the language is scrutinized, challenged, and revised. These drafting sessions will include due diligence investigations. The working group should include the chief executive officer (CEO; or operations manager), chief financial officer (CFO), general counsel (if any), special SEC counsel, managing underwriter, and its counsel. This process usually takes 30 to 45 days or longer, depending on the transaction.

  Once finalized, the registration statement is filed with the SEC. After the registration statement is filed, an SEC examiner will be assigned who will review it. The initial review typically takes at least 30 days. The SEC will provide written comments as to the disclosures and financial statements, which may include legal and accounting questions, comments, and required changes. One or more amendments to the registration statement will be filed in response to the SEC comments. It is not unusual for the SEC to have follow-up or further comments on subsequent amendments.

  At the same time or shortly after the registration statement is filed with the SEC, it will also be filed with the blue sky administrators of the states where the securities will be offered. This is typically handled by the underwriters' counsel. Like the SEC, the blue sky administrators may have comments and require changes to the registration statement.

- *Selling efforts.* After the registration statement is filed and the red herring is printed, the underwriters will commence the marketing of the securities. Under certain circumstances, this process may be delayed until after the first round of comments is received from the SEC and the first amendment is filed. The time between the filing of the registration statement and the time it is declared effective by the SEC is referred to as the waiting period. During this period, the managing underwriter will form the underwriting syndicate and will solicit interest in the securities being registered. No written sales literature other than the red herring may be used during this period, although oral selling efforts may be permitted. The road show is an integral part of the marketing process conducted by the underwriters. Typically, the road show will be conducted over a two- to three-week period. The managing underwriter and the registrant will meet with members of the underwriting syndicate and institutional buyers throughout the United States and, possibly, Europe. Securities counsel does not normally participate in the road show.

■ *Effective date of registration statement and pricing.* After all reviews are completed and a final amendment to the registration statement is filed, the registrant and the managing underwriter will request the SEC to declare the registration statement to be effective. Under applicable current SEC rules, the registration statement may be declared effective before the final price is determined and the underwriting compensation is agreed upon. Typically, on the afternoon this occurs, the registrant and the managing underwriter agree on the price and execute the underwriting agreement. The final prospectus is usually prepared later that evening with the necessary pricing information and the specifics of the underwriting syndicate. The final prospectus must be filed with the SEC within two business days after the date the price is determined, but is often filed the following day.

■ *Closing.* The closing will then occur within three to five business days after the underwriting agreement has been signed. During the interim period, closing documents will be prepared, negotiated, and finalized.

■ *Post-closing matters.* The registrant and its principal security holders will be subject to numerous reporting and other requirements of the federal securities laws after the closing, including periodic reporting obligations under Sections 13, 14, and 16 of the Exchange Act.

Possible Liabilities Faced by a Company and Its Directors and Officers

Before engaging in an IPO, one should carefully consider the potential liabilities the company and its directors, officers, and selling shareholders may face. Both federal and state laws regulate IPOs through laws intended to protect potential purchasers of the offered securities. These laws focus on two areas: (1) ensuring that potential investors know everything about the company that could potentially affect its value and (2) ensuring that the company issuing securities (or anyone on its behalf) does not act fraudulently or deceptively to affect the perceived value of the company.

Liabilities under Federal Securities Laws

Material Misstatements or Omissions of Material Facts   Section 11 of the Securities Act requires that all statements in the registration statement be true and not misleading. If the registration statement contains any untrue statements of material fact that are required to be stated therein or that are necessary to make the statements therein not misleading, then any purchaser unaware of the untruth or omission may sue any of the following parties:

- The company (including anyone acting on its behalf)
- Every person who signed the registration statement (including selling shareholders)
- Every person who was a director of the company at the time of the filing
- Every person who, with his/her consent, is named in the registration statement as being or about to become a director (commonly referred to as a *director nominee*)

Although officers of the company are liable only if they sign the registration statement, the principal executive officer(s), the principal financial officer, and the principal accounting officer are required to sign the registration statement. In order to prove a case under Section 11, plaintiff needs to demonstrate the existence of a material misstatement or omission and that plaintiff was damaged by falling stock prices after the sale. Plaintiff is not required to prove that they acted in reliance on the misstatement or omission, or even that the misstatement or omission caused the drop in the value of the security.

Section 11 provides all persons other than the company with a due diligence defense. To claim this defense, a defendant must show that after reasonable investigation, he/she had reasonable grounds for belief and did believe that the registration statement, at the time it became effective, contained no material untruths and omitted no material facts. This defense is not available to the company itself, which is strictly liable for any material misstatement or omission.

For the directors, officers, and any selling shareholders of the company, the linchpin to this defense is reasonable investigation. It is imperative that these individuals work together, with the help of their counsel, to substantiate all statements (within reason) made in the registration statement. Otherwise, this defense is unavailable, and, like the company itself, these individuals will be strictly liable for *any* material misstatements or omissions in the registration statement.

A plaintiff-purchaser must bring suit against the defendants under Section 11 within one year after discovering the untruth or omission, or the suit will be barred by the statute of limitations. In no case can a plaintiff-purchaser bring suit more than three years after the sale.

Section 12(2) of the Securities Act requires that all information in documents or oral communications be truthful and complete. Any person that offers or sells a security using a prospectus or oral communication that includes a material untruth or omits a material fact will be liable to a purchaser who is unaware of such untruth or omission. Plaintiffs need only show the existence of a material misstatement or omission and falling stock prices after the sale. They need not show that they acted in reliance on the misstatement or omission or even that the misstatement or omission caused the loss in value of the stock.

Section 12(2) has a broader scope than Section 11 and applies not only to the registration statement but to untrue statement or omissions of material fact in any oral communication or other document. Section 12(2) provides the defendant with a reasonable care defense. Specifically, the company or other defendant must prove that after exercising reasonable care, it could not have known and in fact did not know of such untruth or omission. This "reasonable care" standard is generally considered the same as the reasonable investigation standard of the due diligence defense under Section 11.

An action must be brought within one year after discovery of the untruth or omission and not more than three years after the sale.

Fraud in Connection with the Offer and Sale of a Security   Rule 10(b)(5) under the Exchange Act prohibits fraudulent or deceptive acts in connection with the sale of securities. Any act, practice, or course of business that operates or would operate as a fraud or deceit on any person in connection with the purchase or sale of any security is prohibited. Possible defendants under this rule are the same as those listed in Section 11 of the Securities Act, including:

- The company (including anyone acting on its behalf)
- Every person who signed the registration statement (including selling shareholders)
- Every person who was a director of the company at the time of the filing
- Every person who, with his/her consent, is named in the registration statement as being or about to become a director (commonly referred to as a *director nominee*)

"Fraud or deceit" under this rule can be established only by showing the person acted willfully or recklessly. Mere negligence or failure to act with reasonable care is not enough. Unlike Sections 11 and 12(2) of the Securities Act, Rule 10(b)(5) requires plaintiff to prove that defendant's fraud or deceit caused plaintiff to enter into the transaction (transaction causation) and also caused plaintiff to lose money (loss causation). Also in contrast to Sections 11 and 12(2), only purchasers or sellers of securities can bring actions under Rule 10(b)(5).

Similar to Section 12(2) of the Securities Act, this rule is broader than Section 11 and applies not just to statements made in the registration statement, but to all statements made in connection with the purchase or sale of securities. Thus, the rule also applies to statements in the form of a report, press release, or other document.

A suit must be brought within one year from discovery of the fraud and three years from the date of the violation.

Liability under State Blue Sky Laws   The vast majority of states and the Uniform Securities Act have antifraud provisions patterned after Rule 10(b) (5). The provisions are interpreted in the same way as Rule 10(b)(5) but generally have a two-year statute of limitations.

Investor Expectations: The Consequences of an Initial Public Offering Failure   The economic success of the underlying securities offered in an IPO is dependent upon a number of factors. A number of these factors are directly correlated to general economic conditions (e.g., the nature of the public markets and the strength of the economy), and a number of these factors are related to the issuer and its agents (e.g., the ability of the issuer to use the capital generated in an IPO successfully [a majority of IPOs are completed by companies going through a transitory growth period]), the effectiveness of management, and the demand for the individual service and/or good produced. This uncertainty, combined with perhaps the overly ambitious expectations of investors and the investment community at large, can result in securities litigation against the issuer and its officers and directors, and in some cases, each of the financial, legal, and accounting professionals involved in the offering.

A significant percentage of private actions resulting from an IPO are filed by stockholders who have suffered a loss due to the fall of the issuer's share price below the initial IPO price. Therefore, it is fundamentally important that the registration statement and accompanying IPO disclosures are prepared very carefully, particularly with respect to any uncertainties or risks that may adversely affect the issuer and/or related parties in the future.

THE SARBANES-OXLEY ACT AND DODD-FRANK ACT

The requirements of the Sarbanes-Oxley Act (SOX) have both legal and accounting components. Company counsel should advise the directors and officers of the corporate governance aspects; the ban on loans to directors and executive officers (which becomes applicable upon the initial filing of the Form S-1); the post-IPO officer certification requirements; the profit disgorgement provisions applicable to the CEO and the CFO following a restatement of financial statements due to misconduct; the "whistleblower" protection provisions; the rule requiring an attorney to report evidence of a

EXHIBIT 5.3   Timeline for Becoming SOX Ready

SOX Section	Key SOX Activity	Recommended Implementation Timeframe
Section 404	1. Document the company's significant business processes affecting financial reporting	By S-1 filing
Section 404	2. Identify risks, controls, and areas of improvement in internal control over financial reporting	By S-1 filing
Section 404	3. Conduct remediation of internal control structure	3 quarters prior to 404 compliance date
Other key considerations	4. Evaluate the role and composition of board and audit committee	Prior to IPO
Other key considerations	5. Evaluate need for internal audit function	After 404 compliance
Section 404	6. Implement a process to test internal controls and report on that testing	2 quarters prior to 404 compliance date
Other key considerations	7. Establish need for enhanced financial reporting function to support new reporting and disclosure requirements	By S-1 filing
Section 302/906	8. Implement a CEO/CFO certifications process	By first 10-Q
Section 406	9. Make code of ethics and business conduct policy publicly available	Prior to IPO
Section 301	10. Establish whistleblower hotline	Prior to IPO

material violation of securities laws or breach of fiduciary duty or similar violation by the company "up the ladder" within the company; and other legal implications of the act. The company's independent accountants should brief the directors and officers regarding SOX's requirements in the areas of auditor independence; prohibited nonaudit services; preapproval requirements for all services; Section 404 preparation; and other audit and accounting matters. Every detail of SOX need not be tackled up front, but the basic requirements should be factored into the company's decision to pursue an IPO.

Although the vast majority of the Dodd-Frank Act does not directly affect public companies outside of the financial services industry, the Act imposes several significant corporate governance, executive compensation, and disclosure requirements on all public companies. These requirements include say-on-pay (a requirement to hold periodic, nonbinding stockholder votes on executive compensation for public companies that are not smaller reporting companies); enhanced whistleblower protections and a bounty program designed to reward whistleblower tips made to the SEC; and disclosure requirements regarding the company's use of "conflict minerals" (defined as gold, columbite-tentalite, cassiterite, and wolframite). The act also authorizes the SEC to adopt rules regarding proxy access (the ability of stockholders to include director nominees in the company's proxy statement). In addition, all public companies listed on a national securities exchange will be required to adopt "clawback" policies to recover incentive-based compensation erroneously paid to executive officers following an accounting restatement due to material noncompliance with financial reporting requirements.

Public Company Filing Obligations

Company counsel customarily prepares a memorandum for the company describing its public company filing obligations under the federal securities laws. This memorandum usually includes a discussion of the requirement to file periodic reports under Section 13(a) or 15(d) of the Exchange Act, the application of various requirements of the Exchange Act and, if applicable, securities exchange rules arising from registration of a class of securities under Section 12 of the Exchange Act.

Initial Public Offering Alternative: Reverse Mergers

The decision to become a public company should prompt an analysis of the alternatives to an IPO, with reverse merger being the most common alternative. A reverse merger allows a privately held company to go public by acquiring a controlling interest in, and merging with, a public shell company. The SEC defines a shell company as a publicly traded company with (1) no or nominal operations and (2) either no or nominal assets or assets consisting solely of any amount of cash and cash equivalents. Given the popularity of reverse mergers, a separate market for public shells has developed over the past several years, with prices varying based on the age and the history of the shell. Compared to an IPO, reverse mergers have certain advantages and disadvantages.

Advantages Reverse mergers usually allow a company to go faster, and are generally less expensive than IPOs. While reverse mergers, in certain cases, may provide some additional benefits (such as lower dilution), lower cost and faster speed are the two major advantages of reverse mergers. Prior to a final IPO decision, a company should weigh carefully the advantages, the disadvantages, and certain pitfalls involved in the reverse merger transaction.

Disadvantages Although oftentimes overlooked, going public through a reverse merger has several drawbacks.

1. A reverse merger is not a capital raising transaction. Unlike an IPO, a reverse merger is not an "offering" of shares, and it does not provide immediate access to capital. A reverse merger transaction involves no underwriter to develop an active secondary market. While an active trading market could eventually develop for the merged company's shares, without the initial IPO buzz, a new public company will have to work its way up to get noticed in the market.
2. The stock of a company that has become public through a reverse merger is likely to trade at a lower price than that of a comparable IPO-initiated public company. In addition to the initial trading market and publicity created by a new IPO, the price of securities after an IPO is likely to be higher. The involvement of an underwriter generally increases institutional confidence in the offering and supports stock in secondary markets post-IPO. Reverse merger deals, on the other hand, are not underwritten and do not enjoy similar support.
3. The risks associated with the public shell history may cause the issuer to incur additional due diligence costs and expose a company to future unknown liability. This uncertainty may similarly have an adverse impact on the stock price of a company that goes public through a reverse merger.
4. Reverse mergers involve a number of extensive and time-sensitive SEC filings, such as "Super 8-K" beneficial ownership reports and proxy statements. In 2005, the SEC adopted Release 33–8587: "Use of Form S-8, Form 8-K, and Form 20-F by Shell Companies" that requires, no later than four days after the closing of the merger, the filing of the same disclosure information and audited financial statements about the private company as are required in the S-1 filing in an IPO. Consequently, the cost and the time necessary to prepare for the closing of a reverse merger have increased and are now generally comparable to those of an IPO.

Overall, reverse mergers cannot be viewed as adequate substitutes to IPOs and may not be as attractive as oftentimes perceived. The results of numerous studies and articles examining the advantages and disadvantages of reverse mergers are beyond the scope of these materials. Suffice to say that, despite the recent resurgence in the number of reverse mergers, IPOs remain the most traditional and popular method of going public in the United States.

CONCLUSION

The IPO process is an important harvest mechanism in PE and involves numerous legal considerations. In general, a PE fund will look to an IPO as its exit strategy because it believes, based on market conditions in existence at the time, that it can obtain a significantly higher return on its investment as compared to a sale transaction. The decision to take a company public will involve careful consideration of a portfolio company's infrastructure, the IPO window, costs of public disclosure, offering costs, shareholder liquidity, and securities law compliance.

CHAPTER 6

Harvesting Investments Through Mergers and Acquisitions

Harry Cendrowski
James P. Martin

INTRODUCTION

Mergers and acquisitions (M&As) have become an increasingly popular exit vehicle for PE-backed investments. This chapter examines the basics of M&A deals, including types of M&A deals, the sale process, and historical M&A data.

M&A BASICS

Although the term "M&A" is a common one in business, there exist numerous differences between mergers and acquisitions. On a simple level, a merger is a transaction in which multiple parties negotiate the amount of ownership each will hold in a combined firm; by contrast, in an acquisition, an *acquiring firm* will negotiate with a *target firm* over a purchase price for the target. For simplicity, we will sometimes refer to a merger or acquisition as a *takeover*.

When practitioners or academics discuss mergers, they are typically referring to a *forward merger*, or a transaction in which the target firm obtains an equity stake in the acquiring firm or cash in exchange for merging with the acquirer. By contrast, in a *reverse merger,* an acquirer merges into the target company and receives an equity stake in the target. Stock acquisitions are transactions where the acquirer purchases the common stock of the target firm for a negotiated price.

There also exist some descriptive terms that describe the purpose—rather than structure of—an M&A deal. For instance, *horizontal takeovers* take place when two companies in a similar industry merge/are acquired,

111

whereas *vertical takeovers* are those in which members of a supply chain merge/are acquired, creating a single firm. Such a deal eliminates one step in the supply chain (e.g., a supplier and manufacturer merge to create a single company that supplies products to the customer). The term "conglomerate takeover" refers to a merger of companies in dissimilar industries.

Unlike an initial public offering, an M&A deal permits managers and investors to achieve liquidity for their investments without waiting for a lock-up period to expire. In an M&A deal, the target firm's owners generally lose their absolute managerial authority over the firm. However, many acquiring firms will often incentivize the target company's management to stay with the company through lucrative compensation packages containing large equity provisions.

TYPES OF TAKEOVERS

There are generally four types of takeovers: strategic, defensive, growth, and financial. *Strategic takeovers* are those in which the target firm possesses a well-developed product that the acquirer wishes to obtain. This product is usually a service or form of intellectual property that the acquirer deems attractive to its business plan. For instance, there exists an established trend in the pharmaceutical industry for top companies (e.g., Pfizer, Merck, Bayer, etc.) to acquire smaller, venture-backed firms whose products are well on their way to Phase IV Food and Drug Administration approval; years ago, such firms sought to develop such new drugs in their own research and development laboratories. Some automakers are now employing a similar acquisition mentality. General Motors recently started GM Ventures LLC, a $100 million organization tasked with making investments in high-technology products.

Defensive takeovers are those in which the acquirer purchases the target in order to quell eroding market share or market power of the target firm. The robber barons of the late nineteenth and early twentieth centuries (e.g., John D. Rockefeller) typically employed such takeovers in order to squash competitive firms by simply acquiring them and subsequently selling their assets.

In some cases, a firm may employ a "Pac-Man defense" when attempting to stave off a takeover. This term refers to an attempt initiated by a would-be target firm to take over what was formerly an acquiring firm. A popular example of the Pac-Man defense is the attempted hostile takeover of Martin Marietta (MM) by Bendix Corporation in 1982.

When Bendix began purchasing shares in MM, MM began to divest noncore assets, using the proceeds to acquire Bendix stock and launch its own hostile takeover of Bendix. As a result, Bendix was sold to Allied Corporation, while Martin Marietta survived as a separate entity.

Growth takeovers are those in which a usually large, diverse company acquires a target firm with high growth potential. The acquiring firm may use its existing sales and distribution network, along with its management expertise to market the products and/or services of the target firm. International Telephone and Telegraph (ITT) was one such conglomerate that successfully built up and grew many acquired companies in the 1960s and early 1970s. Under the leadership of renowned business executive Harold Geneen, ITT purchased companies such as Sheraton Hotels, Avis Rent-a-Car, the Hartford Financial Services Group, Continental Baking, and nearly 300 others with the hopes of successfully mentoring and growing these firms.

Finally, *financial takeovers* are those in which the acquiring firm is motivated purely by a target firm's financial statements when it seeks to acquire it. Struggling firms may hunt for profitable acquisitions in order to boost earnings, while, conversely, highly successful firms may search for struggling firms (with strong products) to take over in order to offset tax liabilities.

REVERSE TAKEOVERS

Reverse takeovers have become a notably popular exit vehicle for many private equity (PE) portfolio companies in recent years. Harvesting through a reverse takeover allows a privately held company to become publicly traded in a more efficient manner, generally requiring less stock dilution than necessary in an initial public offering (IPO). In a reverse takeover, a firm may go public without raising additional capital; this is not the case in an IPO. Since no shares are required to be sold in a reverse takeover, stock dilution need not occur. Moreover, as discussed in the previous chapter on IPOs, the success of an IPO is particularly dependent on market conditions at the time of the event. In contrast, a reverse takeover is considerably less susceptible to market conditions, over which management has little control.

A company must rely heavily on the faith of many institutional and retail investors in order for its IPO to succeed. If investors become skittish about overall market conditions, an investment bank might experience difficulty in selling the company's shares, and the market may not favorably receive the now-public company's shares once they are listed and trading. In the recent past, particularly during the 2008 through 2009 recession, underwriters pulled IPOs simply because of a *cold period* in the overall market. However, a cold period need not extend to the entire market; a cold period may be restricted to a particular industry, such as biotechnology stocks circa 2003. In contrast, reverse takeovers are largely immune from

IPO market woes as only two parties are involved in such a deal: a target and an acquirer. Moreover, with respect to time, a reverse takeover may be executed in about a month; the process for a conventional IPO typically lasts over a year.

THE TAKEOVER PROCESS AND FINANCIAL ADVISER SELECTION

Entrepreneurs often cringe at the thought of losing control of their once-germinal firm. After many years of devotion and hard work, it is certainly no easy task to "hand over the reins" to the management of another company. Nonetheless, when such an entrepreneur seeks PE funding, he or she must understand that an M&A transaction is a potential exit strategy that a PE investor will likely pursue (in contrast to an IPO, where the entrepreneur may retain control).

Before committing to a merger or acquisition, the management of a target firm should profoundly understand a potential acquirer's business: What are the strengths/weaknesses of the acquirer's business model? How is the organization structured? How can a takeover benefit the target company? Why would the acquirer like to merge with/acquire the target? Does the acquirer have a robust risk management process? These, along with many other questions, can assist the target firm's management in evaluating the economic incentives of acquirers in a potential M&A transaction.

In order to gain further information on potential acquirers, many firms will organize a special committee of the board of directors. This committee will interface regularly with financial and legal advisors, prospective buyers, and even lending institutions. Although the full board of directors must vote on an M&A transaction, this special committee will make its recommendation to the board regarding the deal. Moreover, for larger companies (i.e., those with enterprise values in excess of approximately $100 million), the committee will also need to select an appropriate financial advisor to counsel the board throughout the takeover process.

Selection of an adviser is an intense but brief process. Generally, the special board committee will hold a one or two-day *beauty contest* for investment banks interested in advising the firm. Representatives from these banks will bring with them *pitch books* showcasing their knowledge of the selling company's products, overall market trends, and M&A transactions in the company's industry. Pitch books are specifically tailored for the customer, and are often over 100 pages in length.

When scheduling interviews for the beauty contest, it is important that the selling company's management arrange these meetings with long breaks in between sessions. This will minimize the chance of sale team members running into each other, although some teams may arrive especially early, as doing so may afford them a look at their competition.

Once all of the interviews have been completed, board members will select an appropriate advisor largely based on the experience of the advisor and its access to senior management at potential acquiring firms. Fees are rarely disputed, as all firms will normally charge a similar amount for their services. *Success fees,* or those paid when an M&A arrangement is made, range from around 1 percent of the selling company's enterprise value for smaller deals (i.e., $100 million or less) to about 0.5 percent for larger deals (i.e., over $2 billion). A *retainer fee*—on top of the success fee—of 0.1 percent of the target's enterprise value is also the norm.

One of the most important functions of the financial advisor is to estimate a proper acquisition premium figure for the target company. In the public markets, most acquirers will offer target firms an acquisition premium of between 20 and 25 percent of the share price. Variance in the acquisition premium is particularly high, and the advisor must assist the seller in deriving a proper figure that will be attractive to both the seller and potential buyers.

The acquisition premium is based on numerous factors, including potential synergies with the target, the liquidity of the target's share, and the target firm's growth prospects. For example, an acquiring firm would likely not offer a large acquisition premium to a firm that shares trade infrequently as it would likely be difficult for the target firm's management to monetize its holdings. Additionally, this firm might not be receiving benefits from public company status.

ANALYZING POTENTIAL BUYERS

If a selling company elects to hire a financial advisor for an M&A transaction, this firm will submit lists of strategic and financial buyers to the company for its review. A strategic buyer acquires companies in an industry similar to its own, often in an attempt to realize synergies with the target company; a financial buyer purchases companies expressly for the purpose of reselling them at a later date, usually three to seven years down the road.

When compiling a list of strategic buyers, a financial advisor will look at firms participating in the selling company's industry that possess several characteristics: (1) financial means to complete the deal; (2) potential interest in the seller's products; and (3) opportunities to realize synergies with the target company. Antitrust regulations will also be considered when searching for an acquiring firm. After settling on a group of buyers, the selling company and financial advisor will decide the process by which the company will be sold; most companies are sold either on an exclusive basis or through an auction.

When several strategic buyers exist, each with a high incentive to purchase the target company, an exclusive offering will generally produce the highest valuation. Auctions are generally beneficial when buyers are less ardent in their pursuit of the target company, though strategic buyers are highly adverse to purchasing companies in auction settings: they feel that they have a low probability of acquiring the company in an auction, and, moreover, that such an auction illustrates management's willingness to sacrifice long-term gains for suboptimal, near-term benefits.

While courting buyers, some companies will examine an exit via IPO as a contingency plan, and also to establish a price floor on the company valuation.

THE SALE PROCESS

Once an appropriate list of buyers has been identified, the selling company and its financial advisor will send out a *teaser*. This brief document (frequently less than five pages in length) provides a potential buyer with historical financial statements of the target company, a discussion of its future business plan, and a general description of the industry in which the selling company participates. The selling company is often not identified by name; however, many strategic and financial buyers will likely know the firm that the document describes.

Teasers are sent only to companies that express interest in the would-be target firm. The document serves as a first-level filter for the financial advisor, as some firms who previously expressed interest in the selling company may fail to request a copy of the teaser.

Concurrent with the preparation of the teaser, the financial advisor and selling company will also begin to prepare a lengthy document called the seller's confidential information memorandum (CIM). This document is frequently over 100 pages in length and provides a potential buyer with a plethora of historical and projected information on each of the selling company's products and business lines. Preparation of this document is performed with due care and with the primary goal of transparency. If an acquiring firm uncovers some "skeletons in the closet" after the company sale has gone through, a sizeable lawsuit could result.

A CIM normally contains three sections: an executive summary, a company overview, and a financial review. Within the executive summary is a brief description of the firm's product and/or service lines, and how these offerings compare with those of key competitors. Historical and projected financial statements, typically spanning a period of approximately five years from the date of the CIM, will also be included in this section. The company overview will expand upon the information in the executive summary with 10 years of historical information and five years of projected financial statements. This information will be separated by product line, as well as consolidated.

Financial buyers are often interested in future earnings before interest, tax, depreciation, and amortization (EBITDA) projections, while strategic buyers tend to focus more on net earnings and earnings before interest and tax (EBIT). Financial buyers believe that EBITDA is a good reflection of the cash flow characteristics of the company (as opposed to accrual-based earnings) and, therefore, often use this metric as a barometer to measure the health of a target firm. Moreover, when financial buyers look to resell the company several years down the road, other prospective buyers will generally calculate a market-based valuation for the company using EBITDA multiples, most typically enterprise value-to-EBITDA. As such, it is important that the CIM stress these figures should the field of potential acquirers contain many financial buyers.

However, it is also important to note that a conflict of interest may arise between the financial advisor and the selling company with respect to the types of buyers courted by the CIM. Financial advisors are often enthralled by the sale of a company to a financial buyer, primarily because they may be able to finance the transaction and charge an appropriate level of fees; strategic buyers, in contrast, will generally have financing prearranged with an investment bank of their choice.

Within the final section of the financial summary, detailed five-year projections for revenues, EBIT, EBITDA, and invested capital (i.e., capital expenditures and working capital) will be presented. Validations of these projections will also be provided.

In order to receive a CIM, a potential buyer must sign a bidder confidentiality agreement (BCA). This document requires that the potential acquirer agree to abide by several rules: the buyer (1) is not allowed to hire any of the seller's employees for a stipulated period; (2) may not contact any employees of the seller, members of its board of directors, or its customers without the financial advisor's approval; and (3) may not divulge information contained in the CIM to any third party . The BCA also contains a timeline for the bidding process, specifying when preliminary and final bids are due, along with the dates of management presentations and data room availability.

THE BIDDING PROCESS

After signing the BCA and receiving the CIM, potential buyers will generally take several weeks to comb through the documents and formulate a first-round, nonbinding bid. However, prior to the date preliminary bids are due, buyers will also learn of potential financing through the financial advisor, commonly known as *staple financing*. By employing staple financing, a buyer need only staple a check for the equity portion of the deal to the acquisition agreement. Although this financing will be offered to strategic buyers, these firms generally use their own financiers to provide capital for a deal. Staple financing saves significant time for financial buyers, and also indicates that the financial advisor has confidence in the target firm. However, staple financing may induce the advisor to court financial buyers over strategic buyers, in order to receive the fees associated with securing leverage.

On the day that bids are due, all interested parties will submit offers to the financial advisor, who will then compile this information for the seller. This is the moment of truth for the advisor and the selling company, as both hope that—at a minimum—the highest bids fall within the estimated range projected in the pitch book. Assuming that the preliminary bids are satisfactory and that the seller still wishes to proceed with the deal, the financial advisor will then set up a data room for potential buyers, where they can view detailed data on the company.

The data room is either a physical or virtual room where highly detailed, confidential information will be shown to prospective bidders. (In recent years, many companies and their financial advisors have selected to host an electronic data room, as opposed to renting out a hotel conference room.) These data include customer lists, labor contracts, management compensation contracts, research and development projects, and other highly classified information. Because of the nature of the information contained in the data room, target companies are very cautious about granting entry to nonserious bidders. The last thing a target firm wants is for an employee of a competitive firm—who may have placed a preliminary bid—to obtain access to the data room.

After all potential buyers have had a chance to read the information in the data room, meetings are scheduled for these buyers to meet one-on-one with the target firm's management. At these (often all-day) meetings, buyers listen to a detailed management presentation describing the intricacies of the selling company's business. It is largely after this meeting that buyers begin a deep due diligence analysis on the target firm. This process is often very costly and is a key reason why many strategic buyers drop out of auction-style acquisitions: with a low probability of purchasing the company, the strategic buyer feels that the due diligence costs are just too intensive.

Financial buyers, however, digest this cost as part of their business and, furthermore, are less averse to auctions because they generally cause many strategic buyers to withdraw from the bidding.

REACHING AN AGREEMENT

Subsequent to the management presentations, potential buyers begin to review the definitive merger agreement (DMA) prepared by the seller's legal team. This document includes essential data and operating covenants surrounding the takeover—namely, the date that it will occur, the purchase price and compensation for the target firm, covenants describing how the business will operate prior to the merger, representations by the buyer and seller, and a description of the events that will arise should the deal not go through.

Many provisions in the DMA are designed to prevent buyers from backing out of the takeover after they have signed the agreement, and also to preclude the seller from attempting to find a better deal. Along these lines, there are numerous clauses in the DMA designed to keep the deal moving forward. Perhaps most important among these is the *material adverse clause,* otherwise known as the *MAC-out* clause.

The MAC-out clause specifies the conditions under which the buyer can renege on the deal. Generally, this includes changes in government regulations that bear heavily on the company, a *force majeure*–like event (e.g., hurricane), and other events that would be expected to have a materially adverse effect on the selling company. Terms of the MAC-out clause are negotiated by both parties, with the buyer wanting the option to pull his or her bid for nearly any circumstance, and the seller desiring a virtual "lockbox" on the deal.

A *fiduciary-out* clause, similar to the MAC-out, also exists in the DMA. However, it primarily focuses on the reasons why the seller can back out of the deal. Generally, this clause states that the seller may back out of the deal if it receives an unsolicited bid of a higher amount than the current one specified by the DMA. In the event that the seller terminates the deal, the buyer will receive a prespecified *breakup fee,* typically between 1 and 3.75 percent of the merger sale price.

After all of the preceding events have occurred, and the DMA has been signed, the seller's board of directors must approve the document and the terms within. Furthermore, there is generally a significant time gap between the date a DMA is signed and the time the merger actually takes place. It is during this time that both the seller and the buyer must seek shareholder approval of the takeover.

HISTORICAL M&A TRENDS

While perhaps a bit less spectacular than IPOs, M&A transactions are nonetheless popular exit strategies for funds and managers looking to realize a return on their investment. Moreover, the popularity of M&As has increased significantly since 1999, spurred by the M&A craze of the late 1990s, the passage of the Sarbanes-Oxley Act of 2002, and the dot-com bust of 2001, which put a large damper on the IPO market. Some of the most memorable mergers in history occurred during the dot-com years: Vodafone Airtouch PLC–Mannesmann, Pfizer–Warner Lambert, Exxon-Mobil, BP-Amoco, and Citicorp–Travelers Group all occurred in 1998 and 1999.

As shown in Exhibit 6.1, the number of PE-backed M&A transactions has risen steadily since 1990, and particularly over the past decade. In 2010, there were 170 buyout-backed M&A transactions, up from 65 in 2009, and well above an average of 35 per year from 1990 through 2005. Contrary to popular belief, M&As were a popular harvest mechanism for VCs even prior to the dot-com bust. The level of venture-backed M&A deals has remained cyclical since that time, but relatively steady. In 2010, 438 VC-backed M&A deals occurred.

M&As are the preferred exit vehicle for venture-backed firms. As shown in Exhibit 6.2, the number of VC-backed M&A transactions has far exceeded the number of VC-backed IPOs for the past 10 years. These data suggest that many venture funds, and investment bankers, feel the IPO

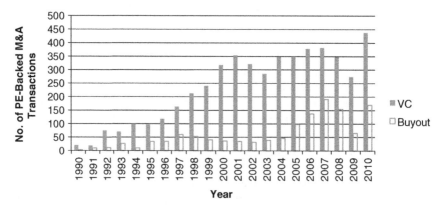

EXHIBIT 6.1 Historical No. of PE-Backed M&A Transactions by Year, 1990–2010
Source: Thomson ONE Banker

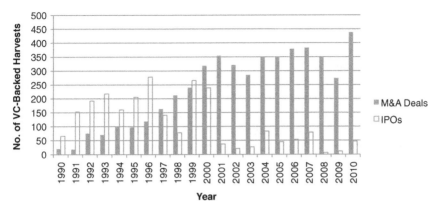

EXHIBIT 6.2   Historical Comparison of Exit Strategies for Venture-Backed Firms
Source: Thomson ONE Banker

market remains a tepid exit vehicle, while harvest through M&A may permit investors to earn better returns.

The number of M&A exits has also surged for buyout-backed firms, as shown in Exhibit 6.3. While the number of buyout-backed M&A deals has exceeded the number of buyout-backed IPOs since 1995, M&A deals are today nearly seven times more popular than IPOs in the buyout arena.

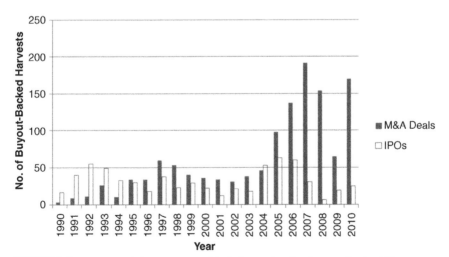

EXHIBIT 6.3   Historical Comparison of Exit Strategies for Buyout-Backed Firms
Source: Thomson ONE Banker

CONCLUSION

M&As are a highly popular harvest mechanism for PE portfolio companies. While the number of VC and buyout-backed IPOs exceeded the number of M&A deals through the mid-1990s, the quantity of M&A harvests today far outweighs the number of IPOs for either asset class. In the coming years, many large buyout-backed firms will need to be harvested by parent PE funds. It remains to be seen whether a merger or acquisition is a viable harvest strategy for these large, market-dominating firms.

CHAPTER 7

Legal Considerations in Sale Transactions

Richard A. Walawender

INTRODUCTION

A private equity (PE) fund does not invest in or purchase a portfolio company with the intent of holding and operating the company in perpetuity. Rather, the PE fund's objective is to exit (i.e., liquefying or cashing out of) its investment in the company at a substantial profit and gain, typically from three to seven years after its initial investment. During that time, the PE fund will seek to maximize the returns on the company. To that end, the PE fund will undertake operational restructuring, add-on acquisitions, divestitures, and other measures with respect to the portfolio company in order to make it as attractive of a potential investment for others as possible at the time of the PE fund's exit.

There are a wide variety of techniques used by PE funds in exiting their portfolio company investments, and other variations depending on what proportion of the company's equity the PE fund owns and controls. But the two most common exit strategies utilized by PE funds involve (1) the sale of the company's stock to the public in an initial public offering (IPO) and (2) the sale of the company's stock or assets to another entity for cash, stock, and debt, in a variety of combinations (the sale transaction). To simplify the analysis, this chapter will focus on the sale transaction model.

When should a PE fund choose as its exit strategy a sale, as opposed to an IPO? Of course, in addition to the current market conditions, including not only the general equity and debt markets, but deal flows, currency and commodity prices, industry sales multiples, and price-to-earnings (P/E) ratios, the following principles should be considered by a PE fund in choosing a sale transaction over an IPO to exit a business:

- *Lack of historical base.* If the target does not have a long record of a consistent, stable pattern of growth and profitability, a sale transaction is probably more feasible than an IPO.
- *Volatile equity market.* The IPO market is volatile and reacts to factors that are outside the target's control. IPO windows may open and close in a cycle different from the target's growth, capital, and liquidity needs. Generally the mergers and acquisitions (M&A) market is not as sensitive to valuations and can offer a more stable pricing platform.
- *Cost.* A public offering is much more expensive than a sale transaction.
- *Liquidity for PE funds.* In many instances, sellers sell relatively few shares in the target's IPO. Furthermore, underwriters will often require the target's shareholders to sign market standoff agreements, agreeing not to sell any of their shares into the public market for at least 180 days after the target's IPO. The target's shareholders may find that, although the target is now "public," its stock is relatively illiquid. If the target's shareholders receive freely tradable acquirer stock that has a significant float, they may receive more real liquidity more quickly than is possible through a target IPO.

SALE TRANSACTIONS

A sale transaction of the target can provide strategic, operating, and financial benefits to both the target and the entity acquiring it (acquirer). Generally, a sale of the target can provide the PE fund with earlier liquidity than an IPO, with less risk and dilution. Optimally, it may also provide the target with important complementary synergies that would otherwise take many years to develop, such as an established manufacturing or distribution infrastructure and new products and technologies necessary to maintain its ompetitive advantage, growth rate, and profitability. Nevertheless, ill-conceived or badly done sales can result in expense and disruption to all parties involved, the discontinuance of good technologies and products, employee dissatisfaction and defection, poor operating results by the combined company, and even delayed distributions to the PE fund's investors.

Prior to the Sale Transaction

Use of an Investment Banker   The target may want to obtain advice from an investment banker when it first considers being sold. The target should select its banker based on its experience in M&As in the target's specific industry doing transactions of similar deal size and its contacts with relevant potential buyers. Before reaching the decision that it should be acquired, the target can have an investment banker review its business, financial, and strategic plans and help it evaluate its business alternatives. With early advice, the target can address value-enhancing or -detracting factors and sometimes improve its valuation. Based on an analysis of the target's business strengths and weaknesses, industry trends, the target's competitive positioning, and recent M&A activity, the investment banker can advise the target on a range of expected acquisition values. These early activities can help the target position itself to command the highest valuation and attract the most qualified prospective purchasers. The investment banker can also prepare a detailed timeline to better prepare the target for the length of the process and how much of management's time will be needed.

Marketing Process Once the target decides to be sold, the seller of the target's business usually prepares detailed marketing materials describing the target's key attributes. An investment banker can greatly assist in this process, as it approaches the marketing process by conducting a detailed analysis of the target, its industry, and the strategic reasons why the acquirer might want to acquire the target. The investment banker will also prepare a detailed list of potential buyers to be contacted during the marketing process. Using a banker at this stage in the process enables the acquirer to ask tough questions of the banker and be more forthright in its evaluation of the target without offending the target's management.

Due Diligence When potential acquirers conduct initial due diligence on the target, the process needs to ensure that the acquirer gets information necessary to submit a binding offer to acquire the target. It is important to anticipate what information will be the most important to the acquirer to avoid embarrassing "surprises" later. An investment banker can assist the target by pointing out sources of synergy and supporting the target's desired valuation by financial analyses based on comparable public and private companies. Familiarity with the target's industry also will allow the banker to suggest alternatives if difficulties arise with a current acquirer prospect.

Negotiations Phase The investment banker can help advise the target as to which offer to accept based on valuation, structure, tax considerations, acquirer currency (if stock is the primary consideration), and other relevant issues. Once an offer is accepted, it is critical to communicate to the investment banker which issues are most important to the target in order to properly position the negotiation discussions. To ensure an efficient final agreement phase, the investment banker can help coordinate communication with the target's attorneys and accountants to make certain all of the target's advisors understand the implications of the definitive agreement. If requested, an investment banker can provide the target's board of directors with a formal "fairness opinion" on the terms offered by the acquirer.

Key Deal Issues

Valuation and Pricing Issues

Target Valuation   Valuation is highly subjective. The "fair" value for the target will vary significantly from one acquirer to another, depending on a variety of factors. An investment banker can assist the target in determining its valuation and in price negotiations with the acquirer. When negotiating its value, the seller should remember that public acquirers, issuing stock in an acquisition or merger, will not want the transaction to be dilutive of their earnings per share (EPS). This means that the acquirer will not want to issue shares to the target's shareholders so that the transaction reduces the acquirer's EPS. Acquirers typically use various methods to arrive at a reasonable target valuation:

- *Comparable public companies.* This involves taking the market value of stocks of comparable, publicly traded companies in the target's industry as a multiple of such companies' earnings and revenues. Those values are then adjusted to account for the size, liquidity, and performance differences between the target and those companies. The challenge with this method is in selecting "comparable" companies and accurately adjusting the target's value to reflect the differences between the target and such companies.
- *Comparable transactions.* This method involves comparing the amount paid in acquisitions of other companies in the target's industry. When using this valuation method, consider the following: While the stock market values all public companies daily, acquisitions occur over time. If a comparable transaction occurred some time before the target's proposed transaction, are the factors essential to that valuation still present? Another factor that can influence valuation is the consideration used in the transaction. An acquirer with a highly valued stock can pay a higher price than an acquirer with a less valued stock. Alternatively, if the seller believes that the acquirer's stock is undervalued by the market, it may be willing to accept a lower price at closing on the expectation of market appreciation in the acquirer's stock after the closing.
- *Discounted cash flow analysis.* This methodology involves assigning a value in today's dollars to the cash flow to be generated by the target's future operations. This type of analysis has two challenges. First, under this analysis, the target's value depends on the credibility of the target's

projections of its future operations. While historical performance is a known quantity, the acquirer and the target may disagree on how the target will perform in the future. Second, a substantial portion of the value represented by this type of analysis is the residual value created by the target's investment in early years. This is another likely source of disagreement between the acquirer and the seller.

Consideration   If the acquirer pays cash for the target, the acquirer will express the purchase price in U.S. dollars or other relevant currency. In an acquisition where the acquirer issues stock to pay for the target, the acquirer may express its offered purchase price in any of the following ways:

- *As dollar value of shares.* If the acquirer expresses the price as a certain dollar value of its shares, the acquirer must specify the mechanism for determining the number of shares to be issued at the closing of the transaction. For example, the acquirer could offer that number of shares determined by dividing $25 million by the average of the closing prices of the acquirer's stock for the 10 trading days ending three days before the closing of the transaction. The acquirer may not want to use this pricing mechanism if it believes that its stock price will fall between the date it signs the purchase or merger agreement and the date it closes the transaction. Such a drop in the acquirer's stock price could result in the target's shareholders receiving a significantly larger number of shares in the transaction. This could be a problem if such an increase would require the acquirer to obtain the approval of its shareholders (which would not be required if fewer shares were issued) or if the acquirer's management believed that the transaction would become EPS dilutive. The target also might worry about a dollar purchase price that calculates the number of shares at the closing date. The target will not want the number of shares issued in the transaction to be reduced if the acquirer's stock market price goes up before the closing date. The target will want its shareholders to share in market appreciation resulting from a favorable response to the announcement that the acquirer is acquiring the target.
- *As fixed number of shares.* These concerns can be reduced if the acquirer denominates its price as a certain number of shares to be issued in the acquisition. However, this pricing method leaves both parties with the risk that the dollar purchase price could go up or down by millions of dollars between signing and closing the deal. Arguably, the dollar purchase price should not matter to the acquirer as long as the transaction will increase the acquirer's EPS. It may matter to the target, however, if the target has outstanding preferred stock

and the acquirer's offered price is not a great deal more than the amount invested in the target by its venture investors. The charter documents of many privately held targets treat an acquisition as a "deemed liquidation." They typically require that the holders of the preferred stock receive their liquidation preferences before any consideration goes to the holders of the common stock. If a sharp drop in the acquirer's stock price resulted in all of the stock having to be paid to the preferred shareholders, the target might find that it would be unable to obtain common shareholder approval of the acquisition. The parties also need to consider how options and warrants will be treated in this calculation. For example, is the number of shares offered by the acquirer intended to be in exchange for outstanding shares, options, and warrants, or only for outstanding shares? This issue is particularly sensitive if options or warrants are significantly "underwater" (i.e., the exercise price to acquire the target shares is far greater than the price offered by the acquirer).

■ *As a percentage of combined entity.* In acquisition and merger transactions between companies of relatively equal size, the acquirer frequently will express the purchase price as that number of shares that will give the target security holders a certain percentage of the combined entity. For example, the acquirer and target security holders will have 55 percent and 45 percent, respectively, of the postclosing capital of the acquirer. Parties use this form of pricing when they want to value the acquirer and the target based on their expected contribution to the combined company's future performance instead of the market price for the stock. Again, the market value of the transaction can fluctuate dramatically from the date of signing until closing. Again, the parties need to delineate clearly which acquirer or target shares, options, or warrants are included in the numerator and the denominator. Again, either the acquirer or the target may argue that underwater warrants and options should be excluded from the calculation.

Net Asset Test   If either the acquirer or the target believes that the target's balance sheet is likely to become significantly weaker or stronger between the date the definitive agreement is signed and the closing date, it may suggest that the purchase price be adjusted to reflect a change in the target's net assets. For example, if the target had $2 million of working capital at the date of signing and the acquirer expected it to decline to $500,000 by the closing date, the acquirer might want to have the purchase price reduced to reflect that change. However, a profitable target might negotiate to have the acquirer increase the purchase price by the amount of any increase in its working capital from the signing date to the closing date.

Earnouts   In an earnout, some portion of the purchase price will be paid by the acquirer only if the target achieves negotiated performance goals after the closing. Parties typically use an earnout when they agree that a higher target valuation would be justified if the target were to meet forecasted performance goals. The seller may propose an earnout when it believes that its future performance will be substantially better than its historical performance. Likely earnout candidates include an early-stage target with a product line separate from that of the acquirer, a turnaround target, or a target in a hot industry sector.

Risk Reduction Mechanisms   There are inherent risks in negotiating, documenting, and closing an acquisition since the parties have to make critical decisions regarding price and terms based on partial knowledge. Following are some mechanisms used by an acquirer and a target to manage these risks:

- *Exclusive negotiating period.* At the time the parties agree on price and the other key deal terms, the acquirer generally will require the seller to cease negotiating with other potential buyers and negotiate exclusively with the acquirer. The acquirer will not want to invest substantial time and resources in performing due diligence and negotiating a deal with the target only to have the seller use the acquirer's offer to start a bidding war by other potential buyers. The seller will want to keep the period during which it has to pull itself off the market as short as possible. To meet its fiduciary obligations, the seller will want to reserve the right to notify its shareholders of other offers and may even reserve the right to accept unsolicited and clearly superior offers. The exclusive negotiating period should be no longer than reasonable for the acquirer to complete due diligence and negotiate the definitive documents—usually between 30 and 60 days.
- *Breakup fee.* Both the acquirer and the seller may be concerned that they will be damaged if the deal fails to close after they have signed definitive acquisition agreements and announced the transaction. As noted in the preceding bulleted entry, the acquirer will not want the target to use the acquirer's offer to start a bidding war. The seller will worry that an acquisition announcement may cause the target's customers to delay orders until they know whether the acquirer intends to continue marketing and supporting existing target products. Similarly, if the announcement causes the target's employees to focus on their resumés instead of on their jobs, the target can be seriously damaged if the acquisition fails to close. Either the acquirer or the seller may propose a breakup fee as a way to address this risk. A breakup fee requires the party responsible for the breakup to pay the other party a negotiated amount of liquidated

damages. The amount of the breakup fee should reflect the damages likely to be sustained by the damaged party.

■ *Acquirer due diligence.* The acquirer will do much of its due diligence under a nondisclosure agreement signed with the seller before the parties agree on a letter of intent. Many sellers, however, will be reluctant to give the acquirer access to the target's most confidential financial, technical, intellectual property, and customer information until a price has been negotiated. As a result, the acquirer must decide whether the target is a strategic fit and arrive at a proposed purchase price based on its own product and market due diligence, without access to the target's more detailed information. Once the parties agree on the basic deal terms and while the acquirer's attorneys are preparing the definitive agreements, the acquirer will conduct due diligence to discover if its assumptions about the target were accurate. The acquirer and target should try to identify and discuss particular sensitivities or unusual problems or liabilities as early in the due diligence process as possible. Early disclosure is more efficient, builds credibility, and is less likely to result in last-minute price renegotiations. The acquirer should avoid placing an unnecessary burden on the target's staff during the due diligence process. The target will rarely have the administrative and financial infrastructure that the acquirer has, and does not maintain the same type of records. It is often preferable to have the acquirer's personnel do much of the due diligence. This enables the acquirer to obtain more accurate information in the form expected, and will reduce the burden on the target. The acquirer also needs to be sensitive to confidentiality concerns. If the acquirer discovers unexpected target liabilities during the due diligence process, it may withdraw from the deal, reduce its offered price, or ask the target's shareholders to indemnify it for damage from special liabilities. The target usually tries to avoid allowing the acquirer to put a "due diligence out" in the definitive acquisition agreement. A *due diligence out* is a condition to closing that allows the acquirer to decide at the closing whether the target is too risky to acquire. To avoid the risks of customer confusion, employee distraction, and the reputation of being "left at the altar," the seller usually requires the acquirer to complete all due diligence before signing and announcing the definitive agreement. The acquirer generally will insist on the right to refuse to close if there is a "material adverse change" in the target's business between signing and closing. If the seller anticipates that a sale announcement will cause such a change, the parties may seek to negotiate a definition of *material adverse change* that will not penalize the target for expected changes to its business, yet will protect the acquirer from unexpected material adverse changes to the target's business.

■ *Target representations and warranties, indemnities, and escrows.* Besides doing its own due diligence, the acquirer's definitive agreement will contain detailed representations and warranties about the target's business, including detailed and specific disclosures to these representations and warranties in a disclosure schedule. The acquirer also will want the disclosure schedules to include detailed lists of the target's assets, contracts, and liabilities to the definitive agreement as part of the target's disclosure schedule. If the acquirer suffers damage because a privately held target failed to disclose any of the requested information, the acquirer will expect the target's shareholders to indemnify it. To mitigate against an unreasonable disclosure burden, however, the target will want to limit some disclosure obligations to those items that are "material" to the target or of which the target has "knowledge.

■ *Baskets and caps.* The seller will want the amount of losses caused by its breaches to cross a certain threshold of damages (called a *basket*) before the acquirer has any right to indemnification, and a maximum indemnification obligation (called a *cap*). Once the basket limit is reached, however, the acquirer will want to recover all its damages, including the basket, while the seller will prefer that the acquirer recover only the damages in excess of the basket. When the target's major shareholders are also its key managers, the seller should expect requests for broader indemnities and escrows. The acquirer also may want to hold a portion of the transaction consideration in escrow as security for such indemnity obligations. Since acquisitions can no longer be accounted for as a "pooling," acquirers are asking for larger and longer escrows.

■ *Seller due diligence.* If the acquirer is paying cash for the target at the closing, there is little need for the seller to do due diligence on the acquirer. If the acquirer is paying for the target with its stock, a promissory note, or an earnout, however, the seller will want to do due diligence on the acquirer. Many of the considerations relating to the acquirer's due diligence will apply when the seller is doing due diligence on the acquirer. If the acquirer is public, its federal securities filings will supply much of the desired information, although the seller may want more detailed information about the acquirer's operations.

■ *Key shareholder preapproval.* One acquisition risk is whether the seller's shareholders will approve the acquisition negotiated by the target's management and approved by the target's board of directors. The seller will have similar concerns if the acquirer must obtain its shareholders' approval. Legal formalities required to obtain shareholder approval mean that there will be a delay between signing the definitive agreement and obtaining shareholder approval to that agreement.

Special Issues in Sales of Private Equity Fund–Owned Businesses

Context   In the process of selling a portfolio company owned by a PE fund, it is important for both the acquirer and seller to keep in mind that the PE fund typically has a fixed life span (e.g., 10 years), after which the PE fund is closed and its assets distributed to investors and the fund's managers. The PE fund owner will want a clean break shortly after the sale of the company, and the acquirer may not have any meaningful recourse for indemnification after the PE fund's liquidation. Accordingly, several provisions in a typical portfolio company purchase agreement, whether it involves an equity or asset purchase, will usually be negotiated and treated differently than would be the case if the seller was not a PE fund.

Survival of Representations, Warranties, Covenants   The basic concern for PE fund sellers is to ensure that the representations, warranties, and covenants of the seller in the purchase agreement survive only for a finite period of time. Ideally, the survival period and indemnification recourse would be coterminous and limited to an escrow fund. Typically, this would also include representations and warranties involving more complicated matters such as environmental, tax, employment, litigation, and employee benefits. More problematic, however, are the representations and warranties covering fundamental representations such as due authority, title to assets, and capitalization, which acquirers usually expect would survive in perpetuity. One possible approach to address this issue regarding fundamental representations, which may also be available for other representations and warranties, is to obtain insurance for the benefit of the acquirer.

Escrow Funds   As mentioned above, a PE fund seller will want to limit the acquirer's recourse in the event of a breach to funds placed in an escrow account for a limited period of time after the closing. Sometimes, there is also an additional amount made available for an additional limited period of time which is backstopped by a third-party guarantee or bank letter of credit. In any case, the seller will want the escrow period to be as short as possible in order to give time to settle or contest any claims asserted by the acquirer against the escrow funds, and in order to leave sufficient time to distribute the funds in escrow to the fund and its investors.

Indemnification Caps and Limited Recourse   The PE fund seller may have a problem distributing the proceeds from the sale immediately to its investors if the purchase price proceeds are at risk because of potential indemnity claims by the acquirer. To mitigate this concern, the fund seller will seek to limit its exposure for breaches of representations and warranties and indemnification claims by capping its indemnification obligations to a smaller percentage of the purchase price, and subjecting them to larger baskets and thresholds, than is typical for strategic sellers. In addition, the purchase agreement may include other mechanisms to limit recourse against the seller, such as a requirement to first apply insurance proceeds to the acquirer's losses, excluding consequential and special damages, crediting any tax benefits the acquirer may receive through tax deductions from the losses, and other benefits the acquirer may receive from the losses. In addition, the fund seller may seek to take more control of the defense of any claims made by third parties.

Joint and Several Liability   In many cases, while the PE fund may be the majority owner of the portfolio company, there are other owners, such as individuals who may have rolled over a portion of their sales proceeds when they sold their company to the PE fund. In such cases, if would be awkward and problematic for these individuals to accept joint and several liability for post-closing indemnification claims relating to the sale of the company, especially if the PE fund was already liquidated. To alleviate such concerns, in addition to the above mechanisms limiting recourse, it is typical for the sellers to enter into a contribution agreement among themselves allocating losses to be paid on a pro-rata percentage basis. In addition, sometimes all the sellers provide the acquirer with limited guarantees pursuant to which each seller's liability is limited to its pro-rata share of the indemnification exposure.

Purchase Price Consideration   PE fund sellers typically want the purchase price to be paid in cash up front. Other payment structures such as earnouts, seller notes, installment payments, or other deferred payments are unusual and frowned upon because they do not provide immediate liquidity for the PE fund to be able to distribute.

Noncompetition, Nonsolicitation Covenants   In a typical purchase agreement, the seller (and its affiliates) will agree to multiyear covenants not to compete with the business it has just sold, as well as not to solicit the business's customers, suppliers or employees, and management. However, a PE fund, which may own many, diversified portfolio companies, may have a difficult time monitoring and ensuring that its portfolio companies (which may even be in different funds, but because they are under common management, may be considered "affiliates" and therefore covered by the covenants) comply with such covenants. Accordingly, PE fund sellers may resist entering into such broad covenants, and may seek to eliminate them from the purchase agreement. Alternatively, these covenants may be written in

EXHIBIT 7.1   Acquisition Structures and Their Impacts

Business Considerations	Merger	Asset Purchase	Stock Purchase
What do you sell/buy?	Target's stock	Specified target assets and liabilities	Target's stock
Can acquirer avoid target liabilities with third parties?	No	Yes, except for certain matters (environmental, employees, taxes)	No
What target shareholder approval is required? Must contract with each target shareholder	Typically	majority vote	Typically majority vote

such ways so as to limit their applicability to shorter time periods and to specifically named target companies and customers.

Sale and Acquisition Structure

Another key issue is how the parties want to structure the transaction. Sometimes the objectives of the seller do not match those of the acquirer. For example, an acquirer may wish to structure the transaction as an asset acquisition (from a tax standpoint) in order to take advantage of basis step-up, but a seller may seek to sell the business as a stock sale to avoid the necessity of having to obtain third-party consents and adverse tax consequences. Exhibit 7.1 shows a summary of possible acquisition structures and their impact on key business considerations.

Merger   In a merger, either the target or the acquirer (or acquirer's subsidiary) merges into the other by operation of law, with the target's shareholders exchanging their shares for acquirer shares. A merger is the simplest mechanism for acquiring another company and results in the acquirer (or acquirer's subsidiary) automatically receiving all of the target's assets. State merger laws typically require majority target shareholder consent to approve a merger. The law also provides a mechanism for cashing out those target shareholders who are unwilling to accept acquirer stock in the merger (dissenting shareholders). A drawback to using a merger is that the acquirer (or its merger subsidiary) will automatically assume all of the target's liabilities. The acquirer can exchange its stock, promissory notes, or cash for the target stock in a merger.

Asset Purchase   If the acquirer wants to avoid unrelated target liabilities, it may prefer to acquire the target's assets rather than merge with the target. Asset acquisitions require that the parties specify the assets and liabilities to be transferred and thus entail more due diligence and transfer mechanics than a merger. The acquirer can exchange its stock, promissory notes, or cash for the target's assets.

Stock Purchase   The acquirer may want to purchase all of the target's outstanding stock from the target's shareholders. This commonly occurs if the target has very few shareholders or if the target or acquirer is a foreign company that cannot legally do a merger. Since the acquirer acquires all of the target's stock, the target remains in existence as the acquirer's subsidiary, with all of its assets and liabilities intact. One significant drawback to a stock purchase is that, unlike a merger, the law does not provide a means of cashing out large numbers of dissenting shares under a stock purchase. Most acquirers are unwilling to have minority shareholders, which could occur if a target shareholder refused to agree to sell his/her shares to the acquirer on the offered terms. As a result, a stock purchase is impractical if the target has either many shareholders or even one shareholder with substantial holdings who strongly disapproves of the acquisition.

Employee Incentive Issues

A target that was venture backed may find that the total liquidation preferences required by its charter to be paid to the holders of the preferred stock on an acquisition exceed any reasonably expected price that could be offered for the target. For example, a company might have raised $50 million in invested capital, yet be worth only $10 million. Employees realize that if the purchase price is allocated in accordance with the preferred stock liquidation preferences, they, as holders of common stock, will receive nothing in the acquisition. Management may become demoralized and may be unwilling to support an acquisition that will benefit only the holders of the preferred stock. This conflict could stall or even foreclose acquisition negotiations.

The target can solve this problem by creating a cash or stock bonus plan or by doing a recapitalization. Frequently, a cash retention bonus plan is the simplest solution. Exhibit 7.2 shows a summary of major considerations in adopting key employee incentive plans.

Cash Retention Bonus   A cash retention bonus plan can be structured to be offered to those employees who are critical to consummating the transaction and to those who are critical to remaining with the target after the

EXHIBIT 7.2   Considerations in Adopting Employee Incentive Plans

Characteristic	Cash Bonus Plan	Stock Bonus Plan	Recapitalization
Tailor to benefit only key players?	Yes	Yes	No
Requires shareholder approval?	Generally, no	Yes	Yes
Requires securities compliance?	Generally, no	Yes	Yes
Employees taxed when?	Receipt	Receipt	Sale of stock
Employees taxed at what rate?	Ordinary income	Ordinary income	Capital gains
Reduces total liquidation preferences?	No	No	Depends

closing, promising them a cash bonus if they stay through the acquisition. The bonus can be a set dollar amount or calculated as a percentage of the purchase price paid. Such a plan is easy to implement, easily understood by the participants, and cost effective, and it generally does not require shareholder approval or securities law compliance. A contractual obligation by the target to pay cash bonuses to its employees can be assumed by the acquirer in an acquisition or merger transaction. The acquirer will, of course, reduce the purchase price offered by the amount of the retention bonus and thus reduce the amount paid to the holders of the preferred stock. In the preceding scenario, the holders of the common stock (including the employees) would receive nothing for their shares in the acquisition. The employees receiving the cash bonus will be taxed at ordinary income tax rates (rather than the capital gains rates they would likely have enjoyed had the employees received payment for their common stock). Note that if the acquirer were to do an asset acquisition and did not assume the obligation, whether the employees got paid would depend on whether there was enough consideration to pay the bonus. Once bonuses have accrued, they are considered "wages" that must be paid by the employer. If the "employer" cannot pay, under some circumstances the individual officers and managers may be individually liable for the unpaid wages.

Stock Bonuses   Stock bonus plans are sometimes used in place of cash bonus plans. In order for the participants to receive anything in the acquisition, however, the stock bonuses must be senior in priority to some or all existing preferred stock, or the bonus plan must require payment in the acquirer's stock in the acquisition. In some cases, the target will adopt a new stock option plan that provides certain key employees with options to buy a new class of stock with senior participation rights. To implement these plans, the company must amend its charter and obtain shareholder approval. Further, the participants will recognize tax upon receipt of the bonused stock valued at its fair market value and, if the acquisition currency is unregistered stock, participants may not be able to sell the stock in time to pay their taxes. Given a stock plan's additional complexities and limited benefit, a cash bonus plan may be preferable.

Recapitalizations The target could also do a recapitalization. If the target has raised $50 million and is now valued at $4 million, it could recapitalize by amending its charter to allow the common stock to receive up to $X in acquisition proceeds before the preferred, but leave the preferred liquidation preferences unchanged. Alternatively, the target could amend its charter to convert outstanding preferred stock (which had $50 million in liquidation preferences) into a new series of preferred stock with, for example, only $3 million in liquidation preferences, leaving $1 million for distribution to the holders of the common stock. This approach reduces total liquidation preferences, in effect restarting the company. Either will require amending the charter and obtaining preferred shareholder approval, which may be difficult to obtain. In addition, note that all common shareholders (including former employees) benefit under recapitalizations, rather than just those employees who are currently critical. A recapitalization is most likely to be used when the target is raising new money and the new investor is not willing to invest unless the employee retention issue is addressed or liquidation preferences of existing preferred stock are significantly reduced to reflect the target's economic condition at the time of the new investment. If it is clear that the target will be sold near term, it is wise for the investor putting in new money to force the cleanup of the overhang of liquidation preferences at the time of its investment, rather than waiting for the acquirer to put an offer on the table and fighting the issue out then.

The Sale Transaction Process

Having considered the major deal issues involved in an acquirer's acquisition of a target, the following section outlines the process to get the parties from their handshake deal to a completed transaction.

Letter of Intent A letter of intent (LOI) is a document in which the acquirer outlines the key deal points of the proposed acquisition. The purpose of entering into an LOI is to set forth the consensus of the parties on the major issues before the acquirer and seller commit major resources to due diligence and detailed negotiations. The LOI typically outlines the proposed form of the transaction, as well as the details of the consideration to be paid. It also includes proposed risk reduction mechanisms; employment or noncompetition provisions; brokers' fees; and the tax, accounting, and securities structures to be used. Except for confidentiality provisions, the no-shop clause, and the need for each party to pay its own expenses, most LOIs are nonbinding.

Disclosure of Acquisitions   The federal securities laws impose certain obligations on a publicly traded company to disclose to the market material facts that could be expected to affect the value of its securities. Whether an acquisition would be material to the acquirer depends on how important the acquisition is to the acquirer (given the importance of the acquirer's other operations) and how probable it is that the acquisition will occur. Acquisitions that represent 10 percent of the acquirer's stock, assets, or revenues may be considered material. If the acquisition is material, the acquirer may be required to make a public announcement of the acquisition if

- The acquirer is responsible for a market leak relating to the deal.
- The acquirer is trading in its own stock (e.g., stock repurchases).
- The acquirer's insiders are trading in acquirer stock.
- The acquirer has recently denied that it was in merger negotiations.

Companies do not want to make premature announcements of a proposed acquisition. They prefer to announce only after they are certain that the acquisition will occur and they have had an opportunity to address the customer and employee questions that will arise because of a public disclosure. When negotiating an acquisition, it is incumbent upon the parties to institute internal controls to avoid creating a disclosure obligation. For example, the acquirer should maintain strict confidentiality to avoid leaks to the public about the negotiations and should have a policy of responding to press inquiries about merger negotiations with "no comment." As an additional precaution, many public acquirers avoid executing LOIs. After exchanging unsigned drafts of the LOI, the parties may go directly to negotiating and executing the definitive agreements. Their position is that, absent a signed LOI, the acquisition first becomes probable when the parties execute the definitive agreements.

Time and Responsibility Schedule   Once the parties agree on the terms of the LOI, the acquirer generally will circulate a time and responsibility schedule. The time and responsibility schedule outlines the items that need to be accomplished to complete the transaction, the parties responsible for each item, and the date on which each item must be completed. Attached to the time and responsibility schedule is the interested parties list, giving the name; address; office telephone, e-mail, and fax numbers; and home address and telephone number of each party who might be needed on a time-critical basis during negotiations. These documents ensure that everyone has the same expectations regarding who is responsible for doing what and when it must be completed.

Definitive Agreements   The next step in the acquisition process is for the acquirer to send out a due diligence request checklist, soliciting detailed information and documentation about the target. This begins the due diligence process in earnest. (See also earlier bulleted entry on *Acquirer due diligence.*) Simultaneously, the acquirer will prepare, and the parties will negotiate, the definitive agreements. The main agreement would be an "agreement and plan of merger" if the acquirer is acquiring the target by a merger, an "asset purchase agreement" if the acquirer is acquiring the target's assets, or a "stock purchase agreement" if the acquirer is acquiring the target's stock directly from the target's shareholders. Each of these agreements will set forth in detail the

- Terms of the acquisition.
- Seller's representations and warranties (which will be very detailed).
- Acquirer's representations and warranties (which generally will be more limited than those made by the target).
- Seller's covenants (generally relating to the target's conduct of its business between signing the agreement and closing).
- Acquirer's covenants (generally relating to taking the steps necessary to close the transaction).
- Conditions to closing.
- Termination provisions.
- Indemnity and escrow provisions.

To supplement its representations and warranties, the seller will be required to deliver to the acquirer detailed schedules itemizing material target property, assets, and liabilities. The target will want to ensure that the schedules are complete and correct, as the target's shareholders could be liable if they are not.

The seller also will want to focus on the conditions to closing contained in the agreement. "Conditions to closing" are things that must be true before the acquirer, target, seller, or several parties are required to close the acquisition (e.g., there must be no injunction outstanding prohibiting the acquisition). The seller will want to avoid acquirer conditions to closing that are subjective or within the acquirer's control. For example, the seller would not want the acquirer to be able to refuse to close because it has determined that the target's prospects no longer look as promising as they did at the time it signed the definitive agreement. (See also earlier bulleted entry on *Acquirer due diligence.*)

In addition to the principal agreement, the parties may negotiate and execute ancillary agreements, such as an escrow agreement, employment agreements, noncompetition agreements, a registration rights agreement, and affiliates agreements.

Necessary Consents   Once they have signed definitive agreements, the parties must comply with legal, regulatory, and contractual requirements in order to consummate the transaction. The following outlines some of the typical governmental, shareholder, and third-party consents necessary to accomplish a sale transaction.

Antitrust Approvals   The parties must verify if the transaction would require a premerger filing with the Federal Trade Commission (FTC) and Department of Justice (DoJ) under the Hart-Scott-Rodino Antitrust Improvements Act of 1976. Unless early termination is granted, the parties must wait 30 days after the filing before they can legally close. During that period, the FTC or DoJ will determine if the proposed acquisition is likely to be anticompetitive. The acquirer and target must maintain their independent operations during the waiting period. Either the FTC or DoJ can request additional information if it concludes, based on the first submission, that the acquisition may be anticompetitive. If there is a second request, the closing may be substantially delayed, and the target may be required to divest itself of certain assets to obtain FTC or DoJ approval of the acquisition, or approval may be denied.

Shareholder Approvals   To have an enforceable agreement, the parties must obtain the necessary shareholder approvals of the acquisition before the closing. The parties must solicit such approval in compliance with state and federal securities and corporate laws.

Target Shareholder Approval   The target's shareholders generally must approve an asset acquisition or a merger with the acquirer. Under most state laws, the approval of a majority of the target's outstanding shares will be required to approve the transaction. Under certain state law (e.g., California), if there are both common stock and preferred stock outstanding, the target generally will need to obtain the approval of a majority of each class of stock, voting separately. Legal counsel should review the target's state law and charter documents to verify whether some different or super-majority vote is required to approve the acquisition.

Acquirer Shareholder Approval   The acquirer's shareholders may have to approve the acquisition if the acquirer issues a substantial amount of its stock in the acquisition. For example, the NASDAQ National Market rules require the acquirer to obtain its shareholders' approval when the number of shares it will issue is equal to or greater than 20 percent of its outstanding stock before the acquisition. Legal counsel should review the acquirer's state law and charter documents to verify the vote required to approve the acquisition.

Shareholder Proxy Statements   If shareholder approval is required, the company seeking shareholder approval must produce a proxy statement describing the two companies and the terms of the acquisition. If a public acquirer is relying on a private placement or fairness hearing exemption, it generally can provide most of the information about itself by attaching its most recent Form 10-K, Form 10-Qs, and proxy statement. The description of the target can be short and simple when there are few target shareholders and all are involved in its management. When the target has shareholders not involved in managing its business, the description of the target should be more complete. If the parties are relying on the Regulation D safe harbor exemption or are preparing a public company proxy statement, the information required is set forth in the SEC's regulations, and the proxy statement will be voluminous and costly to prepare.

Target Appraisal or Dissenters Rights   Under most states' corporation laws, shareholders who vote against a merger and meet specified requirements are entitled to have their shares appraised. Instead of receiving the negotiated consideration set forth in the acquisition agreement, such dissenting shareholders can receive the appraised value of their shares in cash. These rules vary from state to state, and shareholders must strictly comply with the rules to obtain their benefits.

Third-Party Consents   The parties will want to verify whether the transaction would require any third party or governmental consents in advance of the closing. If so, these types of consents are generally included in the purchase agreement as a condition precedent that needs to be fulfilled prior to closing. The target should then obtain any required consents before closing. Agreements that typically prohibit mergers or acquisitions or treat them as a breach of contract include real estate leases, loan agreements, equipment leases, and key license agreements. In addition, certain governmental

permits and licenses of the target may require approval or re-issuance prior
to the closing.

CONCLUSION

This chapter discussed the sale process as a harvest mechanism for PE investments. A sale may be considered advantageous over an IPO when a
portfolio company does not possess a consistent, stable pattern of growth
and profitability; equity markets are volatile; the cost of an IPO is deemed
too high; and rapid liquidity is desirable for investors. While portfolio company sales have increased in popularity in recent times, there are numerous
sale process issues that pertain specifically to PE funds, including survival of
representations, warranties, and covenants; escrow funds; indemnification
caps and limited recourse; joint and several liability; purchase price consideration; and noncompetition and nonsolicitation covenants.

CHAPTER 8

Intellectual Property and Private Equity

Stephen Olson
David McClaughry

INTRODUCTION

Historically, tangible assets such as factories, buildings, equipment, inventory, accounts, and the like represented the value of a company. When faced with the task of increasing the company's value, the conventional thinking was to investigate increasing sales, developing new products or adding assets through mergers and acquisitions. After all, such endeavors had a proven track record for adding to the bottom line.

Intellectual property (IP) and the intangible assets it represents were once considered ancillary matters best left for the legal staff or the company's outside patent counsel. Over the past decade, strategic corporate planning has broadened its focus to include intangible assets as a viable means for improving the financial performance of a company. Successful evaluation and management of a company's IP is critically important in today's climate wherein the rights to new ideas and innovations can drive the company's ultimate value.

This chapter will further explain the rights and remedies associated with these types of IP, as well as address assessment of the value of IP rights prior to a private equity (PE) investment. This chapter will also address how these intangible assets may be used to both protect and create value related to a PE investment.

INTELLECTUAL PROPERTY RIGHTS AND REMEDIES

"Intellectual property" is the general term used to refer to intangible assets derived from human knowledge and ideas. Types of IP include patents, trademarks, copyrights, and trade secrets. IP and the rights they afford are frequently blurred and sometimes misunderstood. Patents, trademarks, copyrights, and trade secrets protect different but often interrelated aspects of a company's IP.

A patent protects an invention. A trademark protects brand names and logos used on goods and services. A copyright protects an original artistic or literary work. A trade secret is information kept confidential by a company to provide a competitive advantage. To help understand these concepts, consider a company that introduces a new widget at its annual trade show. A patent would protect the widget itself or the method of using the widget. A trademark would protect the brand name or trade dress of the widget. A copyright would protect the software or computer code in the widget or the literature on the product packaging or even advertising associated with the widget. Manufacturing details of the widget product would be maintained as a trade secret.

Patents

Patents frequently form the foundation of a technology-based company. Patent rights create a barrier to entry into a marketplace for competitors. As common examples, a patent may cover a structural feature of a product, a method of manufacturing a product, a composition of matter, as well as improvements thereto.

A patent provides the owner with an exclusive right to make, use, and offer for sale, sell, and import the invention covered by the claims.[1] As an exclusionary right, it is only the patent owner or its licensees that can practice under the patent. In exchange for the public disclosure in the patent of all details relating to the invention, the patent owner is given a monopoly for a limited term of years. When the patent expires, the public is free to use any of the subject matter described in the patent. In other words, the invention is dedicated to the public at the end of its term, which is currently 20 years from the date a patent application is filed.

A patent application is filed with the U.S. Patent and Trademark Office (USPTO). The application is examined by a patent examiner for various formalities and patentability requirements. A patent issues from the USPTO after successful prosecution of the application. An issued patent includes one or more claims that define the scope of protection.

The rights to most patents are owned by the employer of the inventors by virtue of their employment arrangement. A formal assignment is typically executed by the inventors to their employer, which is recorded with the USPTO. Recording of the assignment with the USPTO provides constructive notice to third parties and prevents a *bona fide* purchaser for value from acquiring any rights directly from the inventors.

A patent is only granted for inventions that are new,[2] useful,[3] and non-obvious.[4] These requirements for patentability are statutorily defined and can be briefly restated as follows:

- New: an invention must be original to the inventor.
- Useful: an invention must have a useful purpose.
- Nonobvious: an invention must not be obvious to a person having ordinary skill in the relevant art.

There are three types of patents: utility patents, design patents, and plant patents. The most common type of patent is the utility patent, which protects the utilitarian or functional aspect of an invention. Plant patents are directed to asexually reproducing plants. Design patents protect the ornamental appearance of an article.

A utility patent protects a useful process, machine, article of manufacture, or composition of matter.[5] Utility patents are granted for a term of 20 years from the date of the application filing. The owner of a U.S. utility patent must periodically pay maintenance fees (e.g., at $3\frac{1}{2}$, $7\frac{1}{2}$, and $11\frac{1}{2}$ years from issuance) to maintain the patent in force. Otherwise, the patent will expire, and its subject matter will be dedicated to the public. Similarly, most foreign patents require the payment of annual fees or annuities to maintain enforceability.

A design patent may be granted to any person who has invented any new, original, and ornamental design for an article of manufacture.[6] A design patent protects the appearance of the article but cannot protect its functional or utilitarian features. The scope of protection afforded under a design patent is fairly limited. Design patents, however, are often successfully used to stop a competitor from selling an exact copy or knock-off product. The term of a design patent is 15 years from the date the patent issues. No maintenance fees are required during the life of a design patent.

A suit for infringement of a patent must be brought in federal court. Remedies for patent infringement include injunctions, monetary relief, enhanced damages for willful infringement, and attorney fees. Damages for patent infringement should be adequate to compensate for the infringement that may be based on a lost profit analysis, but in no event shall it be less than a reasonable royalty for the use made of the invention.[7] For design patents, damages may alternatively be based on the total profits of the infringer but not less than a statutory amount, which is currently $250 per act of infringement.[8] If an infringer is found to have willfully infringed a patent, the damages may be trebled.[9] In exceptional cases, the court may award reasonable attorney fees.[10]

Trademarks

Trademarks are utilized by companies that develop and maintain brand image to market their goods or services. Over time, customers come to recognize that products sold under a particular brand name come from a particular source or are authorized by the particular source. A customer may reasonably expect a particular level of quality to be associated with goods or services offered under a particular brand name. In this manner, the owner of a trademark acquires goodwill in the trademark as a representation of its brand image.

A trademark may be a word, phrase, symbol, sound, packaging or product configuration, or a combination of these elements that identifies and distinguishes the source of the goods of one party from those of others in the industry. A service mark is the same as a trademark, except a service mark identifies and distinguishes the source of a service rather than goods. Throughout this chapter, the term "trademark" will be used to refer to both trademarks and service marks.

Unlike patents, where only the federal government has the authority to grant patent rights, trademarks exist and can be protected under both state and federal law. Rights in a trademark are based on use of the trademark in commerce for a particular geographic area. While trademark rights do not require a formal registration, owning a registration on the Principal Register of the USPTO confers several advantages. These advantages include

- Public notice of a claim of ownership of the mark.
- A legal presumption of ownership of the mark and an exclusive right to use the mark nationwide (as opposed to a restricted geographic region) on or in connection with the goods/services listed in the registration.
- An ability to bring an infringement action concerning the mark in federal court.
- Use of the U.S. registration as a basis to obtain registration in foreign countries.
- An ability to record the U.S. registration with the U.S. Customs and Border Protection Service to prevent importation of infringing foreign goods.
- A right to use the federal registration symbol ®.
- Listing in the USPTO's online databases.

A trademark must be distinctive. The strength of a trademark will depend on its degree of distinctiveness, which is categorized from strongest to weakest as follows: fanciful, arbitrary, suggestive, descriptive, and generic. An example of a fanciful mark would be "Kodak" for cameras, which had no known meaning prior to its use. The term "PC" would be considered a generic mark for a personal computer, whereas "Apple" would be arbitrary for computer equipment since it existed as a word but had no prior association to those goods. A trademark may become generic over time if it becomes recognized as the common noun for a particular type of goods (e.g., escalator or aspirin). Once a mark becomes generic, it is no longer enforceable as a trademark. An example of a descriptive mark would be "Tastee" for a food product, whereas "Blu-ray" would be suggestive of a high-capacity disc storage technology. Merely descriptive marks and generic marks can never function as a trademark.

A suit for trademark infringement may be brought in federal court for claims arising under the Lanham Act. Claims based on state statutory and common law may be brought in federal court subject to diversity or supplemental jurisdiction requirements, or alternately in state court. Remedies for trademark infringement include injunctions, monetary relief, attorney fees, and destruction of infringing materials. The monetary relief should provide damages as compensation, not as a penalty, and may include (1) the infringer's profits, (2) any damages sustained by the trademark holder, and (3) the cost of the action.[11] In assessing damages, a court may enter judgment, according to the circumstances of the case, for any sum above the amount found as actual damages, not exceeding three times such amount. In exceptional cases, a court may also award reasonable attorney fees to the prevailing party.

Copyrights

Copyrights protect "original works of authorship," including literary, dramatic, musical, artistic, and certain other intellectual works.[12] This protection is available to both published and unpublished works. The owner of a copyright is given the exclusive right to do and to authorize others to do the following:

- To reproduce the work in copies
- To prepare derivative works based upon the work
- To distribute copies of the work to the public by sale or other transfer of ownership, or by rental, lease, or lending
- To perform the work publicly
- To display the work publicly[13]

A copyright exists upon the creation of any work of authorship that is "original" and "fixed" in a tangible form of media. A work is original if the author created it and was not copied by the author. A work is fixed in a tangible form when it is sufficiently permanent or stable to permit it to be perceived, reproduced, or otherwise communicated for a period of time.

Copyrightable works include the following categories:

- Literary works.
- Musical works, including any accompanying words
- Dramatic works, including any accompanying music
- Pantomimes and choreographic works
- Pictorial, graphic, and sculptural works
- Motion pictures and other audiovisual works
- Sound recordings
- Architectural works

These categories are viewed broadly. For example, computer programs and most compilations may be registered as "literary works." Maps and architectural plans may be registered as "pictorial, graphic, and sculptural works."

A suit for infringement of a copyright may be brought in federal court and requires registration with the U.S. Copyright Office. Damages for copyright infringement may be based on actual damages and any additional profits or statutory damages.[14] The court may issue injunctions to prevent or restrain copyright infringement and may order the impoundment and destruction of infringing copies.

Trade Secrets

A trade secret is information not known by the relevant industry that may provide the owner with a competitive advantage. While patent coverage typically provides stronger protection, insofar as it can stop a third party from using independently developed technology, trade secrets have certain advantages worthy of consideration. The trade secret laws may be used to protect a manufacturing process that is difficult to identify by inspecting the final product, for example. If one had a patent on such a process, the patent would disclose the process to everyone and the owner would not be able to identify infringers. Trade secrets also have the advantage of being valid and enforceable for an indefinite time, provided that the information remains a secret. A commonly known example is the formulation for Coca-Cola®, which has been in existence for decades and provides an ongoing commercial advantage.

Trade secrets protection is a creature of state statutory and/or common law. A Uniform Trade Secret Act is a model law that was authored in 1985 and has been adopted, in some form, by at least 45 states. The other states provide protection against trade secret misappropriation based on their *sui generis* statutes or based in common law.

A suit for trade secret misappropriation may be brought in state court or federal court subject to diversity or supplemental jurisdiction requirements. In most states, a claim for misappropriation of trade secrets requires a party to show that (1) the information incorporates a trade secret; (2) the plaintiff took reasonable steps to preserve the secrecy of the trade secret; and (3) the defendant misappropriated the secret information and used improper means, in breach of a confidential relationship, to acquire the trade secret. Remedies for trade secret misappropriation may include damages, profits, reasonable royalties, and an injunction.

PRE-ACQUISITION DUE DILIGENCE

A thorough analysis of the IP rights owned and used by a target company is a critically important part of an investor's pre-investment due diligence. The amount of due diligence conducted prior to a potential acquisition should depend on the value of the prospective acquisition and the perceived importance and relative value of the IP to the transaction. For technology-based companies, a particular emphasis will typically be placed on patent rights. For brand-based companies, emphasis would typically be placed on trademark rights. While copyrights and trade secrets may be important to certain transactions, the due diligence for most acquisitions will focus on patent rights, as will this chapter, or on trademark rights.

Pre-investment due diligence should be conducted with an eye toward an assessment of the value of the IP to a business and also to the associated risks. In this regard, due diligence activities should assess both rights held by the target company that provide a competitive advantage and rights held by third parties that may raise infringement concerns to the ongoing business.

Established Barriers to Entry—Evaluating Investment Value

IP is a key component in the value of a target company. The value of IP rights principally lies in an ability to establish a barrier to entry into an industry or product market, and thereby create a competitive advantage for the IP owner in the marketplace. Patents make up the most popular IP right that leads to business transactions, including PE acquisitions. The primary reason is that obtaining rights to a patent may give the owner exclusive rights within a market.

There has been a recent boom in the sales of companies having significant patent portfolios. Frequently, a technology-based target company is acquired primarily for the IP. An investment opportunity exists where target companies own underutilized or undervalued patents.

At a minimum, pre-investment due diligence should review the expiration dates and maintenance fee payment records for U.S. patents to determine whether the patents have expired or are unenforceable. Similarly, annuity payment records for foreign patents should be reviewed. Commercially important products are often covered in pending patent applications. These pending applications should be reviewed to ensure they are in good standing and progressing satisfactorily at the USPTO.

It is not enough that a product be shown in the drawings of a patent or described in the pending application. The claims of issued patents and pending applications should also be reviewed to determine the extent to which the patent claims cover the target company's products, and the extent they may be used to preclude others from selling competitive products. The value of a patent or a portfolio of patents will depend on the strength of the claims vis-à-vis the target company's products and competitive products. At a minimum, claims in the patents or the patent applications should cover the target company's core technology, which includes both current products and future products.

Patent rights can be valued using various credible and established techniques. Significant value can be assigned to an issued patent that covers a commercially successful product where the claims of the patent are broad enough to cover potentially competitive products. The evaluation, however, remains a forecast based on future potential income streams.

Pre-acquisition due diligence should also consider ownership issues relating to the target company's patents and other IP rights. Patent rights are owned by the inventors until an assignment is made to the target company. If an inventor is an employee that was hired to invent, that inventor will likely be obligated to assign invention rights to the target company. Nevertheless, all patents and pending applications should have an executed and recorded assignment from each of the named inventors.

For significant PE investments, prudent due diligence may include a validity analysis for key patents of the target company. If a significant potential exists to assert one or more patents against a competitor, a validity analysis should be conducted to determine the strength of the patents. Key personnel may be questioned regarding their knowledge of prior art, as well as known modes of practicing the invention that may affect the validity of the patents. Additionally, an independent search for prior art may be considered.

A technology-based target company should offer some type of barrier to entry by its competitors. Most frequently, this barrier to entry will be IP in the form of patents, trade secrets, or both. Specific investment value can be assigned to such assets only through appropriate due diligence that evaluates the scope of the target company's patent portfolio and the validity of trade secrets that may provide a competitive advantage.

It is important to bear in mind that while the size of a patent portfolio may be of some importance to investors, it should not be the determining factor. A large patent portfolio that fails to cover any commercially significant products can only be assigned very limited value. In contrast, a single, industry-respected patent that covers a class of commercially successful products may provide an opportunity to create a monopoly for an entire business for up to 20 years.

Freedom to Practice—Assessing Risk of Proposed Acquisition

Having considered the value of an IP portfolio on the basis of an ability to preclude competition, it is equally important to consider the potential risk associated with commercialization of core technology from third-party rights. Clearance studies, also known as freedom to operate studies, should be undertaken with respect to at least the more important products of the target company. If a target company is only being acquired for its IP rights (i.e., the target company does not make or sell any products), however, freedom to practice may not be relevant or necessary.

Patent clearance studies may include both issued patents and published applications and may consider utility patent rights and design patent rights of third parties, depending on the circumstances. Likewise, foreign patents may be considered in countries of particular commercial importance for the manufacture, distribution, and sale of the particular product.

Even if a product of the target company is covered by its own patent, freedom to make, use, and sell the product cannot be assumed. A patent provides the owner with a right that allows the owner to exclude others from making, using, or selling a product or method covered by the claims of the patent. It does not, however, grant the right to practice the claimed invention. For example, the target company may have a patent for an improvement of an existing product. The existing product may be covered by a third-party patent, which effectively precludes commercialization of the improved product.

Relevant patents and published applications for patent clearance studies may be identified in various ways. A logical place to begin is a search of the records of the USPTO for patents and applications assigned to known competitors. This type of searching may be efficiently conducted and will identify the highest-risk references. For more important products of the target company or products requiring a large capital investment, searching of all third-party patent references should be considered. This more comprehensive searching can be significantly more extensive and time consuming.

A basic checklist for pre-acquisition patent due diligence includes

- Identify all U.S. and foreign patents and pending applications, both utility and design, owned or licensed by the target company.
- Check title to and the expiration dates and maintenance fee record of patents to ensure enforceability.
- Compare the claims of issued patents and pending applications with key products.
- Review the target company's unfiled invention records.
- Identify other research and development that may be appropriate for future patent protection.
- Review the target company's procedures for identifying, harvesting, and protecting inventions, including procedures for determining that an invention should remain a trade secret, making foreign filing decisions, and ensuring the timeliness of patent filings.
- Review claims of patents and pending applications against competitor products.
- Identify and review all litigation involving patents of the target company.

CREATING INTELLECTUAL PROPERTY VALUE DURING MANAGEMENT

With the operation of a company by a PE concern come the objectives and responsibility to optimize the company's current assets and maximize the development of new assets. Once overlooked, IP has become a focal point for these objectives.

To reap the benefits from this fertile ground, an inventory or audit of the company is necessary to get a sense of the current state of affairs. The results of any pre-acquisition due diligence may go a long way in providing an inventory of the acquired company's IP assets. Additional investigation and due diligence may be necessary to fully understand and implement the IP assets of the company.

Leveraging and Monetizing Patent Rights

As noted in an earlier section of this chapter, patents are most frequently exploited by industries (other than the music and film industries), having the greatest effect on protecting the commercial success and market value of a company's technology. While patents may not represent the "be all and end all" to a successful bottom line, proper development and management of a company's patent assets may significantly enhance the value of the company.

One proven approach for adding value is through licensing of the company's current patent portfolio. The objective here is not to dilute the patent protection for the company's core technology but rather to look for opportunities to license technology in alternative, noncompetitive industries or technology that is underutilized.

Another successful approach to increase the company value is to buttress the patent protection of core technologies by developing and patenting improvements that augment the core technology. Improvements that relate to making the core technology more functional, less expensive, and of higher quality are obvious areas of pursuit. Other areas may be the manner in which the core technology is manufactured, marketed, distributed, or purchased. In this way, patents may be clustered together to form a patent barrier around the company's core technology.

A corollary to building a patent wall around the company's core technology is to lay a patent trap around a competitor's technology. Areas ripe for this strategy are similar to those referenced earlier for clustering. In this way, it may be possible to constrain the expansion of a competitor and its technology from the core technology market by patenting technology closely associated with the competitor's products.

Identification and acquisition of third-party rights in technology that complements the company's core technology can also be an effective means for quickly adding value to the company. For this purpose, inquiries should be made into what interfaces with the core technology, how the products are being deployed, and where they are being used. This inquiry should not be limited to companies with commercial products but can include nonpracticing entities such as independent inventors, research institutes, and universities. In this analysis, emphasis should be placed on securing an exclusive position in the complementary technology, and not merely participating in industry licensing practice.

Bolstering Technological Advantages

Innovation and other creative activities are likely occurring at every ongoing enterprise, but perhaps not recognized as such. In order to tap into this resource, it is important to educate the company's workforce about the role and importance of IP rights and protection, to motivate its development, and to incentivize the commercialization of this intangible asset.

Inventors and innovators are, by their nature, eager to explain their work to someone willing to listen. Sometimes, however, they are so close to their work that they fail to appreciate its significance from an IP asset perspective. This is where a little bit of legal counsel can go a long way.

For example, a nonlegal explanation of the patent process will help inventors assimilate the legal world to their work and justify the additional effort that may be required to capture this important asset. Likewise, procedures such as work logs and record of inventions can be developed to document and evaluate an inventor's work. To ensure success, it is important, however, that these procedures fit into the inventor's work flow. Motivational tools such as patent recognitions and monetary awards for patent filings can be used to promote and reward successful efforts since additional effort on the part of the innovator will be required.

Responsibility for development and commercialization of the patent assets may also be delegated to a particular business unit or division, or assigned to management like other, more traditional tangible assets. In this way, the people with the most direct knowledge about a patented technology can explore and exploit the asset, knowing that it will have a direct and positive reflection on their group.

A workforce familiar with patent concepts can also take advantage of the body of knowledge that patents represent. In fact, it is this source of knowledge that motivated the constitutional provision that authorizes the patent laws—the *quid pro quo* of a limited monopoly in exchange for the disclosure of new and useful inventions. An understanding of the state of the art coupled with knowledge of the problems and insufficiency in the technology can be used to direct development efforts towards improvement.

Boosting Brand Development Efforts

Every company, no matter its structure, size, or locale, has a persona—a quality or character that defines the company and its goods or services. Not every company takes advantage of this distinct personality to develop a brand image for itself and its goods and services. The potential for added commercial value associated with a strong brand image, however, should not be underestimated.

For this reason, brand development should be an integral part of the product cycle, and may be used to direct the technological development of goods and services. Developing a brand image should not be a last priority in the development cycle or, worse yet, left to the whims of customers.

A brand image can be narrowly interpreted as the trademarks associated with a particular company and its goods or services. However, it is better to consider the concept more broadly and to include the designs, product configurations, packaging, logo, imagery, quality, and reputation of the company and its goods and services. A brand image carrying all of these qualities can then be summarized and symbolized by the company's trademarks.

Key to this concept is the development of a brand image and hence trademarks that are unique to the company and distinctive within the industry. An analysis of the trademark landscape in a particular industry or for particular goods and services can further focus the development of an effective brand image.

Trademark searches can be used to assess the availability or strength of a mark. In particular, a search is conducted for usage of the same or similar marks in various databases containing federal and state trademark registrations and applications, known common law usage, and domain names. A trademark search can be formulated to focus on specific goods or services. The search results can be interpreted to determine the manner and extent that a particular mark is used.

A trademark search can also be conducted for usage of various trademarks by competitors in a particular industry. Likewise, trademark watch can provide insight into a competitor's current efforts to develop and protect its brand image. A trademark watch periodically surveys the application and registration records to track activity associated with a specific company or particular mark.

Protection and enforcement of the brand image can be achieved by registering and asserting the trademark right associated with that brand image. With a comprehensive trademark management strategy, companies can effectively add strength to the brand image associated with it and its goods and services which, in the end, adds value to the bottom line.

Preserving Knowledge-Based Resources of the Workforce

Technology-based companies often attract employees having an entrepreneurial spirit looking for the right environment to innovate. With this spirit comes a sense of independence and mobility. In addition, these employees have an expectation that they can choose where they live and work. Consequently, assets associated with this mobile human resource can become the target of competitors looking to catch up or gain a competitive advantage. While our culture and legal doctrine respects employment mobility, certain practices can be implemented to protect the institutional knowledge and technological resources embodied in the knowledge and skill of a company's workforce.

Emphasis on certain legal tenets such as trade secrets, nondisclosure obligations, and, where appropriate, reasonable noncompete restriction may be implemented to protect proprietary and highly sensitive information. To be effective, policies and procedures for securing this information must be put in place and followed. To this point, it is important to advise departing employees of their obligations to maintain the trade secrets and confidentiality of proprietary information. If such practices are not followed, there will be little or no recourse when an employee migrates to the competitor.

But what about the general knowledge and experience gained on the job? It is unlikely that information of this type would be protectable as a trade secret or even under obligations of confidentiality. In fact, it is often this skill, knowledge, and experience that make an employee attractive to the competition. To address these circumstances, it is prudent to develop a working environment that promotes the exchange of information and sharing of experience among key personnel so that no one employee has the critical knowledge base.

A basic checklist for development of IP value during management of the operating company by a PE concern includes

- Understand the operating company's IP landscape vis-à-vis its core technology though an audit or similar inventory procedure.
- Promote innovation and improvement surrounding the core technology to reinforce the company's patent position and possibly block a competitor's inroads to the technology.
- Investigate opportunities to complement the core technology with patented products, manufacturing techniques, and business methods.
- Incentivize innovation through education of the workforce and inventor recognition and rewards.
- Expand efforts to identify and exploit brand imagery of the company and its goods and services.
- Encourage the sharing of information and experience among employees while emphasizing the importance of confidentiality outside the company.

POSITIONING THE EXIT—REVERSE DUE DILIGENCE

At the time a PE concern decides to exit an investment, the various IP assets must be reviewed to ensure that everything is in order for maximized return.

This process is referred to as reverse due diligence or sell side diligence. The seller will be at a disadvantage during negotiations without the reverse due diligence if a prospective buyer has conducted its own due diligence of the IP prior to the acquisition (as outlined in an earlier section of this chapter).

Reverse due diligence should identify aspects relating to the IP that will enhance the value of the sale for the PE fund. Perhaps more importantly, reverse due diligence should identify any issues relating to the IP that negatively impact value or could be used by the acquiring party to drive the value down. In many instances, potentially negative issues relating to the IP may be corrected or at least mitigated prior to exposure of the issue to a prospective purchaser.

First and foremost, a verification of ownership of the IP that is to be sold to the prospective purchaser should be made. While this holds true for all types of IP, most often a PE concern is looking to divest value in the form of patented or unpatented technologies. The technologies may relate to products themselves or processes for manufacturing the products.

For patented and patent pending technology, a chain of title should be established for each patent and patent application. There should be an assignment executed by each inventor named on each of the patents and applications. The assignments should be recorded with the USPTO. For any patents and applications acquired from any third parties during management by the PE concern, executed assignments should similarly be recorded with the USPTO. If security interests were granted and recorded against any of the patents or pending applications, a release should be obtained and recorded to clear the title.

Through reverse due diligence, the PE concern may discover that certain IP used in the business is owned by a third party. First, steps should be taken to ensure that such technology is properly licensed to the business and subject to a written agreement. Secondly, the related licensed agreements should be reviewed to confirm that a right exists to transfer the license rights to a prospective purchaser. Appropriate license rights should be negotiated and concluded in the event any shortcomings are identified prior to the due diligence study of any prospective purchaser.

If the acquiring business places value on any trade secrets during negotiations of a prospective sale, procedures for maintaining confidentiality should be reviewed to ensure that the trade secrets are in fact secret. To this end, personnel having knowledge of the trade secrets should be interviewed to determine the extent of disclosure. Confidentially agreements should be in place with any person having knowledge of the trade secrets.

Proper reverse due diligence will aid the PE concern in preparing to negotiate a potential sale of the business. If potentially negative issues identified during reverse due diligence cannot be corrected or mitigated, an opportunity to address such issues now exists prior to establishing a basis for evaluating the business. In this manner, the reverse due diligence may serve to eliminate an opportunity by the prospective purchaser to re-negotiate the price late in the process.

Minimizing Exposure of Representations and Warranties

Exiting a business venture, the PE concern will be forced to make certain covenants, representations, and warranties to the purchaser or its new investors. The wording of these promises and obligations may appear straightforward and innocuous, but they can present serious potential issues after the deal is closed. Results from the reverse due diligence can be exploited to reduce the exposure and potential liability that may be created from certain representations and warranties made in the transaction documents.

For example, the representations and warranties provisions may cover a listing of all IP, ownership and right of use of the subject IP, the adequacy of the subject IP to cover the technology, a clearance of the technology from third-party claims of infringement, the lack of third-party infringement of the subject IP, the validity and enforceability of the subject IP, the lack of any legal proceeding or adjudications involving the subject IP or its associated technology, and/or the maintenance of confidential obligations and trade secrets.

These provisions must be carefully considered to avoid overstating the facts or unduly obligating the sell side of the transaction. The provisions should be made based on actual knowledge as opposed to information and belief or, worse, blanket recitations. The provisions should also be limited to the material aspect of the IP and the technology, be date specific, and be based on reasonable efforts by the seller. Likewise, any exclusions or exceptions to the explicit representations and warranties should be specifically called out.

A basic checklist for positioning the disposition of a PE's interest in a company includes

- Identify IP that will enhance value of the company.
- Verify and document ownership of all IP to be sold.
- Confirm the confidentiality of trade secrets.
- Correct or mitigate any negative issues.
- Analyze the IP representations and warranties from the seller's perspective to minimize potential liability.

NOTES

1. 35 U.S.C. §271.
2. 35 U.S.C. §102.
3. 35 U.S.C. §101.
4. 35 U.S.C. §103.
5. 35 U.S.C §101.
6. 35 U.S.C §171.
7. 35 U.S.C. §284.
8. 35 U.S.C. §289.
9. 35 U.S.C. §284.
10. 35 U.S.C. §285.
11. 15 U.S.C. §1117.
12. 17 U.S.C §102.
13. 17 U.S.C. §106.
14. 17 U.S.C. §504.

Governance Structures in Private Equity

CHAPTER 9

The Private Equity Governance Model

Harry Cendrowski
Adam A. Wadecki

INTRODUCTION

Private equity (PE) firms possess unique governance structures that permit them to be active investors in the truest sense of the term. Through large equity stakes, management interests in PE portfolio companies become aligned with those of all shareholders, and a sense of ambition is instilled in the executives managing these firms.

This chapter explores the PE governance model and the significant differences between it and the governance structures of public corporations. Implications for publicly traded PE firms are also discussed.

A NEW MODEL FOR CORPORATE GOVERNANCE

In 1989, noted Harvard Business School Professor Michael C. Jensen wrote, "The publicly held corporation, the main engine of economic progress in the United States for a century, has outlived its usefulness in many sectors of the economy and is being eclipsed." Jensen appropriately titled his article in the *Harvard Business Review*, "Eclipse of the Public Corporation." Central to Jensen's article was the notion that PE firms, "organizations that are corporate in form but have no public shareholders," were emerging in place of public corporations.[1]

In the late 1980s, the PE market was burgeoning. With the U.S. Department of Labor's clarifications to the Employee Retirement Income Security Act (ERISA) in 1979 came significant inflows to alternative asset classes. As shown in Exhibit 9.1, PE fundraising levels increased from just over $2 billion in 1980 to roughly $14 billion by 1989, a compound annual growth rate of 24 percent.

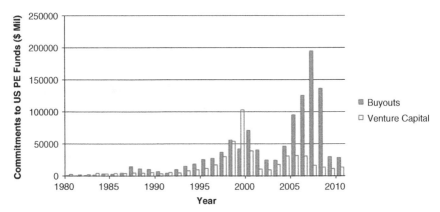

EXHIBIT 9.1 Historical Venture Capital and Buyout Annual Fundraising Levels, 1980–2010
Source: Thomson ONE Banker.

Buyouts gained in popularity throughout the 1980s as interest rates, now available at half the rates of the early 1980s, decreased significantly and the number of distressed corporations grew. With some equity investors earning as much as 60 to 100 percent per year on their investments, the buyout binge was born.[2] Managers overseeing portfolios at institutional investment firms began allocating large portions of their portfolios to PE in an attempt to both diversify their investments and achieve higher rates of return than what was available in public markets.

Entire industries were restructured during this time period, including the automotive supply, rubber tire, and casting industries, among others. The tire industry during this time was characterized by the chief executive officer (CEO) of Uniroyal Goodrich as a "dog-eat-dog business."[3] Those companies that survived these difficult times moved swiftly to counteract the fierce headwinds caused by intense competition; others that failed to perceive these fundamental changes in their external environment experienced significant hardships.

With the growth in PE investments came increased scrutiny from the public—especially for buyout funds—and a general distaste for the tactics employed by leveraged buyout (LBO) shops. A 1989 article in the *Wall Street Journal* expressed investors' growing antipathy for the structure of such transactions:

> *Leveraged buyouts are routinely criticized for being the product of financial engineers with sharp pencils but little appreciation for*

running and improving enterprises. There's little doubt that a number of transactions have been completed at exceptionally high purchase prices by investor groups just hoping to divest divisions at even higher prices. Worse still, some LBOs are so highly leveraged that investment funds for crucially important product, market, and manufacturing improvements are simply unavailable; the burden of debt service takes priority.[4]

During the buyout craze of the 1980s, many saw buyout shops as a new kind of "evil empire," mercilessly slashing costs at portfolio firms in order to increase exit multiples, and hence, a business's valuation. It was during the late 1980s that some of the buyout's largest magnates, like T. Boone Pickens and Carl Icahn, earned their reputation for purchasing distressed firms, laying off employees, cutting research and development (R&D) budgets, and subsequently selling off parts of the company to the highest bidder. Other public company figures like "Chainsaw Al" Dunlap only helped to fuel both Wall Street's and American consumers' distaste for such operational methods.

Working as a CEO at Lily Tulip Corporation, Dunlap "fired most of the senior managers, sold the corporate jet, closed the headquarters and two factories, dumped half the headquarters staff, and laid off a bunch of other workers. The stock price rose from $1.77 to $18.55 in his two-and-a-half-year tenure." Subsequently, while at Scott Paper, Dunlap "fired 11,000 employees (including half the managers and 20 percent of the company's hourly workers), eliminated the corporation's $3-million philanthropy budget, slashed R&D spending, and closed factories. Scott's market value stood at about $3 billion when Dunlap arrived in mid-1994. In late 1995, he sold Scott to Kimberly-Clark for $9.4 billion, pocketing $100 million for himself . . . "[5] However, despite a general disinclination toward such methods, defenders of the buyout boom aptly pointed out that many firms purchased by buyout funds might have gone out of business if it were not for their sometimes cutthroat practices.

Until the past decade, PE funds generally focused on targeting either growing firms or declining businesses participating in mature industries: the former was the focus of venture capitalists, while the latter was the focus of buyout funds. In recent years, however, buyout funds have moved away from purchasing strictly asset-intensive businesses (e.g., manufacturing), seeking out companies in once high-growth sectors (e.g., computer hardware, such as the LBO of Seagate Corporation).

To clarify, an LBO is a transaction in which a private investment group acquires a company by employing a large amount of debt. Companies that have been acquired through an LBO typically have a debt-to-equity ratio of roughly 2:1, although this ratio was as high as 9:1 for some transactions in the late 1980s and as low as 1:1 during portions of 2008 and 2009.

When acquiring a target firm, LBO funds generally look for targets with strong free cash flow and low volatility of these cash flows; when the business produces a significant amount of cash, debt payments can easily be made. Low levels of capital expenditures, a lower debt-to-equity ratio (i.e., conservative capital structure), and market leadership or former market leadership are all traits that LBO funds look for when screening potential companies.

By contrast, a venture capital (VC) deal is a transaction in which a private investment group provides capital to a growing firm primarily through the use of equity. Because many venture-backed firms lack hard assets, banks are often unwilling to lend debt at reasonable interest rates. Moreover, the asset volatility and uncertainty associated with venture-backed portfolio companies does not lend itself well to debt service, where cash stability is a requirement for making periodic interest payments.

Management buyouts, LBOs, hostile takeovers, and corporate breakups—the magnitude of which had never before been seen—have now became commonplace. And many of these deals have successfully transformed the companies they sought to change. Why, then, were so many of these deals successful at transforming declining organizations when previous management faltered? According to Jensen, management in public corporations is controlled by three forces: the product markets, internal control systems, and the capital markets.[6] Of these forces, Jensen argued that only the capital markets have truly imposed discipline on managers, although the product markets have become a strong force for change since Jensen first wrote his article.

For years, the U.S. markets were immune to foreign competition: oligopolistic competition among firms permitted the realization of large economies of scale, and product markets had not yet matured to the point of permitting the global exchange on a massive scale. As these markets developed, many companies failed to react to overseas competition, primarily because these firms believed that the competition was ephemeral and the products were subpar. Consumers, however, soon found that foreign producers offered products of comparable (and sometimes better) quality for a cheaper price. Old-line domestic producers simply couldn't compete against new, nimble entrants to the U.S. marketplace.

In this manner, many domestic firms failed to recognize and properly evaluate the strength of their new competitors—and their products—and did not react to changes in their external environment. It is thus clear that the internal control systems at such corporations were woefully inadequate at instituting a corporate culture committed to properly perceiving changes in its environment and reacting to them in a prompt manner.

An Analogy to Physics

In physics, force is the product of mass and acceleration; an increase in either quantity leads to a commensurate increase in the force. Equation 9.1 presents Sir Isaac Newton's Second Law of Motion, which asserts that force (*F*) equals mass (*m*) multiplied by acceleration (*a*).

$$F = m*a \qquad (9.1)$$

The critical examination of corporations can likewise be applied to this fundamental quantity so well studied by novice scientists. Let us first examine the concept of mass as applied to an organization.

Organizational mass can be defined by numerous factors: the amount of time a firm has been in business; the size of the company's revenues, earnings, interest payments, and the like; the number of people it employs; its market share; and its market leadership position, among other things. It is important to note that, unlike weight for individuals, organizational mass need not carry negative connotations. Much like the blue whale in the ocean, organizational mass can be a symbol of pride for the company and its employees—but it can also be a detriment.

Company managers continually work hard to expand the firm's revenues and grow market share and earnings in an attempt to increase shareholder value. While the achievement of such growth is tantamount to the success of the firm itself, it also creates organizational mass as these accomplishments are realized.

Returning, then, to Equation 9.1, we rearrange to obtain Equation 9.2:

$$a = F/m \qquad (9.2)$$

Here, note that acceleration is equivalent to force over mass. For organizations, this simple relationship carries large implications: In order to accelerate the company toward the achievement of a new goal, larger forces must be applied as organizational mass is increased. In other words, the more mass a company carries, the harder its management team must push in order to change the status quo. The greater the acceleration a management team can induce, the faster the company will move toward its goal.

Extending the analogy a bit further, let us assume that we have the scenario presented in Exhibit 9.2.

In this scenario, a firm is currently moving toward a previously established target. However, management has determined—perhaps due to product markets, capital markets, or a firm's internal control system—that the firm must move to a new target as soon as possible. Achieving this goal requires the firm to reverse entirely its current moving course and accelerate toward the new target.

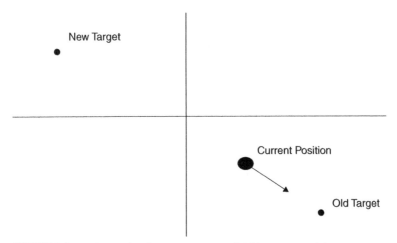

EXHIBIT 9.2   Relationship between New and Old Corporate Targets

For nimble firms of relatively small organizational mass, this task is not particularly difficult: Management need not apply a large organizational force to turn the firm around. However, for a large firm, this is no easy chore: Management must muster an enormous force in order to quickly accelerate the firm toward this new task.

While a large force is required to quickly move the large organization toward this new goal, there exists another way in which this goal may be achieved expeditiously: create a scenario in which the old and new targets are not far apart. This is the job of a well-functioning internal control system.

When a best-in-class internal control system is employed, senior management is very sensitive to movements in the marketplace. Changes in a firm's external environment are swiftly perceived and evaluated, and a course of action is rapidly deployed. Because such changes are sensed quickly, the firm will require less time to achieve newly set targets. If, however, management becomes complacent and fails to react to perceived changes in the environment, a scenario akin to that presented in Exhibit 9.3 may more aptly describe the distance between the old and new business targets. In such a case, management must apply considerably more force to induce a large acceleration toward the new target.

Corporate Governance and the Management of Crisis

The task of successfully identifying change and reacting to it is the goal of corporate governance. In the words of Gerald C. Meyers, past chairman of American Motors Corporation, "Some regard change as a force that is

EXHIBIT 9.3 New and Old Target Position When Best-in-Class Internal Controls Are Employed

inevitable and unmanageable, but this is not necessarily the case. Change can be guided, and the pace of it can be quickened or slowed; to influence change, you must anticipate events and move to dominate them."[7] The idea of management dominating change is essential to the concept of corporate governance: without assuming control of change, management cannot effectively shepherd it through the organization.

Many corporations undertake strategic planning initiatives that examine such planning over long, finite horizons. Frequently, senior management will establish 1-, 5-, and 10-year strategic vision and mission statements for the firm. However, it is important to note that these plans should never be treated as infallible doctrine. As time evolves, the assumptions on which the original strategic plan was based may change significantly, necessitating considerable revisions to the strategy. Without such revisions, the business may soon fall into crisis. Along these lines, Meyers advocates that crisis management and strategic planning "coexist comfortably" as "both deal with the management of change."[8]

Strategic planning should primarily focus on major changes in a business that are gradually implemented; crisis management should also focus on major changes, but only those that must be executed expeditiously. Because many firms fail to properly manage change through strategic and crisis planning, they often struggle to turn around the business before their liquidity dries up. It does not take long before the firm finds itself in a state of financial distress, with buyout offers soon to follow.

PE firms are masters at devising strategic plans and executing them according to plan. PE partners often introduce regular monthly—and, in some cases, weekly—reporting into their portfolio companies in order to promptly detect any performance issues. Because they are identified in this systematic manner, the issue is brought to the forefront, a timetable for remediation is established, and the issue is "nipped in the bud."

Moreover, PE deals incorporate a foundational mechanism for change in the alignment of management and shareholder interests—a sort of corporate governance nirvana. Because of the nature of PE transactions, managers are given large equity stakes for their participation in a buyout deal. As such, they are heavily incentivized to create value within the company in order for it to achieve a successful exit event five to seven years down the road (where they may sell their shares to the public or to a buyer in a mergers and acquisitions deal). Moreover, managers participating in a PE buyout deal need not concern themselves with opinions of outside equity analysts who are continually seeking quarterly earnings guidance; instead, they can focus their efforts on long-term planning without facing short-term penalties for their decisions.

Even before a deal is done, the general partners (GPs) of a fund devise a long-range plan for improvement by examining the future target's operations and financial status. One of the first issues examined by the GPs is the target's cash position; net earnings are not a primary concern of PE partners. Cash is what permits the firm to pay its external bills (including interest payments), meet its payroll, and keep the lights on at all times. Without taking control of cash, the business cannot maintain its liquidity.

Because PE buyouts are often financed with large amounts of debt, cash discipline is paramount to the success of the deal. According to Dick Boyce, a partner at Texas Pacific Group, "Many companies that have not had to cope with the kind of leverage behind private equity investment pay little attention to cash management." To ensure proper management of cash and financial position, Texas Pacific "requires portfolio companies to file weekly flash reports on results and to pay close attention to cash management."[9]

To generate cash flow, GPs will divest unprofitable business lines, sell noncore assets, stretch out payables, reign in receivables, and cut R&D and capital expenditures, among other things. Cash-hungry operations will be closed or sold, with this cash being used to pay down the debt raised in the deal. Rarely are all operations of a distressed corporation unprofitable; there are usually a few lines of business that are cash "bleeders" that hurt the financial position of the company. Because management in a PE deal is heavily incentivized to create value, they are better able to execute these hard decisions than their public company counterparts. Moreover, the institution of rigorous internal controls in PE portfolio companies ensures that managers are continually kept on their toes, always making decisions with an eye toward building shareholder value.

In the case of the Blackstone Group, the firm employs "an automated web-based reporting system that is used by all its portfolio companies to feed information back to the [private equity] firm. That information is then analyzed centrally, allowing Blackstone to detect trends and leading indicators for other companies in its portfolio."[10] Through its rigorous internal controls, firms like Blackstone take control of change and manage it throughout the organization; change is not allowed to cascade throughout the organization unnoticed by management.

Public Corporations and the Private Equity Model

While the model of corporate governance exemplified by PE firms appears to be unique to the industry, there exists no reason why public companies cannot adopt a similar model by which to run their firm—although doing so may prove extremely difficult. Strong internal controls and detailed enterprise resource planning software may be instituted at public and private firms alike. Nonetheless, it appears that many public corporations fail to institute a culture of discipline that rivals that offered by PE firms.

Bebchuk, Fried, and Walker have discussed the issue of managerial power—specifically that of the CEO—as it relates to the issuance of public company stock options and executive compensation. However, this concept may be more broadly applied to examine the reasons why public companies often experience issues related to corporate governance.[11] Overall, Bebchuk et al. identified three reasons why the current public company model, with a CEO overseen by a board of directors, is not optimal for ensuring exemplary corporate governance:

> *First, managers influence the appointment of independent directors, which in many cases enables them to block the appointment of directors who are likely to try to bargain with the managers at arms' [sic] length. Secondly, once appointed, independent directors are influenced by board dynamics that make it difficult for them to deal with managers in a truly arm's length way. . . . Finally, even if directors were otherwise inclined to challenge managers . . . they would likely have neither the financial incentive nor sufficient information to do so.*[12]

The management team of a public corporation wields significant power over the appointment of the board of directors. To this end, Bebchuk et al. asserted that the CEO "dominates" the director nomination process and reinforced this assertion by citing a 1998 survey which found that "only 27 percent of S&P 1500 firms had fully independent nominating committees"; many firms possess nominating committees of which the CEO is a member.[13] In this manner, the CEO's opinion can significantly influence the board's selection of future directors.

Moreover, the overall dynamics of public company boards do not permit a high degree of corporate governance to be maintained. Bebchuk et al. stated, "Most directors believe that their primary responsibility is to monitor the CEO's performance and, if necessary, fire him or her and hire a suitable replacement. Outside of this unfortunate circumstance, however, the directors are expected to support the CEO."[14]

Rather than focus on performance, many boards focus on "mere compliance" with securities laws, material disclosures, and oversight formalities. "Responsibility for a corporation's governance, long treated as secondary to the more important task of nominating directors," is still not viewed as a primary board responsibility by many directors.[15] This culture of tacit support for CEOs permits the executives to hold significant power over the board, despite the fact that the board is supposed to be composed of outsiders who think independently of the CEO. Furthermore, some corporations have CEOs that also serve as chairmen of the board. This is a clear conflict of interest.

In contrast, PE firms present a strong governance model that helps eliminate some of the principal agent problems associated with public company boards. If the PE firm elects to maintain current management when taking over a company, the GPs of the PE fund represent a fully independent board of directors who closely monitor the day-to-day operations of the firm. Additionally, PE funds are not bashful about instituting leadership changes if they feel that current executives are not meeting performance requirements. Some PE shops may appoint firm members to executive positions within a portfolio company if they feel that such action is necessary. In the PE model, all interests are focused on creating shareholder value; all major decisions are made in support of this effort. Furthermore, key executives at PE portfolio companies are heavily incentivized to create shareholder value by the large equity stakes granted to them by their respective PE firms.

In reading the aforementioned praises of the PE governance model, the reader will likely notice that managers of publicly traded corporations are also incentivized through equity stakes, although in a somewhat different manner: stock options. Fifty-one percent of the average S&P 500 CEO's pay package in 2000 was attributable to stock options (up from just 27 percent in 1992).[16] Looking over a longer length of time, roughly 80 percent of executives were granted stock options in 2004, up from approximately 20 percent in 1960.[17] However, stock options differ from the equity incentives offered by PE firms in several important ways. One of the first ways in which stock options differ from PE investment incentives is the time horizon over which the equity (or potential equity) stakes are exercised. By their nature, stock options may be exercised at any point after their grant date before expiry; in contrast, the equity stakes granted to managers of PE firms can be liquidated only after the company has a successful exit event or after the shares vest. In this manner, stock options permit managers to optimize over the short term by exercising and selling their options over significantly shorter periods of time than that facilitated by a PE deal. This is especially true for public company executives who "hop around" from firm to firm without spending large amounts of time at any given company.

Another manner in which stock options differ from the equity stakes granted by PE firms is the size of the equity stake granted through these transactions. In order to attract top-notch talent, PE firms will often offer large compensation packages heavily based on equity incentives. These stakes may range in magnitude depending on the size of the deal (entrepreneurs may retain a majority of the portfolio company's equity in some VC deals), but are generally much larger than the pay packages offered by commensurate public companies. Jensen states that these equity stakes may be 10 to 20 times larger for executives of PE portfolio companies than their public company counterparts.[18] With these large equity stakes, the PE manager can more easily influence his/her pay package by building value in the company.

The Magic of the Private Equity Governance Model

Through large equity stakes, buyout deals foster a sense of proprietorship that acts as a powerful motivator for successful restructuring. It is through these large equity stakes that shareholder interests are aligned with those of executives, and performance is rewarded on a commensurate basis. In fact, some PE professionals believe the more executives who hold equity stakes in a PE deal, the better. These equity stakes can be made to vest over long periods of time (e.g., several years) in order to encourage top management to remain at the firm for a definite period of time.

When a management team is retained from a target company (as opposed to one instituted by the PE firm), the primary function of the PE fund managers is to encourage executives to make the tough decisions without regard to the firm's past; even if a company has been producing a product for decades, it should fix, close, or sell the business rapidly in order to stop this bleeder of cash.

Such actions will generally act as a bruise on management's conscience—especially if the team has been with the portfolio company for a long time. However, without such action, managers must understand that the company may not survive or be able to meet its liquidity constraints imposed by high leverage ratios. This "discipline of debt" acts in concert with management equity stakes to impose a culture of strict cash discipline. Once unprofitable businesses are sold or closed, free cash flow from these entities can then be used to pay down the debt employed in the original buyout transaction.

As the management team in a buyout deal possesses such a large equity stake in the overall transaction, PE fund managers can permit these individuals to act in a rather unregulated manner. Because of these interests, managers focus on creating value, rather than simply "growing the business." Only when such decisions create further financial distress should PE fund managers intervene in the governance of a portfolio company.

No employee enjoys a manager constantly breathing down his/her neck; doing so may lead to short-term optimization by the employee. Managers of the portfolio company should be treated with respect, and reporting transparency should always be stressed. Without this respect, the parent PE firm will soon find it difficult to obtain accurate income statement projections or signals from management of future market difficulties; earnings smoothing and managing to expectations may soon return.

Moreover, it is important to note that PE funds possess contractually limited lifetimes (usually 10 years), after which they must return all investment proceeds to the limited partners in the fund. This finite life of the PE fund further incentivizes managers to act in a manner that is both swift and deliberate: strategic plans must be rapidly implemented in order to realize gains in shareholder value at exit. If a PE firm struggles to realize gains from its portfolio companies, overall fund returns will undoubtedly suffer.

There continually exists a push within the PE arena to achieve returns in the top quartile of all funds targeting similar industries. If a firm achieves this accolade in one of its funds, but fails to do so in a subsequent fund, the consequences can be significant: fund-raising becomes markedly more difficult, debt interest rates may climb, and, in severe cases, the parent PE firm may go out of business.

Corporate governance is entrenched in the PE model at all levels, from portfolio company managers up through the president of the PE firm. On the whole, the PE model stands in stark contrast to the public company governance model, where directors may be appointed simply because they are friends of the CEO. Furthermore, unlike the partners in a PE firm, the board of directors in a public corporation face few consequences when shareholder value is destroyed; only in the bleakest of circumstances are directors removed from the board. In contrast, PE managers must continually achieve high returns in order to perpetuate the existence of their firms and ensure that successor funds can be raised.

PE directors are active investors in the truest sense of the term. They possess large equity stakes in the deal, and they have a constant desire for detailed knowledge of the corporation. In contrast, many large public companies have equity stakes owned by relatively passive investors such as mutual funds, who generally fail to make waves for fear of losing the parent company as a client.

Moreover, Jensen points out that, unlike a public company conglomerate, the cross-subsidization of entities within a PE fund is not permitted. All gains (save the carried interest) realized from portfolio companies must be distributed to the limited partners of a fund.[19] In this manner, the free cash flow of profitable portfolio companies cannot be used to subsidize the losses at another firm. This contractual obligation institutes strict financial discipline at the PE firm level, unlike that possessed at large conglomerates where cross-subsidization is permitted.

With respect to such contractual obligations set forth in the limited partner agreement, the recent trend by some PE firms (e.g., Blackstone, Fortress Investment Group, and Kohlberg, Kravis, Roberts & Company) to raise funds with public money may not be in the best interests of the PE industry or its portfolio companies. The push from these firms to go public has created immeasurable buzz surrounding the industry and a load of criticism for its tactics. It certainly has not helped that some of PE's magnates have been found on the cover of *Fortune* magazine, and in the pages of the *Wall Street Journal*, where details of lavish birthday parties are divulged. The publicity has incited Congress to consider raising the income taxes on the earnings of PE partners, albeit without much success as of late.

One of PE's biggest motivators, the contractually limited lifetime of funds, is lost when PE firms are allowed to raise capital through the public markets: investors cannot demand that proceeds from their investment be periodically returned to them. Moreover, the firm now must file periodic reports with the Securities and Exchange Commission and institute a higher degree of transparency in its reporting practices.

It will be interesting to see how these newly public firms perform in the ever-competitive PE arena, especially amidst the current economic woes PE portfolio companies are facing.

CONCLUSION

The PE model of governance stands in stark contrast to that of public companies. The former model permits the alignment of manager and shareholder interest through large equity stakes granted by the PE firms and imposes strict discipline on management through debt service and frequent monitoring. It remains to be seen, however, how public company PE firms will perform in light of the significant differences in corporate governance caused by the transition to public shareholding and regulation.

NOTES

1. M. Jensen, "Eclipse of the Public Corporation," *Harvard Business Review* (September–October 1989).
2. G. Anders, "An Appraisal: Buyout Funds' Rise Leads to Doubts on Their Effects," *Wall Street Journal*, August 10, 1987.
3. B. C. Ames, "Taking the Risk out of Leveraged Buyouts," *Wall Street Journal*, August 7, 1989.
4. *Id.*
5. D. Plotz, "Al Dunlap: The Chainsaw Capitalist" (1997), www.slate.com/id/1830/.
6. M. Jensen, "Eclipse of the Public Corporation," *Harvard Business Review* (September–October 1989).
7. G. Meyers, *When It Hits the Fan* (Boston: Houghton Mifflin, 1986).
8. *Id.*
9. Wharton Private Equity Review, "Finding Value in a Crowded Market," http://knowledge.wharton.upenn.edu/papers/download/PrivateEquity04262006.pdf.
10. *Id.*
11. L. Bebchuk, J. Fried, and D. Walker, "Managerial Power and Rent Extraction in the Design of Executive Compensation," *University of Chicago Law Review* 63, no. 9 (2002): 751–846.
12. *Id.*
13. *Id.*
14. *Id.*
15. J. Krol, "Driving Board Performance," *Directors Monthly* 31, no. 10: 2–5. 2007
16. K. Murphy, "Explaining Executive Compensation: Managerial Power versus the Perceived Cost of Stock Options." *University of Chicago Law Review* 63, no. 9 (2002): 847–869.
17. C. Frydman and R. Saks, "Executive Compensation: A New View from a Long-Term Perspective, 1936–2005," *Review of Financial Studies* 23, no. 5 (2010).
18. M. Jensen, "The Economic Case for Private Equity," Harvard NOM Research Paper No. 07–02, 2007.
19. *Id.*

CHAPTER 10

Value of Internal Control

James Martin
Louis Petro

Companies at the leading edge of discovering additional value in internal controls have developed techniques proven to drive more predictable revenue, minimize outstanding receivables, reduce operational costs, and even improve a company's performance.
—David R. Campbell et al.[1]

INTRODUCTION

Emphasis on strong internal control has been amplified across organizations of all sizes in recent years. Most notably, regulation such as Section 404 of the Sarbanes-Oxley Act of 2002 (SOX) and subsequently the Public Company Accounting Oversight Board's (PCAOB's) adoption of Auditing Standard No. 5 (AS 5), which together require all publicly registered firms in the United States to receive an audit of management's assessment of the effectiveness of internal control over financial reporting. Though the Dodd-Frank Wall Street and Consumer Protection Act of 2010 exempted some small, publicly traded firms (aka nonaccelerated filers) from portions of Section 404, Section 404 remains a significant element of securities law, and many of its implications have trickled down to private firms.

This chapter will focus on the value of internal control, for both the private equity (PE) firm, and the PE firm's target companies. Internal control will be considered from an operational improvement perspective, financial reporting perspective, and compliance perspective. When internal control is considered in this holistic approach, the value added for PE firms through effective internal controls can be realized.

INTRODUCTION TO COSO AND INTERNAL CONTROL

Internal control has been defined in a variety of ways; in essence, it often has different meanings to different people and when considered in different applications. The gold standard of internal control for organizations is the Committee of Sponsoring Organizations of the Treadway Commission (COSO) publication "Internal Control—Integrated Framework." In fact, 63 percent of publicly held companies utilize the COSO framework of internal control.[2]

COSO Background

COSO was formed in 1985 as a private sector initiative to sponsor the National Commission on Fraudulent Financial Reporting. COSO is sponsored and funded by five major professional associations: the American Accounting Association, the American Institute of Certified Public Accountants (AICPA), Financial Executives International; the Institute of Internal Auditors (IIA), and the Institute of Management Accountants. Originally, COSO was organized to study the causal factors that can lead to fraudulent financial reporting and develop recommendations for public companies and their independent auditors for the Securities and Exchange Commission and other regulators, and for educational institutions.[3]

Since COSO's inception in the mid-1980s, it has published seven major reports:

1. *The National Commission on Fraudulent Financial Reporting* (1987)
2. *Internal Control—Integrated Framework* (1992)
3. *Internal Control Issues in Derivatives Usage* (1996)
4. *Fraudulent Financial Reporting, 1987–1997: An Analysis of U.S. Public Companies* (1999)
5. *Enterprise Risk Management—Integrated Framework* (2004)
6. *Internal Control over Financial Reporting—Guidance for Smaller Public Companies* (2006)
7. *Guidance on Monitoring Internal Control Systems* (2009)

Furthermore, at the end of 2010, COSO "announced a project to update its 1992 Internal Control – Integrated Framework."[4]

Internal Control Defined

COSO defines internal control as "a process, effected by an entity's board of directors, management and other personnel, designed to provide reasonable assurance regarding the achievement of objectives in the following categories: effectiveness and efficiency of operations; reliability of financial reporting; and, compliance with applicable laws and regulations."[5] This definition is intended to mirror four underlying concepts:

1. *Processes.* Internal control is a process (or a multiplicity of processes), a chain of activities, not a singular event or activity. As such, it is subject to change over time and must be properly maintained to remain effective.
2. *People.* Internal control is affected by people at all levels of an organization, and people's actions are affected by internal control.
3. *Reasonable assurance.* Internal control cannot provide absolute assurance to management regarding execution of organizational objectives but can offer reasonable assurance to that end.
4. *Objectives.* Internal control is designed for the accomplishment of an entity's objectives specifically related to operations, financial reporting, and compliance.[6]

It should be noted that no two organizations will (or should) have the same system of internal control. Management's philosophy, the size of the organization, the industry, the level of automation and technology, among others, are all factors that lead to custom systems of internal control. Every organization's internal control system shares the same five components (discussed in the next section) as every other system, but no two will be the same.

COMPONENTS OF INTERNAL CONTROL

Internal control is composed of five complementary and interrelated components that are developed from and integrated with the management process. The five components are intended to permeate all business operations and levels within an organization. All five components must exist and function in order for an organization to attain effective internal controls. Exhibit 10.1 illustrates the relationship of the five components of internal control: control environment, risk assessment, control activities, information and communication, and monitoring.[7]

Control Environment

The control environment component of internal control includes the tone at the top set by management and incorporates elements that influence and

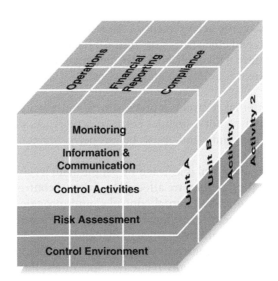

EXHIBIT 10.1   COSO Model of Internal Control
Source: COSO-Internal Control, Integrated
Framework.

support the other internal control components. In essence, the control environment is the foundation that establishes the parameters for which all internal control components operate, an organizational "moral code" of sorts. The control environment encompasses management's philosophy and operating style, management's assignment of authority and responsibility, board involvement, and the organization and development of people within the organization. An internal control system is most effective when it is embedded within the organizational culture through the control environment.[8]

Elements of an effective control environment incorporate activities in support of the organization's objectives, including a competent workforce, integrity across the organization, established and documented policies and procedures, a positive tone at the top, whistleblower protection, fraud deterrence initiatives, compensation programs, and a code of conduct[9] (see Exhibit 10.2). A common thread interwoven among these activities is accountability and integrity.

The COSO model incorporates a number of factors included in the control environment. While all of the factors are important, an organization's characteristics must be considered in determining which factors to emphasize. These factors include:

- *Integrity and ethical values.* The control culture of the organization permeates the organization, and guides employees even in the absence of

EXHIBIT 10.2 Internal Control Components
Source: Adapted from COSO-Internal Control, Integrated Framework.

explicit procedures. The organization's standards of behavior must be supported by management's integrity and commitment to ethical values.

■ *Incentives and temptations.* Minimizing incentives (e.g., pressure to meet targets, performance based rewards, etc.) and temptations (e.g., poor controls, segregation between management and lower levels, etc.) for employees to engage in unethical behavior is a sign of a strong control environment.

■ *Providing and communicating moral guidance.* An organization that exemplifies moral and ethical leadership and communicates these values to employees, often through codes of conduct, likely possesses moral and ethical employees.

■ *Commitment to competence.* Job functions should have specified skill requirements (experience, training, etc.) and positions should be filled by people whose skills match the job's requirements.

■ *Board of directors/audit committee.* An experienced, involved, and independent board of directors and audit committee are all positive factors affecting the control environment.

■ *Management's philosophy and operating style.* Management's risk tolerance, attitudes toward financial reporting, and conservatism toward accounting treatment of transactions all contribute to the control environment.

■ *Organizational structure.* Defining and establishing an appropriate organizational structure through identifying essential functions of authority and responsibility and creating channels for reporting contribute to developing an effective structure.

- *Assignment of authority and responsibility.* Job functions and authority levels should be aligned. Delegation of management-level responsibility should be undertaken only with increased monitoring of results.
- *Human resource policies and practices.* Human resource policies (including compensation) should be designed to reward employees for hard work, uphold a positive morale, and foster an environment whereby employees actively work toward the prosperity of the organization.

Risk Assessment

Following the start of the economic crisis in 2008, the government moved to reduce financial system risks through legislation. For example, the Dodd-Frank Wall Street and Consumer Protection Act of 2010 requires financial services institutions to collect and report on risk exposure in their business. The risk assessment process, however, extends far beyond financial sector firms.

The risk assessment component of internal control relates to an organization's continuous survey of the business environment to identify any risks or threats (internal or external) to the organization's ability to achieve its business objectives and to establish an understanding of how to manage those risks. Risk cannot be reduced to zero, as there are inherent risks in every organization. Effective risk assessment should be a perpetual process where potential risks are identified at every level of the organization and communicated to appropriate levels of management. Other risks, such as strategic risks, are more likely to be assessed at the executive and board level and are typically identified annually or on another periodic basis.[10]

The first step in a risk assessment is the identification of potential threats to the organization. Risk identification is the process by which an organization determines potential risks without evaluating the threat. This is usually accomplished during the planning process and includes identification of entity- and activity-level risks. All levels of the organization should be included in the risk identification process. For example, senior-level employees will be an asset in identifying strategic risks, and entity-level employees will be valuable in identifying operational risks. Consideration of both internal (e.g., communication methods, effectiveness of internal control activities, employee training and competence, etc.) and external risks (e.g., regulatory changes, competition, customer and supplier relationships, etc.) is also important in an effective risk identification process.

Once risks have been identified, an organization must evaluate those risks. Each risk should be analyzed based on its impact and its likelihood. *Impact* refers to the effect the risk occurrence would have on the organization if it were to happen. *Likelihood* refers to the chance that the risk occurrence will actually happen. Any identified risk that is high impact and high likelihood would require prioritized attention and remediation. Likewise, an identified risk that is low impact and low likelihood would receive lower priority for action. After determining the significance of a particular risk, management must determine how to address the risk (i.e., reduce its impact or reduce its likelihood). Reducing a risk's impact can typically be achieved by detective and corrective controls, and reducing its likelihood can be achieved by preventative controls. This must, of course, be done with cost-benefit considerations and the organization's risk tolerance in mind.

Finally, risks can be assessed as either an inherent risk or residual risk. An inherent risk is the amount of risk present before any control procedures have been applied. Residual risk is the remaining risk after a control activity has been executed. Nearly all inherent risks will be assessed as high impact, high likelihood because the evaluation of inherent risk is performed without considering controls. Assessing residual risk typically involves determining the effectiveness of current control activities that are in place to achieve low-impact and low-likelihood results.

Enterprise Risk Management

Enterprise risk management (ERM) is an entity-wide process for analyzing the risks an organization may encounter, including financial, operational, and compliance risks. The COSO 2004 publication, *Enterprise Risk Management—Integrated Framework*, defines ERM as follows:

> *Enterprise risk management is a process, effected by an entity's board of directors, management and other personnel, applied in strategy setting and across the enterprise, designed to identify potential events that may affect the entity, and manage risk to be within its risk appetite, to provide reasonable assurance regarding the achievement of entity objectives.*[11]

ERM is a continuous process that helps an organization achieve continuous improvement. Just as the internal control–integrated framework must be incorporated throughout all levels of an entity, ERM involves all levels of the organization. This is imperative, as the objective of a comprehensive analysis of an organization's risk can be achieved only through cooperation at every organizational level. According to COSO's ERM framework, ERM includes the following concepts:

- *Aligning risk tolerance and strategy.* Strategic decisions, organizational objectives, and risk management should be consistent with management's risk tolerance
- *Enhancing risk response decisions.* Risk responses include risk avoidance, reduction, sharing, and acceptance.
- *Reducing operational surprises and losses.* ERM increases an organization's ability to identify potential risks on the horizon, thereby increasing preparedness and reducing unexpected losses.
- *Identifying and managing multiple and cross-enterprise risks.* Risks that affect multiple units within an organization are more easily managed through integrated responses.
- *Seizing opportunities.* Because management utilizes an enterprise-wide approach with ERM, areas for opportunity and growth are more easily identified.
- *Improving deployment of capital.* Areas within an organization with capital needs are identified through increased information flow, thereby allowing more efficient capital deployment.[12]

These ERM characteristics allow management greater organizational transparency through information flow in regard to operations, financial reporting, and compliance. The information flow results from entity-wide participation in a comprehensive risk analysis. ERM allows management to proactively identify and remediate potential obstacles in the path of achieving organizational objectives (see Exhibit 10.3).

Control Activities

Control activities are most closely aligned with common understanding of internal control. Control activities are the documented policies and procedures that ensure that an organization's objectives are carried out. The processes and subprocesses, as directed by management, for accomplishing organizational objectives are defined within control activities. In essence, control activities are the "how to" guide and blueprint for performing functions of the business. Control activities cannot be considered in a vacuum; even the most detailed control activities are only as effective as the monitoring process that ensures they are functioning.

Due to the dynamic nature of business processes, documented control activities can become obsolete if left stagnant. Organizational units should be encouraged to identify changes to business processes that will result in improved results (efficient and effective operations, asset protection, and

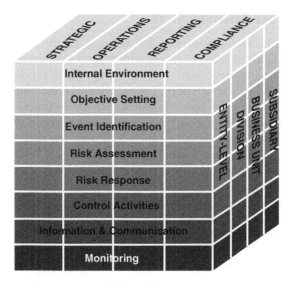

EXHIBIT 10.3 COSO Model—Enterprise Risk
Management
Source: COSO-Enterprise Risk Management,
Integrated Framework.

compliance with laws and regulations); however, management must define
a process to ensure the changes are evaluated and properly documented
prior to implementation.

Control activities are usually categorized into five specific activities:

1. *Separation of duties.* Processes are analyzed and duties assigned
   to appropriate personnel to separate custody and record-keeping
   responsibility.
2. *Proper authorization of transactions and activities.* All transactions
   must be authorized either generally (organization-wide policies for all
   transactions) or specifically (management authorization for individual
   transactions not covered in organization-wide policies)
3. *Adequate documents and records.* Documents and records must be
   adequately maintained and sufficient to provide reasonable assurance
   that events are controlled and recorded.
4. *Physical control over assets and records.* Assets and records must be
   properly protected and maintained.
5. *Independent checks on performance.* Independent, internal verification
   of the previous four control activities is necessary for proper internal
   control.[13]

Information and Communication

Information and communication are integral to properly functioning internal control. Management utilizes information to make operational and strategic decisions, while lower-level employees require certain information in order to perform their activities. Proper channels of communication are necessary to facilitate the flow of information to decision makers. These channels can be both formal and informal communication channels. Most importantly, information must be timely and accurate in order to be most effective: in short, data must have integrity.

Another key element of effective internal control is open communication. Employees at all levels of the organization should be encouraged to notify management regarding process improvement, reporting issues, identification of risks, or inappropriate behavior. Specifically, confidential anonymous reporting and whistleblower protection should be available to all employees. In fact, Section 301 of SOX requires public companies to establish procedures for confidential anonymous reporting of issues regarding questionable accounting or auditing matters.[14]

In addition to openness, information and communication should not be a one-way channel. Information must flow downstream from managers to operations, providing management directives and maximizing operations' activities. Likewise, information must also flow upstream from operations to management, detailing performance and giving feedback to management directives. Furthermore, effective communication with external parties (i.e., customers, suppliers, advisors, etc.) is essential for adequate internal control.

Nearly every organization facilitates information flow through information technology (IT) systems. It is essential for organizations to design and implement adequate internal control over IT systems to ensure information accuracy. The industry's gold standard for IT control was published by the Information Systems Audit and Control Association (ISACA). The ISACA model, Control Objectives for Information and Related Technology (COBIT), was designed in order to provide control objectives for IT processes related to information dissemination requisite for achieving organizational objectives.[15]

Monitoring

Monitoring is an ongoing internal control component that ensures internal control procedures are properly functioning and remain effective. It also verifies that all transactions are processed appropriately. Furthermore, monitoring is the internal control component that ensures an organization's internal control system remains relevant due to the dynamic nature of transactions.

Because of constant change in technology, monitoring of IT controls is integral to an effective internal control system. ISACA's COBIT model includes monitoring procedures and implementation guides to assist management with IT monitoring. The COBIT model provides management with guidance in evaluating IT in the following ways:

- Monitoring the process
- Assessing internal control adequacy
- Obtaining independent assurance
- Providing for independent audit[16]

Ensuring that internal control procedures are properly functioning and remain effective is a key aspect of monitoring. Section 404 of SOX requires this aspect of monitoring (verification of performance of control procedures) for all public companies. Though an auditor attestation pertaining to management's assessment of internal control over financial reporting is not required for nonaccelerated filers (who were recently provided exemption under the Dodd-Frank Wall Street and Consumer Protection Act), managers of these firms should view internal control with no less importance. Furthermore, while the provisions of Section 404 do not apply to private firms, it is considered best practice to ensure that internal control procedures are properly functioning.

There are many approaches management can undertake to verify that control procedures are effective and employees are properly performing them, including

- *Interviews.* Interviews of employees should reveal any deviation from expected process performance. Any variations in the process should be reviewed for appropriateness and either remediated or documented as a process improvement.
- *Process walk-throughs.* In a process walk-through, observations should be made to verify that processes are performed as described in process descriptions and interviews. Any deviation from the process should be assessed in terms of its impact on internal control.
- *Corroboration.* Information gathered in the interview and process walk-through should be corroborated to verify that process descriptions, employee accounts, and actual process execution are aligned.
- *External corroboration.* External parties can be valuable resources in verifying internal processes. Vendors and customers alike can provide independent information about the actual processing execution in an organization.[17]

Monitoring should also incorporate transaction verification. Transaction verification will monitor the integrity of transactional outputs of a system. Independent reconciliation of account balances is an excellent example of transaction verification. Reconciliations should be completed regularly, and any irregularities identified in the reconciliation process should be brought to the attention of management in a timely fashion. In addition, many accounting and information systems have automated monitoring capabilities that can be leveraged to identify irregular or inconsistent transactions.

As a part of the monitoring component, internal control evaluation should be overseen by an organization's audit committee. The audit committee should be responsible for determining the scope and frequency of internal control system evaluation. The audit committee will then direct the evaluation activities to internal audit during the annual internal audit planning process. The internal audit function serves as the primary monitoring activity of management. One essential characteristic of the internal audit is independence from management. The internal audit should report to the audit committee due to potential conflict of interest issues between internal audit and management.[18]

Limitations of Internal Control

As with almost any organizational initiative, there are inherent limitations to COSO's internal control framework. The extent to which any organization's internal control system is effective is limited to those individuals designing, implementing, and performing the controls. Individuals within an organization must be aware of their responsibilities and limits of authority. This can potentially limit the effectiveness of the internal control system due to suspect judgment, decision making, and human error. Moreover, implementing internal controls must be considered within the constraints of their costs and benefits; the relative costs of implementing a particular control must not outweigh the benefits of its implementation.

Internal control is also limited by external forces that cannot be controlled by the organization such as natural disasters, changes in the regulatory environment, and adverse marketplace events external to the firm. Properly designed internal control systems will, however, provide reasonable assurance that management will be made aware of these events in a timely manner and will facilitate remediation processes.

Other limitations of internal control include collusion of two or more people and management override of the internal control system. In order to be effective, the internal control system needs to be aligned with the organization's objectives such that performance of control activities necessary to achieve the objectives is properly designed, implemented, and executed.

CONTROL OBJECTIVES AND
CONTROL COMPONENTS

There is a direct relationship between control objectives and control components (as illustrated in Exhibit 10.4). Control objectives (represented by the vertical columns in Exhibit 10.4) are what an organization works to achieve. The objectives are subdivided into three categories: operations, financial reporting, and compliance. Control components define the control procedures and processes necessary in order for an organization to accomplish its control objectives. As discussed above, the five control components (represented by rows in Exhibit 10.4) include control environment, risk assessment, control activities, information and communication, and monitoring. The third dimension of Exhibit 10.4 represents different activities and units within an organization.

For example, consider the standard organizational control objective of accurate financial reporting related to collecting all valid accounts receivable. Control procedures that an organization could implement in order to achieve the stated control objective might include (1) proposing to write off accounts receivable only after all collection activities have been exhausted; (2) requiring management approval for all write-offs of accounts receivable;

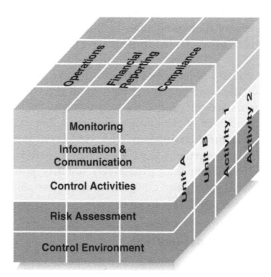

EXHIBIT 10.4   COSO Model of Control
Source: COSO-Internal Control, Integrated
Framework.

and (3) monitoring all write-offs. The first control procedure would ensure that accounts receivable are truly uncollectible before initiating a write-off. The second procedure ensures that management agrees with the determination of delinquency on the account and verifies that all collection efforts have been exhausted. The third procedure allows management to detect any trends or similarities in write-offs to learn about how the accounts became uncollectible and should detect unauthorized write-offs.

As diagramed in Exhibit 10.4, each control objective and control component is interrelated. Building on the previous example of collecting accounts receivable, the diagram and relationship can be further developed. As previously mentioned, collection of all valid accounts receivable is a financial reporting objective. To achieve the objective of receivables collection, the following control components could be utilized:

- Management must monitor receivable write-offs (monitoring).
- Information related to write-offs must be accurate and properly communicated (information and communication).
- Management must approve a specific write-off and document the approval (control activities).
- The impact and likelihood of improper receivables write-offs would be assessed by management prior to assigning the responsibility to employees (risk assessment).
- Management's attitude toward proper treatment of accounting transactions would ensure that competent, high-integrity individuals are handling receivables write-offs (control environment).

Just as each control objective applies to the five control components, each of the five control components applies to all three control objectives. Control components are relevant to the entire entity, each activity or unit within an entity, and each of the entity's objectives. For example, consider the risk assessment control component. Risk assessment is necessary for effective operations management (i.e., evaluate potential process breakdowns), financial reporting (i.e., proactively identify potential areas for financial misrepresentation), and compliance (i.e., assessment and evaluation of regulatory risks applicable to an entity).

Effectiveness of Internal Control

Much of the discussion has centered on the effectiveness of internal control. The idea of effectiveness of internal control cannot be unilaterally applied across all organizations. Furthermore, effectiveness is not an "on-off" switch; there are varying levels and shades of gray. An internal control can be deemed effective at one time and ineffective at a different time. However, an internal control can be deemed effective if it provides management reasonable assurance that

- They have measurable knowledge of how the organization's objectives are being accomplished.
- Financial statements are reliable.
- Conformation with laws and regulations is achieved.[19]

The measurement of internal control effectiveness is subjective. This exemplifies the importance of unique assessments at all organizations and units. Furthermore, with the constantly changing nature of business processes, the effectiveness of internal control will be subject to change, too. However, with an effective internal control system, changes will be monitored and assessment will become a routine function of the organization.

INTERNAL CONTROL AND THE PRIVATE EQUITY FIRM

The value of internal control for a PE firm can be separated into two different focuses: firm value in its fund operations and value of internal control in portfolio companies. Each of these focuses will be examined in terms of the three components of internal control (operations, financial reporting, and compliance); however, the most attention will be given to operations and operational improvement perspective. An effective internal control system provides PE firms a market leadership position related to increasingly effective operations, highly reliable financial reporting, and industry-leading compliance programs.[20]

Value of Internal Control for Private Equity Fund Operations

Effective fund-level internal controls help PE firms in the achievement of objectives. In terms of operational objectives, internal control refers to the effective and efficient consumption of resources. For financial reporting, internal control provides for consistent and reliable financial reports. Finally, with regard to compliance objectives, internal control calls for an identification of regulatory and industry compliance requirements and procedures necessary to reasonably assure that compliance is achieved.[21]

Motivation for effective internal control implementation at the fund level should be considered first. Understanding the "why" will assist in discussing the benefits. There are many obvious benefits to internal control that are at the micro level; however, the main focus will be on the macro value. In a report published by the IIA, five major benefits of control improvement were identified:[22]

1. *Identification of complexities in fiscal year-end closing and journal entry posting processes.* PE funds must have accurate financial reporting in order for managers (and investors) to properly understand returns on investment, value portfolio assets, measure performance of portfolio company teams, and so on.
2. *Increased fraud prevention activities.* Potential investors value firms with strong antifraud initiatives, improved firm image, and perception.
3. *Improved control and control process documentation and evaluation.* Firms will experience easier employee transitions in new job functions, especially valuable in an industry with high job turnover at analyst levels, and facilitation of easy metrics in order to measure performance of business objectives.
4. *Stronger entity-wide control definition and understanding of the control-risk relationship.* Firms that identify and prioritize risks are less susceptible to losses associated with risk activities. Control implementation to mitigate risks achieves this goal.
5. *Encourage a back-to-the-basics approach to controls that may have otherwise been lost due to increasing organizational complexities.* As firms and their funds become larger and more complex, simple controls are often overlooked for the sake of growth. Firms that reevaluate their controls and return to the basics are less likely to run into speed bumps when performing objectives.

The IIA study details five main benefits for control improvement. This study was actually written in response to Section 404 of SOX from research for the benefits of Section 404 implementation at public companies. The key to the report is that the benefits of internal control improvement are real, regardless of whether done as a regulatory mandate like SOX or at any firm looking for operational improvement.

In the PE arena, there is also a need for a sensory device to perceive changes internally and externally at PE funds. This is especially appropriate in PE funds with the complex function of managing many investments simultaneously. Effective internal control system implementation satisfies this need. As previously discussed, each internal control component assists in achieving organizational objectives. With regard to a sensory device within a PE fund, each control component can be easily seen supporting this objective:

- *Control environment.* Fund managers must identify and communicate to the organization that change perception is integral to the fund's success. Employees must be sufficiently trained and competent to recognize changes relevant to the fund.
- *Risk assessment.* Risk assessment is a sensory mechanism in its own right; internal and external threats to the fund are identified and evaluated, and procedures to mitigate these threats are established.
- *Control activities.* Control activities can be either preventative or detective. Preventative control activities are implemented to minimize the chance of threats; detective control activities will "sound the alarm" (i.e., sense) when a specific desired or undesired event occurs.
- *Information and communication.* Management must provide open channels of communication between management and employees for identification of change throughout the firm. Communication between a firm and external parties (limited partners, portfolio companies, etc.) is perhaps the most important method for sensing changes.
- *Monitoring.* Monitoring provides for independent assessment of a firm's operations and performance, detecting where change should be considered or is already occurring.

Perhaps the two most valuable applications of internal control for PE funds are operational improvement and risk management assessment. "Combining business process improvement with [SOX] internal control efforts allows companies to benefit from reengineered business processes, resulting in fewer controls and better downstream business performance."[23] For PE funds, operational improvement translates as efficiency in identifying and evaluating potential portfolio companies. Risk assessment should incorporate the process to identify not only the riskiness of individual investments and portfolios, but also the risk of losing key personnel, market conditions (e.g. changing interest rates, potential regulatory involvement with PE, etc.), or saturation of the PE market due to increased competition.

Value and the Control Environment

PE firms can best derive value from the control environment component of internal control with effective leadership from the board and executives. Leadership should focus on ethics, integrity, and accountability and be entrenched in a firm's culture. In fact, companies with an explicit commitment to ethical standards have been shown to outperform those companies that do not.[24] In addition, human resources policies should be clearly defined and ensure that job functions and individual competencies correspond.

Value and Risk

As identified by the PCAOB, a risk-based approach is one of the most important aspects of an effective internal control system. One major reason a risk-based approach is so important is that it requires an analysis of costs in relation to benefits of internal control. A risk-based approach focuses on those controls that are key controls in determining which controls are tested. This approach ensures that the most important, or "key," controls are tested first thereby giving a firm more bang for its buck.

Another area of value for PE funds related to risk is the implementation of a firm- and fund-level chief risk officer or a risk committee. Few PE firms have these positions today, as many PE professionals assign responsibility for risk mitigation to the general partners and associates in charge of a deal. However, by possessing a centralized chief risk officer or risk committee, a PE firm may be able to more easily perceive risks across the firm's funds, and better analyze the correlation between risky events.

Value and Control Activities

A firm with well-designed and well-implemented control activities can leverage these items into a continuous improvement strategy. A firm that already knows (and has documented) how it accomplishes its objectives will be much more prepared to improve on the processes than a firm that does not. In knowing how objectives are accomplished, areas for improvement are easily identified. Employees with well-defined process functions will have more time to identify ways to improve the efficiency of their tasks.

Preventative controls are more closely associated with business process improvement than detective controls. This is consistent with the idea that proactive firms are better positioned for success than reactive firms. Firms with strong preventative controls have redesigned the business processes in order to deter process breakdowns. The process redesign leads to identification of operational deficiencies and opportunities for increased efficiency. Furthermore, automation of controls and the use of technology are hallmarks of operational improvement through internal control.

Value and Information and Communication

Value and a PE firm's perception are greatly influenced by its information and communication. Communication between the firm and limited partners needs to be timely and accurate in order to maintain investor relations. Operationally speaking, information needs to be appropriately communicated throughout the firm in order to achieve objectives. Firms should encourage open communication among internal auditors, management, and external auditors. Information management is also a valuable aspect of internal control. Without proper information management, virtual mountains of data are compiled, often overwhelming managers responsible for utilizing the information. Use of executive dashboards can assist management in distilling data down to useful metrics.

Value and Monitoring

Monitoring is most valuable when utilizing leading indicators, which provide for time for remediation, rather than lagging indicators, which do not.[25] Much like the discussion of preventative and detective controls, leading indicators are typically more valuable because they allow for proactive efforts to remediate potential concerns, keeping the firm on its toes. Monitoring is also most valuable when internal information is integrated with external information.[26]

One valuable method of monitoring for firms is the use of questionnaires and surveys to determine the efficiency of business processes. As a part of continuous operational improvement, questionnaires and surveys can assist management in determining the functioning and efficiency of existing processes by providing feedback from downstream employees. Employees with operational responsibilities typically have knowledge of how processes can be improved or where they are dysfunctional. The key for success in continuous improvement is leveraging value from previous accomplishments; this can be achieved through effective monitoring.

Value of Internal Control for Target Companies

In an acquisition decision, PE firms have a multitude of measurements that eventually result in a firm's perceived value of a target company. One such measurement should be the value of an effective internal control system in place at the target company. Although the actual value attributed to a specific target company's internal control system is extremely subjective and must be determined on a case-by-case basis, there are certain aspects that should be considered in the value proposition. Just as the value of internal control for a PE firm's internal operations focused on the three objectives of internal control (operations, financial reporting, and compliance), so too will the value of target companies' internal control systems. Moreover, when all other aspects are equal, a target company with an effective internal control system will be more valuable than a target company without an effective internal control system.

Operational Value

Consider the value of internal control with respect to a target company and operations. In the acquisition of a target company, a PE firm is buying more than merely the bricks and mortar and inventory. In most cases, what a PE firm is really buying is a process. The physical assets of a target company are generally not sustainable sources of revenue (with obvious exceptions of certain organizations such as a mining company). As an example, consider a global logistics company like FedEx or UPS. The value in those companies does not lie in delivery trucks or commercial jets (although there is significant value there), but rather in the processes implemented that enable FedEx or UPS to pick up a package at an office in a U.S. city this morning and have it delivered to an international city the next day. Any organization with sufficient monetary resources can acquire trucks, planes, warehouses, and the like, but only a handful of organizations have developed processes to deliver and support online tracking of packages so (seemingly) easily. Clearly, the value in these firms is in the process.

Similar to the preceding example, PE firms must be able to assess the effectiveness of a target company's operational process. When a target company is acquired, the process in place will determine how quickly a transition can be made under new management brought in by the PE firm. If operational processes are not in place, the new management must assess and gain an understanding of operations and then determine their effectiveness, a time-consuming and costly undertaking. Effective and well-documented procedures will help mitigate potential hurdles associated with a target company whose business processes are heavily dependent on a few key people likely to depart once an acquisition takes place. If a target company has well-documented processes for operations, an assessment can be achieved in significantly less time, with considerably fewer resources. Additionally, if a PE firm can identify a potential target company with effective operational processes, a more seamless transition can occur.

In the simplest form, when a PE firm is able to understand a target company's operations prior to acquisition, there should be no surprises after acquisition. Avoiding surprises reduces the risk of an investment. Reducing risk decreases the volatility in return on investment or internal rate of return (and increases likelihood of a positive return) for a PE firm and the limited partners. Avoiding surprises also reduces the time necessary to harvest an investment, another valuable benefit that directly impacts a firm's rate of return.

Financial Reporting Value

In addition to the value internal control systems add to a target company's operations, there exist many valuable benefits for financial reporting processes. First and foremost, PE firms must be able to effectively evaluate financial information presented by a target company. Without reliance on financial information, a PE firm is left without one of the most utilized objective methods for valuing a target company.

Target company financial reporting is only as useful as it is accurate. Without adequate internal controls over financial reporting, a PE firm will not be able to reasonably rely on a target company's financial statements. This concept is actually the foundation behind SOX Section 404. Regulators sought to increase the reliability in public company financial reporting by mandating that the processes used to develop the amounts reported on the financials are operating effectively. Likewise, if a PE firm cannot be assured of a target company's controls over financial reporting, the firm cannot be assured of the outputs of a dysfunctional control system. If a PE firm were to rely on financial information output from a dysfunctional control system, improper information could lead to inappropriate decisions.

The value of internal control systems related to financial reporting is in the reasonable assurance that information relied upon to make investment decisions is accurate. In order to make sound acquisitions, PE firms cannot discover two years down the road that certain previously relied upon financial statements were incorrect. The entire equity investment could be erased in this scenario. Thus, to reduce risks associated with relying on improper financial information, PE firms should properly consider the importance and value of effective internal control systems related to financial reporting.

Compliance Value

One final area of value for private companies in internal control systems related to target companies is that of the compliance objective. Compliance objectives and related control procedures are controls that ensure a target company adheres to all applicable laws and regulations. Furthermore, a target company must meet all industry requirements, loan covenants, and any other relevant obligations. Effective compliance control procedures at a target company should leave a PE firm reasonably certain that the company is in compliance.

Perhaps the most important issue for a PE firm in terms of compliance of target companies relates to the PE's exit strategy for a particular investment. If a PE firm intends to harvest a target company through an initial public offering or sell the target company to an existing public company, there are many additional compliance requirements. The cost of compliance with these exit strategies must be considered when determining a value for a target company. If a target company is engaged in best practices and is compliant to the extent of public company requirements, there can be significant value to the PE firm.

Whichever harvest strategy a PE firm desires for a target company, there is value in procedures related to compliance objectives. Compliance initiatives are usually implemented to increase transparency in a company. The more transparent a target company is, the easier and more comfortable a valuation is for a PE firm as well as a potential acquirer. Additionally, target companies with compliance procedures already in place broaden the scale of harvest opportunities.

CONCLUSION

Despite the fact that certain statutory regulations requiring public companies to address internal control have not been mandated in the PE arena, PE firms would be wise to identify and implement internal control initiatives. As shown, many valuable elements of public company regulations have trickled down to private firms with numerous benefits.

There is considerable value in internal controls, for both the PE firm and the PE firm's target companies.

NOTES

1. David R. Campbell et al., "Adding Significant Value with Internal Controls," *CPA Journal* (June 2006).
2. Larry E. Rittenberg and Patricia K. Miller, "Sarbanes-Oxley Section 404 Work: Looking at the Benefits," *IIA Research Foundation* (January 2005).
3. Committee of Sponsoring Organizations of the Treadway Commission, November 1, 2007, www.coso.org.
4. *Source:* http://www.coso.org/aboutus.htm.
5. Committee of Sponsoring Organizations of the Treadway Commission, *Internal Control—Integrated Framework* (AICPA Publications Division, 1994).

6. *Id.*
7. *Id.*
8. *Id.*
9. Harry Cendrowski et al., *The Handbook of Fraud Deterrence* (Hoboken, NJ: John Wiley & Sons, 2007).
10. *Id.*
11. Committee of Sponsoring Organizations of the Treadway Commission, *Enterprise Risk Management—Integrated Framework* (AICPA Publications Division, 2004).
12. *Id.*
13. Alvin A. Arens et al., *Auditing and Assurance Services: An Integrated Approach* (Upper Saddle River, NJ: Prentice Hall, 2005).
14. Sarbanes-Oxley Act of 2002, Publication No. 107–204, 116 Stat. 745 (codified as amended in scattered sections of 15 U.S.C.).
15. Information Systems Audit and Control Association, *COBIT 4.1 Executive Summary*, November 1, 2007, www.isaca.org/AMTemplate.cfm?Section=Downloads&Template=/ContentManagement/ContentDisplay.cfm&ContentID=34172.
16. COBIT Steering Committee and the IT Governance Institute, *COBIT*, 4th ed. Available at www.isaca.org.
17. *Id.*
18. *Id.*
19. *Id.*
20. *Id.*
21. *Id.*
22. *Id.*
23. *Id.*
24. Simon Webley and Elise More, "Does Business Ethics Pay?" *Institute of Business Ethics* (April 2003).
25. *Id.*
26. *Id.*

CHAPTER 11

Internal Control Evaluation

Harry Cendrowski
Louis W. Petro

INTRODUCTION

The U.S. Companies Accounting Reform and Investor Protection Act of 2002, commonly referred to as the Sarbanes-Oxley Act of 2002 (SOX), requires that both the chief executive officer and chief financial officer of a publicly held company (Securities and Exchange Commission [SEC] registrant) certify the effectiveness of the company's internal control system. They are to certify

- Their responsibility for establishing, maintaining, and evaluating financial reporting controls and procedures.
- That a process exists to assure that all significant internal control deficiencies, material internal control weaknesses, or significant changes in internal controls and the procedures for financial reporting have been disclosed to the company's audit committee.

Companies must establish financial reporting controls and procedures to gather, analyze, and report events, uncertainties, conditions, and contingencies that could materially affect the operating results of the enterprise in order to provide the shareholders with an internal view of the company.

Section 404 of SOX (SOX 404) requires that the management of a publicly held corporation include a report on the corporation's internal control system in their annual reports to shareholders and the SEC. Though the Dodd-Frank Wall Street Reform and Consumer Protection Act of 2010 exempted auditors of small companies from opining on management's assessment of internal control, internal controls remain a paramount risk management tool for public and private companies. Management's report on internal control should present the following:

- A statement of management responsibility for the establishment and maintenance of adequate internal control over financial reporting
- A statement disclosing the process used by management to evaluate internal control effectiveness
- Management's assessment of internal control effectiveness at the end of the fiscal year being reported on
- Disclosure of any material internal control weaknesses (defined below)
- A statement that the company's independent auditor has issued a report on management's assessment of internal control effectiveness

A *material internal control weakness* is a significant deficiency or combination of significant deficiencies that result in more than a remote likelihood that a material misstatement will not be prevented or detected.[1]

SOX 404 requires that the independent auditor of a publicly held corporation (save those of nonaccelerated filers) attest to and report on management's assessment of the effectiveness of the corporation's internal controls over financial reporting. Internal control over financial reporting is defined in SOX 404 as "a process designed by, or under the supervision of, the principal executive and principal financial officers, and effected by the board of directors and management, to provide reasonable assurance regarding the reliability of financial reporting and the preparation of financial statements for external purposes in accordance with generally accepted accounting principles. It includes those policies and procedures for maintaining accounting records, authorizing receipts and disbursements, and safeguarding assets." The role of the independent auditor in evaluating management's assessment of the effectiveness of internal control over financial reporting is specified in the Public Company Accounting Oversight Board (PCAOB) Auditing Standard No. 5, "An Audit of Internal Controls over Financial Reporting that Is Integrated with an Audit of Financial Statements" (AS 5).

Though designed for auditors, AS 5 provides valuable guidance to PE firms when assessing a potential portfolio company's internal controls. PE general partners are not auditors; they can, however, gain insight into portfolio companies by utilizing best practices from the auditing field. Furthermore, the provisions of SOX 404 can be utilized by PE firms as best practices once a portfolio company is under their stewardship, or in conjunction with AS 5 in performing portfolio company due diligence. This best practice framework serves as the motivation for this chapter.

Additionally, this chapter presents PE professionals with an understanding of auditors' work, enabling them to further comprehend how auditors arrive at decisions in evaluating internal control.

When evaluating a company as a potential investment, a PE firm should be concerned with the effectiveness of that company's internal control over financial reporting. Therefore, a PE firm's assessment of the potential investment's internal control effectiveness in such a situation would be greatly enhanced by the availability of both the investment's management report on internal control effectiveness and the investment's independent auditor's report on internal control.

If an independent auditor's report on internal control does not exist, a PE firm should assess a potential portfolio company's system of internal control in its due diligence process. If a management assessment of internal control does not exist, a PE firm should evaluate the portfolio company's tone at the top and discern the reason behind the lack of this assessment. More specifically, the PE firm should attempt to understand whether management places a profound emphasis on internal control, or if internal controls are largely an afterthought to business processes.

The remainder of this chapter will cover the evaluation of internal control effectiveness through a presentation of the requirements of AS 5. Since the standard covers the independent auditor's evaluation, it automatically covers management's requirements for an effective internal control system.

PCAOB AUDITING STANDARD NO. 5

AS 5 states that "Effective internal control over financial reporting provides reasonable assurance regarding the reliability of financial reporting and the preparation of financial statements for external purposes. If one or more material weaknesses exist, the company's internal control over financial reporting cannot be considered effective."[2]

Further, the standard states that:

The auditor's objective in an audit of internal control over financial reporting is to express an opinion on the effectiveness of the company's internal control over financial reporting. Because a company's internal control cannot be considered effective if one or more material weaknesses exist, to form a basis for expressing an opinion, the auditor must plan and perform the audit to obtain competent evidence that is sufficient to obtain reasonable assurance about whether material weaknesses exist as of the date specified in management's assessment. A material weakness in internal control over financial reporting may exist even when financial statements are not materially misstated.

In addition, AS 5 points out that "the auditor should use the same suitable, recognized control framework to perform his/her audit of internal control over financial reporting as management uses for its annual evaluation of the effectiveness of the company's internal control over financial reporting."

Finally, AS 5 prescribes the integration of the internal control audit with the audit of the company's financial statements. It notes that "the auditor should design his/her testing of controls to accomplish the objectives of both audits simultaneously—

- To obtain sufficient evidence to support the auditor's opinion on internal control over financial reporting as of year-end, and
- To obtain sufficient evidence to support the auditor's control risk assessments for purposes of the audit of financial statements."

AS 5 discusses six phases in an audit of internal controls:

1. Planning the audit
2. Using a top-down approach
3. Testing controls
4. Evaluating identified deficiencies
5. Wrapping up
6. Reporting on internal controls

Each of the six phases will be covered, and similar phases should be used by PE firms in evaluating potential portfolio companies. For expositional simplicity, we will refer to an "auditor" when discussing subsequent phases of internal control audits. However, auditor actions might be replicated by PE professionals in the due diligence process. The term "auditor" can thus be interchanged with "PE professional" in the proceeding discussion.

PHASE 1: PLANNING THE AUDIT

Any engagement entered into by an accountant, including an internal control audit, should be properly planned. Adequate planning should be based on the auditor's consideration as to whether the following matters are important to the organization's financial statements and the internal control over financial reporting:

- The auditor's knowledge of the organization's internal control system
- The effects of accounting practices, economic conditions, laws and regulations, and technology on the organization's operating environment
- The organization's operating characteristics, organization structure, and capital structure (a particular consideration in leveraged buyouts)
- Recent changes in the organization, its operations, and its internal control system
- The auditor's preliminary risk and materiality assessments and his/her assessment of the firm's own risk assessment and other factors relating to internal control
- Internal control deficiencies previously communicated to the organization's audit committee and or management
- The awareness of legal or regulatory matters affecting the organization
- The availability of evidence relating to the effectiveness of the organization's internal control system
- The auditor's preliminary assessment of the effectiveness of the organization's internal control system
- The auditor's awareness of public information relevant to his/her judgment as to the likelihood of material financial statement misstatements and/or the likelihood of significant or material internal control deficiencies
- The auditor's concern about the risks of client acceptance and retention
- The relative complexity of the organization's operations

Factors affecting complexity of operations include, among other things,

- The number of business lines involved.
- Business processes.
- Financial reporting systems.
- The centralization or decentralization of accounting functions.
- The extent of management involvement in the day-to-day activities of the organization.
- The number of levels of management.
- Management's span of control.

The preceding considerations influence how the auditor should look at the five major segments of audit planning. The segments, each of which will be discussed, are

- Risk assessment.
- Scaling the audit.

- Fraud risk.
- Using the work of others.
- Materiality.

Risk Assessment

In an audit, the determination of significant accounts and disclosures and relevant assertions is based upon risk assessment. Risk assessment involves the following:

- The determination of threats to the internal control system and the probabilities of the threats
- The determination of the internal controls against the threats and the probabilities that the controls might fail
- The estimated amounts of losses that would occur from the execution of and lack of detection of threats

Threats to the system consist of errors and irregularities. Irregularities consist of asset misappropriations and fraudulent financial reporting. Errors relate to the competence of employees, while irregularities are a function of employee honesty and integrity.

Scaling the Audit

The organization's internal control objectives are a function of its size and the complexity of its business operations and processes. The size and complexity affect the organization's risks and the controls needed to address the risks. The audit, therefore, needs to be scaled to the size and complexity of the organization. A "one size fits all" approach is not appropriate.

Fraud Risk

The auditor must consider the risk of fraud in the design of audit procedures and tests. He/she should determine whether the organization's internal controls adequately address identified risks of material misstatements due to fraud. Examples of controls that might address fraud risk include

- Related-party transaction controls.
- Controls over significant management estimates.
- Controls over unusual transactions and unusual journal entries.
- Adjusting and correcting entry controls.
- Controls limiting the incentives for, and pressure on, management to fraudulently manage and report financial results.

Using the Work of Others

In planning the audit, the auditor should adequately consider the extent of his/her reliance on the work of others in conducting the internal control audit. Auditing Standards AU §322, "The Auditor's Consideration of the Internal Audit Function in an Audit of Financial Statements," applies in an integrated audit of internal controls and the financial statements. The auditor, in performing an internal control audit, may use the work performed by, or receive assistance from, internal auditors, organizational personnel other than internal auditors, and third parties working under the direction of the organization's management or audit committee provided the work is performed by competent and objective persons.

AS 5 states that

> *For purposes of using the work of others, competence means the attainment and maintenance of a level of understanding and knowledge that enables that person to perform ably tasks assigned to them, and objectivity means the ability to perform those tasks impartially and with intellectual honesty. To assess competence, the auditor should evaluate factors about the person's qualifications and ability to perform the work the auditor plans to use. To assess objectivity, the auditor should evaluate whether factors are present that either inhibit or promote a person's ability to perform with the necessary degree of objectivity the auditor plans to use. The auditor should not use the work of persons who have a low degree of objectivity, regardless of their level of competence. Likewise, the auditor should not use the work of persons who have a low level of competence, regardless of their degree of objectivity. Personnel whose core function is to serve as a testing or compliance authority at the company, such as internal auditors, normally are expected to have greater competence and objectivity in performing the type of work that will be useful to the auditor.*

The extent that the auditor uses the work of others in performing a particular audit procedure or test is a function of the risk associated with the control being tested. The higher the risk, the more the need for the auditor to perform his/her own work as opposed to relying on the work of others.

Materiality

AS 5 states, "In planning the audit of internal control over financial reporting, the auditor should use the same materiality considerations he or she would use in planning the audit of the company's annual financial statements."

PHASE 2: USING A TOP-DOWN APPROACH

A top-down approach to the evaluation of internal control over financial reporting begins at the financial statement level and works down to the organizational levels responsible for preparing the statements. The starting point is the auditor's understanding of the overall risks associated with the client's financial reporting. The auditor first focuses on entry-level controls and then on significant accounts, disclosures, and assertions. Significant accounts, disclosures, and assertions, as noted in AS 5, are those "that present a reasonable possibility of material misstatement to the financial statements and related disclosures." The auditor's next step is the verification of his/her understanding of the client's process risks and the selection of tests addressing the assessed risk of misstatement for each relevant assertion. The main concerns in the top-down approach are

- Identifying entry-level controls.
- Identifying significant accounts and their relevant assertions.
- Understanding likely sources of misstatement.
- Selecting controls to test.

Identifying Entry-Level Controls

The auditor's testing should focus on the entry-level controls that determine whether the client has effective internal control over financial reporting. As stated in AS 5, entry-level controls include the following:

- Controls related to the control environment
- Controls over management override
- The organization's risk assessment process
- Centralized processing and controls, including shared service environments
- Controls to monitor the results of operations
- Controls to monitor other controls (the audit committee, the internal audit function, and self-assessment programs)
- Controls over the period-end financial reporting process
- Policies that address significant business control and risk management processes

Two of the most important of these controls, the control environment and the period-end financial reporting process, will be discussed in detail.

Control Environment   The control environment provides the pervasive framework within which all other controls operate. It is imperative that the auditor evaluate the overall effectiveness of the control environment. In particular, AS 5 states that the auditor must assess whether

■ Management's philosophy and operating style promote effective internal control over financial reporting.
■ Sound integrity and ethical values, particularly those of top management, are promoted, developed, and understood.
■ The board of directors of the audit committee understands and exercises effective oversight over internal controls and financial reporting.

Period-End Financial Reporting Process   Because of the close connection of end-of-period processes to the overall fairness of the financial statements, the auditor must thoroughly evaluate these processes. As noted in AS 5, the period-end financial reporting process includes procedures

■ Used to enter transaction totals into the general ledger.
■ Related to the selection and application of accounting policies.
■ Used to initiate, authorize, record, and process journal entries in the general ledger.
■ Used to record recurring and nonrecurring adjustments to the annual and quarterly statements.
■ For preparing annual and quarterly financial statements and related disclosures.

In evaluating the controls over the period-end processes, the auditor should assess

■ The inputs, processes, and outputs of the annual and quarterly financial statement production processes.
■ The extent that the information technology function is involved in the period-end financial reporting processes.
■ Management participants in the period-end processes.
■ Organization locations participating in the process.
■ The types of adjusting and consolidating entries made in the process.
■ The period-end oversight processes employed by management, the board of directors, and the audit committee.

AS 5 states, "The auditor should obtain sufficient evidence of the effectiveness of those quarterly controls that are important to determining whether the company's controls sufficiently address the assessed risk of misstatements to each relevant assertion as of the date of management's assessment. However, the auditor is not required to obtain sufficient evidence for each quarter individually."

Identifying Significant Accounts and Disclosures and Their Related Assertions

Management in the publishing of financial statements makes five assertions:

1. *Existence or occurrence.* All assets, liabilities, and equities shown exist and all revenues, expenses, gain, losses, taxes, dividends, and cash flows occurred.
2. *Completeness.* All of the previously noted items are accounted for.
3. *Valuation or allocation.* All of the previously noted items are properly valued and all interperiod allocations such as depreciations and amortizations are properly made.
4. *Rights and obligations.* The organization has the rights to the assets shown, and all obligations are shown.
5. *Presentation and disclosure.* The financial statements have proper classifications and formats, and full and adequate disclosures have been made.

The determination of significant accounts and disclosures and their relevant assertions is a function of the quantitative and qualitative risk factors related to the financial statement line items and disclosures. Relevant risk factors include

- The size and composition of the account.
- Susceptibility to misstatements due to errors or fraud.
- The volume of activity, complexity, and homogeneity of the individual transactions processed through the account or reflected in the disclosure.
- The nature of the account or disclosure.
- Accounting and reporting complexities associated with the account or disclosure.
- The exposure to losses in the account.
- The possibility of significant contingent liabilities arising from the activities reflected in the account or disclosure.
- The existence of related-party transactions in the account.
- Changes from the prior period in account or disclosure characteristics.

The auditor needs to approach the determination of the potential for misstatement with an inquisitive attitude. He/she needs to ask, "What could go wrong?" within a significant account or with a disclosure.

Understanding Likely Sources of Misstatement

According to AS 5, the auditor, in order to understand the likely sources of potential financial statement misstatements, should achieve the following objectives:

- An understanding of the flow of transactions, including transaction initiation, authorization, processing, and reporting
- Identification of the points within the organization's processes at which a material misstatement, whether intentional or unintentional, could arise
- Identification of the internal controls that management has implemented to prevent, detect, or correct the potential misstatements

Performing transaction walk-throughs will often be the most effective way of achieving the above objectives. Walk-through procedures include inquiry, observation, document inspection, and control re-performance.

Selecting Controls to Test

AS 5 states:

> *The auditor should test those controls that are important to the auditor's conclusion about whether the company's controls sufficiently address the assessed risk of misstatement to each relevant assertion. The decision as to whether a control should be selected for testing depends on which controls, individually or in combination, sufficiently address the assessed risk of misstatement to a given relevant assertion rather than on how the control is labeled (e.g., entry-level control, transaction-level control, control activity, monitoring control, preventive control, detective control).*

PHASE 3: TESTING CONTROLS

The testing of controls includes four steps:

1. Testing design effectiveness
2. Testing operating effectiveness

3. Relationship of risk to the evidence to be obtained
4. Special considerations for subsequent yearly audits

Testing Design Effectiveness

Control design effectiveness is tested by determining whether the controls are being executed as prescribed and that they are executed by personnel having the required authority and responsibility. Effective controls will satisfy control objectives by preventing and detecting errors and frauds that would result in material misstatements in the financial statements. The auditor would use the following procedures in testing control effectiveness:

- Inquiry of personnel
- Observation of operations
- Inspection of relevant documentation

Walk-throughs using these three procedures would normally satisfy the sufficiency of design effectiveness evaluation.

Testing Operating Effectiveness

Operating effectiveness can be tested simultaneously with the testing of design effectiveness.

Relationship of Risk to the Evidence to Be Obtained

The evidence needed for the auditor to conclude that a control is effective depends on the risk associated with the control. As control risk increases, the amount of evidence required when testing the control increases. AS 5 notes the following factors affecting control risk:

- The nature and materiality of misstatements that the control is meant to prevent or detect
- The inherent risk associated with accounts and assertions related to the control
- Changes in the nature or volume of transactions that might affect control effectiveness
- The history of errors or irregularities in accounts related to the control
- The effectiveness of entry-level and monitoring controls
- The nature of the control itself and the frequency of its operation
- Whether the control relies on the effectiveness of other controls
- The competence of the personnel performing or monitoring controls

- Whether the control is manual or automated
- The complexity of a control
- Whether judgment is required in a control's execution

The evidence the auditor obtains in control testing is a function of the nature (type), extent (sample size), and timing (interim versus year-end testing) of the audit procedures used. When a control is evaluated at an interim date and it is assessed as effective, the auditor may use roll-forward procedures to evaluate the control effectiveness over the remainder of the period. Additional evidence required for the roll-forward depends on the following:

- The nature of the control, the risks associated with it, and the results of the interim control test
- The sufficiency of the interim evidence obtained
- The timing of the interim test relative to the end of the audit period covered
- The possibility of changes in internal control between the interim date and the end of the audit period

Special Considerations for Subsequent Yearly Audits

In an ongoing audit situation, the auditor should incorporate prior audit experience in determining the nature, extent, and timing of the control tests performed. In particular, the auditor should consider the following:

- The nature, extent, and timing of control test procedures performed in prior audits
- The outcomes of prior audit control tests
- Whether there have been operating and/or control changes made by the client since the previous audit

The information available from prior audits may allow the auditor to assess control risk at a lower level than in the prior year, resulting in a reduction in the amount of control testing required. However, prior audit results might cause the auditor to assess control risk at a higher level, resulting in increased control testing.

PHASE 4: EVALUATING IDENTIFIED DEFICIENCIES

The auditor is required to evaluate the severity of each control deficiency found to determine whether the deficiencies, either individually or in combination, are material as of the date of management's assessment of internal control over financial reporting. The severity of a deficiency depends on two factors. First, is there a reasonable possibility that the control will fail to prevent or detect a misstatement of an account balance or a disclosure? Second, what is the magnitude of the potential misstatement resulting from the deficiency or deficiencies?

There are many risk factors that indicate whether there is a reasonable possibility that a deficiency, or combination of deficiencies, will fail to prevent or detect a misstatement. The risk factors covered in AS 5 are the following:

- The nature of the accounts, disclosures, and assertions involved
- The susceptibility of the related asset or liability to fraud
- The subjectivity, complexity, or extent of judgment required to determine the amount involved
- The relationship and/or interaction of the particular control with other controls
- The interaction of the deficiencies found in the audit
- Possible future consequences of the deficiency

AS 5 notes:

> *Multiple control deficiencies that affect the same financial statement account balance or disclosure increase the likelihood of misstatement and may, in combination, constitute a material weakness, even though such deficiencies may individually be less severe. Therefore, the auditor should determine whether control deficiencies that affect the same significant account or disclosure, relevant assertion, or component of internal control collectively result in a material weakness.*

Indicators of material weaknesses in internal control of financial reporting include the following:

- The identification by management of any indication of fraud
- Restatements of prior financial statements to correct material misstatements
- Indication of a current period material misstatement that the auditor believes would not have been detected by the client's internal control system
- Ineffective audit committee oversight of the client's internal controls and financial reporting

The standard states:

When evaluating the severity of a deficiency, or combination of deficiencies, the auditor also should determine the level of detail and degree of assurance that would satisfy prudent officials in the conduct of their own affairs that they have reasonable assurance that transactions are recorded as necessary to permit the preparation of financial statements in conformity with generally accepted accounting principles. If the auditor determines that a deficiency, or combination of deficiencies, might prevent prudent officials in the conduct of their own affairs from concluding that they have reasonable assurance that transactions are recorded as necessary to permit the preparation of financial statements in conformity with generally accepted accounting principles, then the auditor should treat the deficiency, or combination of deficiencies, as an indicator of a material weakness.

PHASE 5: WRAPPING UP

Wrapping up the audit of internal controls over financial reporting consists of the following:

- Forming an opinion on the effectiveness of the controls
- Obtaining written representations
- Communicating certain matters

Forming an Opinion

The auditor's opinion is supported by evidence obtained from testing of controls, misstatements detected during the financial statement audit, and any identified control deficiencies. The auditor may form an opinion only when there have been no restrictions on the scope of his/her work. Scope restrictions require that the auditor either disclaim an opinion or withdraw from the engagement. Failure to obtain written representations from management is a scope limitation.

Obtaining Written Representations

In conducting an audit of internal control over financial reporting, the auditor should obtain a management representation letter. The letter, in addition to acknowledging management's responsibility for maintaining effective internal control over financial reporting, should include the following:

- A statement that management has evaluated and assessed the effectiveness of the organization's internal control system
- A statement that management, in performing the assessment noted above, did not use the auditor's procedures as a basis of management's assessment of internal control effectiveness
- A statement that management's assessment of internal control effectiveness is based upon the control criteria as of a specified date
- A statement that management has disclosed to the auditor all deficiencies in the design and operation of internal controls that were identified by management as part of their internal control evaluation
- Descriptions of any frauds involving management or other employees having a significant role in the internal control over financial reporting
- A statement that control deficiencies identified and communicated to the audit committee or board of directors from prior engagements have been resolved
- A list of unresolved control deficiencies identified and communicated to the audit committee or board of directors from prior engagements
- A statement as to whether there have been any changes in internal control over financial reporting since the date of the auditor's report

The statement on subsequent changes in internal control should include any corrective actions taken by management with regard to any significant control deficiencies and/or material control weaknesses.

Communicating Certain Matters

AS 5 states:

> *The auditor must communicate, in writing, to management and the audit committee all material weaknesses identified during the audit. The written communication should be made prior to the issuance of the auditor's report on internal control over financial reporting. If the auditor concludes that the oversight of the company's external financial reporting and internal control over financial reporting by the company's audit committee is ineffective, the auditor must communicate that conclusion in writing to the board of directors.*

Any significant control deficiencies identified during the audit must be communicated in writing to the audit committee. The auditor should also communicate in writing any internal control deficiencies to the client's management.

PHASE 6: REPORTING ON INTERNAL CONTROLS

According to the standard, the auditor's report on internal controls over financial reporting must include the following:

- A title including the word "independent"
- A statement that management is responsible for maintaining effective internal control over financial reporting and for assessing the effectiveness of internal control over financial reporting
- Identification of management's report on internal control
- A statement that the auditor's responsibility is to express an opinion on the internal control based on his/her audit
- A statement that "Internal control over financial reporting is a process designed by, or under the supervision of, the company's principal executive and principal financial officers, or persons performing similar functions, and effected by the company's board of directors, management, and other personnel, to provide reasonable assurance regarding the reliability of financial reporting and the preparation of financial statements for external purposes in accordance with GAAP and includes those policies and procedures that—
  1. Pertain to the maintenance of records that, in reasonable detail, accurately and fairly reflect the transactions and dispositions of the assets of the company;
  2. Provide reasonable assurance that transaction are recorded as necessary to permit preparation of financial statements in accordance with generally accepted accounting principles, and that receipts and expenditures of the company are being made only in accordance with authorizations of management and directors of the company; and
  3. Provide reasonable assurance regarding prevention or timely detection of unauthorized acquisition, use, or disposition of the company's assets that could have a material effect on the financial statements."
- A statement that the audit was conducted in accordance with the standards of the PCAOB (United States)
- A statement that PCAOB standards require that the auditor plan and perform the audit to obtain reasonable assurance as to whether effective internal control was maintained in all material respects

- A statement that the audit includes obtaining an understanding of internal control over financial reporting, assessing the risk that a material weakness exists, testing and evaluating the design and operating effectiveness of internal control based on the assessed risk, and performing such other procedures as the auditor considered necessary in the circumstances
- A statement that the auditor believes that the audit provides a reasonable basis for the opinion
- A paragraph stating that, because of inherent limitations, internal controls over financial reporting may not prevent or detect misstatements and that projections of any evaluation of effectiveness to future periods are subject to the risk that controls may become inadequate because of changes in conditions, or that the degree of compliance with the policies or procedures may deteriorate
- The auditor's opinion on whether the company maintained, in all material respects, effective internal control over financial reporting as of the specified date, based on control criteria
- A manual or printed signature of the auditor's firm
- The city and state (or city and country, in the case of non-U.S. auditors) from which the auditor's report has been issued
- The date of the audit report

The auditor may choose to issue a combined report containing both an opinion on the financial statements and an opinion on the internal controls or separate reports—one for the financial statements and one for the internal control over financial reporting.

CONCLUSION

This chapter has presented a number of considerations employed by auditors in evaluating and reporting on an entity's level of internal control. Though PE professionals are not auditors, this chapter serves to provide a best practice framework by which PE professionals can evaluate portfolio company internal controls, and also provides these professionals with an understanding of how auditors arrive at internal control opinions.

NOTES

1. See SAS No. 112 for additional information.
2. *Source:* http://pcaobus.org/Standards/Auditing/Pages/Auditing_Standard_5 .aspx.

CHAPTER 12

Financial Statement Fraud and the Investment Decision

Harry Cendrowski
James P. Martin

INTRODUCTION

Private equity (PE) investment decisions are made under the premise that the target entity has the ability to meet predetermined financial goals. Certainly, there are unforeseen circumstances and unidentified risks that overcome the organization's ability to maintain its business plans and adhere to the expectations, but generally, given a fair chance to evaluate the organization's business situation, the PE firm should be able to evaluate the target company's earnings potential. At the same time, fraud is a very real threat to every organization's ability to meet its financial objectives, and it can remove the chance of fair evaluation of the business situation. Given the increasing incident rate of fraud across all segments of business, it is no longer feasible to consider fraud an "unidentified risk." PE firm managers and financial institutions must consider the risk of fraud when evaluating financial statements and organizational operations for the purposes of making an investment decision.

Fraud is broken down into two main categories. Additionally, there is an overarching risk of financial distortion due to money laundering activities, either by the principals of an organization or as a service provided to third parties. Money laundering can make an organization appear to have increased sales and revenues, without any services actually being performed.

MONEY LAUNDERING

Money laundering is traditionally thought of as a banking issue, but the Bank Secrecy Act states, "Money Laundering involves transactions intended to disguise the true source of funds; disguise the ultimate disposition of the funds; eliminate any audit trail and make it appear as though the funds came through legitimate sources; and evade income taxes. "

The scope of anti–money laundering programs was expanded across the financial services industry by the Uniting and Strengthening America by Providing Appropriate Tools Required to Intercept and Obstruct Terrorism (USA-PATRIOT) Act of 2001. Title III of that act, titled "International Money Laundering Abatement and Anti-Terrorist Financing Act of 2001" adds the coverage of "investment companies" (e.g., PE firms) to the list of covered entities. This amendment was intended to help prevent, detect, and prosecute not only money laundering, but also the financing of terrorist activities. There are currently hundreds of thousands of financial institutions subject to Bank Secrecy Act reporting and record-keeping requirements for which the Financial Crimes Enforcement Network is authorized responsibility.[1] These include

- Depository institutions (e.g., banks, credit unions, and thrifts).
- Brokers or dealers in securities and/or futures.
- Money services businesses (e.g., money transmitters; issuers, redeemers, and sellers of money orders and travelers' checks; check cashers and currency exchangers).
- Casinos and card clubs.
- Insurance companies.
- Mutual funds.
- Individual(s) transporting over $10,000 in currency or other monetary instruments into/out of the United States.
- Shippers/receivers of over $10,000 in currency or other monetary instruments into/out of the United States.
- Individuals or entities that receive more than $10,000 in cash in one or more related transactions in a trade or business.
- U.S. persons who have a financial interest in or signature or other authority over a foreign financial account if the aggregate value exceeds $10,000 at any time during the reporting year.

On September 26, 2002, the Treasury Department's anti–money laundering enforcement division, the Financial Crimes Enforcement Network (FinCEN), issued a proposed rule that excluded PE funds from Title III of the USA-PATRIOT Act.[2] The primary reason for this was that lock-up periods typically imposed by PE funds make them inherently illiquid, and thus not suitable for money laundering activity. FinCEN proposed that Title III would include those companies that allowed investors to redeem a portion of their investment within two years after that investment was made, and exclude those with a longer lock-up period.[3]

In addressing the proposed rule, FinCEN also believed that entities with less than $1 million in assets pose a significantly lower risk for money laundering and excluded companies below that capitalization level; thus, the proposed rule excluded investment pools such as investment clubs and other small entities.

Greg Baldwin, a partner in the Miami, Florida office of Holland and Knight and former federal prosecutor, believes that the lock-up aspect of PE funds is not an exclusionary provision for money laundering activity. "I think it's analogous to the sleeper cells the U.S. government reports that terrorist organizations create," he said. "If terrorist organizations are willing to take their investment in people that they've enlisted, trained, created a mission or potential mission for, and leave them in place for years at a time, why wouldn't they do the same thing with money? And that money would become very hard to track if it has the appearance of a regular investment."[4]

While PE firms have so far been excluded from the provisions of the USA-PATRIOT Act, it does not mean that they are necessarily free from money laundering risk. FinCEN is not limited from proposing rules that would cover PE firms in the future, should there be additional interest in controlling such activities.

CATEGORIES OF FRAUD

The first category of fraud is asset fraud, where a perpetrator removes assets (typically cash) from the organization. Hopefully, the organization has some sort of monitoring control in place to identify the actions of the perpetrator, but unfortunately, in many cases, the fraud is discovered when checks begin to bounce. Thus, it may be difficult or impossible for the organization to meet its solvency requirements. In essence, the perpetrator has stolen funds needed to successfully operate the business.

The second category of fraud is financial statement fraud. In this type of fraud, management creates fictional or erroneous entries to the financial statements with the intention of creating financial statements that will mislead the user. There are many different ways to accomplish this and many different rationalizations for such actions. Among the most telling: "If I don't make these entries and show a profit, I'll never receive this round of financing." Management has tilted the table through deception and created a situation where the firm could take an investment decision that, but for more accurate information, it would never take.

Fraud schemes can be quite complex, and perpetrators seem to demonstrate boundless creativity in developing schemes to mislead and quickly cover their tracks. Management of an organization has all the tools at their fingertips that they need to be able to create fictional statements. But not all hope is lost. Fortunately for the fund, fraud schemes leave telltale signs, almost like latent fingerprints at a crime scene, which, with a little diligence and awareness, can be detected and interpreted by the equity firm management and other key personnel.

WHAT IS FRAUD?

Black's Law Dictionary describes fraud as "the intentional use of deceit, a trick or some dishonest means to deprive another of his/her/its money, property or a legal right"; in other words, fraud involves intent, profit, and misrepresentation. Financial statement fraud can conceal a sham organization or an organization's inability to maintain its repayment obligations. For a capital provider, be it a commercial lender, PE source, or equity market, a primary concern has always been distortions of financial position and results from misrepresentations in financial statements. Unfortunately, statistics maintained by law enforcement as well as the Association of Certified Fraud Examiners indicate that all types of fraud, including financial statement fraud, are increasing, perhaps because of current economic conditions. The good news is that a PE firm with an understanding of the causal factors as well as the warning signs of fraud can become better prepared to spot potential issues with financial statements and understand how to make more informed investment decisions.

Distortions in the financial statements may be direct or indirect. In either case, the distortion can project a false image of the strength of the organization or hide severe operational and financial issues.

In a direct distortion, a perpetrator, typically management or company ownership, makes unsubstantiated entries in the financial statements for the purpose of altering key financial indicators, such as asset values, revenues, or expenses. The reward for this is often indirect: loans or capital based on strong asset values or revenues, increased salary levels for positive business performance, bonuses for meeting financial metrics. The perpetrator receives a legitimate reward based on falsely reported figures.

Indirect distortion occurs as a by-product of asset fraud. Asset fraud results in a direct reward to the perpetrator: They are removing cash or other valuable assets, and they need to hide what they have done. Successful fraud requires concealment, and perpetrators must develop a means to hide the financial effects of their actions; the entries to conceal the fraud can distort the financial statements. Imagine a case where a bookkeeper is writing checks to herself and cashing them. A credit entry will naturally be made to cash, but where can the debit entry be made to successfully hide it from management? In smaller frauds it might be possible to charge the debit to an expense account, as it might go unnoticed by management. For larger frauds, this might be possible too if the perpetrator can identify an expense center that is not regularly monitored. For larger frauds, the perfect destination is a high-balance asset account that is not regularly reconciled or monitored, or where the perpetrator also is responsible for reconciling the asset account. This is another good reason for regularly performing a fixed-asset reconciliation: it is a perfect hiding spot for a large debit entry. In either case, the debit entry to offset the unauthorized withdrawal will distort the financial statements, and unless they are involved, management will likely be unaware of the distortion.

THE REQUIRED ELEMENTS OF FRAUD

Criminologist Donald R. Cressey proposed in the 1950s that three elements must be present in every situation where there is fraud; these elements have been interpreted by the American Institute of Certified Public Accountants (AICPA) for financial statement fraud as (1) incentive or pressure, (2) attitude, and (3) opportunity. Financial statement fraud involves an indirect reward. The perpetrator receives additional funds; thus, the perpetrator has an incentive or is under pressure to misstate the financials. Attitude describes the attitude of the perpetrator of the need for accuracy in financial representations, and opportunity is the opportunity of the perpetrator to distort the financials.

Financial statement fraud is typically committed by senior members of the organization, including senior management and ownership. In most organizations, there is a built-in incentive or pressure to show positive operating results in the financial statements: salary levels, bonuses, and perquisites are often based on the financial results reported by the organization. The expectations of a PE firm for operating results also create such pressure. Additionally, where the financial statements are used to support an application for financing or investment, positive financial statements will typically affect the amount, rate, and covenant terms and conditions associated with the capital. It is important to remember when evaluating financial statements of a portfolio company that portfolio company management is not independent with respect to those financial statements.

Senior members of an organization have tremendous opportunity to affect the numbers in the financial statements. In every organization, as part of the normal financial accounting process, management decisions and judgments directly affect account balances, including reserves, allowances, and estimates. The critical factor in such decisions and judgments is the intent of management. Hopefully, management is committed to correctly reflecting the underlying economics of a transaction and making appropriate entries to do so. However, ill-intentioned management could also use those entries as an opportunity to distort the financials. Additionally, management can direct subordinates to make journal entries or override internal control procedures; management may even threaten or coerce employees into such actions. Given that management already has incentive to produce positive financial statements and opportunity to adjust the financial records, the actions taken by management will be determined by the third element: attitude.

Attitude describes the mind-set of management as they perform their duties, including the calculation and recording of financial entries. Do recorded entries honestly reflect the economic substance of a transaction and represent management's true and best judgment, or are they mere building blocks meant to support a predetermined target? Attitude determines if management will take an extreme position with a transaction or maintain a commitment to fair presentation. Attitude also covers management's rationalization of why an inappropriate entry may actually be tolerable. For example, assume management is attempting to obtain a capital investment, and management has represented stable revenue, when, in actuality, it has declined over the past year. Management may rationalize that without the investment proceeds the business may fail, resulting in employee layoffs and damage to their personal reputation, and perhaps distorting actual sales a bit by recording sales activity that hasn't actually quite happened yet is a better alternative to the business failing. The investment proceeds are the incentive to distort, and management has assumed the attitude that the possible negatives associated with the distortion are preferable to the other outcomes. A proper management attitude is essential; for this reason, the capital provider needs to be concerned with the integrity of management and the control culture of the organization, as this is a primary driver of management's attitude toward accuracy in financial reporting.

Management's lack of independence, combined with the opportunity to directly manipulate the financial statements, drives the need to have an objective party perform an analysis and attestation on the financial statements; this is also why a sound understanding of the entity's internal control structure is essential. Fraud involves concealment: the perpetrator actively tries to hide his/her actions by creating misleading transactions, destroying documentation, creating fictional documentation, or other nefarious means. The prospect of concealment means that even a properly planned and executed attestation engagement is not guaranteed to discover a fraud.

FINANCIAL STATEMENT ATTESTATION

Certified public accountants (CPAs) perform attestation engagements on financial statements to provide greater assurance that the numbers reflected in the financial statements are fairly represented. However, not all attestation engagements are the same, and it is important to understand the type of attestation and the limitations of the work performed by a CPA under that engagement. The engagements naturally become more expensive as the diligence applied in each type increases, and often the decision on engagement type involves balancing the risk mitigation of increased diligence against higher engagement costs.

Also, keep in mind that most CPAs do not have specialized training in fraud detection or investigation and may not be prepared to recognize the warning signs of fraud, should they exist.

Tax Return Preparation

Tax return preparation is not actually an attestation engagement; however, some capital providers receive tax returns as a surrogate financial statement, and often they assume a higher degree of analysis on the part of the preparer than is actually performed. Tax preparation software can print copies of the entire return on images of the forms and create a very presentable package; the return even bears the signature of the preparer. Professional standards for tax return preparation indicate the practitioner generally may rely in good faith without verification upon information furnished by the client. In this case, the client would likely be the chief executive officer or chief financial officer of the portfolio company.

It is important to ensure that tax returns provided to the PE firm actually correspond to tax returns filed with the Internal Revenue Service (IRS)—tax return software also allows a user to easily create fictional returns that appear official as well. Tax returns are not required to be prepared by a CPA, and even when one is, the CPA does not provide an opinion on the accuracy of the numbers or the underlying financial statements. If the client provides permission, the firm can obtain copies of the actual returns filed from the IRS; this permission could be included in investment terms or operating agreements in certain situations where additional verification is needed.

Compilation

Compiled financial statements look official because they are nicely formatted and accompanied by a letter from the CPA. As reflected in the AICPA standards, however, "The accountant is not required to make inquiries or perform other procedures to verify, corroborate, or review information supplied by the entity."[5] The accountant is required to note any information from other engagements that might allow him/her to question the financial statements, or the entity could provide financial information that on its face would cause the accountant to question the financials; however, the accountant is not required to verify any of the numbers, and no opinion on the accuracy of the numbers is expressed. Thus, a compilation is not an attestation engagement either. A PE firm should be very cautious when decisions are based on compiled financial statements.

Review

In a review, a CPA performs limited procedures to "obtain a basis for communicating whether he or she is aware of any material modifications that should be made to the financial statements for them to be in conformity with generally accepted accounting principles."[6] In other words, the CPA expresses the limited assurance that he/she is not aware of any material modifications that should be made to the financial statements. A review does not include analysis of internal control procedures or any detailed testing of transactions. It is important to remember that the limited procedures performed in a review engagement, including the lack of analysis of internal controls, mean that it would be extremely difficult for a CPA to detect fraud in the financial statements.

Audit

Audit standards for public companies are defined by the Public Company Accounting Oversight Board (PCAOB); the AICPA defines standards for nonpublic companies. Despite the different focus of each group, the two standard sets currently remain fairly consistent and compatible. Auditing standards require the CPA to plan and perform the audit to obtain reasonable assurance about whether the financial statements are free of material misstatement.[7] Note that a CPA does not guarantee an absence of fraud in the financial statements; in fact, a CPA is not charged with actively looking for fraud in the course of the audit. According to standards, CPAs must consider where there is a risk of fraud based on their understanding of the business and alter their audit procedures to consider that risk of fraud. The standards require that CPAs report any fraud that comes to their attention during the course of the audit to management, based on the procedures performed. During an audit, a CPA analyzes the company's internal control system, tests detailed transactions, performs analytical procedures, and performs verification and substantiation procedures (discussions with debtors, inventory tests, investment verification, etc.) to gain the described assurance. While audit procedures have been strengthened over the past several years through new auditing and oversight standards, it is important to remember that an audit is not infallible: Enron, WorldComm, Rite Aid, and Tyco all issued financial statements that had been audited by a Big Five accounting firm.

RECOMMENDATIONS

> *Enron has built unique and, in our view, extraordinary franchises*
> *in several business units in very large markets.*
> —Goldman Sachs analyst David Fleischer[8]

No one really discovers "fraud." Fraud is a complex legal issue that must be proven in a court of law. An investigation typically begins when someone discovers a warning sign that some impropriety could have occurred, commonly called a "red flag," which would need to be investigated, documented, and presented in a court of law to allow the trier of fact to rule on the issue of fraud. Since fraud involves concealment, perpetrators are actively trying to hide the red flags from all parties, including their CPA and capital provider. The battle against fraud begins with an educated professional who understands the red flags of fraud and what they potentially mean, and applies the diligence to follow-up on questionable items. Lamentably, fraud investigations frequently reveal clues and evidence of the illicit actions that were also plainly visible prior to the actions being discovered— if only those clues and evidence were noticed and pursued, the illicit actions could have been revealed much sooner.

Do Not Rely Solely on Financial Statements

Financial statements present a point-in-time summary of activity over a given interval. As the old saying goes, they are not an indicator of future performance. PE firm management should have an understanding of their portfolio company's business, especially related to exactly how the organization creates value. This will allow the PE firm to independently evaluate the representations in the financial statements. Do the results make sense given the overall environment of the industry in which the organization operates? Additionally, an understanding of the organization's internal control procedures will provide insight into the processes in place to both create value and ensure that financial entries accurately represent the results of the organization. Portfolio company management should be able to clearly demonstrate that they have appropriate control procedures given the industry and size of the organization. In certain circumstances, portfolio company management or the PE firm itself may choose to hire an outside firm to document and evaluate the internal control structure. Additionally, portfolio company management should be aware of their control structure and rapidly remediate any control weakness that is discovered.

Pay Attention to Details

Consider the case of a small law firm that suffered a major embezzlement by its CFO; the embezzlement scheme lasted more than a decade. The plot was quite clever: The CFO opened a personal line of credit at the same bank where the firm conducted all its business, drew on the line of credit, and repaid the line with a check from the firm. No fictional vendor, no complicated lapping, just a single check per month payable to a bank that received a dozen or so checks per month anyway. On the bank side, however, they needed legitimate income to support repayment of the line of credit, so the CFO provided fictionalized tax returns. As the level of fraud grew, the CFO increased his personal credit line, which meant that he needed to show the bank higher legitimate income as well on the tax returns. Finally, a loan supervisor asked why the CFO of a small law firm would be paid a salary of over $500,000 per year as was represented on the tax returns; this just didn't make sense. Upon further review of the loan file, they found tax returns listing two separate Social Security numbers for the CFO, a fact that had gone unnoticed for years. Unfortunately, in any organization, it is possible for people to lose sight of the important details that cross their desk on a daily basis—they begin to focus on processing documents rather than looking for nuances and anomalies. The details that go unnoticed are often indicators that something major is lurking beneath the surface.

Information received from the portfolio company or other information source should be evaluated in the context of the overall understanding of the entity. Does it make sense? If not, additional follow-up questions are in order; the answers to those questions should be scrutinized.

Follow Up on Unexpected or Interesting Items

A bank lost several million dollars in a wholesale floor plan fraud and wanted additional fraud awareness training for its loan officers. To develop the training the bank offered one of the business owners' personal financial statements that had been provided to the bank, in case there was anything of note that should be included in the training. The financial statements listed, among other things:

Ownership interest in dealership $155,000

Salary from dealership $72,000

House $240,000

Property $175,000

Automobiles $910,000

Interestingly, the bank was unaware of the amount reported for automobiles, even though the financial statements had been reviewed by the bank as part of the loan underwriting process. This is not to say that the business owner did not actually own $910,000 in automobiles, but that representation in the financial statements certainly raises several questions, given the amounts listed under salary and house. Is that one car or several? Where does he store them? How did he pay for them? Often, the answers to such follow-up questions do not satisfy the question, and expand the mystery of the situation. The seemingly isolated anomaly is often a red flag of fraud—the perpetrator has worked hard to conceal his actions, except for one overlooked item. Of course, that is the time to continue to ask additional follow-up questions until the true circumstances are understood.

This does not only apply to representations on documents: other details are important, too. If you ask for a document that should be readily available, say a financial statement for the period just ended, and it takes an extraordinary amount of time to produce that document, take note. The concern, of course, is that the extra time is needed to create or clean up the information prior to releasing it. Likewise, if asking for additional information or details raises a defensive attitude, levels of concern should rise as well.

Maintain Professional Skepticism

After working with a client or organization for a number of years, it is natural to achieve a sense of comfort with regard to documents and representations. Sometimes this means details that might otherwise raise concern are ignored. The 1992 adventures of John McNamara and General Motors

Acceptance Corporation (GMAC) is a good example. During the course of this floor plan fraud, GMAC loaned McNamara over $5 billion on fictional van purchases and eventually lost $436 million to the scheme. During the course of the scheme, McNamara was purportedly purchasing over 17,000 vans per month for conversion and eventual export (through a closely related company). The scheme continued despite the fact that the volume of vans supposedly purchased exceeded the production of the entire industry, no one had ever seen the conversion factory, and no vehicle ID numbers had ever been provided for any of the vans. Several credit analysts at GMAC raised concerns, but they were turned away by branch management because McNamara was a good client who always paid on time; he had a long-standing relationship with the branch.

The branch management eventually learned that no amount of history should override concerns about seemingly impossible representations. The optimism of the branch management was fueled by the false financial numbers and loan activity by McNamara: his loan activity, and his prompt repayment, allowed the branch management to make their numbers.

Explanations Should Be Rational, Reasonable, and Verifiable

Many times, warning signs of fraud are discovered, only to be explained away by the perpetrator. Unfortunately, this provides additional time for the fraud to continue and further harm the organization. In one organization, fraud was finally revealed when checks started being returned for insufficient funds: the money had all been stolen. During the investigation it was revealed that the perpetrator/controller had continued to record the payroll tax expense and payroll tax liability, even though the money to pay the liability had been stolen. The payroll tax liability account showed an increasing balance over four years on the financial statements, eventually reaching approximately $1.5 million. When this was discussed with the business owner, he acknowledged that he was aware of the liability, but the controller had explained that an "arrangement had been made with the state" to take care of the issue. While that answer opens even more questions to be explored, even if it were true, it does not explain why the balance originated in the first place.

What Do the Financial Statements Say about the Entity's Ability to Meet Its Objectives?

At the end of the day, the financial statements should be a barometer for the operational success of the portfolio company. Don't lose the big picture in all the details in the financial statements.

During a series of training workshops with a regional bank, one of the senior loan officers asked if the bank had a duty to report tax issues with a client to the IRS. It seems that during a recent loan review it had come to the loan officer's attention that a tax liability had not been satisfied and had continued to grow. The IRS was apparently close to placing a lien on the organization. In this case the officer's concern for the IRS had overshadowed the concern he should have had for the bank. If the entity is so cash strapped that it is incurring a large liability to the IRS, it is unlikely that it will be able to repay its debt to the bank. Additionally, if the IRS were to discover the liability, the bank debt would almost certainly be subordinated to the IRS lien that could eventually be placed on the business. In any case, the likelihood of debt repayment is gloomy, and the bank should consider whether the account should be placed in workout.

FRAUD AND DUE DILIGENCE PROCEDURES

Unfortunately, traditional due diligence procedures focus on financial transactions and records, and do not fully investigate underlying situations that could reveal anomalies in the financial records. In addition to the general guidance offered above, application of investigational and forensic accounting procedures will be helpful in revealing potential issues with the target, and could help prevent surprises later.

Background Investigation of Key Employees

Target company management will be key to the success of the organization, and will be responsible for safeguarding the company assets, including invested capital. The due diligence process should include investigation of key employees to identify any potential concerns.

- *Public information search.* A variety of information can be revealed through Internet keyword search activities using search engines such as Google or Yahoo! Articles, quotes, news stories, and other information can provide insights into the history and background of an individual.
- *Public records search.* Many public records have been stored electronically and can be searched via the Internet. For example, many states have their felony-level conviction records stored in a searchable database. Additionally, public records search providers can accumulate information from these public databases for a reasonable fee.
- *Other investigative techniques.* In certain situations, additional procedures such as surveillance may be appropriate. Additional information on such activities is contained in Chapter 11.

The investigation process should be reasonable for the investment considered and, prior to initiation of any investigative activities, should be reviewed with counsel.

Testing of Journal Transactions

Top-side journal entries are the most susceptible to manipulation by management. In most financial reporting fraud situations, it is not the detailed, recurring entries that are manipulated, but the month-end adjusting journal entries, or those that record estimates and accruals. Such entries should be scrutinized for supporting detail and reasonable explanation of the entry. Additional follow-up questions are appropriate where detail and explanation are not adequate.

Additionally, since revenue recognition is a common area where numbers can be easily skewed, it is important to understand the underlying business model of the organization and the methods under which revenue is recognized. To be recorded, revenue must be earned and realized/realizable; in other words, the service needs to have been performed and the amounts due collected or collectable. Recording revenue where the revenue is not fully earned (i.e., where the organization still has obligations to perform to earn the revenue) can inappropriately increase earnings in the current period. Again, this is why it is essential to understand the business model of the target firm and how it actually creates value for its underlying clients or customers.

Journal entries can be efficiently analyzed for anomalies or outliers using automated data analysis tools. These tools allow the analyst to define statistical thresholds and comparisons and rapidly analyze thousands of records. Additionally, these tools can automate the time checking of journal entries, for example, to identify all entries posted within a certain interval after the period close, which should include the adjusting journal entries. Other statistical tests are virtually boundless, including identification of the largest journal entries, the most frequent journal entries, or the dollar volume or entry count of journal entries each period.

Check File Metadata

Metadata are data; for common business documents such as word processor files or spreadsheet files, this includes time stamp information that is created and modified as the file is created and modified. These metadata provide a history of the file that can be accessed and viewed through the electronic version of the file. A well known example of metadata is the date and time stamp of the file that can be viewed through the folder view. This represents the operating system date and time the file was last saved, and unfortunately, it is easy to modify. This, however, is not the only metadata of interest.

Many file formats also contain additional information about document history. For example, Microsoft Excel files contain document properties that include the date created, date modified, and date last accessed. It also includes the author and person who last saved the file, according to the user information passed by the operating system.

This information is useful in due diligence to help verify the information received as legitimate. For example, if management represents that a spreadsheet is used to track receivables, and has been used for several years, the spreadsheet should have actually been created several years ago. If the metadata reveal it was just recently created, or was created subsequent to the request to provide the file to the due diligence team, additional follow-up would be in order.

CONCLUSION

The existence of one or more red flags does not necessarily mean that a fraud actually has occurred—red flags are just possible warning signs. As the number of red flags noted begins to grow (e.g., the controller with the really nice car can't get you the financial statements right away and is very defensive about it), the level of concern should grow as well, but red flags can also be revealed for other reasons. For example, if the financial statements cannot be produced in the expected amount of time, it may only be because the accounting staff is disorganized or the bookkeeper is overworked or maybe just not qualified for the position. Such red flags can be ascribed to a "conspiracy of incompetence" that, while an interesting fact in its own right, does not reveal a fraud. Given the wide variety of causal events that can lead to a red flag, the PE firm should be careful in interpreting the underlying facts and not leap to any conclusions or make accusatory statements while continuing to explore the situation.

Also, many organizations maintain separate and different sets of books for legitimate purposes. For example, an organization could maintain a cash basis set of books for tax purposes, and an accrual basis set for financial reporting purposes. Companies with foreign operations may also need to maintain books according to the accounting standards in that country. The existence of multiple books of entry does not necessarily mean there is a fraud, but it does demand that the requestor of financial information understand what they are receiving and why it is maintained by the organization. Again, it comes back to understanding the organization's business.

A relationship with an external expert in fraud investigation and forensic accounting will also be invaluable to the capital provider. This resource can help interpret red flags, suggest possible follow-up actions, and, should the need arise, investigate the underlying transactions within the organization to determine what actually has happened. This relationship will typically pay for itself over time: A single bad deal avoided will generate savings far in excess of the professional fees.

NOTES

1. *Source:* Financial Crimes Enforcement Network, U.S. Department of Treasury, available at www.fincen.gov/reg_bsaforms.html.
2. "A Report to Congress in Accordance with § 356(c) of the USA PATRIOT Act," December 31, 2002.
3. *Id.*
4. John Baldwin, "AML Law for Venture Capitalists Still under Study at FinCEN," March 12, 2007. Available at www.actimize.com/index.aspx?page=news53
5. *Source:* AR 100
6. *Id.*
7. *Source:* AU 316
8. David Fleischer, "Is Enron Overpriced?" *Fortune* 143, no. 5: 122. 2006

CHAPTER 13

Professional Standards

Harry Cendrowski
Louis W. Petro

INTRODUCTION

Though private equity (PE) appears to float under the regulation radar of the Securities and Exchange Commission (SEC), it is not entirely unregulated. As detailed in Chapter 1, the Dodd-Frank Wall Street Reform and Consumer Protection Act of 2010 (Dodd-Frank) significantly increased the regulation of PE firms, particularly those that manage one or more private funds with greater than $150 million in assets under management. However, PE funds are subject to rules and regulations that have resulted from decades of legislation. This chapter introduces securities legislation pertinent to PE funds as well as relevant policing bodies.

FEDERAL TRADE COMMISSION

The Federal Trade Commission (FTC) is charged with investigations regarding federal antitrust legislation and investigations involving federal consumer protection legislation.

Federal Antitrust Legislation

The FTC enforces the following U.S. antitrust statutes:

- Sherman Antitrust Act (1890)
- Clayton Antitrust Act (1914)
- Federal Trade Commission Act (1914)
- Robinson-Patman Act (1936)
- Celler-Kefauver Antimerger Act (1950)
- Hart-Scott-Rodino Antitrust Improvement Act (1976)

Sherman Antitrust Act (1890)   The Sherman Antitrust Act of 1890 was the first U.S. statute passed that deals with business practices used by companies to create monopolies. Several states had already passed similar laws, but such laws are limited to intrastate commerce. A federal law was needed to handle companies engaged in interstate commerce.

The act prohibits restraints of trade leading to monopolies. Specifically, it prohibits the following acts:

- Vertical price fixing (resale price maintenance)—agreements with customers obligating them to resell at manufacturer mandated prices
- Horizontal price fixing—agreements among competitors dictating quantities produced, offered for sale, or bought
- Bid rigging by competitors
- Boycotts
- Market allocation by competitors

PE firms should be aware of the Sherman Antitrust Act as they engage in the acquisition process. The Department of Justice began investigating numerous PE firms after the class-action lawsuit of *L. A. Murphy v. Kohlberg Kravis Roberts & Company, et al.* was filed with the U.S. District Court on November 7, 2006. The complaint alleges PE bid clubs violate antitrust laws through corresponded pricing and bid valuing to keep prices low.

Clayton Antitrust Act (1914)   The 1890 Sherman Act did not outlaw attempts to limit competition. It focused only on the creation of monopolies. The Clayton Act amends and clarifies the Sherman Act by making illegal certain acts that tend to lessen competition. The Clayton Act added the following restraints of trade to those enumerated in the Sherman Act:

- Acquisition of a competitor when such acquisition would tend to limit competition
- Interlocking directorates
- Price discrimination
- Tie-in sales agreements unless such an agreement is needed to protect the selling company's goodwill

The nation's largest PE firms should keep in mind the Clayton Act's focus on limiting competition as well as monopolization when considering mergers and acquisitions.

Federal Trade Commission Act (1914)   The 1914 FTC Act prohibits certain unfair acts and practices not covered by the Sherman Act and Clayton Act.

In addition, the FTC Act created the Federal Trade Commission, a bipartisan commission composed of five presidential appointees, to enforce its provisions as well as the provisions of the Sherman Act and the Clayton Act. The practices prohibited by the FTC Act include:

- Unfair competition such as price discrimination or using size or market position to coerce suppliers to grant price concessions
- Deceptive practices such as false or misleading advertising

The FTC Act provisions and the creation of the FTC allow sanctions to be imposed on PE firms that do not abide by the antitrust acts.

Robinson-Patman Act (1936) The purpose of the Robinson-Patman Act, sometimes referred to as the Anti–Chain Store Act, is to protect smaller, independent retailers from larger, chain-store pricing practices. The act was supported by wholesalers wanting to stop the chain stores from buying directly from manufacturers at prices lower than those charged by the wholesalers. In other words, the wholesalers wanted to lessen competition from the chains.

The Robinson-Patman Act prohibits price discrimination that is not cost justified or that is not based on a response to a competitor's price. The act allegedly deters competitors from using unfair pricing practices.

Celler-Kefauver Antimerger Act (1950) The 1950 Celler-Kefauver Act closed a loophole in the antimerger provisions of the 1914 Clayton Act. The Clayton Act prohibits stock purchases that result in reduced competition but does not prohibit asset purchases accomplishing the same end. The Celler-Kefauver Act prohibits the acquisition of a competitor's assets that lessens competition.

Hart-Scott-Rodino Antitrust Improvement Act (1976) The Hart-Scott-Rodino Act prohibited so-called "midnight mergers" by providing a notice period of a merger or acquisition. According to the act, all persons contemplating certain mergers and acquisitions must provide notification to the FTC and the Assistant Attorney General for the Antitrust Division of the Department of Justice of their intentions. This begins a 30-day waiting period, during which time those regulatory agencies may request additional information or perform investigations to determine if the proposed transaction would violate antitrust laws. The filing requirement is triggered by the value of the transaction, which is adjusted annually based on the change in gross national product.

According to Peter W. Rodino, Jr., former U.S. Congressman from New Jersey, "Hart-Scott-Rodino was intended to give the anti-trust agencies two things: critical information about a proposed merger and time to analyze that information and prepare a case, if necessary. From what I hear, the legislation absolutely has transformed merger enforcement. Competition, as well as the consumer, has benefited."[1]

Federal Consumer Protection Legislation

The FTC is charged with enforcing consumer protection legislation as well as with enforcing antitrust legislation. Consumer protection legislation is directed at deterring business practices aimed at deceiving consumers. There are numerous consumer protection acts. Among them are the following:

- Wool Products Labeling Act (1939)
- Fur Products Labeling Act (1951)
- Textile Fiber Products Identification Act (1958)
- Federal Cigarette Labeling and Advertising Act (1966)
- Fair Packaging and Labeling Act (1966)
- Truth in Lending Act (1968)
- Fair Credit Reporting Act (1970)
- Postal Reorganization Act (1970)
- Dolphin Protection Consumer Information Act (1972)
- Hobby Protection Act (1973)
- Fair Credit Billing Act (1974)
- Magnuson-Moss Warranty–Federal Trade Commission Improvements Act (1975)
- Consumer Leasing Act (1976)
- Petroleum Marketing Practices Act (1978)
- Drug Price Competition and Patent Term Restoration Act (1984)
- Comprehensive Smokeless Tobacco Health Education Act (1986)
- Fair Credit and Charge Card Disclosure Act (1988)
- Federal Deposit Insurance Corporation Improvement Act (1991)
- Energy Policy Act (1992)
- Telephone Disclosure and Dispute Resolution Act (1992)
- Telemarketing and Consumer Fraud and Abuse Prevention Act (1994)
- Violent Crime Control and Law Enforcement Act (1994)
- Home Ownership and Equity Protection Act (1994)
- Home Equity Loan Consumer Protection Act (1995)
- Electronic Fund Transfer Act (1996)
- Telecommunications Act (1996)

- Credit Repair Organizations Act (1996)
- Identity Theft Assumption and Deterrence Act (1998)
- Equal Credit Opportunity Act (1999)
- Fair Debt Collection Practices Act (1999)
- Gramm-Leach-Bailey Act (1999)
- Children's Online Privacy Protection Act (2000)
- College Scholarship Fraud Protection Act (2000)
- Crimes Against Charitable Americans Act (2001)
- Sports Agent Responsibility and Trust Act (2002)
- Do-Not-Call Registry Act (2003)
- Do-Not-Call Implementation Act (2003)
- Fair and Accurate Credit Transactions Act (2003)
- Controlling the Assault of Nonsolicited Pornography and Marketing Act (2003)

The list of consumer protection acts administered by the FTC is long and quite inclusive. PE firms' diverse portfolios may be covered in any number of these acts.

SECURITIES AND EXCHANGE COMMISSION

The stock market crash of October 29, 1929, aside from ushering in the Great Depression, encouraged the U.S. Congress to enact legislation regarding the interstate sale of securities and publicly held company financial reporting. Several federal acts are administered by the SEC:

- Securities Act (1933)
- Securities Exchange Act (1934)
- Public Utility Holding Company Act (1935)
- Trust Indenture Act (1939)
- Investment Company Act (1940)
- Investment Advisers Act (1940)
- Foreign Corrupt Practices Act (1977)
- Sarbanes-Oxley Act (2002)[2]

Securities Act (1933)

The 1933 Securities Act, often referred to as the Truth in Securities Law, has two primary objectives. First, the act prohibits any type of fraud, misrepresentation, and deceit in the interstate sale of securities. Second, the act, through its required registration process, requires that investors be provided with information, both financial and nonfinancial, regarding securities offered for public interstate sale.

The registration process requires that the organization offering the securities for sale provide the following to investors:

- Descriptions of the corporation and its properties
- Descriptions of the securities being offered for sale
- Information about the corporation's board of directors and management
- Certified financial statements

Not all securities offerings are subject to registration with the SEC. Exemptions include the following:

- Offerings of limited volume
- Private offerings to a restricted number of investors or institutions
- Intrastate offerings
- Governmental securities

Private placement investments are subject to scrutiny under the Securities Act, and as PE funds are generally sold through private placements, PE firms should be aware of the limitations. Fund investment opportunities must be limited to accredited investors with a preexisting relationship to the fund or its sponsor.

The Dodd-Frank Act of 2010 redefined the term "accredited investor." Prior to Dodd-Frank, a person was an accredited investor if (1) such person had an individual income in excess of $200,000 in each of the two most recent years or joint income with their spouse exceeding $300,000 in each of those years and has a reasonable expectation of reaching the same income level in the current year; or (2) such person's net worth, together with their spouse, exceeds $1 million at the time of purchase. For the purpose of determining net worth, individuals previously could include the value of their primary residence. Under Dodd-Frank, individuals may no longer include the value of their primary residence for the purpose of determining net worth under the accredited investor definition.

Securities Exchange Act (1934)

The 1934 Securities Exchange Act, among other things, created the SEC. The SEC has regulatory authority over brokerage firms, transfer agents, clearing agencies, security self-regulatory organizations (SROs), and the stock exchanges. The stock exchanges are SROs. The act specifies appropriate conduct in the securities markets and prohibits fraudulent activities, such as insider trading, relating to the offer, purchase, or sale of securities. The act gives the SEC the power to set generally accepted accounting principles (GAAP) for SEC registrants. Periodic, such as quarterly, and annual reporting requirements are also mandated by the 1934 act. Corporate SEC filings are publicly available through the SEC's Electronic Data Gathering and Retrieval System (EDGAR).

SEC filings include significant events (8-K or 8-Q) such as the acquisition or sale of a subsidiary, a change in officers or directors, addition or deletion of a product line, and a change in auditor, as well as annual (10-K) and quarterly financial reports (8-K). The reporting requirements apply to corporations with more than $10 million in assets and more than 500 shareholders.

Finally, the 1934 act covers regulations regarding information requirements for proxy solicitations and for tender offers.

Public Utility Holding Company Act (1935)

The 1935 Public Utility Holding Company Act has requirements designed to protect utility customers from, among other things, utility company fraudulent behavior. Specifically, the Act requires public utilities to be incorporated in the state in which they operate or to be regulated by the SEC if they operate in more than one state. The former requirement allows the individual state to regulate them. In addition, the Act prohibits nonpublic utility companies, such as investment banks or oil companies, to own public utilities.

The 1935 Act was repealed by the Energy Policy Act (EPACT) in 2005 and replaced by the Public Utility Holding Company Act of 2005. The EPACT moved jurisdiction over public utilities from the SEC to the Federal Energy Regulatory Commission (FERC).

The repeal of the 1935 Act opened the door to investment in public utilities, and PE firms struck quickly. With FERC as the oversight body, utility assets have become a target for PE investment.

Trust Indenture Act (1939)

The 1939 Trust Indenture Act applies to debt securities, such as bonds and notes, offered for public sale. It requires that registered debt securities be accompanied by a formal indenture agreement between the debtor and the creditor. The agreement, known as the trust indenture, must conform to the provisions of the Act. The trust indenture covers the reciprocal rights and duties of the debt security issuer (debtor) and the debt security buyer (creditor) and is publicly available. The Act helps to deter the making of fraudulent debt agreements.

Investment Company Act (1940)

The 1940 Investment Company Act gives the SEC authority to regulate the organization and operation of companies engaging in the trading of publicly traded securities. The Act includes mutual funds. A primary purpose of the law is to minimize potential conflicts of interest that might arise in the principal/agent relationship between the trading company and the actual owner(s) of the securities being traded. In addition, the Act requires investment companies to disclose their financial condition and investment policies when initially selling securities, and, thereafter, on a regular basis. The Act does not give the SEC authority to mandate investment decisions and activities to investment companies.

In order to avoid registering as an investment house, and therefore becoming subject to SEC regulation, PE funds must be aware of the exemptions to the Investment Company Act:

- Section 3(c)(1) allows domestic funds limited to 100 total investors and offshore funds of 100 U.S. investors to avoid SEC registration.
- Section 3(c)(7) nullifies the limitation of 100 investors so long as every investor is a qualified purchaser, characterized as an individual or family with $5 million of net worth, or an entity with $25 million net worth.

Generally, funds will limit investor size to 499 to avoid conflict with the Securities Exchange Act, as described in an earlier section of this chapter.

Investment Advisers Act (1940)

The 1940 Investment Advisers Act requires investment companies operating as agents for security purchasers and sellers to register with the SEC and to conform to appropriate SEC regulations. The regulations include the provisions of the 1940 Investment Company Act, as well as this Act. The Investment Advisers Act was amended in 1996 to cover, in general, only those having over $25 million in assets under management.

Effective February 1, 2006, under SEC Rule 203(b)(3)(a) to the Investment Advisers Act, many hedge fund advisors were mandated to register with the SEC as investment advisors. However, on June 23, 2006, the rule was vacated by the U.S. District of Columbia Court of Appeals ruling over *Goldstein v. SEC*. Though some hedge fund managers have chosen to deregister, others have decided to remain registered, often citing sunk compliance costs, best practices, and increased investment interest as reasons for remaining compliant.

Dodd-Frank makes numerous changes to the registration and reporting and recordkeeping requirements of the Investment Advisers Act. According to the SEC,

> *Among these is the requirement that advisers to most private funds (hedge funds and private equity funds) register with the Commission. Historically, many of these advisers had been exempt from registration under the so-called "private adviser" exemption. The Dodd-Frank Act replaces this exemption with several narrower exemptions for advisers that advise exclusively venture capital funds and advisers solely to private fund with less than $150 million in assets under management in the United States. Foreign private advisers and advisers to licensed small business investment companies also are exempted.*[3]

Foreign Corrupt Practices Act (1977)

The 1977 Foreign Corrupt Practices Act (FCPA) was precipitated by the bribery of foreign officials by agents for U.S. companies or their employees, officers, or directors. The bribes were for the purpose of obtaining foreign business. Many of the bribes were made without the authorization or knowledge of the bribing company's officers or directors. The FCPA has two major provisions. First, the FCPA prohibits companies, their subsidiaries, directors, officers, employees, and agents from bribing foreign officials. Second, the act mandates that SEC registrants maintain an adequate internal control system, something PE firms considering going public or with the exit strategy of IPO for investments must consider.

The definition of "internal" used in the FCPA follows the one used in the American Institute of Certified Public Accountants (AICPA) Statement on Auditing Standards No. 1 (SAS 1). The FCPA provisions require that the SEC registrants maintain an internal control system that provides reasonable assurance of the following:

- Transactions are executed in accordance with management's general or specific authorization.
- Transactions are recorded as necessary (1) to permit preparation of financial statements in conformity with GAAP or any other criteria applicable to such statements, and (2) to maintain accountability for assets.

- Access to assets is permitted only in accordance with management's general or specific authorization.
- The recorded accountability for assets is compared with the existing assets at reasonable intervals and appropriate action is taken with respect to any differences.[4]

The internal control requirements are to help deter the prohibited bribery of foreign officials. Violations of the FCPA may result in both criminal and civil penalties.[5]

Sarbanes-Oxley Act (2002)

President George W. Bush, on July 30, 2002, signed into law the U.S. Company Accounting Reform and Investor Protection Act of 2002. He characterized the act, commonly referred to as the Sarbanes-Oxley Act (or SOX) after its two sponsors, Senator Paul Sarbanes of Maryland and Representative Michael Oxley of Ohio, as "the most far-reaching reforms of American business practices since the time of Franklin Delano Roosevelt."[6] SOX amends the 1934 Securities Exchange Act and gives the SEC additional authority and responsibility for the deterrence of management fraud. The enactment of SOX was precipitated primarily by the collapse of Enron. Problems involving corporate governance and/or audit issues at Adelphia Communications, Merrill Lynch, WorldCom, Imclone, Tyco, and Salomon Smith Barney helped encourage the passage.

SOX covers six areas:

1. The Public Company Accounting Oversight Board (PCAOB)
2. Auditor independence
3. Corporate governance
4. Chief executive officer/chief financial officer (CEO/CFO) certifications
5. Enhanced financial disclosure
6. Civil and criminal penalties

All of the provisions are designed to improve corporate governance and audits and to deter fraudulent financial reporting.

Public Company Accounting Oversight Board   The PCAOB's role is to protect the interests of investors in the preparation of accurate and independent audit reports. It has taken over what was the AICPA's role in the setting of auditing standards for public company audits and in the oversight of public company audits. In particular, the PCAOB is responsible for

- Registering certified public accountant (CPA) firms that audit public companies.
- Establishing auditing, quality control, ethical, and independence standards for such CPA firms.
- Inspecting such CPA firms.
- Conducting investigations of such CPA firms.
- Disciplining such CPA firms.
- Enforcing CPA firm compliance with the act, with PCAOB rules, with professional standards, and with security laws relating to the preparation of financial statements and audit reports.

Auditor Independence SOX has provisions to improve the perception of auditor independence as well as the actuality of auditor independence. It intends to do this in four ways. First, the PCAOB prohibits CPA firms from offering certain services to publicly held audit clients. The prohibited services are as follows:

- Bookkeeping/accounting
- Financial information systems design and implementation
- Appraisal/valuation services
- Actuarial services
- Internal auditing outsourcing
- Management/human resource functions
- Broker/dealer/investment advisor/investment banker services
- Legal/expert services unrelated to the audit
- Other services that the PCAOB proscribes

The first additional service proscribed by the PCAOB is the advising of a publicly held audit client to engage in "aggressive" tax shelters. Second, SOX requires that all nonaudit services provided to a publicly held audit client be approved by the client's audit committee.

Third, SOX requires that the both the audit partner in charge and the review partner on a public company audit be rotated out in five years or less.

Finally, SOX mandates that a CPA firm may not audit a publicly held company if any of the following worked for the CPA firm on an audit of the client during the past year:

- CEO
- CFO
- Controller
- Chief accounting officer

Corporate Governance The primary corporate governance provisions of SOX are the mandating of a board of directors–level audit committee and the provision of whistleblower protection rules. The audit committee members must not be affiliated with the corporation even as a consultant or an advisor. The members may receive only a normal director's fee. No additional compensation is allowed. At least one of the audit committee members must be a designated financial expert. The expertise areas consist of the understanding of the following:

- GAAP and financial statements
- The preparation and audit of financial statements for a comparable company
- Internal controls
- The role and functions of an audit committee

The mandated duties of the audit committee consist of the following:

- Approving the selection of the external auditor
- Liaison with the external auditor
- Determining the external auditor's compensation
- Overseeing the external auditor's work
- Resolving auditor disputes and disagreements

In addition, SOX requires CPA firms auditing publicly held clients to report to the client's audit committee.

SOX enhances employee reporting of complaints regarding accounting, audit, and control issues by mandating whistleblower protection and by mandating that publicly held corporations provide confidential, anonymous mechanisms for employee submission of accounting, audit, and control matters. Procedures must be established for receiving, retaining, and responding to complaints.

SOX has added provisions banning corporate loans to officers and directors, decreasing the time allowed between the execution of and the reporting to the SEC of insider stock trading, and the disgorgement by recipients of bonuses and other compensation gained by fraudulent behavior.

Finally, SOX requires publicly held corporations to have a code of ethics for senior financial officers. The corporation is required to disclose whether the corporation has adopted such a code, and if not, the reason why not. The Act also requires immediate disclosure to the SEC of any change in or waiver of the code of ethics for senior financial officers.

CEO/CFO Certifications SOX requires both the CEO and a CFO of a publicly held company to certify both the company's financial statements and its internal control system. The CEO and CFO have to certify that the financial statements have been reviewed by them and that, to the best of their knowledge, the statements have no material errors or omissions and that the statements fairly present the company's financial position and results of operations in accordance with GAAP or other appropriate reporting criteria.

Regarding the company's internal control, the CEO and CFO certify management's responsibility for establishing and maintaining the internal control system and that the internal control system has been evaluated within 90 days, and whether the system is effective. Effectiveness is compromised if there are one or more material weaknesses in the internal control system. A material weakness is defined by the PCAOB as "a significant deficiency or combination of deficiencies that could result in more than a remote likelihood that a material misstatement of the annual or interim financial statements will not be prevented or detected."[7]

Enhanced Financial Disclosure SOX has the following enhanced financial statement disclosure requirements:

- An internal control report confirming management's responsibility for the establishing and maintaining of the internal control system and management's evaluation of the effectiveness of the system
- The auditor's opinion on the effectiveness of the internal control system
- Management's statement that no material or immaterial employee and/ or management fraud occurred during the period covered by the financial statements
- The reporting of all material audit corrections and all material off-balance-sheet financing arrangements in SEC filings
- Enhanced management discussion and analysis (MD&A) disclosures in the company's annual report

The MD&A requirements include disclosure of significant trends, demands, uncertainties, and commitments confronting the corporation.

Civil and Criminal Penalties SOX has amended U.S. Federal Sentencing Guidelines, mandating harsher penalties for fraud and for obstruction of justice. These penalties are dictated to a large extent by the Federal Sentencing Guidelines.

"PRIVATE" EQUITY GOING PUBLIC

Some PE industry giants have gone public in recent years, including the Blackstone Group and Kohlberg, Kravis, Roberts & Company. The Blackstone Group's decision to go public was not accomplished overnight. Blackstone needed to overcome an array of issues that are shrouded for private company counterparts, issues that will be discussed presently.

Even PE groups that have no aspirations of hitting Wall Street need to be knowledgeable of public company regulations. A common strategy for PE funds is to offer investments to the public. Before making an IPO, an investment needs to be compliant with public company regulations.

Introduction to Public Standards

The assessment of the governance and operations of a potential investment target by a PE firm requires an understanding of the target's internal control system. The understanding of an organization's internal control system is the first step in the financial audit of the organization. The purpose of an organization's internal control system is to provide reasonable assurance that

- The organization's assets are safeguarded.
- The organization maintains accurate and reliable records.
- The organization's operations are efficient.
- The organization's policies are adhered to.
- The organization complies with laws, rules, and regulations.

A primary concern of the PE firm is that the target's internal control system provides assurance that the objectives listed above will be accomplished.

Best practices for public companies result from a combination of the efforts by management and outside professionals and consultants, such as external and internal auditors (CPAs and CIAs), certified fraud examiners (CFEs), and certified fraud deterrence professionals (CFDs). Although most PE firms themselves are not subject to the same regulations as public companies, their investments may not enjoy the same benefits. Investments with an IPO exit strategy must prepare for eventual compliance with the same regulations inasmuch as any other public company. Further, PE firms should be aware of public company regulations as the giants of the industry have either gone public or are debating going public.

The professional standards affecting public companies by outside professionals are covered as follows:

- PCAOB
- AICPA Auditing Standards
- AICPA Accounting and Review Standards
- Institute of Internal Auditors
- Information Systems Audit and Control Association

Additionally, numerous acts resulting from the creation of the FTC will be discussed. These acts relate to corporate business practices, including PE firms.

PUBLIC COMPANY ACCOUNTING OVERSIGHT BOARD STANDARDS

The PCAOB, a provision of SOX, through January 2011 has issued 15 auditing standards.

Although the PCAOB auditing standards legally apply only to audits of publicly held companies (SEC registrants), they provide a benchmark for the audit of any type of organization. They are seen by many as best practice.

PCAOB Auditing Standard No. 1

The first standard released by the PCAOB, "References in Auditors' Reports to the Standards of the Public Company Accounting Oversight Board," has two major provisions. First, the standard states that the PCAOB has adopted as standards, on an initial, transitional basis, the generally accepted auditing standards, described in the AICPA's Auditing Standards Board's SAS 95, "Generally Accepted Auditing Standards," in existence on April 16, 2003. Therefore, the PCAOB has adopted SAS 82, "Consideration of Fraud in a Financial Statement Audit," which, as superseded by SAS 99, will be discussed later.

The second issue in PCAOB No. 1 notes that in the auditor's report on either an audit or a review of a public company, the auditor should note that the engagement was conducted "in accordance with the standards of the Public Company Accounting Oversight Board (United States)."

PCAOB Auditing Standard No. 2

PCAOB Auditing Standard No. 2, "An Audit of Internal Controls over Financial Reporting Performed in Conjunction with an Audit of Financial

Statements," has been replaced by PCAOB Auditing Standard No. 5, "An Audit of Internal Control over Financial Reporting that Is Integrated with an Audit of Financial Statement."

PCAOB Auditing Standard No. 3

PCAOB Auditing Standard No. 3, "Audit Documentation," provides guidelines for the documentation of any type of external audit, including an audit of internal controls. The primary purpose of audit documentation is to provide the evidence to support the auditor's opinion. The documentation also provides evidence that the auditor followed generally accepted audit standards in planning, supervising, executing, reporting, and reviewing the engagement. The requirement that audit engagements be adequately documented encourages the auditor to exercise due care in the performance of the engagement.

PCAOB Auditing Standard No. 4

PCAOB Auditing Standard No. 4, "Reporting on Whether a Previously Reported Material Weakness Continues to Exist," applies to engagements geared solely to reporting on whether a previously reported material weakness has not been corrected and, therefore, continues to exist. Such engagements are performed at management's discretion and as of a reasonable date selected by the management. The engagement need not be in conjunction with an audit or review and may cover more than one allegedly corrected material weakness. In order to perform the engagement, the auditor must receive a written statement from management noting that the specified weakness or weaknesses no longer exist as of the date specified by management.

PCAOB Auditing Standard No. 5

PCAOB Auditing Standard No. 5, "An Audit of Internal Control over Financial Reporting that Is Integrated with an Audit of Financial Statement," contains standards and guidelines for independent auditors to attest to and report on the effectiveness of an organization's internal control over financial reporting under Section 404(b) of SOX. It replaces PCAOB Auditing Standard No. 2, "An Audit of Internal Controls over Financial Reporting Performed in Conjunction with an Audit of Financial Statements." The new standard should make Section 404 audits more effective and efficient by promoting risk-based audits scaled to the size and complexity of the organization being audited. Improvements over PCAOB Auditing Standard No. 2 include the following:

- The standard is less prescriptive.
- It recommends scaling the audit to fit the size and complexity of the organization being audited.
- It advises the auditor to focus on high-risk control issues, eliminating unnecessary audit procedures.
- It applies a principles-based rather than rules-based approach to determine when and to what extent the auditor can use the work of others is used.

The Standard Is Less Prescriptive PCAOB Auditing Standard No. 5 is a principles-based standard. It directs the auditor to engage in dialogue with the organization's management and audit committee. The purpose of the dialogues is that the audit focuses on high-risk, material items rather than merely complying with a detailed rulebook. The result is that the auditor can focus testing in areas where his/her judgment deems it necessary. PCAOB Auditing Standard No. 5 is less than half the length of PCAOB Auditing Standard No. 2 and is considered to be more readable.

Scalable Audits PCAOB Auditing Standard No. 5 contains guidance explaining how the auditor should apply control evaluation and testing procedures to smaller or less complex organizations. Instead of designing the internal control audit to the standard, the auditor can design it to the organization and to improving that organization's financial reporting. The auditor can reduce the amount of control testing and can rely on mitigating and compensating controls. For example, if separation of duties is limited due to lack of personnel, the auditor may rely on inquiry, observations, and/or reperformance when there is limited documentary evidence.

Audit Focus PCAOB Auditing Standard No. 5 advises the auditor to focus on high-risk, material concerns. In particular, it recommends evaluating and testing those controls designed to prevent material misstatements and fraudulent financial statements. It suggests that the auditor

- Focus on identifying control weaknesses most likely to result in material misstatements or management fraud.
- Follow a top-down approach to the audit, beginning with the financial statements and working down to the detailed transactions.
- Emphasize the organization's control environment—how the organization is managed and staffed, management integrity, the code of ethics, and the audit committee.
- Focus on the high-risk stages of financial statement preparation such as the adjusting entry process.

The standard notes that the audit focus should be on the effectiveness of internal controls over financial reporting and not on other management processes.

Using the Work of Others   PCAOB Auditing Standard No. 5 allows external auditors to use their professional judgment in deciding when and how they will use the work of others, such as internal auditors, in conducting their internal control evaluations and testing. The standard goes so far as to allow external auditors to rely on testing done by persons other than internal auditors. The reliance is predicated on the external auditor's evaluation of the person's competence and objectivity.

PCAOB Auditing Standard No. 6

PCAOB Auditing Standard No. 6, "Evaluating Consistency of Financial Statements," establishes requirements and offers guidance to auditors evaluating the consistency of financial statements. It suggests the auditor should evaluate "whether the comparability of the financial statements between periods has been materially affected by changes in accounting principles or by material adjustments to previously issued financial statements." Furthermore, it states that auditors should evaluate consistency between audits covering two or more periods, and that auditors should "recognize" changes in accounting principles and adjustments to correct misstatements in previously issued financial statements in their report.

PCAOB Auditing Standard No. 7

PCAOB Auditing Standard No. 7, "Engagement Quality Review," describes the objective and procedures necessary for an engagement quality review for an audit. It also describes the qualifications of an engagement quality reviewer. An engagement quality reviewer performs "an evaluation of the significant judgments made by the engagement team and the related conclusions reached in forming the overall conclusion on the engagement and in preparing the engagement report . . . "

PCAOB Auditing Standard No. 8

PCAOB Auditing Standard No. 8, "Audit Risk," discusses the auditor's consideration of audit risk. It states the auditor must "plan and perform the audit to obtain reasonable assurance about whether the financial statements are free of material misstatement due to error or fraud," and discusses two forms of risk auditors should be aware of:

1. Inherent risk—refers to the susceptibility of an assertion to a misstatement, due to error or fraud, that could be material, individually or in combination with other misstatements, before consideration of any related controls.
2. Control risk—refers to the risk that a misstatement due to error or fraud that could occur in an assertion and that could be material, individually or in combination with other misstatements, will not be prevented or detected on a timely basis by the company's internal control.

PCAOB Auditing Standard No. 9

PCAOB Auditing Standard No. 9, "Audit Planning," establishes requirements regarding planning an audit. It states the engagement partner is responsible for the engagement and its performance as well as planning the audit. The standard describes preliminary engagement and planning activities for audits, including the knowledge base an audit should possess. Audit strategies and plans are also discussed.

PCAOB Auditing Standard No. 10

PCAOB Auditing Standard No. 10, "Supervision of the Audit Engagement" specifies the requirements regarding the supervision of the overall engagement and the work of engagement team members. It outlines the responsibility of the engagement partner for supervision, and provides guidance to these individuals in their supervision of engagement team members.

PCAOB Auditing Standard No. 11

Among other items, PCAOB Auditing Standard No. 11, "Consideration of Materiality in Planning and Performing an Audit" defines materiality in the context of an audit. The standard states a fact is material if there is "a substantial likelihood that the . . . fact would have been viewed by the reasonable investor as having significantly altered the 'total mix' of information made available." Determinations of materiality require "delicate assessments of the inferences a 'reasonable shareholder' would draw from a given set of facts and the significance of those inferences to him . . . " The standard also mentions procedures an auditor should undertake to obtain reasonable assurance about whether the financial statements are free of material misstatement.

PCAOB Auditing Standard No. 12

PCAOB Auditing Standard No. 12, "Identifying and Assessing Risks of Material Misstatement" discusses the performance of risk assessment procedures that "are sufficient to provide a reasonable basis for identifying and assessing the risks of material misstatement, whether due to error or fraud, and designing further audit procedures." Risk assessment procedures include

- Obtaining an understanding of the company and its environment;
- Obtaining an understanding of internal control over financial reporting;
- Considering information from the client acceptance and retention evaluation, audit planning activities, past audits, and other engagements performed for the company;
- Performing analytical procedures;
- Conducting a discussion among engagement team members regarding the risks of material misstatement; and
- Inquiring of the audit committee, management, and others within the company about the risks of material misstatement.

PCAOB Auditing Standard No. 13

PCAOB Auditing Standard No. 13, "The Auditor's Responses to the Risks of Material Misstatement" sets forth procedures for auditors to follow in responding to the risks of material misstatements. It states the auditor should design and implement overall responses to address the assessed risks of material misstatement in the following manner:

a. Making appropriate assignments of significant engagement responsibilities;
b. Providing the extent of supervision that is appropriate for the circumstances, including, in particular, the assessed risks of material misstatement;
c. Incorporating elements of unpredictability in the selection of audit procedures to be performed; and
d. Evaluating the company's selection and application of significant accounting principles.

Procedures for testing controls in an audit are also defined.

PCAOB Auditing Standard No. 14

PCAOB Auditing Standard No. 14, "Evaluating Audit Results" establishes requirements regarding the auditor's evaluation of audit results and determination of whether he or she has obtained sufficient appropriate audit evidence.

According to the standard, "the auditor's evaluation of audit results should include evaluation of the following:

a. The results of analytical procedures performed in the overall review of the financial statements ("overall review");
b. Misstatements accumulated during the audit, including, in particular, uncorrected misstatements;
c. The qualitative aspects of the company's accounting practices;
d. Conditions identified during the audit that relate to the assessment of the risk of material misstatement due to fraud ("fraud risk");
e. The presentation of the financial statements, including the disclosures; and
f. The sufficiency and appropriateness of the audit evidence obtained."

Sufficient appropriate audit evidence requires consideration of

a. The significance of uncorrected misstatements and the likelihood of their having a material effect on the financial statements;
b. The results of audit procedures performed in the audit of financial statements;
c. The auditor's risk assessments;
d. The results of audit procedures performed in the audit of internal control over financial reporting, if the audit is an integrated audit; and
e. The appropriateness of the audit evidence obtained.

PCAOB Auditing Standard No. 15

PCAOB Auditing Standard No. 15, "Audit Evidence" explains what constitutes audit evidence and establishes requirements regarding designing and performing audit procedures to obtain sufficient appropriate audit evidence.

The standard defines audit evidence as, "all the information, whether obtained from audit procedures or other sources, that is used by the auditor in arriving at the conclusions on which the auditor's opinion is based. Audit evidence consists of both information that supports and corroborates management's assertions regarding the financial statements or internal control over financial reporting and information that contradicts such assertions."

AMERICAN INSTITUTE OF CERTIFIED PUBLIC ACCOUNTANTS AUDITING STANDARDS

Frequently, companies will provide audited financial statements as part of the due diligence process, and the PE firm should understand the underlying audit procedures performed and the limits of those procedures, at least at a high level. In addition, when the exit strategy includes an IPO, the PE firm should be familiar with the audit process.

There are several statements on auditing standards of interest to a PE firm when evaluating a potential investment:

- SAS 99, "Consideration of Fraud in a Financial Statement Audit"
- SAS 104, "Amendment to Statement on Auditing Standards No.1, 'Codification of Auditing Standards and Procedures ("Due Professional Care in the Performance of Work")' "
- SAS 105, "Amendment to Statement on Auditing Standards No. 95, 'Generally Accepted Auditing Standards' "
- SAS 106, "Audit Evidence"
- SAS 107, "Audit Risk and Materiality in Conducting an Audit"
- SAS 108, "Planning and Supervision"
- SAS 109, "Understanding the Entity and Its Environment and Assessing the Risks of Material Misstatement"
- SAS 110, "Performing Audit Procedures in Response to Assessed Risks and Evaluating the Audit Evidence Obtained"
- SAS 111, "Amendment to Statement on Auditing Standards No. 39, 'Audit Sampling' "
- SAS 112, "Communicating Internal Control Related Matters Identified in an Audit"
- SAS 113, "Omnibus Statement on Auditing Standards"
- SAS 114, "Auditor's Communication With Those Charged With Governance"
- SAS 116, "Interim Financial Information"

The major points in each of these standards will be discussed.

SAS 99, "Consideration of Fraud in a Financial Statement Audit"

The primary AICPA audit standard of interest to PE firms is SAS 99, "Consideration of Fraud in a Financial Statement Audit." SAS 99, issued in 2002, replaced SAS 82, which had the same title. SAS 99 emphasizes that the auditor consider the client's susceptibility to fraud in the planning of an audit of the client's financial statements. Specifically, the standard

- Replaces SAS 82.
- Amends SAS 1, "Codification of Auditing Standards and Procedures."
- Amends SAS 85, "Management Representations."

SAS 99 has been in effect for financial statements for periods beginning on or after December 15, 2002. The amendments to SAS 1 and SAS 85 will be discussed first, followed by the replacement provisions to SAS 82.

SAS 1 Amendments

The SAS 99 amendments to SAS 1 add new language regarding, first, due professional care in the performance of work and, second, the concept of reasonable assurance. SAS 99 notes that due professional care in the performance of a financial statement audit should include audit staff discussions regarding the potential for client fraud. The fraud could be either asset misappropriation or fraudulent financial reporting.

SAS 99 requires the auditor to recognize that reasonable assurance is affected by both the characteristics of fraud and the inherent ineffectiveness of audit procedures in detecting fraud. The characteristics of fraud noted in particular are

- Concealment and/or collusion by management and/or employees.
- Documents withheld, misrepresented, altered, or falsified.
- The ability of management to override the control system.

SAS 85 Amendments

The amendments to SAS 85, "Management Representations," add new language to the management representation letter and require the auditor to inquire of management regarding fraud and the risk of fraud. Specifically, the new language requires that management acknowledge the following in the written management representation letter:

- Management's responsibility for fraud prevention and detection
- Management's knowledge of suspected management and employee frauds
- Management's knowledge of employee allegations of fraud and the follow-up on the allegations

SAS 82 Replacements

SAS 99 covers the following areas relating to fraud:

- Descriptions and characteristics of fraud
- Professional skepticism
- Discussions of fraud with audit engagement personnel

- Fraud risks
- The evaluation of audit evidence
- Auditor communication with client management, the audit committee, and others
- Documenting the auditor's consideration of fraud during the audit engagement

Each of these areas will be discussed.

Descriptions and Characteristics of Fraud   The two basic types of fraud are fraudulent financial reporting (management fraud) and misappropriation of assets (employee fraud). Fraudulent financial reporting involves the following:

- Manipulation, falsification, or alteration of documents or records
- Misrepresentations
- Omissions
- Misapplication of GAAP

Asset misappropriation involves misstatements arising from employee theft and/or embezzlement. Fraud characteristics should be considered within the fraud triangle framework of incentive, opportunity, and rationalization (attitude).

Professional Skepticism   SAS 99 mandates that the auditor conduct a financial statement audit with an attitude of professional skepticism. Professional skepticism in auditing consists of a questioning mind and the critical assessment of audit evidence. The auditor must recognize that in any audit engagement the possibility of fraud exists, regardless of the auditor's previous knowledge and beliefs about the client management and employee integrity and honesty. In addition, professional skepticism requires the auditor to extend audit procedures should an indicator of fraud be noticed. Finally, the auditor should not accept less than pervasive evidence about an audit assertion just because he/she believes the management to be honest.

Engagement Team Discussions   SAS 99 requires that there be audit team discussion and communication throughout the engagement. The standard requires brainstorming during the planning phase of the audit. The brainstorming sessions should cover how and where the client's financial statements might be susceptible to fraudulent misstatement. The sessions should reinforce the skeptical mindset mentioned earlier. The sessions should also encourage effective communication of fraud indicators during the execution and evaluation phases of the audit.

Fraud Risks SAS 99 requires the auditor to consider the following regarding fraud risk when conducting a financial statement audit:

- Obtaining information to identify risks
- Identifying risks
- Assessing risks
- Responding to the risk assessment

Obtaining information requires the following:

- Inquiries of the audit committee management, employees, and client's in-house legal counsel
- Analytical review procedures designed to indicate possible areas of fraud
- Consideration of the three fraud triangle elements (incentive, opportunity, and rationalization)

In addition, the information from the results of the following may be relevant to the assessment of possible fraud risk:

- Client acceptance and continuance procedures
- Interim financial statement reviews

Identifying Risks SAS 99 requires that risks identified by the information-gathering procedures covered earlier be segregated by type (management or employee), significance or materiality, likelihood or probability, and pervasiveness. Pervasiveness relates to whether a fraud misstates only a part of the financial statements or the statements taken as a whole.

Assessing Risks SAS 99 refers to SAS 55, "Consideration of Internal Control in a Financial Statement Audit." SAS 55 has been amended by SAS 78, "Consideration of Internal Control in a Financial Statement Audit: An Amendment to SAS No. 55." First, the standard requires that the auditor obtain an understanding of the five components of the client's internal control sufficient to adequately plan the audit. The five components specified in SAS 78 are from the Committee of Sponsoring Organizations of the Treadway Commission (COSO) Integrated Framework, and include the following:

1. Control environment
2. Risk assessment

3. Control activities
4. Information and communication
5. Monitoring

SAS 55 listed the following five components that were replaced by the above:

1. Segregation of duties
2. Authorizations
3. Documentation
4. Safeguards
5. Independent checks

Second, SAS 55 notes that the auditor should recognize the two primary inherent internal control limitations. They are management override and the collusion of two or more people. Third, the standard mandates that the auditor evaluate whether client controls addressing risks of material misstatements due to fraud have been implemented and are operating effectively. Finally, the auditor should assess the risks of fraud based on the evaluation and respond to the risk.

Responding to the Risk Assessment   The auditor's response to the risk assessment consists of the following six activities:

1. Adjusting the planning, staffing, and supervising the audit
2. Modifying the nature of audit tests covered in SAS 31 and SAS 80, "Evidential Matter"
3. Changing the extent of audit tests covered in SAS 39, "Audit Sampling"
4. Moving the timing of audit tests covered in SAS 45, "Substantive Tests Prior to the Balance Sheet Date"
5. Reviewing journal entries and adjustments
6. Reviewing management estimates

The review of journal entries, among other things, should focus on the following:

- Entries to unrelated, unusual, or seldom used accounts
- Entries made by personnel not usually making journal entries
- End-of-period and/or postclosing entries
- Entries made right before or during financial statement preparation, in particular, any entries to unnumbered accounts
- Entries whose dollar amounts are round or inconsistent with expectations

- Complex journal entries
- Intracompany and related-party transaction journal entries
- Unusual entries involving such things as mergers and acquisitions, impairments, abandonments, restructurings, extraordinary gains or losses, and discontinued operations

The preparation of financial statements requires management to make many accounting estimates. When perpetrating a fraud involving financial statement misstatement, management often accomplishes the fraud by manipulating accounting estimates. SAS 99 requires the external auditor to obtain persuasive evidence to support any significant management estimates. Estimates that should be reviewed include the following commonly made ones:

- Actuarial parameters and imputed interest rates used in accounting for pensions and other postretirement benefits
- Imputed interest rates used for lease capitalization
- Contingent liabilities related to environmental and health and safety issues
- Cash flows used for property, plant, and equipment impairment present value calculations
- Fair values for goodwill impairment calculations
- Warranty liabilities
- Uncollectible account expense and the related allowance for doubtful accounts
- Allowances for sales returns, sales allowances, and sales discounts
- Inventory obsolescence values
- Useful lives and residual values for buildings and equipment
- Useful lives for amortizable intangible assets

The preceding list contains the more common management estimates. It is not all inclusive.

Evaluating Audit Evidence   SAS 99 requires the external auditor to review evidence as it relates to the overall audit and to apply analytical procedures to determine the reasonableness of the financial statements. The evidence review should focus on the following:

- Discrepancies in accounting records
- Untimely information or data
- Conflicting or missing evidence
- Problematic or unusual auditor/client relationships

Examples of evidence discrepancies include

- Incomplete data, information, or documentation.
- Unsupported entries or management assertions.
- Significant last-minute adjusting entries.
- Tips from or complaints by employees regarding financial reporting issues.

Conflicting or missing evidence includes such things as

- Missing or altered documents.
- Unusual documents.
- The use of photocopies of documents when originals would be the norm.
- Inconsistent, vague, or implausible auditor inquiry responses made by management or employees.
- Missing evidence such as assets, data in electronic form, program change records, and data destruction inconsistent with client document retention policies.

Problematic or unusual auditor/client relationships include, but are not limited to, the following:

- Client denial of access to records, assets, facilities, or personnel
- The unwillingness of the client to assist with or to facilitate the audit
- Client intimidation of the auditor
- Delays in responses to auditor inquiries or requests for access to records, assets, facilities, or employees
- The unwillingness of the client to make auditor-requested adjustments to the financial statements
- The unwillingness of the client to make adequate financial statement disclosures

SAS 99 requires the auditor of financial statements to use analytical review procedures such as financial ratio analysis to determine the overall reasonableness of the financial statements. In particular, the auditor should look for and follow up on any unusual or unexpected relationships. Relationships to be reviewed would include such things as

- Current and quick ratios.
- Net income to cash flow from operations.
- Gross margins on sales.

- Margins on sales.
- Return on assets.
- Inventory and receivables turnovers.
- Inventory days on hand and receivables collection periods.
- Uncollectible account expense and the allowance for doubtful accounts.
- Asset turnovers.
- Interest and fixed charge coverages.

The ratios should be reviewed over time as well as compared to industry averages and ranges for reasonableness. Significant changes or discrepancies in the ratios indicate the possibility of fraud. The auditor is required by SAS 99 to follow up on the possibilities.

SAS 99 requires the external auditor to evaluate the materiality of any detected misstatements. If any misstatements are material, the auditor must, first, determine the implications regarding the gathering of additional audit evidence. Second, the auditor should advise management of the finding and further investigate the finding. Finally, the auditor should advise the client to consult its legal counsel about the matter. If the misstatements are immaterial, the auditor should consider its implications regarding his/her evaluation of management and/or employee integrity.

Auditor Communication   SAS 99 requires the auditor of financial statements to communicate any fraud-related issues to management, the client audit committee, and others. Auditor communications are covered in three other statements on auditing standards:

- SAS 60, "Communication of Internal Control Related Matters Noted in an Audit"
- SAS 61, "Quality of the Entities Accounting Principles"
- SAS 84, "Communications Between Predecessor and Successor Auditors"

In addition, the auditor needs to consider legal and regulatory reporting requirements such as responses to subpoenas or to requests from governmental funding agencies. Government funding agency requests are covered in the Governmental Accountability Office Auditing Standards ("The Yellow Book").

Audit Documentation   The standard requires the auditor of financial statements to document fraud issues related to the audit. Specifically, SAS 99 requires the auditor to document the following:

- Fraud discussions with audit and among the audit engagement personnel
- Risk procedures used during the engagement
- Audit evidence and/or analytical procedures leading to the need for additional audit procedures
- The nature of fraud communication resulting from the audit

The discussion documentation must cover how the discussions were conducted, who was involved, when the discussions occurred, and what was discussed.

Risk procedures documented must include the following:

- How risk information was obtained
- The identification of specific risks
- The assessment of the risk of material misstatements
- The assessment of the risk of management override of internal controls

All fraud communications with management, the audit committee, or others regarding the audit must be documented.

SAS 104, "Amendment to Statement on Auditing Standards No.1, 'Codification of Auditing Standards And Procedures ("Due Professional Care in the Performance of Work")'"

SAS 104 expands the SAS 1 definition of *reasonable assurance*. The literature prior to SAS 104 provides no definition of the term "reasonable assurance." However, reasonable assurance has been presumed to be something less than certainty or absolute assurance but more than a low level of assurance. SAS 104 states:

> *The auditor must plan and perform the audit to obtain sufficient audit evidence so that audit risk will be limited to a low level that is, in his or her professional judgment, appropriate for expressing an opinion on the financial statements. The high, but not absolute, level of assurance that is intended to be obtained by the auditor is expressed in the auditor's report as obtaining reasonable assurance about whether the financial statements are free of material misstatement (whether caused by error or fraud).*

SAS 105, "Amendment to Statement on Auditing Standards No. 95, Generally Accepted Auditing Standards"

SAS 105 changes the scope of the second standard of field work from "understanding the entity's internal control system" to "understanding the entity and its environment, including its internal control." In addition, the standard amends the third standard of field work to read, "The auditor must obtain sufficient appropriate audit evidence by performing audit procedures to afford a reasonable basis for an opinion regarding the financial statements under audit." The standard provides guidance regarding

- Defining audit evidence.
- Defining relevant management assertions.
- Covering the qualitative aspects of audit evidence.
- Covering audit procedures and why they are to be performed.

SAS 106, "Audit Evidence"

SAS 106 notes that "audit evidence is all the information used by the auditor in arriving at the conclusions on which the audit opinion is based and includes the information contained in the accounting records underlying the financial statements and other information." Specifically, the standard

- Defines audit evidence.
- Defines relevant management assertions and covers their use in risk assessment and the design of appropriate audit procedures and tests.
- Covers qualities the auditor should consider in the determination of the appropriateness and sufficiency of audit evidence.
- Discusses audit procedures and their purposes.

SAS 107, "Audit Risk and Materiality in Conducting the Audit"

SAS 107 provides the auditor with guidance regarding the documentation of risk and materiality considerations encountered in the conduct of a financial statement audit. First, the standard requires the documentation of the following:

- Materiality and tolerable misstatement levels used in the audit and any changes in those levels

- The aggregate of uncorrected misstatements related to both known and likely misstatements
- The auditor's conclusion, and the basis for the conclusion, regarding whether uncorrected misstatements, either individually or in aggregate, cause the financial statements to be materially misstated
- The correction of all known and likely misstatements identified in the audit that have been corrected by management

Uncorrected misstatements are to be documented so that the auditor can determine whether they cause the financial statements to be materially misstated.

SAS 108, "Planning and Supervision"

SAS 108 states that planning is an interactive process, and that along with supervision it should be continuous throughout the audit. The audit is to be planned and executed so that it responds to the risk and materiality assessments made by the auditor. The assessments should be based on the auditor's understanding of the entity's environment and internal control system.

SAS 109, "Understanding the Entity and Its Environment and the Risks of Material Misstatement"

SAS 109 covers the procedures and tests that the auditor should perform in obtaining an understanding of an entity's environment and internal control system and in assessing the risks of material misstatements. The standard states that the auditor should

- Understand the types and classes of transactions, account balances, and relevant management disclosures.
- Relate identified risks to relevant management assertions and how the risks affect the assertions.
- Consider the likelihood of material misstatement for each risk identified.

The SAS provides auditor guidance for documentation and for determining significant risks. It requires the auditor to evaluate the entity's internal controls for adequate design and implementation.

SAS 110, "Performing Audit Procedures in Response to Assessed Risks and Evaluation of the Audit Evidence Obtained"

SAS 110 provides auditor guidance regarding

- How to address risks of material financial statement misstatements.
- The design and performance of audit procedures related to the assessed risks of material misstatement.
- The determination of whether the risk assessments are appropriate and whether sufficient appropriate evidence has been obtained.
- The proper documentation of risk assessment, audit procedures, and evidence obtained.

SAS 111, "Amendment to Statement on Auditing Standards No. 39, 'Audit Sampling'"

SAS 111 amends SAS 39 by incorporating SAS 99 fraud considerations, SAS 107 risk and materiality considerations, and SAS 110 audit procedure considerations in the design and implementation of audit sampling procedures. The statement provides the auditor with guidance related to his/her judgment in establishing tolerable misstatement levels. It also supplies guidance in the applying sampling techniques to tests of internal control.

SAS 112, "Communicating Internal Control Related Matters Identified in an Audit"

SAS 112 replaces Statement on Auditing Standards No. 60, "Communication of Internal Control Related Matters Identified in an Audit." In addition to communicating internal control related matters identified in an audit, SAS 112

- Requires the auditor to communicate significant internal control deficiencies or material internal control weaknesses identified in the audit to the client's management and those charged with governance. Communication should also include uncorrected significant deficiencies and material weaknesses communicated in previous audits.
- Contains auditor guidance on evaluating the severity of internal control deficiencies.
- Requires the auditor to conclude whether prudent officials given the same facts under the same circumstances would classify deficiencies into the same categories as was done by the auditor.

SAS 112 notes that the body charged with governance may be different for different entities. The body could be any of the following:

- The board of directors
- A board-level committee such as an audit or oversight committee
- A management committee such as a finance, executive, or budget committee
- Partners

SAS 112 uses the following definitions:

- "A *significant deficiency* is a control, or combination of control deficiencies, that adversely affects the entity's ability to initiate, authorize, record, process, or report financial data reliably in accordance with generally accepted accounting principles such that there is more than a remote likelihood that a misstatement of the entity's financial statements that is more than inconsequential will not be prevented or detected."
- "A *material weakness* is a significant deficiency, or combination of control deficiencies, that results in more than a remote likelihood that a *material* misstatement of the financial statements will not be prevented or detected."

The definitions are those used in the PCAOB Auditing Standard No. 2, "An Audit of Internal Controls over Financial Reporting Performed in Conjunction with an Audit of Financial Statements." Remember that PCAOB Auditing Standard No. 2 has been replaced by PCAOB Auditing Standard No. 5, "An Audit of Internal Control over Financial Reporting that Is Integrated with an Audit of Financial Statement" The definitions, however, have been maintained.

SAS 113, "Omnibus Statement on Auditing Standards"

SAS 113 clarifies the terms used to describe professional responsibilities imposed on auditors by SASs 99 and 104 through 112. The standard adds two footnotes to SAS 99:

- Footnote 15 links the auditor's consideration of fraud to his/her assessment of risk.
- Footnote 21 links the auditor's consideration of fraud to his/her response to assessed risks.

SAS 114, "The Auditor's Communication With Those Charged With Governance"

SAS 114 supersedes Statement on Auditing Standards No. 61, "Communication With Audit Committees." It provides guidance on matters that should be communicated with those charged with governance. SAS 114 defines "those charged with governance" as "those with responsibility for overseeing the strategic direction of the entity and obligations related to the accountability of the entity, including overseeing the entity's financial reporting process." Examples of parties charged with governance are noted in SAS 112, previously covered. The SAS uses the term "management" to refer to "those who are responsible for achieving the objectives of the enterprise and who have the authority to establish policies and make decisions by which those objectives are to be pursued." The standard notes that management is responsible for the entity's financial statements.

SAS 114 identifies the communication matters noted in SAS 61 as well as additional matters. Specifically, from SAS 61, SAS 114

- Describes the primary purposes of communication with those charged with governance.
- Stresses the importance of effective two-way communication and mandates that the auditor evaluate the effectiveness of the two-way communication.
- Requires the auditor to determine the appropriate governance personnel with whom to communicate matters.
- Recognizes the variations in governance structures among organizations.
- Encourages the auditor to exercise professional judgment when deciding with whom to communicate.
- Requires the auditor to recognize unique concerns when those charged with governance are also involved in managing the entity. This often occurs in small entities.

In addition, SAS 114 adds the following requirements:

- The auditor must communicate
  - An overview of the audit scope and timing.
  - The representations that the auditor is requesting from management.
- It provides guidance on the communication process regarding
  - The forms and timing of communication.
  - The need to communicate audit findings in writing.
- It mandates that required communications with those charged with governance be documented.

SAS 116, "Interim Financial Information"

SAS 116 provides guidance on the nature, timing, and extent of procedures to be performed when conducting a review of interim financial information. These procedures may be applicable in the event a PE firm acquires a smaller private firm that has not received an audit in between two fiscal year ends.

According to the standard, interim financial information "means financial information or statements covering a period less than a full year or for a 12-month period ending on a date other than the entity's fiscal year end."

In performing a review of interim financial information, SAS 116 (in conjunction with AU 722, the professional standard modified by SAS 116) states the accountant "should have sufficient knowledge of the entity's business and its internal control." Furthermore, the accountant "should perform procedures to update his or her knowledge of the entity's business and its internal control," including the consideration of any

- Corrected material misstatements.
- Matters identified in any summary of uncorrected misstatements.
- Identified risks of material misstatement due to fraud, including the risk of management override of controls.
- Significant financial accounting and reporting matters that may be of continuing significance, such as significant deficiencies or material weaknesses.

AMERICAN INSTITUTE OF CERTIFIED PUBLIC ACCOUNTANTS ACCOUNTING AND REVIEW STANDARDS

A financial statement review includes a lower level of assurance than an audit, and is intended to be a faster and less expensive process than an audit. Many smaller firms obtain reviewed financial statements. Compiled financial statements have no expression of assurance whatsoever; however, they are accompanied by a letter from the CPA firm. The standards that cover review and compilation services are defined in the Statement on Standards for Accounting and Review Services (SSARS). Specifically of interest to the PE firm are two recent statements: SSARS 10, "Standards for Accounting and Review Services" and SSARS 12, "Omnibus Statement on Standards for Accounting and Review Services—2005." The two SSARSs will be discussed separately.

SSARS 10

SSARS 10 amends SSARS 1, "Compilation and Review of Financial Statements." Among other things, SSARS 1 covers the performance and documentation of review engagements. SSARS 10 does not apply to compilations.

Among other things, SSARS 10 provides for inquiries regarding fraud in a review engagement. Under the new standard, accountants performing a review engagement will need to develop an understanding of the client's business, understand the potential for misstatement of the financial statements due to fraud, and be able to apply additional inquiries or analytical procedures to identify any material adjustments needed to bring the financial statements into conformity with GAAP.

The illustrative inquiries in SSARS 10 have been expanded to include questions that seem to assess the operation of the underlying business processes. If the accountant is not prepared to judge the responses to the inquiries, recognize the warning signs of fraud, and develop appropriate communication to company ownership, he/she could be exposed to professional liability.

The risk to the accountant highlighted by the revised standard is that a fraudulent situation could exist within the organization that is not uncovered during the review. SSARS 10 reiterates that an understanding of internal controls is not part of a review engagement. However, fraud studies claim that about 90 percent of fraud would be prevented by appropriate internal controls. This means the single most powerful tool to understand the potential for fraud in the organization is not available to the accountant performing the review. The accountant is left with the responsibility for considering fraud without the ability to identify conditions that present the opportunity for fraud.

SSARS 12

SSARS 12, "Omnibus Statement on Standards for Accounting and Review Services—2005," amends SSARS 1. It requires the external accountant to have an understanding with a compilation or review client regarding the reporting to the client of fraud or illegal acts that come to accountant's attention during the performance of the compilation or review engagement. The standard recommends, but does not require, that the understanding be in writing. The accountant must report any evidence or information that comes to his/her attention regarding fraud or illegal activities to the appropriate level of management.

SSARS 12 also includes a footnote that defines fraud: "For purposes of this Statement, fraud is an intentional act that results in a misstatement in compiled or reviewed financial statements."[8]

INSTITUTE OF INTERNAL AUDITORS STANDARDS

Statement on Internal Auditing Standards 3 (SIAS 3), "Deterrence, Detection, Investigation, and Reporting of Fraud (1985)," provides guidance for the performance of financial, compliance, and operational audits by internal auditors. SIAS 3 requires internal auditors to determine if their organization has fraud deterrence policies and procedures in place. The standard notes the following:

- Effective internal controls are the principal way to deter fraud.
- The control system is management's responsibility.
- The role of the internal auditor is to assist management in deterring fraud.

In fulfilling the role, the internal auditor reviews and evaluates the adequacy and effectiveness of the organizations internal controls.

In determining the effectiveness of the internal control system in deterring fraud, the internal auditor considers the following:

- Does the organization's management have the proper attitude toward internal controls?
- Does the management set the proper control "tone" for the organization?
- Does the organization establish realistic goals and objectives for the management and employees?
- Does the organization have a code of conduct?
- Does the code adequately cover prohibited activities and the consequences of code violations?
- Is the code communicated to all employees?
- Do appropriate authorization policies exist and are they followed?
- Are procedures to monitor activities in place, and are they followed?
- Are asset safeguarding procedures in place, and are they followed?

Finally, the internal auditor must make recommendations, as appropriate, to improve fraud deterrence controls.

INFORMATION SYSTEMS AUDIT AND CONTROL ASSOCIATION

Information Systems (IS) Auditing Procedure: Irregularities and Illegal Acts Standard P7, section 3.2.4, details provisions of an effective internal control system. The standard states that the "IS Auditor should be aware that management can override controls and this may facilitate fraud by senior management."

Audit Considerations for Irregularities Standard G9, section 1.2.1, establishes the potential guidelines with regards to irregularities. The standard states that, ultimately, fraudulent activities depend on the definition of fraud in the jurisdiction of the audit. However, nonfraudulent irregularities may include the following:

- Intentional violations of established management policy
- Intentional violations of regulatory requirements
- Deliberate misstatements or omissions of information concerning the area under audit or the organization as a whole
- Gross negligence
- Unintentional illegal acts

CONCLUSION

This chapter has presented a survey of selected professional standards for PE professionals. While PE professionals are generally not accountants or auditors by trade, an understanding of professional standards applicable to PE assists a professional in better understanding the procedures performed in compilations, reviews, and audits.

NOTES

1. Statement of Peter W. Rodino, Jr. on the 25th Anniversary of Hart-Scott-Rodino, available at http://www.ftc.gov/bc/hsr/rodinostmt.shtm.
2. *Source:* Sarbanes-Oxley Act of 2002.
3. *Source:* http://www.sec.gov/spotlight/dodd-frank/hedgefundadvisers.shtml.
4. "The Laws that Govern the Securities Industry," http://sec.gov/about/laws/.shtml, March 3, 2006.
5. "Anti-Bribery and Books and Records Provisions of the Foreign Corrupt Practices Act," U.S. Code, Title 15, Commerce and Trade, Chapter 2B—Securities Exchanges.
6. "The Laws that Govern the Securities Industry," http://sec.gov/about/laws/.shtml, March 3, 2006.
7. "Anti-Bribery and Books and Records Provisions of the Foreign Corrupt Practices Act," U.S. Code, Title 15, Commerce and Trade, Chapter 2B—Securities Exchanges.
8. SSARS 1, effective for compilations and reviews of financial statements for periods ending after December 15, 2005, by Statement on Standards for Accounting and Review Services No. 12.

Understanding Operations

III

Understanding
Operations

CHAPTER 14

Contemporary Business and Competitive Intelligence

Theresa B. Mack
James P. Martin

An automatic system is being developed to disseminate information to the various sections of any industrial, scientific, or government organization. This intelligence system will utilize data-processing machines for auto-abstracting and auto-encoding of documents and for creating interest profiles for each of the "action points" in an organization. Both incoming and internally generated documents are automatically abstracted, characterized by a word pattern, and sent automatically to appropriate action points.
—H. P. Luhn, *IBM Journal*, October 1958

INTRODUCTION

Business intelligence, a term first coined by H. P. Luhn in 1958, was formerly used to describe a computer system that acted as a repository for information centered on corporate strategy. Within this system were compilations of publicly available data and action points for various entities within the firm. These data would be automatically disseminated to appropriate parties by the system for efficiency and to encourage more expedient responses to the incoming data.

However, with time, the concept of business intelligence has broadened significantly. It now refers to the act of perceiving changes in a firm's external environment, and subsequently formulating a plan to shepherd these changes throughout the organization. Moreover, contemporary business intelligence refers to the gathering of quantitative data and the use of unique methods to analyze this information. In essence, contemporary business intelligence is highly intertwined with the principles of corporate strategy and marketing: businesses must perceive changes in their environment and then formulate a plan for action based on these events.

Throughout this chapter, the tenets of contemporary business intelligence and corporate strategy will be discussed, along with unique methods of analysis that may assist the reader in formulating more educated decisions. Statistical techniques, options analysis, and consumer behavior will all be examined with the hope that such a discussion may shed light on the necessity for businesses to undertake profitable projects that generate economic profit, while positioning the firm in a unique manner with its competitors. Applications to private equity (PE) will also be discussed.

CONTEMPORARY BUSINESS INTELLIGENCE

Firms operating in today's global economy participate in a highly dynamic environment that both influences and constrains their activities. As such, in order to ensure survival and future profitability, firms must continually perceive their external environment and formulate educated business decisions based on quantifiable data. The following sections describe these principles of contemporary business intelligence in detail, along with selected sample applications of the techniques.

Sources of Information

Business intelligence professionals view information as the gateway to sound, strategic decision-making practices. In this manner, we will now briefly describe a variety of sources by which business intelligence professionals may accumulate data, including public records searches, news archives, legal proceedings, patent awards and applications, social networking sites, (collectively known as "open source information") as well as employees.

Public Records Searches A number of companies will provide a cost-effective search of public records on a target individual or company, delivering near-immediate results via a web page. These searches collate information available in public databases to paint a picture about the target. For example, automobile registration records, property tax documents, boat registrations, and business registrations are all public records; when properly assembled, they can reveal quite a bit about a target's net worth, behavior patterns, and lifestyle.

Since these searches are based on public records, there is typically no special permission needed from the target to run such a search, and the target will not even know such a search was run. Credit histories, however, are not public records and typically cannot be accessed.

The Federal Credit Reporting Act was enacted in 1970 and provides strict guidelines as to when there is "permissible purpose" for gaining access to a personal credit file. An example of such permissible purpose exists when a potential investor or current insurer intends to use the information in connection with a credit risk assessment of an existing obligation.

News Archives The Internet is a tremendous resource, and many periodicals maintain online archives of articles. Additionally, news archival sites and databases maintain stories well beyond the archival periods of the original publication source. Searches can be applied based on the names of entities, the principals of the target company, members of senior management, or potential events.

Different search engines employ dissimilar algorithms to execute searches and frequently yield different results; for this reason it is important to utilize a variety of search engines. Obviously, searches are more effective when searching based on a more specific term, rather than a more general one.

Web site search engines also cache information as they "crawl" the Web for content. When searching, notice the hyperlink "cached" included as part of the search results. Even if the linked content is no longer available, the cached version of the content may still be viewable.

The Internet archive also can yield historical web site content long after changes have been made to the web site. Available at www.archive.org, the Internet archive "is building a digital library of internet sites and other cultural artifacts in digital form."[1] Entering a URL in the Internet archive search will return the archive pages captured at various points in time.

Legal Proceedings Court filings are in the public domain, absent an order to seal the file or other protective order. Consider the case of Richard S. Bobrow, then global chief executive at the Big Four accounting firm of Ernst and Young (E&Y). As a privately held firm, E&Y has no obligation to disclose details of its finances; however, on January 13, 2003,[2] every detail provided to partners internally through late 2000 became public as part of Mr. Bobrow's divorce trial. Mr. Bobrow was compelled to provide financial information as part of the case, and his attorneys failed to have the file sealed. A request for the information was made by the *New York Times*, and the judge ordered the information released. Mr. Bobrow retired from E&Y on October 11, 2003, with no comments on the reason for his departure.[3]

Similarly, financial and other information on private companies is often included in other public records, including hearings held by government agencies (e.g., hearings held by the Environmental Protection Agency regarding environmental impact), city council meetings, and other public forums.

Many courts have now made their legal records available through an Internet portal; this provides rapid access to legal information, including the names of parties to litigation, dates, attorneys of record, filing dates, and also the ability to request copies of documents.

Keep in mind that while the Internet is a source of voluminous information, simple Internet searches are not enough to adequately analyze a portfolio company or its executives. Information on the Internet could be dated, or completely erroneous, and thus should be verified with a primary source. Also, the information on the Internet is typically available to everyone else; thus, Internet information does not have a tremendous potential for competitive advantage over others.

Patent Awards and Applications The U.S. Patent and Trademark Office maintains an Internet database of granted patents and published applications. The database is searchable by multiple fields, including issue date and key words. Search results return the inventors as well as the assignee. The database is available at patft.uspto.gov.

The database can reveal patents issued relating to technologies relevant to an investment strategy, or directly issued to competitors. Additionally, new patents may be issued related to complementary technologies that could present a business opportunity: consider the case of an investment in a company that makes lightweight, high-torque electric motors learning that a patent has just been issued for a new fuel cell technology.

Social Networking In the past few years, Facebook, Twitter, LinkedIn, and other networking sites have grown in prominence. Individuals frequently post pictures, résumé details, and their daily thoughts on these sites for numerous individuals to see. While some sites, including Facebook, have provided users with additional features to protect their privacy, social networking sites contain a significant amount of information surrounding an individual.

Employees Employees are a wealth of information. They attend the trade shows and speak to customers, suppliers, and vendors. They often possess exemplary ideas about what is going on in the business and with the competition—your competition. Spend time interviewing your employees or, put another way, debriefing your employees at all levels, talking to them on a regular basis. Too many companies underestimate the amount and value of the information their employees (no matter what level) have. One needs to interact with the employees and maintain a communication channel whereby information of value can be obtained in a timely manner.

COMPETITIVE INTELLIGENCE AND THE EXTERNAL ENVIRONMENT

Competitive intelligence is the process of gathering, analyzing, and assimilating data about competitors, business trading partners, investment targets, or other entities of a firm's external environment in order to obtain some sort of competitive advantage. The techniques employed in a competitive intelligence process are, by definition, legal.

The practice of gathering this information is based on the supposition that there exists a tremendous amount of data available within the public space that can be located with persistence and used to a firm's advantage. Also, since the techniques are legal and the information is within the public space, organizations that fail to apply competitive intelligence techniques as part of their investment process are missing a vital component that is likely being applied by their competitors participating in their external environment.

An organization's external environment is defined as "all elements that exist outside the boundary of the organization and have the potential to affect all or part of the organization." All firms participate in a chosen "domain" that defines the firm's niches and "external sectors with which the organization will interact to accomplish its goals."[4]

In order to ensure survival and maintain profitability, firms must continually perceive their external environment and make appropriate changes to their "organizational domain" as necessary. Richard Daft provides an example of a company called Guiltless Gourmet, which experienced significant hardships because its managers were not focused on analyzing the firm's external environment. In the early 1990s, many businesses in the food and nutrition sector sought to develop low-fat products that satisfied discriminating consumer palettes in a healthy manner. One such company was Guiltless Gourmet of Austin, Texas, a maker of fat-free tortilla chips that "grew from the founder's kitchen into a $23 million enterprise operating out of an 18,000 square foot facility." Market share continued to grow through the mid-1990s, but by 2000 the company "was all but dead."[5]

In 1994, Frito-Lay, a snack-food heavyweight, had introduced a new line of low-fat Baked Tostitos chips to much fanfare: the company deployed "an army of 13,000 sales people" to promote its newly developed tortilla chips. Within six months of Frito-Lay's introduction, Guiltless Gourmet's orders "plummeted by 25 percent." The company "tried to compete, improving the taste of the chips and developing new packaging," but none of its efforts proved effective. Additionally, the low-fat craze gave way in the 1990s to the fat-loving Atkins diet, further impacting Guiltless Gourmet. By 2000, revenues had fallen below $9 million.[6]

Daft's example of Guiltless Gourmet manifests the necessity for firms to continually perceive their external environment and act upon these changes. In a little more than six years, the company had gone from riches to rags, primarily because it was not able to effectively position itself as a unique product that differed significantly from cheaper Frito-Lay offerings. Moreover, a shift in market demand away from low-fat foods further solidified the company's fate.

Too often firms react in an untimely manner to such changes and, in doing so, quickly lose consumers who turn to substitutable products. Once this shift begins, it reaches a critical tipping point at which consumers simply do not turn back. Malcolm Gladwell, in his book that popularized the "tipping point" phrase, gave the example of a glass, restaurant-style ketchup bottle that is being shaken by a hungry patron: When the bottle is first shaken, little or no ketchup emerges. The famished diner then proceeds to shake the bottle more vigorously until, suddenly, a voluminous glob of red goop lands on the plate, in the process peppering the patron's shirt with crimson splotches from the overspray.[7]

There are two elements to this story that relate well to the competitive marketplace. First, a "shakeup" of the market by a new entrant (in this case the diner's hand). Second, if this agitation fails to produce results, competitors often "shake" more vigorously to obtain favorable results. This latter action may have dire consequences for firms not quickly perceiving its environment.

Overall, shifts in a firm's external environment must be quickly and thoroughly analyzed. However, given the speed at which markets change, this information must be effectively prioritized in order for it to be valuable. In this manner, there are two dimensions in which issues should be classified: size and scope. By classifying shifts along these lines, the chance that the organization will experience "paralysis by analysis" will be effectively minimized.

NORMALIZING PERFORMANCE

Many companies routinely analyze and track their performance in a detailed manner. However, an important facet of this analysis is often overlooked: that of normalizing performance. When companies examine trends showcased by measured metrics, it is paramount that these metrics are compared against other leading competitors and across industries.

If a firm has been able to grow its net earnings at a compound annual growth rate (CAGR) of 5 percent over the past five years, management may applaud themselves for achieving such a feat. If, however, a pure-play competitor grew its earnings at a CAGR of 10 percent over the same time period, should management remain proud of their accomplishment? What if this firm was located in an emerging market economy, in which the gross domestic product had a CAGR of 15 percent over the same time period? Suddenly the once-lauded managers now appear to be underachievers.

Statisticians long ago developed metrics for comparing two similar distributions with varying means and standard deviation—namely, through the use of standardizing data. If a particular distribution possesses a mean of 5 and a standard deviation of 1, while another, similar distribution has a mean of 10 and a standard deviation of 8, standardization affords a way of comparatively analyzing the performance of data within both samples.

Let us first assume that the above figures represent the average and standard deviation of net earnings growth in two distinctly different industries. We will now employ this concept of standardization to understand how two firms may compare their performance, despite the fact that the distributions of these data have varying parameters. Suppose that Firm A operates in an industry where earnings have followed the first distribution, and Firm B's industry has earnings following the latter distribution. If Firm A's earnings grew by 7 percent (2 percent better than the industry average), and Firm B's grew by 13 percent (3 percent better than average for both firms), which firm performed better with respect to its industry?

If we assume that the earnings of both industries follow a normal distribution, then we can easily calculate each firm's performance using the concept of a Z-score and the standard normal distribution.[8] Using this statistical concept, we find that Firm A performed better than 98 percent of its peers, while Firm B performed better than roughly 65 percent of its peers. Thus, while Firm B was able to grow earnings at a faster rate (13 percent versus 7 percent for Firm A), Firm A's management deserves special praise for their achievement. In all likelihood, Firm A is the leader in its industry.

To further solidify this point, Exhibits 14.1 and 14.2 present simulated histograms of data with the aforementioned population mean and standard deviation (these figures will need to be estimated from sample firm data). Note that in Exhibit 14.1 almost no data points exist at an earnings growth of 7 percent, while in Exhibit 14.2 there are a large number of data points above Firm B's 13 percent.

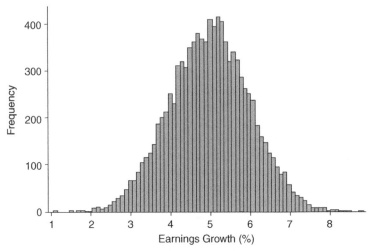

EXHIBIT 14.1 Histogram of Normally Distributed Random Data with Mean 5 and Standard Deviation of 1

Data normalization is also an important concept for businesses operated in seasonal and cyclical industries. Many retailers experience the highest sales levels of the year between late November and the end of December. Toy companies, chocolatiers, restaurants, computer firms, and many others see their demand levels peak during this time of year. Given this information, how can firms determine appropriate metrics for sales and earnings

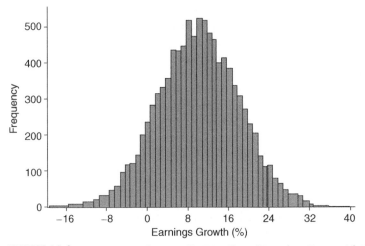

EXHIBIT 14.2 Histogram of Normally Distributed Random Data with Mean 10 and Standard Deviation of 8

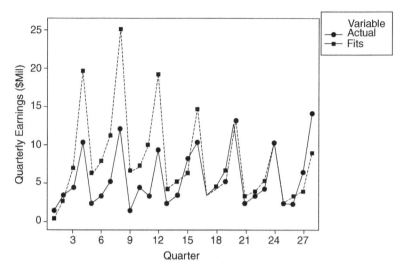

EXHIBIT 14.3 Example Using the Holt-Winters Method of Prediction

goals throughout the remainder of the year? How can they assess their performance during the holiday season with those of past years? The answer lies in parsing data and normalizing them according to this seasonality.

For firms operating in the above scenario, this analysis may involve parsing yearly data into smaller time periods (e.g., quarters) for better analysis. In doing so, many methods become available to the data analyst, one of which is the Holt-Winters method. This particular method takes into account both seasonality and linear trends over time to forecast data.[9]

Exhibit 14.3 presents sample data for a firm that experiences seasonality in earnings over a four-quarter period. The plot shows that, after about four periods of data (16 quarters), the Holt-Winters method gives relatively reliable predictions of firm performance. These predictions may then be used by management as a baseline to forecast future earnings, which may be further honed by incorporating the impact of novel management goals and initiatives in the forecast.

For the especially ambitious data analyst, use of the Box-Jenkins method for forecasts may also be appropriate.[10]

COST OF CAPITAL AND THE OPTION TO INVEST

Many established firms employ capital budgeting techniques such as net present value (NPV), internal rate of return (IRR), and payback period as the basis for capital allocation decisions. Among these methods, NPV is generally preferred by many businesses, while the IRR method is frequently employed by PE firms. Despite their near ubiquity, these methods are often used in a suboptimal manner when making business decisions. One of the most egregious errors used by businesses is often an incorrect cost of capital when formulating business decisions.

Research has shown that many firms use a prespecified hurdle rate as their cost of capital proxy when discounting cash flows. This hurdle rate, in some cases, was seen to be three to four times higher than the actual cost of capital, significantly impacting business decisions.[11] The justification for this hurdle rate is often that the company wants to err on the side of caution with respect to future projects; however, there exist alternative methods for supplementing a typical NPV analysis, which we will now discuss.

In spite of its frequent use, loyal fans of the NPV rule forget that it tacitly assumes that a project is a now-or-never proposition; that is, the project must be undertaken now or the opportunity will not exist in the future. This assumption is simply untrue for many business projects: the ability to invest at a later date generally exists for a majority of capital budgeting projects. Consider a simple example, similar to the one proposed by Dixit and Pindyck (1994).[12]

A pharmaceutical firm (Firm X) is looking to acquire a relatively young, private firm that currently has a drug awaiting Phase III approval from the Food and Drug Administration (FDA). While the young company has performed well in the past, the FDA approval process has negatively impacted the firm's cash flow and resources, forcing it to seek a joint venture partner. This partner will have to commit to an investment of $500 million immediately after signing the joint partnership agreement.

If the drug is approved, Firm X believes that the future cash flows from the project will be on the order of $150 million per year; if the drug is not approved, cash flows are estimated at roughly $20 million per year. We will assume that these cash flows begin one year from today and extend to perpetuity. Moreover, Firm X currently believes that the drug will be approved with a probability of 20 percent. If Firm X's cost of capital is 10 percent, should it approve the project?

Using the expected net present value rule, we find that the expected NPV of the project is $6 million; our calculations state that we should accept this project. See Equation 14.1 below for more details.

$$NPV = 0.2\left(-\$500 + \sum_{t=0}^{\infty} \frac{\$150}{1.1^t}\right) + 0.8\left(-\$500 + \sum_{t=0}^{\infty} \frac{\$20}{1.1^t}\right) = \$6 \quad (14.1)$$

However, while our NPV calculation was technically correct, it ignores the value of the option Firm X possesses in selecting when to enter the project. Suppose now that Firm X waits a year and will invest only if the drug meets Phase III FDA approval; it will not invest if the drug is rejected. Equation 14.2 presents the NPV calculation for this scenario.

$$NPV = 0.2\left(\frac{-\$500}{1.1} + \sum_{t=1}^{\infty} \frac{\$150}{1.1^t}\right) = \$210 \qquad (14.2)$$

Based on these calculations, it is clearly better to wait a year than invest now, should the opportunity be available. In essence, this option to wait a year is valued at $204 million—a very significant amount. As such, when examining future business opportunities, those well versed in business intelligence should examine not only the net present value of the project but also the value associated with delaying the investment and how this may impact the project.

Furthermore, in possessing a concrete understanding of a company's current cost of capital, managers may better project the economic profit associated with the project. This quantity is defined in Equation 14.3.

$$\text{EconomicProfit} = (\text{ROIC-WACC})^*\text{Capital} \qquad (14.3)$$

In Equation 14.3, *ROIC* denotes the return on invested capital for a particular project, *WACC*, the appropriate weighted-average cost of capital, and the final term, the capital consumed by the project. Clearly, without the ability to accurately determine a firm's weighted average cost of capital, managers may make improper judgments of a project's expected economic profit. As a consequence, total shareholder value may fail to grow as intended or, in the worst case, may even decrease.

DEVELOPING UNIQUE INTELLIGENCE

Microeconomic theory teaches us that in perfectly competitive markets prices approach the marginal cost of production; that is, in the long run, no firm will be able to make a profit. This result assumes that all firms in a market produce homogeneous goods (i.e., they are perfectly substitutable with each other), and that there are enough firms so that each is a price taker: no firm is able to influence the price for the goods.

Other models in economics support this conclusion in an even stricter sense. In 1883, Bertrand proposed a model of competition often used in contemporary game theory in which two firms produce identical goods that they then sell in a downstream market. In the model, each firm is able to select the price at which it sells its product to customers, and then supplies the demanded quantity of goods at the proposed price. Overall, using this model, Bertrand found that with just two noncooperating firms in the market, prices would equal marginal cost.

According to Bertrand's two-firm model, if Firm A sold a good at a given price \$X, while the other firm sold the homogeneous good at a price \$Y, customers would simply shop at whatever firm was selling the good at the lowest price; if X were equal to Y, both firms would get half of the demand. Therefore, in the long run, firms would compete against each other until they had sufficiently depressed prices to the marginal cost level, where neither firm would have an incentive to deviate from selling at marginal cost. If either firm raised the price, it would see no customer demand because it could not guarantee the other firm could do the same. Likewise, neither firm would sell goods at a price below marginal cost because that would prompt a shutdown of the business.

Although Bertrand's model makes numerous assumptions in arriving at this result, it nonetheless demonstrates the necessity for firms to produce unique products for sale in the marketplace. The global economy has drastically lowered the industry average marginal cost of production for many substitutable goods; some firms are able to compete in this aggressive environment, while others are not. Decreasing material and labor costs cannot provide a long-term solution for companies hurt by such competition. Instead, corporate retrenchment, and an overall "refocus" on a commitment to delivering unique products is the only long-run equilibrium solution. In successfully carving out a niche for products, the price a firm is able to charge for its goods will drift toward the monopoly price (i.e., away from the perfectly competitive scenario where price approaches marginal cost).

To this end, each business must develop its own unique intelligence in order to ensure its ultimate survival. This organizational deftness must focus on continually analyzing market movements and positioning the company to succeed in light of these changes. The onslaught of new competitors, breakthroughs in production technology, and changes in consumer demand must all be quantifiably measured and deliberately analyzed. Only after an analysis of these changes has occurred can a plan of remedial action be outlined; this document should include a proposal that details the manner in which the firm may retain its uniqueness in order to ensure future profitability. It is important to note that this uniqueness need not be based solely on proprietary technologies or techniques alone. One manner in which firms may successfully carve out an exclusive niche for their goods is by competing on product quality.

AN ECONOMIC VIEW OF QUALITY

If two firms produce goods that serve identical consumer needs, but one possesses a reputation for quality while the other's goods are known to have a limited life, consumers will often pay significantly more for the other firm's products. Although many consumers may not realize it, they are effectively performing a back-of-the-envelope NPV analysis when purchasing a good. Expected future utilities are estimated by the consumer, and these are then discounted back to the present time in order to arrive at an estimate of the price they are willing to pay for a good: a consumer will be willing to incur a cost for which the overall NPV of this particular purchase is not less than 0. Let us now formalize this example mathematically. Equation 14.4 presents an economic view of quality from the perspective of the buyer.

$$E(NPV) = E\left(\sum_{t=0}^{N} \frac{Utility}{(1+r)^t}\right) - Cost + E(Salvage) \qquad (14.4)$$

In this equation, N denotes the number of periods, r the buyer's discount rate, and E the expected value operator. In layman's terms, Equation 14.4 states that the expected NPV of a purchase is equal to the expected value of the discounted utility flows received from it, minus the product's cost, plus the expected salvage value. It is important to note that N, r, the periodic utility flows, and the salvage value are all random variables.

When a consumer purchases a good that he/she believes to be more durable, the expected number of periods over which the asset will operate, N, increases; this has the effect of increasing the consumer's expected NPV. Likewise, the utility derived from the product may increase with quality simply because the consumer associates higher utility with the comfort of knowing the product will last a long time: he/she worries less (i.e., incurs less disutility) that the product will break while in service. Lastly, the discount rate that the consumer applies to his/her "utility flows" is decreasing in quality: higher quality products are seen to be less risky, hence the discount rate decreases with quality.

Given the above relationships, it is important to note that an increase in quality provides a commensurate three-pronged increase in the expected NPV of the product. Thus, a very high valuation may be arrived at for a good of high quality solely on the basis of this trait. Holding constant a product's salvage value, an NPV-maximizing consumer will then be willing to pay more for a more durable good.

In using the options analogy from a previous section, one could make an argument that buying a more risky asset affords the consumer an implicit put option (i.e., an option to sell) on an early salvage: since the good may cost significantly less, a consumer may simply discard it if it breaks rather than pay to have it fixed. This put option serves to increase the expected NPV of a low-cost good, but, as this option's value is decreasing in the good's price, a product would have to cost significantly less than its competitor in order for this option value to eclipse the effect of the good's initial cost. This notion is formalized in Equation 14.5.

$$E(NPV) = E\left(\sum_{t=0}^{N} \frac{Utility}{(1+r)^t}\right) - Cost + E(Salvage) + E(Option_{Salvage})$$

$$(14.5)$$

DEVELOPING RELATIONSHIPS AND NAVIGATING CRISES

The old adage, "It's not what you know, it's who you know" rings especially true in today's super-connected age of businesses. Networking provides not only an opportunity for business development, but also affords a business the ability to withstand unforeseen shocks that may hit a firm.

Developing good relationships with key members of the firm's supply chain can prove especially valuable should short-term events impact the business. When firms experience financial difficulty, all participants in the supply chain change their perception of the manufacturer. Suppliers become wary that a potential customer will default on payments, and may require up-front compensation for delivery of goods. Likewise, downstream retail customers may forgo the purchase of the manufacturer's goods for fear that it may go out of business.

Relationships can significantly mitigate these supply chain risks and serve to assist companies should they get into trouble. If a manufacturer has developed long-standing ties with its suppliers, the manufacturer may be more sympathetic to the current situation and even assist the business in boosting its livelihood. Likewise, if a business has a long-standing relationship with its financial institution, tripped covenants may not trigger default but instead a renegotiation of terms that permits the business to get back on its feet.

When a firm faces a crisis, it is likely the case that the media will jump at the opportunity to cover the story. More often than not, these stories will portray the company in dire straits and incite fear in potential customers and employees. If a firm faces such a crisis, it is important that it use the media to its advantage: Using television and radio to broadcast the company's future plans and actions for change may help to instill confidence in potential consumers. Moreover, upbeat speeches detailing the company's future may also quell employee fears of impending financial distress.

APPLICATION TO PRIVATE EQUITY

PE investments are made based on financial representations and strategic plans, and investment decisions are hopefully backed by careful research and analysis. Strategic information can be gained through competitive intelligence techniques that can help support the PE life cycle.

Investment Decision

Enhanced due diligence describes the application of intelligence and forensic procedures to validate assertions made during the investment analysis phase. While traditional due diligence focuses on financial information, enhanced due diligence includes analysis of underlying internal control procedures, centers of expertise within the organization, and the capacity of the organization to grow and achieve projected targets. Additionally, since the principals of the PE fund will often be involved with the management of the portfolio company after the investment is made, a background investigation is often helpful in identifying potential issues that could affect the long-term relationship with the equity firm.

Competitive intelligence techniques can also be applied to identify business strategies of potential competitors, alternative investment targets, or the industry as a whole. Such information can help validate or, in some cases, refute evidence suggesting the investment should be made.

Strategic Management of Portfolio Companies

Risk assessment is a continuous survey of the business environment to identify any events or uncertainties that could affect the accomplishment of the organization's business objectives. As part of the risk assessment process, it is important to consider all possible types of risks and apply any available information to refine the assessment of the potential impact and likelihood of risk occurrence. Such assessment can be enhanced by understanding information accessible through competitive intelligence procedures, including industry expectations, competitive marketing plans and strategies, and pricing decisions.

Exit Strategy

Forensic valuation is a term used to describe the application of forensic procedures as part of a business valuation. It is important in a business valuation to make sure that all major representations are accurate and verified prior to determining the valuation amounts. Often, the persons responsible for maintaining the financial records of an organization, and for making representations about business operations, have a direct financial interest in determining a higher or lower value figure. Forensic procedures can help ensure an objective determination of value is achieved, rather than one motivated by revenue.

CONCLUSION

This chapter has presented selective elements of competitive intelligence that may benefit PE fund managers in selecting and overseeing portfolio companies. While business intelligence once connoted a repository for a business's strategic information, the term today refers to a process designed to help ensure a business remains ahead of its competitors.

NOTES

1. Internet Archive Mission, www.archive.org.
2. "Ernst and Young Financial Details Are Disclosed in Divorce Case," *New York Times*, January 14, 2003.
3. "Ernst and Young Chief Leaves after Holding Post a Year," *Accountancy Profession News*, added October 12, 2003, www.accountancy.com.pk/newsprac .asp?newsid=402.
4. Daft, R.
5. *Id.*
6. *Id.*
7. For further information, *see* Devore, J.
8. "Ernst and Young Financial Details Are Disclosed in Divorce Case," *New York Times*, January 14, 2003.
9. For further information, *see* S. Nahmias.
10. For further information, *see* C. Chatfield, "The Holt-Winters Forecasting Procedure," *Applied Statistics* 27, no. 3 (1978): 264–279.
11. L. Summers, "Investment Incentives and the Discounting of Depreciation Methods," in *The Effects of Taxation on Capital Accumulation*, ed. Martin Feldstein (Chicago, IL: Chicago University Press, 1987).
12. For further information, *see* A. Dixit, and R. Pindyck, *Investment Under Uncertainty* (Princeton, NJ: Princeton University Press, 1994).

CHAPTER 15

Organizations as Humans

Harry Cendrowski
James P. Martin

INTRODUCTION

Organizational theorists have long devised descriptive tools for analyzing businesses. For instance, in his seminal work, *Images of Organization*, Gareth Morgan critically examines firms by relating organizations to machines, brains, and even "psychic prisons," among other metaphors. Through these analogies, an analyst can gain an acute understanding of how a business works, and also how it can improve. Such a topic is particularly pertinent for private equity (PE) professionals because they often act as change agents for an organization.

Along these lines, this chapter will, in effect, serve as a "mental pause" for the reader: a break from the analyses of past chapters and a segue into those forthcoming on organizational improvement and operations assessments. After reading this section, one should be better equipped to understand and analyze the needs of organizations and how those needs are currently being met or evaded. Moreover, a new metaphor for organizations—in the vein of Gareth Morgan's work—will be introduced, that of organizations as humans.

An organization is a complex manifestation of a once original idea. Many of today's most prominent organizations are quite large in size, allowing for unwieldy analyses of their inner workings if a structured framework for investigation is not provided. This complexity and the search for a tangible metaphor are the motivation behind this chapter's central theme, organizations as humans.

Many businesses falter because their leaders fail to understand the intricacies of the environments in which they participate. It is hoped that by using this metaphor as a tool, the reader will be better prepared to dissect the somatic systems of the organization and to understand their interaction with each other and the environment surrounding the firm.

PURPOSE OF THE ORGANIZATION

Before delving too deeply into the organizations as humans metaphor and examining the stages of organizational life, it is first necessary to analyze the purpose of organizations and their reason for being. Organizations are "sociotechnical systems" with a high degree of "interdependence of technical and human needs"; within an organization, both needs must be firmly kept in mind.[1] Organizations must be cognizant of their own humanness and realize that all decisions will in some way impact their staffs. In this manner, they must serve to provide a working environment for employees that is both safe and stimulating in order to ensure employee contentment.

In his 1943 paper, "A Theory of Human Motivation," Abraham Maslow detailed a hierarchy of needs that each human seeks to satisfy over his/her lifetime. Maslow described a "pyramid" composed of five essential types of needs: (1) physiological, (2) safety, (3) love/being, (4) esteem, and (5) actualization. (See Exhibit 15.1 for a pictorial representation of Maslow's hierarchy of needs.)

Maslow believed that as humans fulfilled the lower-level needs (i.e., physiological, safety, etc.), they then sought gratification through achievement of higher-level needs.[2]

In using Maslow's framework to analyze employee contentment, the reader may notice that once lower-level needs are satisfied, people then seek esteem. Humans long for respect and also wish to respect themselves: recognition for deeds done assists the employee in promoting his/her own self-worth. Unfortunately, if one's workplace provides no way of fulfilling this need, as is sometimes the case in highly bureaucratic organizational structures, employees will never perform to the best of their ability.

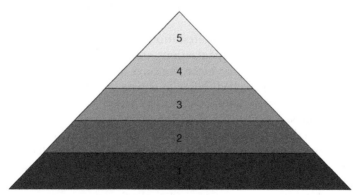

EXHIBIT 15.1 Maslow's Hierarchy of Needs

PE firms, especially those specializing in buyout transactions, should pay particular attention to the manner in which employees' needs are fulfilled when evaluating target businesses: if employees are not given a chance to shine, and, hence, fulfill their need for esteem, the efficiency of the business can likely be improved by rectifying this situation.

Moreover, in addition to satisfying the needs of employees, the ultimate goal of an organization is to please its shareholders and investors. For public companies, this means performing well relative to competitors and informing financial analysts at investment banks of the firm's goals, both immediate and long-term. For private companies (e.g., those run by PE firms), this means that the organization must serve the financial goals of those who hold ownership in the company. However, for both types of firms, the ultimate vehicle that makes both realizations possible is organizational survival.

Much as the goal of a man or woman is to raise a successful family (somewhat akin to shareholders in a company), organizations must ultimately survive to become successful and please shareholders. This is the ultimate goal of organizations, from conception to death.

GENESIS

Humans begin life as the realization of an idea: Both mother and father must make a conscious decision to conceive life in order for a baby to be born. They must have a passion and desire for one another and for life to bring a newborn into this world. While sometimes the execution of this idea may be arrived at "accidentally," the process of human conception involves a sequence of conscious decisions, all of which are the realization of one's innermost ideas and passions.

Much in a similar manner, an organization begins life as a realization of an individual's ideas and passions. Venture capital–backed companies like Apple Computer came to life because Steve Jobs and Steve Wozniak believed that the personal computer would someday replace large mainframes; Google was started by two Stanford students who developed a new search algorithm for the World Wide Web; General Motors (GM) was born of Billy Durant's vision to build the largest car company in the world.

Once conceived, humans and organizations are initially reliant on key figures during their gestation periods: neither can survive entirely on their own. Organizations require much wisdom and savvy of their founders to continue development during this crucial period.

Painstaking attention to all details is necessary for the organization's survival. If the finances run out, the organization is left powerless and paralyzed, with no way to communicate or realize its novel idea. What was once a promising idea is now nothing more than a stillborn thought forever etched in the minds of but a few people. Similarly, if the founder of an organization lacks the conviction to spearhead the development of his/her new product, the organization ends up in much the same state.

Organizations are dependent on their founding entrepreneur's ability to communicate his/her vision to investors in order to receive the funding needed to pursue an original idea. Venture capitalists typically accept only 1 in 2,500 proposals. As such, it is imperative that an entrepreneur be able to clearly communicate his/her thoughts to potential investors in order to ensure success for the company.

In much the same way, a baby is heavily reliant on its parents for nutritional and financial support. Both mother and father must carefully watch over their offspring to ensure that he/she receives the proper amount of food, shelter, and warmth. The child is fully dependent on its parents for fulfillment of its needs and requires the parents to pay extreme attention to every detail when caring for it.

This idea of interdependence between the parent-child and entrepreneur-organization model is crucial to the understanding of initial phases of organizations. Both babies and organizations are fully dependent on their creators for their maturation and development.

DEVELOPMENT AND SPECIALIZATION

Organizations and humans on the simplest level are a conglomeration of parts that must effectively work together to ensure survival. However, such a statement is not true when one examines the initial phases of both humans and organizations.

Humans begin life as a single cell when a male's sperm and a female's egg both meet in the female's body. Once this cell is formed, the process of mitosis begins, and the cell rapidly divides into two, then four, then eight cells, and on and on as the process of life begins to unfold. After several months, cells become more specialized in their workings and begin to divide their labor as the baby develops in the mother's womb. The beginnings of somatic systems are formed within the body, the cardiovascular, sensory, and nervous system being examples of the many specialized systems present within the body that must come together to produce a salubrious human being. Each system must eventually operate effectively in order to maintain the health of an individual.

Much in the same manner, an organization, at its core, is the idea of one person. While one may argue that some organizations are started by groups of people, it is invariably the work of a single individual (perhaps working with a team of individuals) who ultimately has the idea to start something new. This individual then begins the process of *organizational mitosis*, convincing others of the feasibility of his/her idea, until several people become committed to a unified idea.

At this point, the organization becomes incorporated and begins to form specialized units. Initially one person may specialize in engineering, while another concerns himself/herself with the day-to-day finances. As the organization continues to grow, staffs may be formed to specialize in key areas, much as cells do in the body. Somatic systems and their specialization are quite similar to the staffs of an organization. While each has a specific duty to perform, they are nonetheless reliant on other systems for sustenance and direction. If it were not for the brain, involuntary actions such as a heartbeat would not be possible. Furthermore, the interdependence of somatic systems symbolizes this intertwined aspect of organizations. For instance, while the pancreas is tasked with producing insulin to help break up sugars in the digestive tract, it is also reliant on the cardiovascular system for key nutrients such as oxygen in order for its survival.

Just as each human has its own set of unique DNA, so, too, does an organization: no two are exactly alike. For instance, while one may initially view all car companies as simply producers of cars who transform raw inputs into large outputs, upon further examination, one discerns the unique differences between organizations that result from their "organizational DNA." Toyota is run much differently from Ford Motor Corporation, although both produce automobiles.

Before imparting their fiscal knowledge upon newly acquired companies, PE firms should first seek to thoroughly comprehend an organization's "DNA" prior to formulating a strategic plan for the business. Failure to perform such an analysis may result in the creation of unreasonable/unwise goals for the business, given its current "genetic makeup."

PARTS OF THE WHOLE AND MATURATION

Progressing further toward the maturation of organizations and humans, one can see parallels between the degrees of specialization that arise for both objects. No organization can survive in an undeveloped state for long, especially in a capitalistic economy. With increased funding from financial sources comes a responsibility to meet milestones, as they are called in the venture capital business. The only way to meet these targets is for the organization to mature into a well-organized form. This is quite a challenge for both a human and an organization. A fetus must prepare for physical separation from its mother, while an organization must begin to separate itself (in terms of dependency) from its creator. During this separation, both organization and human first begin to take on a personality of their own, albeit still heavily influenced by their creators.

Organizations and humans, once they begin to mature, develop specialized parts that, when combined, form the complete whole. Moreover, there exist many parallels between the parts of the body and the parts of an organization.

The eventual chief executive officer (CEO) of an organization is much akin to a person's brain, the ultimate leader who is responsible for all actions of the organization. All functions of both the body and organization must continuously report to their CEO. The heart is much like the mission statement of an organization, its reason for continuation and further development. The skeletal system is similar to an organization's infrastructure in that it provides a rigid form for the organization, which is necessary for survival. The sensory system of the body is akin to the strategic planning and marketing arm of an organization, always perceiving the wants of the customer and translating these into actions for the organization to undertake.

Furthermore, once the maturation process starts, the organization begins to change from one that requires constant supervision to a learning organization that is able to think and perform actions at least partially by itself. Just as a toddler is able to scan and perceive its environment, and, in the process, react to such stimuli, an organization that develops this learning attribute becomes a much stronger player in its environment.

Morgan specifically notes, in his organizations as brains metaphor, that "successful learning organizations need to be skilled in the art of representation. They need to be able to create appropriate maps of the reality with which they have to deal." Morgan further notes that, this process "has to be active rather than passive."[3]

As the human progresses further into maturation, he/she becomes ever more aware of his/her surroundings, until the once-small child develops into a self-thinking adolescent. It is at this stage where further intellectual ties begin to break with respect to the child-parent system (and hence the organization-founder system), as the child develops critical thinking skills. These critical thinking skills allow both the human and organization to better perceive their environment, and, in the words of Morgan, "engage and experience the environment as fully as possible."[4]

The goal for any successful entrepreneur should be to create a company that, after a given gestation period, can survive on its own, even without further nurturing from its founder. Processes and policies should be instituted so that, should something happen to the entrepreneur, the organization may continue to operate. Similar to the child-parent relationship, the organization can always learn from the entrepreneur, but it should not be entirely dependent on a single individual for sustenance.

This is where the nurture versus nature argument separates, where adaptation to the present environment drives behavior, and reliance on developmental nature (founder's orientation) diminishes as a major evolutionary driver.

ENVIRONMENTAL ADAPTATION

Once both an organization and a human have reached suitable maturation, they must learn to adapt to their environment. The idea of one person, by now, is the foundation of a sound business plan, a plan that is developed in response to stimuli occurring in the environment surrounding the business.

Furthermore, as an organization matures, it comes to develop its own personality, hopefully in accordance with the products it produces or services it delivers in a given environment. As Morgan points out in discussing organizations as organisms, "Just as we find polar bears in arctic regions, camels in deserts, and alligators in swamps, we notice that certain species of organizations are better 'adapted' to specific environmental conditions than others."[5] This analogy also rings true for people in that some of us are better adapted to certain tasks than others. People typically classify themselves into two overly simplistic categories, left-brained and right-brained, with the former denoting someone who is logical, analytical, and objective, and the latter typifying one who is random, intuitive, and subjective. Some of us are instinctively good at mathematics, while others excel at art and English.

Likewise, organizations that survive in their environments are usually adapted to do so. Richard Daft's summary of an earlier work by Robert Duncan elegantly classifies organizations into four categories, characterized by two levels of environmental change and complexity. With respect to environmental change, Duncan discusses two levels of such change, stable and unstable; with respect to complexity, he discusses both simple and complex levels of this idea. For further information on the Duncan Framework, see Exhibit 15.2.[6]

In this exhibit, the stable-unstable dimension describes the manner in which change occurs in the environment, while the simple-complex dimension refers to the number of external factors affecting the firm.

Using this framework, Duncan is able to group companies into each of the four categories based on their environment, and identifies companies that are successful in each. For instance, computer and aerospace firms operate in both a complex and unstable environment, while beer distributors and container manufacturers operate in a simple and stable environment.

Environmental Complexity

	Simple	Complex
Stable	**Simple/Stable** 1. Small number of external elements, and elements are similar 2. Elements remain the same or change slowly Examples: Soft drink bottlers, beer distributors container manufacturers, food processors	**Complex/Stable** 1. Large number of external elements and elements are dissimilar 2. Elements remain the same or change slowly Examples: Universities, appliance manufacturers, chemical companies, insurance companies
Unstable	**Simple/UnStable** 1. Small number of external elements and elements are similar 2. Elements change frequently and unpredictably Examples: E-commerce, fashion clothing, music industry, toy manufacturers	**Complex/UnStable** 1. Large number of external elements, and elements are dissimilar 2. Elements change frequently and unpredictably Examples: Computer firms, aerospace firms, telecommunications firms, airlines

(Left axis label: Environmental Change)

EXHIBIT 15.2   Duncan Framework of Environmental Change and Complexity

In much the same vein as Duncan, Christensen groups people into four styles—analyzer, controller, supporter, and promoter—in his stylistic test "Lifescripts."[7] He further identifies the most effective environment for a person with each style. A matrix illustration of Christensen's framework is presented in Exhibit 15.3.

Here, individuals are classified according to whether they are task or people centered, and also whether they possess an introverted or

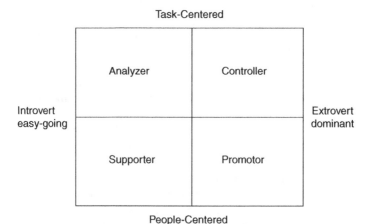

Task-Centered

	Analyzer	Controller	
Introvert easy-going			Extrovert dominant
	Supporter	Promotor	

People-Centered

EXHIBIT 15.3   Matrix Form of Christensen's Four Styles

EXHIBIT 15.4   Effective Environments for Christensen's Four Styles

Person with:	Supporting Style	Controlling Style	Analyzing Style	Promoting Style
Most effective environment is:	Supporting Reassuring Idealistic Unchanging	Competitive Open Challenging Opportunistic	Factual Scientific Practical Unemotional	Social Changing Youthful Optimistic

extroverted personality. Further characterizations of effective environments for each of Christensen's four styles are presented in Exhibit 15.4.

Drawing on parallels between the four categories, one can begin to analyze the similarities between Christensen's four styles and the modified Duncan framework. For instance, a "promoter" would feel quite comfortable in a complex-unstable environment.

"Promoters," according to Christensen, are most effective in an ever-changing environment that requires high degrees of interaction. Indeed, many computer firms that participate in a complex-unstable environment often have a stigma of embracing change and promoting social activities at work. The historic food fight at Apple Computer between developers of the Lisa and Macintosh computers further attests to the "promoter" style such organizations seek to foster.

"Analyzer" organizations are most comfortable in environments that are both simple and stable. These organizations are masters at understanding their current processes and the facts behind the business, which they then use to improve efficiency. Furthermore, these organizations are often "introverted" in the sense that they largely do not pay attention to the specific needs of their customer, nor do they necessarily need to in the short term.

"Supporter" organizations are somewhat akin to "promoter" organizations, except they are heavily introverted and operate in a complex-stable environment. Much like the "analyzer," they do not need to pay constant attention to their customers' wants and desires, but they are heavily centered on their employees.

"Controller" organizations typically participate in a simple-unstable environment. These organizations, and the industries in which they do business, are highly competitive and dynamic, yet customers have relatively few demands, most of which are similar in nature.

By using both the Duncan framework and Christensen's styles of people from "Lifescripts," one can form a unique perspective of organizations through personification and better understand their "human" personalities.

ENVIRONMENTAL INFLUENCE AND INTERACTION

While some organizations participate in a simple and stable environment, and largely do not have to worry about changes within their immediate sphere of operation, this number is decreasing significantly. The global economy has brought with it a renewed sense of urgency to firms that once operated in highly stable industries. Some firms are able to adjust to their changes in environment, while others are not able to do so without the assistance of a third party (such as a PE firm). Nonetheless, all organizations, irrespective of the type of environment they participate in, are shaped by and influence their environment.

Organizations live to produce products or deliver services to wanting customers. In order to survive, they must both understand and serve to shape their immediate environment. In describing the way humans interact with their environment, postmodernist French philosopher Michel Foucault used the term "discourse" to symbolize a construction that defines and produces objects of knowledge. Discourse, as Foucault believed, helps to shape the culture within which each human lives, and furthermore, each individual affects the discourse.

In recent years, many companies have become enamored with focus-on-the-customer techniques such as Total Quality Management (TQM) or Quality Function Deployment (QFD). But, in embracing these techniques, organizations have failed to acknowledge that they themselves participate in a discourse. They have the power to influence people and other organizations through inventions or new technology, as opposed to reacting to historical tastes.

For instance, while many watch customers were content with their fine Swiss or Danish timepieces, the industry was turned upside-down when Seiko "managers made the bold, proactive decision to substitute their quartz watch for their existing mechanical watches."[8] It did not help, of course, that these watches were both cheaper and more accurate than their counterparts.

Within this organizational discourse are any number of technology cycles at a given point in time, with each cycle being shifted by technological discontinuity. Venture capital firms often attempt to finance firms that they feel can produce such technological discontinuities, although, strangely, many venture capitalists dislike completely unproven, novel technology.[9]

Such features of organizational discourse provide for ripe comparative analyses to humans, who are typically involved in a number of learning cycles at any given point in one's life. While under the careful umbrella of our parents, we each hold values unremarkably similar to their own—we've been participating in a rather small discourse consisting of immediate family and a few friends. However, once exposed to a diverse student body at a major university, we begin to come out from under the umbrella and into a larger discourse, one that includes not only the college campus and its environs, but also the world itself, as many students on U.S. college campuses have roots in countries other than the United States. We make a discourse leap—just as a business makes a technological leap—when we hear about a new philosophy or reason for being that touches us in a unique way, and we embrace it as never before. It is these discontinuities that bring newfound ways of thinking to both humans and organizations, and on which each builds upon.

This exciting time of rising environmental awareness is particularly uplifting for both humans and organizations, and can characterize the adolescent stage of both organizations and humans as during this stage both items are involved in an intense process of learning. This is the ultimate state for organizations.

MATURITY CREATES "THE MACHINE"

While up to this point the analogy between humans and organizations has largely chronicled success, this module serves to discuss the middle to "over the hill" age for both items.

Having passed the adolescent stage of development, humans typically begin to settle into a life characterized by ordinariness. We become situated in the workplace, in the home, and in our lives in general. In short, it is during this phase of our lives that we most resemble machines. We tend to operate in a banal, efficient, reliable, and predictable way. Moreover, we tend to fail in recognizing many fresh ideas and approaches and instead engage in mechanistic thinking.

From an organizational perspective, middle age is a by-product of the paradox of success. Because an organization has been successful in the past, management believes that it must therefore be successful in the future. Nonetheless, as Etling Morrison notes, "We are . . . a society based on technological advance, and a civilization committed irrevocably to the theory of evolution."[10] These things mean that we believe in change; they suggest that if we are to survive in good health we must become an adaptive society. In short, in order to ensure success in both our personal lives and for our organizations, we must become adaptive participators in our environment.

If a human fails to adapt to his/her environment, he/she may suffer as others continue to grow in the wake of the prevailing discourse. In much the same way, an organization that soldiers on not thinking about its customers will ultimately fail as its consumers shift to new products not examined by the organization. Morgan summarizes this occurrence nicely when he says,

> *Mechanistic approaches to organization often have severe limitations. In particular they: (a) can create organizational forms that have great difficulty in adapting to changing circumstances; (b) can result in mindless and unquestioning bureaucracy; (c) can have unanticipated and undesirable consequences as the interests of those working in the organization take precedence over the goals the organization was designed to achieve; and (d) can have dehumanizing effects upon employees, especially those at lower levels of the organizational hierarchy.*[11]

These thoughts ring especially true when one considers the current state of the American automotive industry and its suppliers; the environment surrounding IBM and Xerox in the early 1980s; and even the encyclopedia industry as online, free reference sources such as Wikipedia continue to gain popularity. The parallels to human life are endless: If we neglect to notice changes in our spouses and their desires, we may soon lead a solitary life; if we neglect the changes in our children as they mature, we may soon become too domineering and pushy and repel them away from our environment; if we neglect changes in our friends, and fail to comfort them in times of need, they may question once loyal ties.

All in all, in today's global environment, there are few straightforward tasks to perform, and environments are rarely stable enough to ensure that the products produced will be the appropriate ones. The mechanistic middle-age years have dangerous consequences for both humans and organizations if not tread upon quite carefully.

DEATH OF THE ORGANIZATION AND REBIRTH

As is the case with all natural things, an organization at some point must pass away. While some organizations invariably last longer than some of their peers, no organization has been present since the dawn of man. At some point, all things pass on, and like humans, an organization must prepare to effectively die. For a human, identification of death is a simple, unchanging binary process: a person is either alive or dead. However, organizations in the modern world may effectively die, or go into bankruptcy, and reemerge several years later as a healthy, adept organization. This notion of death is somewhat akin to a Buddhist's belief in reincarnation, although to the authors' knowledge, no organization has yet achieved spiritual nirvana.

Nonetheless, it is often quite easy to identify an organization teetering on the edge of death. Unstable cash flows, plummeting stock price, excessive debt, investor unrest, and high turnover in the executive ranks all signal what may be inevitable. How does an organization come to be on the verge of death? Quite simply, by not understanding and learning from its environment.

Some organizations are born of great ideas and begin to flourish, but because of financial oversights and poor management, they pass quite quickly from the adept adolescent stage into a pre-death state. Conversely, older, more mature organizations may arrive at this stage in their life by failing to adapt to a changing environment and by treating their day-to-day operations in a mechanistic manner.

If, rather than filing for Chapter 7 bankruptcy (liquidation—and hence ultimate death), an organization is given a new shot at life through Chapter 11, a chance exists for the organization to be reborn and start anew. Such is the case with many automobile suppliers and airline companies today. Chapter 11 affords businesses the opportunity to restructure and reorganize, to shed the plaguing problems associated with the past, and begin the organizational life cycle anew.

Moreover, PE firms provide an important role in the life of organizations: they permit older, "mature" firms to drink from the "fountain of youth" and, hence, return to a more inquisitive, adolescent state. They also shepherd start-up firms through their nascent years. PE firms are change agents for companies of all organizational ages, although they invariably try to return an organization to a stage of adolescence, where firms may once again embrace and even create technological leaps.

STRENGTHS AND WEAKNESSES OF THE ORGANIZATIONS AS HUMANS METAPHOR

A complex metaphor like "organizations as humans" allows for rich comparisons and juxtapositions between something that is quite tangible for a reader (i.e., human life) and something that may be rather abstract (i.e., organizational theory). A primary strength of the metaphor is its ability to pinpoint the exact stage of an organization in its life.

For instance, with all the flurry (and talk of bankruptcy) surrounding GM a few years ago, including comments by President Bush, who said, "[GM] needs to build cars that are relevant," one might argue that they were in the middle to over-the-hill age of an organization. For years, a mechanistic approach to car building brought them success, largely because they were only one of a few competitors participating in an ever-growing market. They failed to challenge their own organizational norms and shunned many fresh ideas because they were deemed too costly. In the end, the organization briefly died when it filed for bankruptcy in June 2009.

However, the GM of today is much different from that of several years ago. After emerging from bankruptcy, GM's management has re-devoted itself to building products that are highly prized by consumers, and also to embracing technological leaps, such as vehicles propelled by alternative technology (e.g., the Chevrolet Volt). While GM remains a mature company, management is succeeding in rejuvenating a once over-the-hill firm. Additionally, one may look at a large, mature organization like Toyota and see that, while mature, it is still relatively young and agile at heart. One could, however, make an argument that Toyota has begun to reach the maturation phase of its organizational development, given several recent missteps concerning product recalls.

While years and age have a direct correlation in life, they do not have an identical relationship in organizations. Specifically, a company may be quite old in years, but if its state of mind serves to keep pushing it ahead of the competition, it may be deemed quite young in age.

Another strength of the metaphor is the way it exposes the needs of an organization if it is to achieve survival, its ultimate goal. In order to be successful, an organization must fully understand its discourse, how it both participates in and influences its environment. This environment is not static, but rather dynamic and ever-changing. As Morgan states when referring to organizations as organisms, "The focus on 'needs' also encourages us to see organizations as interacting processes that have to be balanced internally as well as in relation to the environment."[12]

Yet another strength of the metaphor is the way it emphasizes the importance of stressing innovation and overall adeptness in order for the organization to be successful. Organizations cannot become overly mechanistic and set in their ways if they are to be forever successful. They must remain in a state of constant learning, much like that of a maturing adolescent, in order to survive in the global economy.

On the weakness side, the metaphor is, unfortunately, not able to accurately describe the correct way to shape and mold an organization from a bureaucracy standpoint. It is largely unable to comment on symptoms of structural deficiency, or how to remedy them, but it does showcase the importance of the humanness each organization must possess in its infrastructure to be successful.

A further weakness can be showcased by the fact that the metaphor rests many of its key assumptions on what Morgan calls "functional unity."

In short, "if we look at organisms in the natural world we find them characterized by a functional interdependence where every element of the system under normal circumstances works for all the other elements." That is to say that an organization is extremely dependent on the operation of its parts to be a successful "whole."[13] Conversely, in real life, one finds that different parts of organizations often lead separate lives themselves and still find success (however, if this phenomenon becomes too pronounced, the organization can be in serious danger of becoming stale).

CONCLUSION

While the organizations as humans metaphor does have some limitations, it provides a tangible—though complex—viewpoint from which one can critically examine an organization with success. Just as many people wish they could forever remain 21 years of age, it is important for organizations to try and remain in such a state of "mature adolescence," no matter how many years they have been in business. Doing so will allow the organization to achieve its ultimate goal of survival and to please both its employees and shareholders as it continues through life.

Reshaping mature organizations into inquisitive adolescents should be the focus of buyout fund managers as they embark on their quest to generate returns. Likewise, venture capitalists should shepherd their organizations through the maturation process so that they may become successful, independent entities.

NOTES

1. For further information, *see* G. Morgan, *Images of Organization* (Thousand Oaks, CA: Sage Publications, 1997).
2. A. H. Maslow, "A Theory of Human Motivation," *Psychological Review* 50 (1943): 370–396.
3. *Id.,* p. 91.
4. *Id.,* p. 92.
5. *Id.,* p. 33.
6. Reproduced from Richard L. Daft, *Organization Theory and Design* (Mason, OH: Thomson Learning, 2004). For further information, *see* Robert B. Duncan, "Characteristics of Perceived Environments and Perceived Environmental Uncertainty," *Administrative Science Quarterly* 17 (1972): 313–327.
7. For further information, *see* T. Christensen, *Lifescripts: An Inventory of Personal Strengths* (South Bend, IN: STS Management Resources, 1981); or www.shrm.org/testing/products/Lifescripts/lifescripts.asp.

8. For further information, *see* M. Tushman, P. Anderson, and C. O'Reilly, "Technology Cycles, Innovation Streams, and Ambidextrous Organizations: Organization Renewal Through Innovation Streams and Strategic Change," *Administrative Science Quarterly* 35, no. 4 (1990): 604–633.

9. *Id.*, p. 9.

10. For further information, *see Etling Morrison,* "Gunfire at sea," Chapter 2 in *Men, Machines, and Modern Times* (Cambridge, MA: MIT Press, 1968).

11. For further information, *see* G. Morgan, *Images of Organization* (Thousand Oaks, CA: Sage Publications, 1997).

12. *Id.*

13. *Id.*

CHAPTER 16

Beginning the Lean Transformation

Harry Cendrowski
James P. Martin

INTRODUCTION

Much like past quality initiatives, lean manufacturing initiatives have cropped up at numerous firms across the nation—and, indeed, the world. While some companies (notably Toyota) have succeeded in implementing lean manufacturing and its beliefs, other companies have failed miserably in realizing the benefits this discipline can offer. Given its importance in reshaping buyout-backed firms, this chapter explores lean transformation and common reasons why organizations fail to properly implement it successfully.

One of the most prominent reasons for the collapse of lean transformation initiatives is the failure of the entire organization to adopt the tenets of lean manufacturing; it is not simply a manufacturing initiative. It is for this reason that this chapter will refer to the beliefs of this discipline as lean operations, and not lean manufacturing.

As buyout funds often look for distressed companies to acquire, a profound understanding of lean operations (aka Lean) and its principles can assist managers of these funds in turning around their portfolio companies. At its core, Lean is a process improvement tool, centered on improving the efficiency of the organization at every level and in every department. Its primary goal is the deliberate reduction of waste throughout all facets of the organization. When implemented properly, Lean creates a corporate culture driven by feedback and continuous improvement. It is this culture—not the tools of Lean—that will drive the organization forward to success.

While there exist many books and papers written on the implementation of lean manufacturing processes—and the tools commonly used in doing so—it is not the goal of this chapter to supplement this body of existing work. Rather, in reading this chapter, the reader should gain an understanding of the common pitfalls associated with the implementation of Lean and its proper method of implementation. As such, this chapter primarily focuses on laying the foundation for a lean transformation, a crucial series of steps that is often missed by organizations and frequently leads to less-than-satisfactory results.

Hiring external consultants to implement Lean is not enough. These ephemeral employees will not remain with the corporation long enough to ensure that the organization exudes a commitment to continuous improvement at all levels (a primary goal of Lean). Instead, it is essential that management themselves are well versed in the tenets of Lean, and that they are the main force driving it throughout the organization; tacit management compliance and/or support for external consultants will lead to disastrous results.

The Origins of Lean Operations: Lean Manufacturing

It is unfortunate that Lean precedes the word "manufacturing" in nearly all settings in which it is used. At its core, Lean is a process of guiding principles by which an organization should be run—not just the manufacturing arm of a business. Accounting, finance, engineering, manufacturing, and all other facets of the organization need to embrace the mentality of Lean before it can deliver results.

However, despite the many advantages that Lean offers, numerous companies have failed to implement it in a manner that delivered consistent, positive results—and for good reason. Too many companies jump head first into the implementation of lean tools before their organization is ready.

One of the main tenets of Lean is the elimination of unnecessary waste throughout the manufacturing process. And, many firms today still employ manufacturing methods that are obese: bloated inventories and wasted time at both the shop floor and management levels characterize the operations at the firm's facilities.

Implementing Lean processes without first training employees and management in the tenets of this philosophy can lead to dismal results. The consequences of such action are somewhat similar to an overweight man or woman buying an undersized pair of pants in order to lose weight without first changing his/her diet: in addition to proving difficult to wear, after a short time, the too-small trousers will create immeasurable discomfort for the owner. Moreover, many passersby will likely be quite appalled by the sight of the skin-tight vestment.

Potential Pitfalls of Lean

Before delving into the proper method of implementing Lean philosophy in one's company, it is important to first review the numerous pitfalls associated with becoming lean.

It is no secret that many manufacturers have spent large sums of money trying to convert their organization from one that embraces mass production to Lean. Some of these implementations achieve high levels of success, while many others do not achieve the results management initially expected to realize through this transition. Too many firms try to "push" Lean throughout the organization instead of "pulling" it through when the organization is ready.

Consider a typical scenario in which an organization begins its implementation of Lean by reducing inventories on the plant floor (a key tool of Lean). If machine uptime is low, a reduction of buffers between stations will starve the system, causing production delays and, hence, an increase in costs. Moreover, such a poorly executed attempt at a Lean transition will inevitably degrade employee morale and incite a general loathing for Lean within the minds of workers.

In this scenario, many manufacturers return to the drawing board and select a new Lean tool to push through their firm's production system; they fail to realize that they have skipped several necessary steps on the path to Lean implementation. In the process, morale continues to sink, and cost benefits are rarely realized.

Similar to the J-curve of a private equity (PE) portfolio, the implementation of Lean tenets at a portfolio company will undoubtedly require tremendous resources for a minimum of two years following the start of such an initiative. During this period, benefits will not outweigh the costs, and significant teething problems will arise; Lean is not a quick fix. As such, its implementation within PE portfolio companies must be made with deliberation and constant monitoring.

Toyota, arguably the world's foremost expert in lean manufacturing, has devised and implemented their system of production over the course of 30 years; it did not transform its facilities overnight. This is not to say that a grassroots implementation of Lean will take 30 years. Many companies can begin to see success after only two to three years—if the process is properly implemented.

Too often, those who are tasked with executing Lean initiatives are not well versed in its tenets. These individuals frequently focus solely on realizing immediate financial rewards brought about by Lean, and fail to center the initiative on changes in the overall process. Such a focus on monetary rewards leads to short-term optimization of the entire initiative. In order to properly implement Lean, a company must not only develop a new process to deploy the initiative throughout the organization, but must also institute safeguards to ensure that successes realized through Lean will be sustained. In this manner, it is essential that, prior to the implementation of Lean, a firm is genuinely ready to accept a major shift in its status quo and embrace a new method of thinking.

In the following sections, a general methodology will be described for laying a Lean foundation at organizations. Two distinct steps associated with this process, organizational development and discipline building, will be described in detail.

Organizational Development

To say that a Lean transformation begins with management is a gross under-statement. While many organizational theory textbooks and articles detail a need for management to embrace change, few companies adhere to this mantra when instituting Lean practices. (Even the Committee of Sponsoring Organizations of the Treadway Commission describes a necessity for setting a tone at the top.) All too often, executives who believe Lean is a panacea for organizational issues attempt to force it through the establishment without first understanding the discipline themselves and important components of the Lean transformation process. Educating management and conditioning the entire organization for change are perhaps the most important parts of a Lean transformation—and the first steps in such an initiative.

Lean transformations will achieve the best results when the aforementioned tasks are rolled out to the entire organization—not just manufacturing. Obtaining uniform support for the initiative requires constant teamwork between not only manufacturing employees, but also between those within all departments of the organization. A manufacturing division of an organization can employ best-in-class methods and have top-notch management, but if the accounting department fails to pay the electricity bill on time, the plant will still shut down.

Hiring outside consultants expressly for the purpose of a Lean transformation is a good start, but in doing so, managers are not given a chance to demonstrate their desire to learn the tenets of Lean, nor their ability to sustain the process once consultants leave. Bringing in a group of temporary consultants can only lead to disaster if management lacks a thorough understanding of Lean. Once the consultants leave to institute change at another company, management is left standing without its former crutch of knowledge.

For PE funds, the Lean transformation of a portfolio company first begins with talent at the PE firm level. All PE firms participating in the manufacturing arena should have a well-trained staff whose sole function is the institution and maintenance of Lean at portfolio companies. If a fund does not currently possess a staff, a team of individuals should be hired from reputable firms in industry. These individuals should demonstrate a thorough understanding of Lean, and also be able to point to numerous projects where they championed such initiatives prior to being hired by the firm.

In possessing such a staff, the PE firm effectively has its own group of consultants. Their purpose should not include implementation of Lean at portfolio companies; instead, they must focus on management education. Management at each portfolio company should be tasked with the actual execution of Lean initiatives.

Once a portfolio company's management is well versed in Lean, the executive team should begin to formulate vision, mission, and values statements to guide the organization in the coming years. The vision statement should define the future of the organization, while the mission statement should describe the manner in which this vision will be achieved. Statements describing the company's values should reflect the firm's organizational culture and priorities. (See Chapter 15 for further discussion on these statements.)

All of these statements should be brief but detailed, and should be displayed throughout the organization as a constant reminder to employees. Following are examples of such statements for an automotive components manufacturer:

- *Vision statement.* Our firm strives to be the technological market leader of high-quality automotive components for our customers.
- *Mission statement.* We will deliver our products on time and in accordance with our customer expectations. We will commit significant resources to our research and development staff in order to bring these products to market. Employees at all levels will demonstrate a commitment to quality.
- *Values.* We believe an emotionally rewarding, safe work environment is of highest importance to our employees. We value our employees' suggestions and will implement them wherever possible.

In addition to formulating such statements, it is of paramount importance that management continually reinforce the beliefs behind these words through their actions, or the words could serve to debase employee morale. If, for example, the firm that developed these statements has failed to implement any employee suggestions in the past year, the values statement will serve as a constant reminder to employees of management's indifference to their concerns.

After the vision, mission, and values statements have been developed, management should begin to focus on the formulation of short-term (three to five years) and long-term (10 or more years) business plans, a robust policy deployment process, well-defined roles and responsibilities, and a system that rewards behavior and performance that supports a Lean environment. It is important to note that while a PE firm will not likely possess a portfolio company for more than five to seven years, the implementation of long-range planning and goals will help buoy valuations and increase exit multiples.

In a Lean environment, every employee must understand his/her role in the company, and management must direct employees toward their goals through an established policy deployment processes, such as a Plan-Do-Check-Act (aka Deming or Shewhart) cycle. See Exhibit 16.1 for further details.

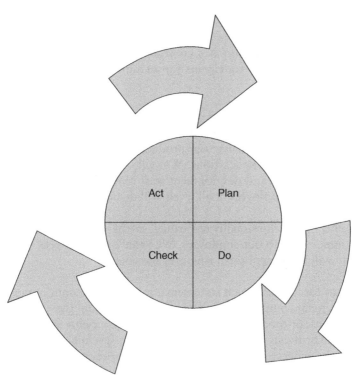

EXHIBIT 16.1   Plan-Do-Check-Act or Deming Cycle Representation

In this cycle, the four phases are characterized in the following manner:

- *Plan.* Establish objectives and processes in accordance with the firm's vision, mission, and values statements.
- *Do.* Execute the plan.
- *Check.* Monitor the process and variance to the established plan.
- *Act.* Apply corrective actions if necessary.

In a sense, the Deming cycle is somewhat akin to the cruise control function on a car. The driver establishes a desired cruising speed (Plan); the driver depresses the cruise control button after the desired speed has been established (Do); the vehicle's onboard computer monitors the car's speed and calculates any variance in desired speed from actual speed (Check); and, if road conditions change, the vehicle's throttle is increased or decreased in order to speed the vehicle up or slow it down (Act).

Additionally, when implementing plans using the Deming cycle, managers and employees should be monetarily compensated on their implementation of such initiatives and the success they achieve in establishing them; employees must be held accountable for their actions and the implementation of strategic initiatives.

Discipline Building

Once top management and employees recognize the need for change—and Lean's role in this transformation—another step must take place before Lean is implemented in the company: discipline building. This often represents the biggest challenge an organization must overcome on the road to Lean.

This phase of a Lean transformation requires the institution of a framework to convert a mass production facility into one that embraces Lean. Without such a deliberate approach, many companies will fail to sustain the gains in productivity that they realize from early Lean initiatives.

The first step in instituting a culture of discipline throughout the organization is winning employee support for management decisions. Without a respect and appreciation for management, line workers will resist change and may even sabotage the initiative. Resolving lingering safety and ergonomic issues, along with the creation of a visible employee suggestion box, will signal to employees that management cares about their health and well-being. If recreation areas for employees do not exist, they should be created. Moreover, the corporation should sponsor sporting and social events in order to keep employees involved in the workplace—even when they are not physically in the building.

For years, employees at Delta Airlines were known for wearing their employee uniforms while off duty, and even ordering personal checks with corporate logos, symbolizing their pride for the company.[1] Such corporate pride should be the envy of company executives everywhere. It provides validation for management by tangibly demonstrating that employees feel valued in the workplace.

Once worker morale has improved, a principal practice may be instituted throughout the company that will set the foundation for future use of Lean tools: standardized work. Standardized work is the bedrock of Lean, and of efficient operation in general. For line workers, devising a standardized work procedure means the creation of a single, best-practice process for workers to follow at every station on the line. This process should be posted at the worker's station and frequently updated to accommodate production changes.

In order to do this, manufacturing tasks should be broken down into essential movements. These movements should then be timed several times in order to obtain an overall average for each movement. A document with these processes should be posted at the worker's station and frequently updated to accommodate production changes.

The implementation of standardized work procedures ensures that the current state of the facility is documented, and future improvements can be readily measured against the status quo. For instance, if a standardized work process sheet is revised and includes the elimination of a step from the job, the overall improvement can be easily measured.

Standardized work is also beneficial for nearly every part of the organization. For instance, in the accounting department, its implementation can assist new employees in quickly understanding the ropes of their new job. When new employees are provided with detailed worksheets outlining their roles and responsibilities—and how to properly perform them—few questions will exist regarding an employee's duties.

Continuous improvement, or *kaizen,* is the goal of standardized work. As time goes on, and employees progress in their skills, standardized work methods should be updated by the employees in order to provide them with ownership of the process, and also to create a personal incentive for them to improve their performance on the job. For instance, if a worker suggests an improvement to a business process that he/she believes may save the company money, this worker should be compensated for such a suggestion.

As mentioned at the beginning of this chapter, Lean is a process improvement tool. This improvement is facilitated by a thorough understanding of the current state in the form of developing standardized work because, if the current state cannot be determined, managers can never measure improvement.

Once standardized work has been implemented, and employees genuinely believe that the company wants to improve, the tools of Lean may be introduced into the workplace.

What Private Equity Means for Lean

As discussed in the opening chapters of this book, PE funds (save those that are evergreen) are legally obligated to liquidate their assets and distribute returns at the end of a set period, typically 10 years. In light of this obligation, PE fund managers should be particularly vigilant when attempting to institute Lean at one of their facilities.

The implementation of Lean tenets at a portfolio company will require tremendous resources before the financial gains from the initiative can be measured. However, despite these unavoidable issues, the implementation of Lean within a portfolio company will eventually begin to pay dividends, and also provide an excellent selling point for the business (especially with strategic buyers).

In order to reap the greatest financial benefits, PE fund managers should decide whether or not to implement Lean shortly after the portfolio company has been acquired. Doing so will permit the portfolio company to realize gains in earnings before interest, tax, depreciation, and amortization (EBITDA) from the initiative, while facilitating the future sale of the company at a higher enterprise value-to-EBITDA exit multiple. Moreover, private equity firms can realize a significant amount of benefits from the implementation of Lean if they simply lay the foundation for Lean tool usage (e.g., *kanban cards, visual management, 5 S workplace, pull system, etc.)* by following the above steps to change the current corporate culture.

One aspect of Lean that is generally forgotten by "green-in-Lean" implementers is that Lean is a *people* system: employees are responsible for the implementation of Lean, and also for ensuring that the system remains focused on continuous improvement. If employees are not treated satisfactorily— or feel that they will not benefit from a Lean transformation—they may, knowingly or unknowingly, sabotage the initiative. This implication is particularly important for PE firms.

It is no secret that PE ownership brings with it connotations of job layoffs and sharp reductions in costs, both of which serve to unsettle employees and make them feel uneasy. In order to combat this corporate zeitgeist, it is essential that PE firms cultivate a sense of employee pride; every little thing counts.

Better cafeteria food, small subsidizations of meal costs, periodic employee gatherings and social events—even better toilet paper in company restrooms—can all instill a feeling within employees that they are genuinely valued by the firm. Moreover, in implementing the aforementioned suggestions, employees will feel that executives are trying to break down the "brass ceiling" that bifurcates so many corporations. Instead of employees being grouped into two classes—workers and management—all employees will begin to believe that they are part of a single class, working toward a common goal of corporate success.

When individuals feel that they share common motivations, and are a genuine part of the corporate whole, they will instinctively make decisions to benefit the corporation: this is management's ultimate goal. No amount of safeguards or clichéd corporate banners (e.g., those displaying trite sayings like, "Is what I'm doing good for the company?") can effectively augment the collective conscience of individual employees. Only when these workers privately possess a desire for the company to succeed will the brass ceiling be broken; this enables PE firms to achieve a high internal rate of return.

When a company invests in its employees, its employees will, in turn, feel that they possess a vested interest in the company. As such, they will make nonhedonistic decisions that—to borrow a term from economics—maximize not only their personal utility but also the utility of the corporation. The achievement of this state of pareto-optimal decision making will enable PE firms to more expediently achieve their distributions, while concurrently benefiting employees at all levels of the corporation.

CONCLUSION

Lean provides a mechanism by which organizations can improve their efficiency in nearly every aspect of the business. While frequently employed in manufacturing, Lean tenets can be used in accounting, finance, program management, and other areas. Lean, however, is not without its pitfalls. When these pitfalls are mitigated and Lean is properly implemented, it can help PE firms achieve greater rates of return and also provide a more rewarding environment for PE portfolio company employees.

NOTE

1. C. Dade, "After Delta's Recovery, New Turbulence Stirs," *Wall Street Journal*, October 4, 2007.

CHAPTER 17

Performing Manufacturing Due Diligence Assessments

Harry Cendrowski
Adam A. Wadecki

INTRODUCTION

An extremely important—and sometimes overlooked—aspect of private equity (PE) investment due diligence is the portion that focuses on the operations of a manufacturing firm. While many financial buyers will often pore over the numbers, it is also important that the buyer thoroughly understand the current state of a target firm's manufacturing operations prior to purchase. Along these lines, visits to each of the company's facilities will provide the buyer with great insight into the efficiency of the target's plants. These visits need not require a large amount of time. In some cases, even an hour-long tour can provide sufficient information for a detailed analysis.

PERFORMING THE ASSESSMENT

After introducing the tenets of several manufacturing processes and philosophies in a previous chapter, we now describe a detailed methodology for performing manufacturing plant assessments. Although plant assessments do not require a significant amount of time, experience is required in order to perform them proficiently. The best way to learn how to properly assess plants is to actually perform the task.

A facility tour is the first step in performing an assessment. The tour will demonstrate to the analyst how the facility is run, in addition to visually conveying its strengths and weaknesses. Notes should not be taken by assessors while on the tour. This can be especially distracting, and, furthermore, it does not permit the assessor to get a true sense of the plant floor dynamic. Instead, immediately following the tour, assessors should congregate in a conference room and share/record their ideas.

In addition to a plant tour, interviews should be scheduled with members of the management team, financial staff, and operators in order to get a sense of how these individuals interact on a daily basis—and to understand their perceptions about the facility.

Following are several areas of importance that assessors should seek to address when performing facility assessments.

Employee Satisfaction

Nearly every management textbook discusses the necessity of employee satisfaction; however, few books describe how such a metric can be measured. Employees are the foundation of every business, and shop floor employees are the basis of a firm's production. As such, it is imperative that employee satisfaction be assessed at each plant visited by an assessor.

One of the first signals an assessor will receive about the level of employee satisfaction is the attitude of the employees giving the plant tour. It is suggested that assessors briefly tour the facility at least twice: once with management and again with shop floor employees if at all possible. These tours should be separated in order to glean more information about the management-employee relationship from line workers, who often open up to outsiders when their superiors are not around. Moreover, touring the facility solely with the workers will permit an assessor to better perceive the employees' pride in their workplace.

Likewise, a tour with management will also provide the assessor with much information about employee satisfaction. In some cases, management may assert that the management-worker relationship is strong, but an assessor can easily discern the truth about this relationship. While on the facility tour, the assessor should observe whether or not workers greet their superiors or simply ignore them as they pass by. If the latter scenario best describes what was seen on the tour, it is clear that the management-worker relationship is strained, at best.

Moreover, while on the tour with management, an assessor should inquire about current worker absenteeism rates and whether these rates have changed over the past few years. Plants in which employees feel undervalued often exhibit high absenteeism rates, especially around holidays and the first day of hunting season. Also, such plants will generally possess higher levels of medical incidences as workers may seek treatment for minor (or even nonexistent) illnesses in order to obtain a break from the banalities of their job.

Some newer facilities—especially those without labor union representation—train workers in multiple job functions in order to minimize the boredom associated with repetitive work. Workers can then rotate between jobs up to several times per day in order to "keep them on their toes." Cross-training can also assist in mitigating the risks of absenteeism as multiple workers can fill in for a missing worker.

It is imperative that all employees involved in making a finished product feel satisfied with their job; yet, this is especially difficult in a typical factory environment where workers continuously perform repetitive jobs for eight hours or more per day. However, when employees feel valued, they will make better decisions on the job, perform to higher standards, and even generate product sales as they spread the enjoyment of their job to company outsiders.

The employee suggestion box (or lack thereof) is also a great indicator of employee satisfaction within a plant. If the facility has a high level of suggestions received, and also regularly implements such suggestions, this is a signal that management values its employees and that they likely, in turn, feel appreciated. The number of employee suggestions and their implementation should also be tracked by management.

The following questions are an excellent starting point for evaluating overall employee satisfaction:

- Do the employees leading the plant tour appear excited about showing the facility or indifferent?
- While on the tour, do line-level workers greet/acknowledge management?
  - Do they acknowledge their superiors by their first name?
- If the plant is unionized, how would one characterize the union-management relationship?
- Are workers organized in teams?
  - Are these teams supervised by hourly or salary personnel?
  - Do these teams have regular meetings?
- Does management identify worker absenteeism as a problem?
  - What percentage of workers are absent around holidays and the first day of hunting season?
- What percentage of workers receive medical treatment of any form on a daily basis?
- Are workers cross-trained (this may not be possible in union facilities)?
- Are there recreational areas for employees?
  - Are pictures of employee sports leagues posted on the walls?
  - Does the company sponsor employee social events (e.g., picnics or car shows)?

- Is there an employee suggestion box?
  - Where is it located?
  - What percentage of suggestions are implemented?
  - Are the number of employee suggestions tracked by management?
- Off the tour, do line workers visibly display pride in the products they are making?
  - How often do they mention conflicts with management?

Customer Satisfaction and Perceived Quality

Customer satisfaction is the *raison d'être* for the existence of any business: without an end market for demand, businesses would not be able to generate the revenues necessary for survival. Many of today's companies recognize customer satisfaction as being paramount to the success of the business, and yet the methods by which firms translate this metric to the plant floor vary widely—even within factories owned by the same company.

Although facilities may track customer satisfaction, it is essential that management translate aggregate customer satisfaction to the shop floor level, where employees feel they can make a tangible contribution to the issue. For instance, senior managers may set a goal for the plant of attaining a given score on an industry-wide quality survey; however, mid-level managers must decide what such a survey means to each individual operator on the floor.

Consider the case of an automobile manufacturer. Many such firms participate in J. D. Power's Initial Quality Study (IQS), which measures the number of defects per 100 vehicles in the first 90 days of ownership. J. D. Power derives these figures from surveys sent out to customers. At the end of the survey period, results are tallied and are reported for each make and model in a firm's portfolio. J. D. Power also presents quality awards to individual plants making the automobiles. Through vehicle identification numbers, the research firm can trace a car all the way back to the facility from which it originated. In 2011, Toyota's Cambridge South, Ontario, and Kyushu 2, Japan, plants in addition to Honda's Greensburg, Indiana, plant won J. D. Power's Platinum Plant Quality Award "for producing vehicles yielding the fewest defects."[1]

While the number of defects per plant is an effective metric for customer quality, this aggregate figure means little to the operator on the line installing parts. In order for this individual to measure his contribution to customer satisfaction, a metric should be devised for each individual workstation that assists employees in measuring the customer satisfaction and quality associated with their job. For instance, while an assembly plant may be measured on its IQS score, the operator responsible for installing door seals may be tracked by the number of wind noise or water leak complaints reported by customers; the operator responsible for headlight installation may be tracked by the number of customers reporting improperly aimed headlights; and so on. Scores for these operator-centric issues should be tracked in-station (if possible) and in a visual manner. In this way, employees can feel greater ownership of the processes on which they are measured.

Moreover, employees should have a keen sense of the immediate customer for their products. When asking operators where their product moves after they finish assembling it, they should not reply, "We fill up this tray, and it's picked up every hour. We don't really know who uses it." If they instead reply, "We fill this tray, and then it's moved to Fred in the trim department," then the assessor knows that these employees have a good sense of the overall process flow.

While on a plant tour, the assessor should review the following questions in order to gauge the plant's commitment to customer satisfaction:

- How is customer satisfaction measured?
  - Are customer satisfaction ratings clearly displayed so that employees can readily see them?
  - Do operators have knowledge of warranty costs?
- How is quality measured within the plant?
  - Are these metrics readily visible to employees?
- Are aggregate quality and customer satisfaction metrics translated to the workstation level?
  - Do employees at each station understand critical customer quality issues?
- Do employees know their immediate downstream customer?

Corporate Vision and Mission

Whether or not it is displayed, every facility serves a purpose in producing products for its parent company. However, it is not always the case that a plant prominently displays vision and mission statements to its employees.

Every employee needs to understand the vision for his/her facility and how they are supposed to achieve this vision; this is the purpose of the mission statement. Vision and mission statements should be short, pointed, and lack generic terms. Both should lucidly convey the role the facility plays in a firm's operations as well as specific goals for how this role will be fulfilled.

Consider the following mission/vision statement:

This facility will provide its customers with low-cost, world-class products of the highest quality. We strive to produce our products in a timely manner while maintaining our commitment to the

environment. We believe a rewarding, safe work environment is of
highest importance to our most important asset: our employees.

While likely well intentioned, this statement provides too general of a
vision for the facility. Does it strive to produce low-cost products or those
of highest quality? The reader will note that these goals generally differ dia-
metrically. With such a blanket goal, employees on the line may not understand whether they should maximize quality or efficiency.

Moreover, the closing sentence can be somewhat of a double-edged
sword for the facility: If management demonstrates to the employees that
they are indeed valuable, this statement's inclusion is warranted. If, however, management fails to express their appreciation for their staff, this
statement serves as a continual slap in the face to employees. The reader
need only rent the comedic movie *Office Space* in order to realize how such
statements can debase workers.

When visiting any facility, it is imperative that vision and mission statements be displayed, understood, and agreed to by employees. For this reason, it is suggested that all employees—not just management—participate
in their creation. This provides workers with a sense of ownership over the
process, which further creates an incentive for them to support and understand the goals.

An assessor should seek to answer the following questions related to
mission and vision statements when visiting a facility:

- Are the corporate vision and mission statements visible?
  - Do they contain specific goals?
  - Do they lack generic terms?
  - Are they brief?
  - Do the operators comprehend these statements?
- Were the mission and vision statements developed with input from all
  employees?
- How does management reinforce the goals set forth in the vision and
  mission statement?
- Do the employees agree with these goals?

Equipment and Facility Maintenance

Manufacturing facilities are often filled with expensive equipment that requires frequent, periodic maintenance in order ensure reliable operation.
In the best plants, manufacturing equipment is kept clean and is maintained using a well-documented preventative maintenance (PM) program,
as opposed to one that merely reacts to machine failures. PM refers to

the act of repairing a machine before it breaks, and maintaining it to a high standard.

Machines in plants with PM programs are generally free of dirt and debris, and maintenance records are located directly on the machine for easy use. The date of purchase and initial cost are stenciled on the machine, and the maintenance records are maintained and up to date.

When touring a facility, look for examples of machines that are both old and new. If it appears that new machines are dirty and the area around them is unkempt, then the plant likely does not value the equipment as a prized asset. By contrast, if one sees a relatively old machine that appears as if it were just installed, this is a signal to the assessor the machines are generally well maintained.

Plants following maintenance best practices will require line workers to perform periodic, routine maintenance on machines in order to give them a sense of ownership of the process. Such a procedure is frequently called *autonomous maintenance*. With operators performing the bulk of routine maintenance, dedicated maintenance workers can focus on repairing machines that fail unexpectedly, and also on planned machine downtimes. Operators should also have a say in what type of equipment is purchased, as they will inevitably be using this equipment on a daily basis.

Moreover, when PM programs are aggressively followed, less expensive pieces of equipment will receive the same amount of attention as costly machines. This practice signals to employees that management values the equipment as well as the activities operators perform that are critical to equipment maintenance.

When performing an operations assessment, the cleanliness of the overall facility should also be evaluated. A clean workplace signals to employees that the company values their safety and happiness. In this manner, an assessor should evaluate the overall facility by asking himself/herself a simple question: Would the assessor be proud if he/she managed the facility?

Restrooms should be clean and tidy, lights should not be burned out, ventilation filters should be relatively clean (indicating that they have been recently changed), and the exterior of the building should largely be free of blemishes. The food in the cafeteria should not resemble Oliver Twist's gruel, and all functions requiring food should be catered by the cafeteria (indicating that management eats the food).

On the whole, an assessor should seek to address the following questions when assessing a plant's commitment to equipment and facility maintenance:

- Does the facility have a PM program?
  - Do operators directly perform PM (autonomous maintenance), or is this done by a central maintenance department?

- Does the facility have planned downtime for machine maintenance, or does it simply replace parts when machines have failed?
- Are maintenance activities logged on an in-station worksheet, or in a central location?
- Are tools and maintenance equipment organized in an orderly fashion?
- What is the machine uptime percentage of critical equipment?
  - Is machine uptime tracked in station?
- Are expensive machines more readily maintained than their less expensive counterparts?
- Are purchase dates and prices recorded directly on the machine, or on a worksheet immediately near it?
- Are production employees involved in the purchase of equipment and tools?
- Is the facility clean and tidy?
  - Are the restrooms clean?
  - Are any lights burned out?
  - Is the facility dust free?
    - Are the dust filters clean or dirty?
  - Is the exterior free of blemishes?
- Is the food in the cafeteria satisfactory?
  - Do caterers supply food for management meetings (as opposed to the employee cafeteria)?

Visual Management

Visual cues are the heart of any best-in-class facility. At any point in time, employees should be able to instantly discern inventory levels, quality rates, and customer satisfaction. When performing an operations assessment, an assessor should ask the following questions that address a facility's visual management system:

- Are organizational tools, such as kanban cards, visible?
- Are inventory levels maintained through use of visual cues?
  - Can inventory be counted "at a glance"?
- Are workstation tools clearly labeled and organized in an orderly manner?
- Are operational goals prominently displayed?
  - Is it easy to determine the current status of actual performance versus goals?
  - Are these charts up to date?
  - Are audit results clearly visible?
- Can the status of machine PM be readily determined?

- Do operators have a sense of the pace of production?
- Do workstations have clearly defined borders?
- Is scrap properly tagged and readily visible?
  - Is scrap separated by part, or aggregated?
- Are Andon boards present and functioning?

Workstations should have clearly defined borders (sometimes called pitch lines) in order to maintain workplace organization and to give operators the sense of ownership over their own area of the facility. In the same manner, operational goals (such as in-station quality levels) should be displayed in an obvious manner. Operators should be able to see these goals—and the current status of the facility's performance to these targets—with ease. Within the workstation, visual cues for PM should be used so that operators can instantly know the status of maintenance on the machine.

Across the facility, display boards showing the performance of each workstation to overall *takt* time should be visible. This permits operators to easily sense whether or not they are ahead or behind the production schedule. Moreover, if the facility employs a pull system, these display indicators can indicate to the operator whether a downstream workstation requires more goods.

In the best facilities, scrap parts are tagged and are readily visible; scrap is not hidden away where operators (and management) cannot see it. Making scrap parts visible permits management and floor operators to discern at a glance which areas of the facility are experiencing quality issues.

Andon boards are also an essential tool in monitoring problem areas of the facility. They provide operators and maintenance personnel with an instantaneous readout of any problems within the facility and indicate whether a response team is on its way.

Inventory Management and Product Flow

Lean manufacturing initiatives have attempted to transform many mass-production facilities with typical batch and queue workstations into just-in-time production plants. However, as discussed in the previous chapter, many such initiatives have failed because of poor implementation approaches.

One of the first aspects of production that many lean initiatives seek to change is the methodology according to which inventory is handled: large stockpiles of parts being pushed downstream are removed, and a pull system is implemented.

The first step in evaluating a plant's inventory management is to look for any large build-up of work-in-process (WIP) inventory between workstations. If an assessor sees such a build-up, he should try to estimate the number of WIP pieces and the station's overall cycle time. Using this information, an assessor can discern the amount of inventory in the pile. In most instances, no more than a few minutes of WIP inventory should exist. Should large stockpiles exist, the assessor should investigate if the inventory is being caused by scheduling issues, or because of a bottleneck process. Furthermore, when observing inventory, the assessor should also examine the amount of WIP transported by forklifts. If the plant is cluttered with these vehicles, it is likely that the facility's layout is inefficient.

In this manner, it is important that the plant be laid out in continuous flow lines, where products flow downstream with little transportation around the facility, as opposed to machine shops, where groups of machines are simply clumped together because they produce similar parts. The latter form of organization is not conducive to lean manufacturing's tenet of one-piece flow.

Most facilities will have an inbound freight area where inventory is temporarily stored before it is transported to the line. The assessor should analyze whether material is organized in a manner that facilitates first-in, first-out (FIFO) flow. For instance, if a factory stores inbound freight directly against a wall, it may be difficult to pull the oldest items from storage, as access to the backside of the inventory is not possible.

Overall, the assessor should seek answers to the following questions when analyzing inventory management and product flow:

- Are there any stations with excessively large WIP inventory build-ups?
- Are products "pulled" downstream rather than "pushed"?
  - Do workstations produce to a schedule, or to replenish inventories?
  - If schedules exist, are schedules for workstations independent of one another?
- Is the facility organized in a manner that facilitates minimal material movement?
  - Are there many forklifts transporting items throughout the facility?
- Are there any observable bottleneck processes?
  - Are there any machines that exhibit poor uptime?
- How many deliveries per day does the plant receive?
- What is the amount of raw material on hand at any one point in time?
- Is inventory organized in a way conducive to FIFO flow?

OPERATIONAL DATA AND COST OF SALES

Aside from answering the preceding questions, an assessor should also gather basic operational data on a given facility. Some suggested data to gather are presented in Exhibit 17.1. These data are from Professor R. E.

EXHIBIT 17.1   Suggested Plant Assessment Operational Data

Measure	Metric
Sales volume	Yearly customer sales dollars
Unit production	Number of yearly production units
Production employees	Number of hourly employees
Average wage rate	$ per hour
Fringe benefits	% of wage rate
Salaried employees	Number of employees
Average salary	Yearly base pay plus fringes
Total employees	Total production & salary people
Employee turnover	% employees that leave each year
Direct/indirect ratio	Ratio of direct labor to indirect labor
Overhead rate	Direct labor rate multiplier
Workforce grievances	Number outstanding for union workforce
Average overtime	% overtime by employees over year
Direct material cost	Actual $ or COS%
Average working capital	Inventory + Accounts receivable − Accounts payable
Order fulfillment	% of orders delivered on time
PP&E	$ Book value of property, plant, & equipment
Equipment state	Old technology or up to date
Equipment condition	Preventive maintenance effectiveness
Plant size	Square footage
Product complexity	Number of different product families
Process complexity	Number of different process types
Operations type	Job shop, line flow, batch, assembly
Operations mix	What mix of operations types?
Daily demand variability	Short-term variability—peak to average
Yearly demand variability	Seasonal variability—peak to average
Equipment utilization	Average equipment utilization
Finished goods inventory	$ or units of finished goods
WIP inventory	Raw material & WIP inventory levels
Bottleneck process?	What is the operation's bottleneck?
Theoretical flow time	Theoretical time to produce products
Actual flow time	Actual time to produce products
Environmental issues	Noise, air, effluents, etc.
Safety record	Incidents per employee per year

COS, cost of sales; PP&E, property, plant, and equipment; WIP, work-in-progress inventory.

Source: http://webuser.bus.umich.edu/Organizations/rpa/RPARATINGSHEETs.xls.

Goodson of the University of Michigan, a former head of Johnson Control, Inc.'s (JCI) automotive seating business, and also past chief scientist at the U.S. Department of Transportation. (Professor Goodson helped grow JCI's seating business from $150 million in revenue to $1.3 billion.)

These data can be used not only to compare the facility to its peers, but also to produce an estimate of its cost of sales (COS). For instance, while on the plant tour, an assessor can gather the preceding information from interviews with management and the financial staff, and then use this information in a manner similar to that presented in Exhibit 17.2. Where information cannot be gleaned from a plant tour, the assessor may use information in Exhibit 17.3.[2]

EXHIBIT 17.2 Cost of Sales Example for a Facility

Plant Data	Value	Plant Data	Value
Yearly sales	$100,000,000	Material % of COS	56%
Gross margin	15.0%	Freight in % of material	4.0%
Total production workers	350	Scrap & rework in material	3.0%
Indirect workers (in above)	110	Plant size sq ft	150,000
Salaried staff	55	Plant fixed cost $/sq ft	$5.00
Standard hours/yr	1,800	Plant variable cost $/sq ft	$4.50
Average direct labor rate	$15	Equipment fixed cost	$4,000,000
Average indirect labor rate	$17	Equipment variable cost	$750,000
Average hourly overtime	10.0%	PP&E	$6,175,000
Fringe %	42.0%	Manufacturing O/H rate	300%
Average salary	$50,000	Salaried O/H rate	60%
Salaried fringes	30.0%	Corporate allocation %/sales	2.00%
Salaried overtime	10.0%	Tour evaluation 55 (Table 1) rating; 5 yes's for Table 2	

COS RPA "Cut"	RPA COS	% COS	Traditional COS Computation	Value	% COS
Yearly sales	$100,000,000		Sales	$100,000,000	
Direct materials + freight in	$48,156,077	56.7%	Material % of COS	$49,645,440	58.4%
Production people costs	$15,379,452	17.1%	Direct labor	$7,128,000	8.4%
Salaried people costs	$3,932,500	4.6%	Manufacturing overhead	$21,384,000	25.2%
Total people costs	$19,311,952	22.7%	Salaried O/H	$4,840,000	5.7%

PP&E	$6,175,000	7.3%	Corporate allocation	$2,000,000	2.4%
Other	$9,356,971	11.0%	COS	$85,000,000	100.0%
Corporate allocation	$2,000,000	2.4%			
COS	$85,000,000	100.0%			
Gross profit	$15,000,000				
Gross margin	15%				
Sales per employee	$ 246,914				

Note: direct labor is 8.4% of COS, while total people costs are 19.2%.
COS, cost of sales; O/H, overhead; PP&E, property, plant, and equipment RPA, rapid plant assessment

Source: http://webuser.bus.umich.edu/Organizations/rpa/RPAtablecost.xls.

EXHIBIT 17.3 Typical Data for Operations Assessments

No.	Variable	Low Side	High Side	Nominal
1	Yearly sales per employee—Manufacturing	$10,000	$560,000	$340,000
2	Yearly sales per employee—Assembly	$280,000	$1,680,000	$560,000
3	Production hourly wage rate—Manufacturing	$10	$27	$18
4	Production hourly wage rate—Assembly	$10	$25	$13
5	Hourly wage rate—Retail	$7	$17	$10
6	Production hours per year (less vacation & holidays; see Note [2])	1,732	1,920	1,850
7	Fringe—FICA & Medicare taxes (employee portion only—1/2 of total)			9.4%
8	Fringe—Medical for family per year	$4,200	$9,100	$5,300
9	Fringe—Workmen's compensation per year—production employee	$300	$1,000	$400
10	Fringe—Insurance, AD&D, other per year % of hourly wage rate	5.0%	12.0%	7.5%
11	Fringe—Vacation, holiday, sick leave/production employee—days/year	15	30	22
12	Fringe—for hourly employees—% of yearly base pay	25%	95%	40%

(continued)

EXHIBIT 17.3 (*Continued*)

No.	Variable	Low Side	High Side	Nominal
13	Annual average salary for plant employees	$40,000	$90,000	$50,000
14	Fringe—for salaried employees—% of yearly base pay	20%	40%	25%
15	Plant fixed costs per sq ft per year	2	7	5
16	Plant variable costs per sq ft per year	3	6	5
17	Yearly equipment fixed costs—% of COS—Heavy manufacturing	4%	10%	6%
18	Yearly equipment fixed costs—% of COS—Assembly	2%	6%	4%
19	Yearly equipment variable costs—% of COS	1%	7%	4%
20	Sales per sq ft per year—Manufacturing	$110	$560	$220
21	Sales per sq ft per year—Assembly	$220	$1,120	$560
22	Gross margin—Manufacturing	10%	55%	30%
23	Gross margin—Assembly	7%	30%	15%
24	Material % of COS—Manufacturing	25%	60%	45%
25	Material % of COS—Assembly	60%	80%	70%
26	Manufacturing overhead rates—% of direct labor hourly cost	200%	500%	275%
27	Salaried overhead rates—% of direct yearly salary	30%	100%	60%
28	Corporate allocations—Percent of sales	1%	5%	3%
29	"Other" plant costs % of COS—Manufacturing (see Note [3])	5%	20%	12%
30	"Other" plant costs % of COS—Assembly	6%	15%	8%
31	Working capital to sales	−5%	35%	18%
32	Inventory to sales	5%	30%	15%
33	Accounts receivable—Days outstanding	15	120	45
34	Account payable—Days outstanding	20	90	45
35	Inventory turns per year—Assembly	10	125	20
36	Inventory Turns per year—Heavy manufacturing	3	20	10
37	Hours to assemble an automobile	20	80	35
38	Hours to assemble a typical seat set for an automobile	0.5	2.5	1.0
39	Hours to assemble a PC	0.1	0.5	0.3

40	Hours to manufacture a heavy-duty truck	50	100	60
41	Typical manufacturing overhead variances	3%	20%	7%
42	Property, plant, & equipment investment to yearly sales	15%	100%	25%
43	Equipment depreciation—Years	3	15	7
44	Indirect to direct labor ratio	10%	150%	33%
45	Salary to production worker ratio	10%	50%	18%

AD&D, accidental death and disability; COS, cost of sales; FICA, Federal Insurance Contributions Act; PC, personal computer.

Although constructing a COS analysis is beyond the scope of this chapter, the reader is encouraged to review Professor Goodson's online examples of how to construct such an analysis.[3]

CONCLUSION

Facility assessments are an essential part of due diligence for PE firms looking to purchase any firm that produces products for an end consumer. When performing an assessment, the assessor should attempt to evaluate employee satisfaction, customer satisfaction and perceived quality, the company's vision and mission statements, equipment and facility maintenance procedures, inventory and product flow, and the visual management techniques used by the facility.

Moreover, by performing an on-site assessment, a PE firm can devise a detailed cost of sales analysis for the facility.

NOTES

1. For further information, *see* http://businesscenter.jdpower.com/news/pressrelease .aspx?ID=2011089.
2. For further information, *see* http://webuser.bus.umich.edu/Organizations/rpa/ COSTemplates.xls. Data updated using CPI values from the Bureau of Labor Statistics, www.bls.gov.
3. For further information, *see* http://webuser.bus.umich.edu/Organizations/rpa/ RPAtablecost.xls.

About the Authors

Harry Cendrowski, CPA, ABV, CFF, CFE, CVA, CFD, CFFA
President, Cendrowski Corporate Advisors, LLC, Chicago, IL, and
Bloomfield Hills, MI

Harry Cendrowski is a founding member and Managing Director of Cendrowski Corporate Advisors (CCA). He is also a founding member of Cendrowski Selecky PC and The Prosperitas Group. Over his 30-year career, Harry has worked hand-in-hand with businesses, private equity and venture capital funds, attorneys, and nonprofit organizations to address their needs. He has helped businesses mitigate risks, streamline their operations, and deter fraud. He is a veteran of the private equity and venture capital industries, where he has implemented back and middle office operations and performed due diligence assessments of potential portfolio companies. In the legal community, Harry's experience has allowed him to serve as an expert witness in numerous economic damages analyses, contract disputes, lost profit analyses, business valuations, and partnership disputes.

Harry sits on boards of numerous nonprofit and charitable organizations. A passionate advocate for assisting families and children in need, Harry is an Advisory Board member of the Schiller DuCanto & Fleck Family Law Center at DePaul College of Law and an Active Trustee for La Rabida Children's Hospital. He is also a supporter of higher-level education and serves as the Chairman of the Madonna University Foundation, Vice Chairman of the Madonna University Board of Trustees, and Chairman of their Finance Committee and Investment Committees. Harry received a "Committed" award from the Association of Fundraising Professionals for his dedication to the educational community.

Theresa B. Mack, CPA, CFF, CAMS, CFCI, PI
Senior Manager, Cendrowski Corporate Advisors, LLC, Chicago, IL, and
Bloomfield Hills, MI

During her 22 year career with the Federal Bureau of Investigation (FBI), Theresa was instrumental in solving high-impact and extensive white collar crime investigations. The majority of her career as a Special Agent was

devoted to the investigation of bank fraud, corporate fraud, money laundering, wire and mail fraud, identity theft schemes, copyright infringement,
and bankruptcy fraud. She also developed and honed her interviewing techniques during her tenure at the FBI by conducting thousands of eye-witness
and confidential informant interviews. Theresa is a member of the American Institute of Certified Public Accountants, the FBI Agents Association,
the Association of Certified Anti-Money Laundering Specialists, and the International Association of Financial Crimes Investigators. A graduate of
Aquinas College, Theresa began her professional career with Pannell Kerr
Forster, CPAs.

James P. Martin, CMA, CIA, CFE
Managing Director, Cendrowski Corporate Advisors, LLC, Chicago, IL,
and Bloomfield Hills, MI

Jim specializes in providing comprehensive risk assessments, focusing on the
evaluation of operating effectiveness of business processes and the internal
control structure along with the development of recommendations for
improvement. In many cases, these services were provided to companies
where basic internal control lapses had led to financial reporting and operational issues. Jim has performed forensic examinations of numerous
business arrangements to determine the accuracy of recorded transactions
and presentations, including the health care, durable equipment, real estate,
and construction industries.

Jim holds a B.B.A in Accounting and an M.S. in Accounting Information Systems from Eastern Michigan University. Jim has served on the facul-
ties of Davenport University, Walsh College, and the University of Detroit-
Mercy, where he instructed courses in Fraud Examination, Managerial
Accounting, Internal Auditing, and Information Technology. Jim is a
coauthor of *The Handbook of Fraud Deterrence* published by John Wiley
& Sons, Inc.

David A. McClaughry
Principal, Harness, Dickey & Pierce PLC, Troy, MI

David A. McClaughry has practiced exclusively in the field of intellectual
property law since 1993. Mr. McClaughry represents clients in a diverse
range of legal and technical matters. He has litigated numerous patent,
trademark, and copyright cases in federal courts to successful conclusions.
He has also represented numerous clients before the U.S. Patent and Trademark Office by preparing and prosecuting hundreds of utility and design
patents.

Stephen T. Olson
Principal, Harness, Dickey & Pierce PLC, Troy, MI

Mr. Olson is a member of the Executive Committee at Harness Dickey. His practice is devoted to all areas of intellectual property law with a particular emphasis on the creation and management of both patent and trademark portfolios, as well as the clearance of new products. Mr. Olson is a graduate of the University of Michigan College of Engineering and the Michigan State University Law School (cum laude). Mr. Olson is registered to practice before the U.S. Patent and Trademark Office.

Louis W. Petro, PhD, CPA, CMA, CFE, CIA, CISA, CFM, CCP, PE
Senior Manager, Cendrowski Corporate Advisors, LLC, Bloomfield Hills, MI

Since 1969, Dr. Petro has taught auditing, systems, accounting, and finance courses at a number of colleges and universities in Michigan and Ontario, Canada. He was the Dean of the Lawrence Technological University (LTU) School of Management from 1979 through 1989.

From 1971 through 1979, Dr. Petro held consulting and auditing positions at the CPA firms of Ernst & Young, Plante & Moran, and Grant Thornton. He was a Management Advisory Services Manager at Grant Thornton in Chicago immediately prior to becoming the Dean at LTU.

Prior to his auditing and consulting career, Lou was a manufacturing engineer at the Chevrolet Division of General Motors (GM) and the GM Manufacturing Development Staff. Lou is a coauthor of *The Handbook of Fraud Deterrence*, published by John Wiley & Sons, Inc.

Phillip D. Torrence
Partner, Honigman Miller Schwartz and Cohn LLP, Kalamazoo, MI

Phillip D. Torrence is managing partner of the Kalamazoo office of Honigman Miller Schwartz and Cohn LLP. Along with being the managing partner of the local office, Torrence is a member of Honigman's board of directors, chairman of its Financial Institutions Practice, and a partner in Honigman's corporate department. He represents public and private companies in a wide range of industries, including the medical device and life sciences industries and the financial services sector. He has particular expertise in handling acquisitions of publicly traded companies and hostile takeover transactions, most recently representing the Special Committee of the Board of Directors of Fremont InsuraCorp in connection with the unsolicited takeover bid received from Biglari Holdings Inc. He said his work ranges from such things as closing on a large PIPE (private investment in a public company) financing deal for a medical device company and running bank merger and acquisition transactions, to advising the directors of a public company of their fiduciary duties while facing a hostile takeover bid. Torrence, 37, has handled more than 40 bank merger and acquisition transactions and more than 100 venture capital financings totaling more than $400 million worth of investment proceeds.

Adam A. Wadecki, PhD
Manager, Cendrowski Corporate Advisors, LLC, Chicago, IL, and Bloomfield Hills, MI

Adam Wadecki is a Manager with CCA and specializes in operational analyses, business valuations, litigation, and quantitative risk management modeling. Adam has helped numerous Fortune 500 companies assess, improve, and monitor the operations of their production facilities. In conjunction with the CCA team, he has provided business valuations that have served as the basis of legal cases of publicly traded and privately held firms. Adam has also worked with the CCA team to provide quality of earnings analyses of potential portfolio companies for private equity funds, forensic accounting analyses of documents for legal cases, and business valuations of startup firms. In addition to his professional experiences, Adam is active in academia. He is a lecturer at the University of Michigan, and his academic research focuses on uncertainty, competition, and barriers to entry in private equity fundraising and investment.

Richard A. Walawender
Senior Principal, Miller, Canfield, Paddock, and Stone, PLC, Detroit, MI

Mr. Walawender is Director of the Corporate Group, and his practice focuses on the areas of mergers and acquisitions, corporate finance, and corporate governance for public companies, private equity funds, and privately held companies. He also specializes in complex, multinational and international mergers, acquisitions, and strategic alliances involving the automotive industry, and heads up the firm's Automotive Group. Mr. Walawender received his law degree from the University of Michigan Law School, where he also received his B.A. with high distinction. He is admitted to practice in New York and Michigan and is a member of the American Bar Association, the New York State Bar Association, the State Bar of Michigan, and the International Bar Association.

Glossary

AAA   American Accounting Association.

Accredited Investors   Individuals with historical income in excess of $200,000 per year, individuals whose net worth exceeds $1 million, or families with joint income of over $300,000. This also includes entities with assets in excess of $5 million. Under Dodd-Frank, individuals may no longer include the value of their primary residence for the purpose of determining net worth under the accredited investor definition.

Acquisition   Transaction in which an acquiring firm will negotiate with a target firm over a purchase price for the target.

Acquisition Premium   A price paid in excess of the market value of the firm. Acquisition premiums are often used to entice shareholders to sell their shares to a potential buyer.

AICPA   American Institute of Certified Public Accountants; governs the practice of public accountancy except for standards related to the audit of public companies, which are defined by the Public Company Accounting Oversight Board (PCAOB); www.aicpa.org.

Auditing Standard No. 5   Requires all publicly registered firms in the United States to receive an audit of management's assessment of the effectiveness of internal control over financial reporting.

Bankruptcy Code   The U.S. Bankruptcy Code; law containing numerous provisions governing bankruptcy proceedings.

Blank Check Company   A development stage company without a specific business plan or purpose.

Blue Sky Laws   Laws that regulate the offer and sale of securities at the state level.

Break-Up Fee   Requires the party responsible for a break-up in an acquisition to pay the other party a negotiated amount of liquidated damages.

Bridge Financing   Transactions in which a bank will hold an equity stake in a target company until the PE fund can find investors willing to purchase the equity.

Broker-Dealer   Person who engages in the business of effecting transactions in securities for his/her own account or for the account of others.

Business Intelligence   Knowledge of what is going on in one's business so that it remains alive and stable while protecting it from competition.

Capital Calls   Request for funds by the general partners to which the limited partner contractually adheres throughout the life of a private equity fund.

CAPM   Capital Asset Pricing Model; believes that returns to a well-diversified portfolio should increase linearly in risk. Investors are paid for the systematic, nondiversifiable risks they bear with greater returns. When an investor bears no risk, he/she should receive only the market risk-free rate of return.

Carried Interest The portion of realized fund profits the general partners will retain in exchange for managing the fund. The standard used in many private equity agreements is 20 percent of the fund's profits. Sometimes called the carry.

Clayton Antitrust Act Added restraints of trade to those specified in the Sherman Antitrust Act to limit monopolizing.

COBIT Control Objectives for Information and Related Technology; standard for information technology control published by the Information Systems Audit and Control Association.

Competitive Intelligence Knowledge of one's competitor as compared to his/her own company so the company can still be profitable.

Control Acquisitions When a private equity firm seeks to own or control a majority of the voting equity, as well as a majority of the board of directors of the portfolio company.

Control Environment The foundation of the internal control structure in an organization, including management's tone at the top; it is one of the five elements of the COSO model of control.

Cooling Off Period During this time, issuers may not solicit potential investors of the offering.

COSO Committee of Sponsoring Organization of the Treadway Commission; considered the gold standard of internal control for organizations as its framework is utilized by 63 percent of publicly held companies.

CPA Certified public accountant; an accounting professional licensed by his/her respective state administrative board.

Disinvestment Period Period in which the general partners focus on realizing returns on the fund's assets.

DMA Definitive merger agreement; document that includes extensive data and surrounding covenants regarding a takeover.

Dodd-Frank Wall Street Reform and Consumer Protection Act An act of Congress passed in 2010 that, *inter alia*, requires many private equity firms with over $150 million in assets under management to register with the Securities and Exchange Commission. An exemption does exist for venture capital funds. Also changed the definition of "accredited investor."

Dog-Eat-Dog Business Phrase characterized by the chief executive officer of Uniroyal Goodrich to describe the fierce and competitive business practices that occurred in the tire industry.

Earnout Instance in which a portion of the target company's purchase price will be paid by the acquirer only if the target company has achieved negotiated performance goals after being achieved.

Equity Financings Financings that typically have a high initial cost, have significant control features, and often require transfer of ownership and operational control of the company; structurally subordinate to both senior loans and mezzanine loans.

ERISA   Employee Retirement Income Security Act of 1974; a federal law that sets minimum standards for most voluntarily established pension and health plans in private industry to provide investment protection for individuals in these plans.

ERM   Enterprise Risk Management; the analysis of all risks facing an organization, it includes financial, operational, and comprehensive risks.

Exit   *See* Harvest.

FEI   Financial Executive International.

FinCEN   Financial Crimes Enforcement Network; the anti–money laundering enforcement division of the U.S. Treasury.

Forward Merger   Transaction in which the target firm obtains an equity stake in the acquiring firm in exchange for merging with the acquirer.

Fraud   As defined by *Black's Law Dictionary*, the intentional use of deceit, a trick, or some dishonest means to deprive another of his/her/its money, property, or a legal right. Fraud can be categorized into two categories: financial statement fraud and asset fraud.

FTC   Federal Trade Commission. The FTC was created in 1914; its purpose was to prevent unfair methods of competition in commerce as part of the battle to "bust the trusts." Over the years, Congress passed additional laws giving the agency greater authority to police anticompetitive practices. In 1938, Congress passed the Wheeler-Lea Amendment, which included a broad prohibition against "unfair and deceptive acts or practices." Since then, the Commission also has been directed to administer a wide variety of other consumer protection laws, including the Telemarketing Sales Rule, the Pay-Per-Call Rule, and the Equal Credit Opportunity Act. In 1975, Congress passed the Magnuson-Moss Act, which gave the FTC the authority to adopt trade regulation rules that define unfair or deceptive acts in particular industries.

GP   General partner; the manager of private equity funds.

Harvest   An event in which investors and management of a company sell at least a portion of their shares to public or corporate buyers.

Hierarchy of Needs   Idea proposed by Abraham Maslow in which the needs a human attempts to satisfy in his/her life are demonstrated by a pyramid consisting of five layers: psychological, safety, love/being, esteem, and actualization.

Horizontal Takeover   Occurs when two companies in a similar industry merge/are acquired.

IMA   Institute of Management Accountants.

Internal Control   As defined by COSO, a process, effected by an entity's board of directors, management, and other personnel, designed to provide reasonable assurance regarding the achievement of objectives in the following categories: effectiveness and efficiency of operations, reliability of financial reporting, and compliance with applicable laws and regulations.

ISACA   Information Systems Audit and Control Association; www.isaca.org.

LBO   Leveraged buyout; a transaction where a group or entity gains control of a target company's equity using a large amount of debt or borrowed money; typically involves a recapitalization of the target company.

Lead Investor   One who contributes a large portion of a private equity fund's capital, and in exchange, he/she will receive a portion of the fund's carried interest in addition to an already substantial portion of the fund's distributions.

Lean   Management tool that uses the standardization of processes to reach efficiency and organizational relevance.

Limited Partnership Agreement   Document in which the lifetime and minimum size of a private equity firm is specified; binds both the limited partner and general partner.

LOI   Letter of intent; a brief document in which the acquirer outlines the key deal points of the proposed acquisition. The primary reason for such a document is to ensure agreement on the major issues before the parties involved commit major resources to due diligence and detailed negotiations.

LP   Limited partner; investors with limited liability in private equity funds.

MAC-Out Clause   Material adverse clause; numerates the conditions under which a buyer can renege in a takeover.

Mega Funds   Private equity funds larger than $5 billion.

Merger   Transaction in which multiple parties primarily negotiate the amount of ownership each will hold in a combined firm.

Mezzanine Financing   Mid-level financing on a company's balance sheet between secured debt and equity.

Organizational Mass   Defined by numerous factors, including the amount of time a firm has been in business; the size of the company's revenues, earnings, and interest payments; the number of people it employs; its market share; and its market leader position.

Pac-Man Defense   An attempt by a would-be target firm to take over what was formerly an acquiring firm.

Patent   An invention that contains enough novelty to warrant the government to grant a monopoly to the inventor for 20 years.

PCAOB   Public Company Accounting Oversight Board; responsible for setting audit standards for public company audits.

PE   Private equity; investment of capital by private individuals and companies.

Pitch Books   Books prepared by banks containing information on a selling company's products, overall market trends, and mergers and acquisitions transactions in the company's industry.

Placement Agents   Firms that the general partners hire in order to attract capital.

Prospectus   The principal selling document; prior to the registration statement being declared effective by the Securities and Exchange Commission (SEC), it is commonly called the "red herring," which refers to the fact that the document is subject to completion. Shortly before or after approval by the SEC, it becomes the final prospectus and is called a "black," which is the definitive offering document for the securities.

Prudent Man Rule   Maintained in ERISA that pension plan managers should invest plan assets in a careful and prudent manner. A 1979 clarification to this rule by the

U.S. Department of Labor specifically permitted fund managers to invest in private equity.

Registrant Counsel   The counsel with securities law expertise that assists the registrant in the preparation of the required disclosure documents and in negotiating the underwriting arrangements with the managing underwriter and its counsel.

Regulation D of the Amended Securities Act of 1993   Specifies that a fund may have only 35 unaccredited investors and imposes restrictions on the solicitation funds that may be used to raise capital.

Reverse Leveraged Buyouts   The act of offering new, publicly traded shares in a firm that was previously taken private through a buyout transaction.

Reverse Merger   Transaction in which an acquirer merges into the target company and receives an equity stake in the target.

S-1 Registration Document   Form filed by companies with the Securities and Exchange Commission when they are seeking to become public companies.

Sarbanes-Oxley Act   Momentous reform of corporate governance and reporting requirements for issuers of financial statements enacted in July of 2002 due to numerous corporate scandals such as Enron and WorldCom; it included many reforms and regulations to improve the corporate oversight process, including strengthening the role of the audit committee in corporate governance, management certification of financial results, and detailed reporting of internal controls for financial reporting.

SEC   Securities and Exchange Commission. Congress passed the Securities Act of 1933 and the Securities Exchange Act of 1934 to restore investor confidence in capital markets by providing more structure and government oversight. Congress established the SEC in 1934 to enforce the newly passed securities laws, to promote stability in the markets, and to protect investors.

SEC v. Ralston Purina Co.   Case in which the U.S. Supreme Court decided that the primary purpose of the Securities Act was to protect investors by promoting full disclosure of information believed to be necessary to make an informed investment decision.

Section 11 of the Securities Act   Important requirement of the Securities Act that requires that all statements in the registration document be accurate and truthful; if a misleading statement is discovered, the purchaser may legally sue various parties involved in the transaction.

Section 12 of the Securities Act   Similar to Section 11 of the Securities Act in that it protects the purchaser; however, it has a broader scope as it requires that all information in documents or oral communications be truthful, not just contained in the registration statement.

Securities Counsel   Expert in securities laws who assists an issuer in preparing the registration statement and prospectus in negotiating the underwriting arrangements with the underwriters.

Senior Loans   Senior secured loans; credit facilities that represent the top tier of the company's balance sheet.

Sherman Antitrust Act   Passed to prevent business practices leading to monopolies, for example, horizontal price fixing, vertical price fixing, boycotts, etc.

Small Business Investment Incentive Act of 1980   Added an exemption to the Securities Act for transactions involving offers and sales of securities by any issuer to one or more accredited investors.

Stale Pricing Problem   Instance in which partners record a firm's value at cost until it nears harvest, the time in which the true market value of a portfolio becomes observable.

Staple Financing   A prearranged financial package prepared by the investment bank that is advising the selling company. It is given to possible bidders in an acquisition and includes principal, fees, and loan covenants.

Teaser   Brief document that provides a potential buyer with historical financial statements of a target company, a discussion of its future business plan, and a general description of the industry in which a selling company participates.

TQM   Total Quality Management; management approach developed by W. Edwards Deming that centers on quality. Initially popular in Japan and subsequently in the United States, TQM says success is based on participation from all members of the company and recognizes the company's long-term success through customer satisfaction.

Trademark   A distinctive design, picture, emblem, logo, or wording (or combination) affixed to goods for sale to identify the manufacturer as the source of the product. Words that just name the maker without particular wording or a generic product name are not trademarks.

ULOE   Uniform Limited Offering Exemption; developed by the North American Securities Administrators Association to coordinate a state transaction exemption with the exemption for private offerings under Rule 505 of Regulation D.

Underwriter   Provides financial advisory services to companies with no specific plans for an offering.

Uniform Commercial Code   A uniform act developed to harmonize the laws of sales and commercial transactions within the 50 states; it has been enacted by 49 states, with Louisiana as the sole holdout.

USA-PATRIOT Act of 2001   Uniting and Strengthening America by Providing Appropriate Tools Required to Intercept and Obstruct Terrorism; in regard to business conduct, it contains provisions that prevent, detect, and prosecute money laundering.

Vertical Takeover   Occurs when members of a supply chain merge/are acquired, creating a single firm.

Index

A

Accountants, 92, 223–226
Accredited investors, 16, 339
Acquisition, 339
Acquisition Premium, 339
Advisors, selection of, 91–92
Akerlof, George, 48
American Accounting Association
  (AAA), 339
American Institute of Certified
  Public Accountants (AICPA),
  339
  accounting and review standards,
    270–271
    SSARS 10, 271
    SSARS 12, 271
  auditing standards
    SAS 1, 243
    SAS 1 amendments, 257
    SAS 82, 249
    SAS 82 replacements,
      257–264
    SAS 85 amendments, 257
    SAS 95, 249
    SAS 99, 256–257
    SAS 104, 264
    SAS 105, 265
    SAS 106, 265
    SAS 107, 265–266
    SAS 108, 266
    SAS 109, 266
    SAS 110, 267

    SAS 111, 267
    SAS 112, 267–268
    SAS 113, 268
    SAS 114, 269
    SAS 115, 270
American Jobs and Closing Tax
    Loopholes Act of 2010, 54
American Research and
    Development Corporation
    (ARD), 31
American waterfall model, 10
Angel investing, 20–21
Antitakeover provisions, 93
Antitrust legislation, federal
    235–238
  Celler-Kefauver Antimerger Act
    (1950), 237
  Clayton Antitrust Act (1914),
    236
  Federal Trade Commission Act
    (1914), 236–237
  Hart-Scott-Rodino Antitrust
    Improvement Act (1976),
    140, 237–238
  Robinson-Patman Act (1936),
    237
  Sherman Antitrust Act (1890),
    236
Apollo Global Management, 53, 55
Assessments, manufacturing,
    319–333
  corporate vision and mission,
    323–324

Assessments, manufacturing
  (*Continued*)
  customer satisfaction and
    perceived quality, 322–323
  employee satisfaction, 320–322
  equipment and facility
    maintenance, 324–326
  inventory management and
    product flow, 327–328
  operational data and cost of sales,
    328
  visual management, 326
Audit, scaling, 206
Auditing Standards. *See also* Public
  Company Accounting
  Oversight board (PCAOB)
  standards
  AU §322, 207
  No. 5, 202–204, 214–215, 216

B

Baldwin, Greg, 221
Bank Secrecy Act, 219–220
Bankruptcy code, 339
Baskets and caps, 131
Bendix, 112–113
Bertrand's two-firm model, 288
Best effort, 74
Bidder confidentiality agreement
  (BCA), 117
BlackRock Inc., 55
Blackstone Group, 4, 6, 11, 15, 19,
  51–54, 62, 65, 170, 248
Blank check company, 339
Blue sky laws, 339
  liabilities under, 105
Bobrow, Richard S., 279–280
Book building, 73
Boutique investment bank, 74
Breaking issue, 77
Breakpoints, 13

Breakup fee, 129–130, 339
Bridge financing, 339
Broker-dealer, 339
Bulge bracket bank, 74
Business development companies
  (BDCs), 54
Business intelligence, 277–292, 339
  application to private equity,
    291–292
  exit strategy, 292
  investment decision, 291
  portfolio companies, strategic
    management of, 291
  competitive, 281–282
  contemporary, 278–281
  employees, 280–281
  legal proceedings, 279–280
  news archives, 279
  patent awards and
    applications, 280
  public records searches, 278–279
  social networking, 280
  cost of capital and option to
    invest, 285–287
  developing relationships and
    navigating crises, 290–291
  developing unique intelligence,
    287–288
  normalizing performance,
    282–285
  quality, economic view of,
    289–290
Buyout funds, 13
  returns by fund size, 43–45
Buyouts, 21, 164–166

C

California Public Employees'
  Retirement System
  (CalPERS), 6
Campeau, Robert, 32

Capital Asset Pricing Model
(CAPM), 339
Capital, drawing down, 8
Capital calls, 8, 339
Carried interest, 10, 14–15, 339
current tax framework for,
63–64
Celler-Kefauver Antimerger Act
(1950), 237
Chief executive officer (CEO), 15,
101, 171–172, 298
certifications, 244, 247
Chief financial officer (CFO), 15,
101, 228
Certifications, 244, 247
Chief operating officer (COO), 15
Chief legal officer (CLO), 15
Chief recruitment officer, 15
Christensen's framework, 300–301
Clawback provision, 10
Clayton Antitrust Act (1914), 236,
339
Cleantech investments, 41
Club deal, 9–10
Committee of Sponsoring
Organizations of the
Treadway Commission
(COSO), 178–179, 340
Competitive intelligence, 340
Compound annual growth rate
(CAGR), 283
Comparable public companies,
126
Comparable transactions, 126
Confidential information
memorandum (CIM),
116–117
Confidentiality, 100
Consumer protection legislation,
federal, 238–239
Control acquisitions, 340
Control environment, 340

Control Objectives for Information
and Related Technology
(COBIT), 186–187, 339
Cooling off period, 340
Copyrights, 147–148
Corporate housekeeping matters, 93
Covenants, 27–28
Cressey, Donald R., 223
Crisis management, corporate
governance and, 168–171
Cullman, Lewis, 31

D

Dagres v. Commissioner, 63
Data room, 118
Definitive merger agreement
(DMA), 119, 340
Deming cycle, 314–315
Denominator effect, 38
Directors and officers questionnaire,
99
Disclosure of acquisitions, 138
Discounted cash flow analysis, 126
Disinvestment period, 340
Dodd-Frank Wall Street Reform
and Consumer Protection
Act, 6–7, 16–17, 58, 61–62,
71, 105–109, 182, 187,
201–202, 235, 240, 243, 340
Doriot, General Georges, 31
Dot-com companies, 35–37
Dow Jones' Private Equity Analyst,
55, 62
Draper Fisher Jurvetson, 41
Due diligence
assessments, manufacturing,
319–333
corporate vision and mission,
323–324
customer satisfaction and
perceived quality, 322–323

Due diligence (*Continued*)
employee satisfaction, 320–322
equipment and facility maintenance, 324–326
inventory management and product flow, 327–328
operational data and cost of sales, 328
visual management, 326
intellectual property, 149–152
assessing risk of proposed acquisition, 151–152
evaluating investment value, 149–151
reverse, 157–158
IPO, 100
sale transaction, 125
acquirer, 130
seller, 131
Duncan framework, 299–300
Dunlap, "Chainsaw Al," 165

E

Earnouts, 129, 340
Earnings before interest and tax (EBIT), 117, 317
Earnings before interest, tax, depreciation, and amortization (EBITDA), 21, 117, 317
Earnings per share (EPS), 73, 126–127
Electronic Data Gathering and Retrieval System (EDGAR), 241
Employee Retirement Income Security Act of 1974 (ERISA), 17–18, 31, 79, 163, 341
Prudent Man Rule, 18, 31, 342

Employees, as source of information, 280–281
Energy Policy Act (EPACT), 241
Enterprise risk management (ERM), 183–184, 341
Equity financing, 340
European waterfall model, 10
Evergreen funds, 7
Exit, 341. *See also* Harvest

F

Fairness opinion, 126
Federal Energy Regulatory Commission (FERC), 241
Federal Trade Commission (FTC), 235–239, 341
federal antitrust legislation, 235–238
Celler-Kefauver Antimerger Act (1950), 237
Clayton Antitrust Act (1914), 236
Federal Trade Commission Act (1914), 236–237
Hart-Scott-Rodino Antitrust Improvement Act (1976), 140, 237–238
Robinson-Patman Act (1936), 237
Sherman Antitrust Act (1890), 236
federal consumer protection legislation, 238–239
Federal Trade Commission Act (1914), 236–237
Fiduciary-out clause, 119
Financial Executive International (FEI), 341
Financial Crimes Enforcement Network (FinCEN), 220–221, 341

Financial statement fraud, 219–234
  categories of fraud, 221–222
  definition of fraud, 222–223
  and due diligence procedures,
    231–233
    background investigation of
      key employees, 231–232
    file metadata, checking,
      232–233
    journal transactions, testing of,
      232
  financial statement attestation,
    225–227
    audit, 226–227
    compilation, 226
    review, 226
    tax return preparation, 225–226
  money laundering, 219–221
  recommendations, 227–231
  required elements of fraud,
    223–225
Firm commitment, 74
Follow-on fund, 10–11
Force majeure, 119
Foreign Corrupt Practices Act
  (1977), 243–244
Forensic valuation, 292
Form SB-2, 78–79
Forward merger, 341
Fraud
  categories of, 221–222
  in connection with offer and sale
    of a security, 104–105
  definition of, 222, 341
  financial statement, 219–234
  required elements of, 223–225
  risk, 206
Free writing prospectus, 76
Frito-Lay, 281–282
Fund of funds (FoF), 4, 18
Fundraising
  levels, 1980–2010, 3

process, 22–25
recent trends in, 25–26, 54–60

G

Gatekeepers, 8, 22
Gates, Bill, 71–72
General Motors (GM), 305–306
General Motors Acceptance
  Corporation (GMAC),
  229–230
General partner
  incentives, 12–15
  investment restrictions, 26–28
Gladwell, Malcolm, 282
"Green Shoe," 77
Guiltless Gourmet, 281–282
Gun jumping, 76

H

Hart-Scott-Rodino Antitrust
  Improvement Act of 1976,
  140, 237–238
Harvard Management Company,
  46–47
Harvest, 341
Hierarchy of needs, 341
Historical trends, overview of, 29–49
  private equity
    brief history of, 29–33
    at the turn of the century,
      33–39
    secondary funds, 45–48
    venture capital
      and buyout returns by fund
        size, 43–45
      investment and returns by fund
        stage, 39–43
Holt-Winters method of prediction,
  285
Horizontal takeovers, 111, 341

I

Icahn, Carl, 32, 165
Images of Organization (Morgan),
    293
Industry Little Hawk, 56–57
Information Systems Audit and
    Control Association
    (ISACA), 272–273, 341
Initial public offerings (IPOs)
    advance planning opportunities,
        91–94
        accountants, 92
        advisors, selection of, 91–92
        antitakeover provisions, 93
        corporate housekeeping
            matters, 93
        management, 94
        securities counsel, 92
        underwriters, 93
    advantages, potential, 87–89
    disadvantages, potential, 89–91
    harvesting investments through,
        69–83
        basics, 69–72
        historical trends, 79–83
        initial steps in process, 72–75
        post-IPO underwriter
            responsibilities, 77
        registration documents, 78–79
        role of SEC and state policing
            bodies, 75–77
    liabilities, possible, 102–105
        fraud in conection with offer and
            sale of a security, 104–105
        material misstatements or
            omissions of material facts,
            102–104
        under state blue sky laws, 105
    process, 94–102
        key components of, 95
        principal documents, 96–98

principal parties, 94, 96, 97
registration process, 100–102
selling security holder
    documents, 98–99
Sarbanes-Oxley Act and
    Dodd-Frank Act, 105–109
    filing obligations, 107
    reverse mergers, 107–109
Institute of Internal Auditors (IIA),
    178, 192
    standards, 272
Institutional Limited Partners
    Association (ILPA), 10
Institution of Management
    Accountants (IMA), 341
Institutional-quality investments, 19
Intellectual property, 143–159
    creating value during
        management, 152–156
        brand development efforts,
            boosting, 154–155
        knowledge-based resources of
            the workforce, preserving,
            155–156
        patent rights, leveraging and
            monetizing, 153
        technological advantages,
            bolstering, 153–154
    pre-acquisition due diligence,
        149–152
        assessing risk of proposed
            acquisition, 151–152
        evaluating investment value,
            149–151
    reverse due diligence, 156–158
        representations and warranties,
            minimizing exposure of, 158
    rights and remedies, 143–149
        copyrights, 147–148
        patents, 144–146
        trade secrets, 148–149
        trademarks, 146–147

Internal control, 177–218, 341
  Committee of Sponsoring
    Organizations of the
    Treadway Commission
    (COSO), 178–179
  components of, 179–188
    control activities, 184–185
    control environment, 179–182
    enterprise risk management
      (ERM), 183–184
    information and
      communication, 186
    limitations, 188
    monitoring, 186–188
    risk assessment, 182–183
  evaluation, 201–218
    PCAOB Auditing Standard
      No. 5, 203–204
    Phase 1: Planning the Audit,
      204–208
    Phase 2: Using a Top-Down
      Approach, 208–211
    Phase 3: Testing Controls,
      211–213
    Phase 4: Evaluating Identified
      Deficiencies, 213–215
    Phase 5: Wrapping Up, 215
    Phase 6: Reporting on Internal
      Controls, 217–218
  objectives and components,
    189–191
    effectiveness, 190–191
  and the private equity firm,
    191–198
    compliance value, 197–198
    financial reporting value, 197
    operational value, 196–197
    value and control activities, 194
    value and control environment,
      193–194
    value and information and
      communication, 195
  value and monitoring, 195
  value and operations, 191–193
  value and risk, 194
  value for target companies,
    195–196
Internal rate of return (IRR), 8
  predicted, by fund size, 57
International Telephone and
  Telegraph (ITT), 113
Investment adviser, SEC definition
  of, 60–61
Investment Advisers Act of 1940,
  17, 242–243
Investment agreement, 16
Investment Company Act of 1940,
  17, 30, 54, 242

J

J-curve, 47
J. D. Power's Initial Quality Study
  (IQS), 322
Jensen, Michael C., 163, 173, 175
Junk bonds, 32

K

Kaizen, 316
Khosla, Vinod, 26
Kleiner Perkins Caulfield & Byers, 41
Kohlberg Capital Corporation, 55
Kohlberg, Kravis, Roberts &
  Company (KKR), 32, 52–53,
  62, 248
Kravis, Henry, 53

L

*L. A. Murphy v. Kohlberg Kravis
  Roberts & Company, et al.,*
  236
Lead investor, 342

Lean transformation, 309–318
  discipline building, 315–317
  Lean manufacturing, 310
  organizational development,
    312–315
  potential pitfalls, 311–312
  private equity and, 317–318
League tables, 73
Legal proceedings, as source of
    information, 279–280
Lerner, Josh, 57
Letter of intent (LOI), 137–138, 342
Leveraged buyouts (LBOs), 22, 31,
    164–166, 342
  reverse, 80
Limited liability companies
    (LLCs), 5
Limited partner agreement (LPA),
    10, 11–15, 342
Limited partnerships (LPs), 5,
    57–60
Liquidity events, 9–10
Lock-up agreement, 98–99
Lowenstein, Douglas, 62

M

Management fees, 12–13
Management discussion and
    analysis (MD&A), 247
"The Market for Lemons"
    (Akerlof), 48
Martin Marietta, 112–113
Maslow, Abraham, 294
Material adverse (MAC-out) clause,
    119, 342
Material misstatements or
    omissions of material facts,
    102–104
Materiality, 208
McNamara, John, 229–230
Mega funds, 25, 44, 342

Mendillo, Jane, 46
Mergers and acquisitions,
    harvesting investments
    through, 111–122
  agreement, reaching, 119
  basics, 111
  bidding process, 118–119
  historical trends, 120–121
  potential buyers, analyzing,
    115–116
  process, and financial adviser
    selection, 114–115
  sale process, 116–117
  types of, 112–114
    defensive, 112–113
    financial, 113
    growth, 113
    reverse, 113–114
    strategic, 112
Metrics, normalizing performance,
    283
Meyers, Gerald C., 168–169
Mezzanine financing, 342
Milken, Michael, 32
Mini-public offering, 79
Money laundering, 219–221
Morgan, Gareth, 293, 298, 304,
    306–307

N

Net asset test, 128
Net present value (NPV) budgeting
    technique, 285–287
News archives, 279

O

Offering expenses, 99
Organizations as humans, 293–308
  death and rebirth of organization,
    304–305

development and specialization, 296–297
environmental adaptation, 299–301
environmental influence and interaction, 302–303
genesis, 295–296
maturity, 303–304
parts of the whole and maturation, 297–299
purpose of the organization, 294–295
strengths and weaknesses of organizations, 305–307
Overallotment option, 77
Organizational mass, 342

P

Pac-Man defense, 112, 342
Patents, 144–146, 153, 342
awards and applications, as source of information, 280
rights, leveraging and monetizing, 153
Period-end financial reporting process, 209–210
Pfizer Inc., 65
Pickens, T. Boone, 165
Pitch books, 114, 342
Placement agents, 7, 23
Plan-Do-Check-Act cycle, 314–315
Portfolio companies, strategic management of, 291
Power of attorney and custody agreement, 99
Preferred return, 14
Price-to-earnings (P/E) ratio, 73
Private equity
brief history of, 29–33
fund, typical stages of, 7–12.
See also Venture capital

harvest or disinvestment period, 9
investment stage, 8
management phase, 8–9
organization/fundraising phase, 7–8
governance model, 163–176
analogy to physics, 167–168
crisis, management of, 168–171
magic of, 173–175
public corporations and, 171–173
historical trends, overview of, 29–49
introduction to, 3–27
definition, 4–5
firm structure and selected regulations, 15–19
fundraising process, 22–25
general partner investment restrictions, 26–28
general terms and brief overview, 5–12
investment, types of, 20–22
limited partner agreement and general partner incentives, 12–15
recent fundraising trends, 25–26
Private investments in public equity (PIPEs), 4,
process, 15
trends in, 51–68
milestones, 51–54
overall industry and fundraising trends, 54–60
regulatory changes and proposals, 60–64
strategic buyers, rise of, 64–66
at the turn of the century, 33–39

Prospectus, 75
  final, 97–98
  free writing, 76
  preliminary, 97
Professional standards, 235–273
  American Institute of Certified
    Public Accountants (AICPA)
    accounting and review
      standards, 270–271
    auditing standards, 255–270
  Federal Trade Commission
    (FTC), 235–239
    federal antitrust legislation,
      235–238
    federal consumer protection
      legislation, 238–239
  Information Systems Audit and
    Control Association,
    272–273
  Institute of Internal Auditors
    standards, 272
  private equity going public,
    248–249
  Public Company Accounting
    Oversight board (PCAOB),
    342
    standards, 249–255
    Auditing Standard No. 1, 249
    Auditing Standard No. 2,
      249–250
    Auditing Standard No. 3, 250
    Auditing Standard No. 4, 250
    Auditing Standard No. 5,
      250–252
    Auditing Standard No. 6, 252
    Auditing Standard No. 7, 252
    Auditing Standard No. 8,
      252–253
    Auditing Standard No. 9, 253
    Auditing Standard No. 10,
      253
    Auditing Standard No. 11, 253
    Auditing Standard No. 12,
      253–254
    Auditing Standard No. 13, 254
    Auditing Standard No. 14,
      254–255
    Auditing Standard No. 15, 255
  Securities and Exchange
    Commission (SEC), 239–247
    Foreign Corrupt Practices Act
      (1977), 243–244
    Investment Advisers Act
      (1940), 242–243
    Investment Company Act
      (1940), 242
    Public Utility Holding
      Company Act (1935), 241
    Sarbanes-Oxley Act (2002),
      244–247
    Securities Act (1933), 239–240
    Securities Exchange Act (1934),
      240–241
    Trust Indenture Act (1939),
      241–242
Prudent Man Rule, 18, 31
Public Company Accounting
  Oversight Board (PCAOB),
  177, 202–204, 226, 244–245
  Auditing Standard No. 1, 249
  Auditing Standard No. 2,
    249–250
  Auditing Standard No. 3, 250
  Auditing Standard No. 4, 250
  Auditing Standard No. 5, 250–252
    audit focus, 251–252
    purpose, 251
    scalable audits, 251
    using work of others, 252
  Auditing Standard No. 6, 252
  Auditing Standard No. 7, 252
  Auditing Standard No. 8, 252–253
  Auditing Standard No. 9, 253
  Auditing Standard No. 10, 253

Auditing Standard No. 11, 253
Auditing Standard No. 12,
    253–254
Auditing Standard No. 13, 254
Auditing Standard No. 14,
    254–255
Auditing Standard No. 15, 255
Public records searches, 278–279
Public Utility Holding Company Act
    (1935), 241

Q

Quality, economic view of, 289–290
Quality Function Deployment
    (QFD), 302
Quiet period, 75–76, 87

R

Recapitalizations, 137
Reconstruction Finance
    Corporation (RFC), 30
Red herring, 75, 87
Registrant counsel, 343
Registration process, IPO, 100–102
    closing, 102
    confidentiality, 100
    due diligence, 100
    post-closing matters, 102
    registration statement, 101
        effective date of and pricing,
        102
    selling efforts, 101
    timeline, 100
Registration statement, 75, 96–97,
    101
    effective date of and pricing, 102
Regulation A offering, 79
Regulation Fair Disclosure, 90
Regulatory changes and proposals,
    60–64

Reverse due diligence, 156–158
Reverse leveraged buyouts, 80, 343
Reverse mergers, 107–109, 111,
    113–114, 343
    advantages, 107–108
    disadvantages, 108
Risk assessment, 206, 291
Robinson-Patman Act (1936), 237
Rockefeller, Lawrence, 31

S

S-1 registration document, 75,
    78–79, 343
Sale transactions, legal
        considerations in, 123–142
    deal issues, key, 126–134
        consideration, 127–128
        context, 132
        earnouts, 129
        escrow funds, 132
        indemnification caps and
            limited recourse, 132–133
        joint and several liability, 133
        net asset test, 128
        noncompetition,
            nonsolicitation covenants,
            133–134
        purchase price consideration,
            133
        risk reduction mechanisms,
            129–131
        survival of representations,
            warranties, covenants, 132
        target valuation, 126–127
    employee incentive issues,
        135–137
        cash retention bonus, 135–136
        recapitalizations, 137
        stock bonuses, 136–137
    prior to, 124–126
        due diligence, 125

Sale transactions (*Continued*)
  investment banker, use of,
    124–125
  marketing process, 125
  negotiations phase, 125–126
  process, 137–142
    definitive agreements,
      139–140
    disclosure of acquisitions, 138
    letter of intent (LOI),
      137–138
    necessary consents, 140–142
    time and responsibility
      schedule, 138–139
  sale and acquisition structure,
    134–135
    asset purchase, 135
    merger, 134
    stock purchase, 135
Sanofi-Aventis US, 65
Sarbanes-Oxley Act of 2002, 55, 71,
    105–109, 177, 186, 187,
    192, 201–202, 244–247, 342
  provisions of
    auditor independence, 245
    CEO/CFO certifications, 247
    civil and criminal penalties,
      247
    corporate governance, 246
    enhanced financial disclosure,
      247
    Public Company Accounting
      Oversight Board (PCAOB),
      244–245
    Section 301, 186
    Section 404, 177, 187, 192,
      201–202
    timeline for becoming
      ready, 106
Schoar, Antoinette, 57
Schwarzman, Stephen, 51–52
Secondary funds, 12, 45–48

Securities Act of 1933, amended,
    16, 76, 86–87, 89, 102–104,
    239–240
  Regulation D, 16, 342
  Section 5, 87
  Section 11, 102–103, 343
  Section 12, 343
  Section 12(2), 103–104
Securities counsel, 92, 343
Securities Exchange Act of 1934,
    90, 104, 240–241
  Rule 10(b)(5), 104
Securities and Exchange
    Commission (SEC),
    239–247
  registering with, 61–62, 71
  role of, in IPOs, 75–77
SEC v. Ralston Purina Co., 342
Selling security holder documents,
    98–99
  directors and officers
    questionnaire, 99
  lock-up agreement, 98–99
  offering expenses, 99
  power of attorney and custody
    agreement, 99
Senior loan, 343
Sherman Antitrust Act (1890), 236,
    343
Shorting, 77
Sidecar fund, 55
"Skin in the game," 19, 23, 71
Small Business Act of 1953, 30
Small Business Investment
    Company (SBIC) Program,
    30–31
Small Business Investment Incentive
    Act of 1980, 344
Small Defense Plants
    Administration (SDPA), 30
Smaller War Plants Corporation
    (SWPC), 30

Social networking, as source of information, 280
Staged capital, 21
Stale pricing problem, 344
Standards, professional. *See* Professional standards
Staple financing, 118, 344
Stieger Amendment, 32
Strategics, 64–66
Syndicate, 74
Syndicated investment, 9

T

Tax Act of 1981, 32
Tax Reform Act of 1986, 19
Tax return preparation, 225–226
Teaser, 344
Term sheet, 16
Texas Pacific Group, 170
Thomas H. Lee Partners LP, 55
Time and responsibility schedule, 138–139
Tombstone ads, 16, 77
Total Quality Management (TQM), 302, 344
Trade secrets, 148–149
Trademarks, 146–147, 344
searches, 155
Trust Indenture Act (1939), 241–242

U

Underwriters
IPO, 93
selecting, 72–74
post-IPO responsibilities, 77
Underwriting agreement, 98
Uniform Commercial Code, 344

Uniform Limited Offering Exemption (ULOE), 344
Uniting and Strengthening America by Providing Appropriate Tools Required to Intercept and Obstruct Terrorism (USA-PATRIOT) Act of 2001, 220–221, 344
U.S. Companies Accounting Reform and Investor Protection Act of 2002. *See* Sarbanes-Oxley Act of 2002
U.S. Federal Sentencing Guidelines, 247
U.S. Patent and Trademark Office (USPTO), 144, 146, 152
U.S. Pension Protection Act of 2006, 18, 25–26

V

Venture capital, 20, 29–31, 39–45, 56–58, 80–81, 165
and buyout returns by fund size, 43–45
early-stage, 20
investment and returns by fund stage, 39–43
Vertical takeovers, 112, 344
Vintage year, 14
Vision statement, 313
Volcker Rule, 58–59

W

"Walking dead" investment, 27
War Finance Corporation, 29–30
Whitney, J. H. "Jock," 31
Work-in-process (WIP), 328

Printed and bound by CPI Group (UK) Ltd, Croydon, CR0 4YY

23/04/2025

14661000-0002